ISRESILIENCE

What Israelis Can Teach the World

To Judy

Wishing you health, happiness
success, strength — and
resilience!

Michael Dickson

Naomi Baum

PRAISE FOR ISResilience

I have long marveled at the ability of Israelis to face adversity and move beyond it. In *ISResilience*, Michael Dickson and Naomi Baum tell compelling stories that illustrate this remarkable Israeli national characteristic. This wonderful book profiles inspiring Israelis and their spirit, with a message that will resonate for everyone. Israel has been referred to in many ways – from ancient times as the Holy Land, to modern times as the Start-Up Nation. Now this book gives the Israeli people a new name that they have earned – "ISResilience."

Joe Lieberman
former United States Senator

The extraordinary resilience of the Jewish people in the face of adversity through every generation since Moses is one of the keys to our collective identity and sense of purpose. This idea is beautifully captured by Michael Dickson and Dr. Naomi Baum in *ISResilience* through a series of inspiring stories that demonstrate the power of the modern State of Israel, not just as a country or as the homeland of the Jewish people, but as a shining example of resilience for the world.

Rabbi Lord Jonathan Sacks
international religious leader and author

As terrorists have turned the home front into the front lines, and a global pandemic has disrupted our lives, Israelis have shown tremendous resilience in dealing with these challenges. Having served as Israel's Minister of Public Security, Homeland Defense, and in other positions of national leadership, I have seen how our resilience has been the key to our strength and success. Michael Dickson, an expert in telling Israel's story, and Dr. Naomi L. Baum have done a great service in sharing the stories and secrets of Israeli resilience with their readers, and as Ambassador to the UN and US, I intend to share these inspiring stories with others as well.

Gilad Erdan
Israel's Ambassador to the United States and United Nations

By elegantly weaving together the fascinating accounts of women and men who underwent and overcame unimaginable conflict, in *ISResilience*, Michael Dickson and Dr. Naomi Baum examine the very heart of the Jewish people's enigmatic survival.

Isaac Herzog
Chairman, Jewish Agency for Israel

ISResilience is a rich, rewarding, multidimensional work. The dynamic duo of Naomi Baum and Michael Dickson have coauthored a collection of delightful, insightful, and inspiring stories showing the charm, diversity, depth, and sheer grit of Israelis today. At the same time, they have produced a more resonant, universal work exploring just what it means to be resilient – and what it takes – which is particularly welcome during these trying, plague-scarred times.

Well written, well told, well paced, and well worth your time, this book will move you to tears – while teaching you how to "fall forwards," facing adversity with a smile on your face and a glint in your eye, mastering the human – and very Israeli – ability to overcome the toughest of challenges.

Professor Gil Troy
author, *The Zionist Ideas*

Israelis are resilient people – they have to be, since they live with the constant threat of terrorist attacks, and the ever-present possibility of war. *ISResilience* tells truly remarkable stories of Israelis whose strong spirit and resilience has not only led them through difficult times, but has allowed them to achieve remarkable success despite what seem like insurmountable odds. This is a book that will engage and inspire you, particularly during these times of great challenge and uncertainty.

Yael Eckstein
President, International Fellowship of Christians and Jews

The determination of the Israeli spirit is the theme of this book. As a daughter of Holocaust survivors, I have often wondered how Jews have picked up the pieces of their shattered lives and have not only survived but have thrived in cities around the world, including Israel. How? What makes it possible for the Jewish persona to compartmentalize pain and move forward with joy, grace, determination, and creativity? And in Israel, despite all the challenges from wars and terrorism, the Israeli spirit soars above the very real threats and succeeds in areas from technology to humanitarian aid and everything in between. Israel is consistently listed as one of the happiest places in the world to live! Why? We owe a debt of gratitude to Michael Dickson and Dr. Naomi Baum, who have written *ISResilience*, because in doing so, they have given us the gift of insight and inspiration throughout the pages of this book.

Roz Rothstein
International CEO and Cofounder, StandWithUs

Resilience has long been one of the secrets of the Israeli people. It is a characteristic that has helped this war-torn nation overcome more than seventy years of daunting threats and challenges. The portraits chosen by Dickson and Baum reveal a diverse group of Israelis who have each, in their own way, achieved greatness through grit, devotion, and a belief in the Jewish state. Their stories are inspiring.

Yaakov Katz
Editor-in-Chief, *Jerusalem Post*; author, *Shadow Strike: Inside Israel's Secret Mission to Eliminate Syrian Nuclear Power*

Michael and Naomi have penned a series of revelatory portraits of remarkable Israelis – some of them well known, others less so. What they have in common is a combination of exceptional personal drive and extraordinary commitment to their country's well-being.

Israel has not merely survived but thrived, in the toxic, precarious Middle East, because of characters like the Israelis we meet on these pages. So if you want to understand quite how Israelis consistently beat the odds and face down the challenges, while constantly innovating, questioning, and pushing the frontiers of knowledge and achievement, read this book.

David Horovitz
Founding Editor, *Times of Israel*

The stories in this book are the stories of the Jewish people through the generations. Stories of perseverance, faith, resilience. These are the amazing stories of people who took on some of the world's toughest challenges and withstood them. They represent all parts of Jewish and Israeli society and exemplify the ancient saying "All of Israel are responsible for one another." Michael Dickson and Naomi Baum have taken these stories and turned them into lessons that everyone can and should learn, lessons that everyone – Israeli or not – can benefit from.

Ambassador Ron Prosor
Director, Abba Eban Institute of International Diplomacy,
IDC Herzliya

ISResilience is a perfect guide for these tough times: a panoply of stories and lessons from Israelis, both famous and unknown, who inspire us to stand together to weather this difficult moment in history. Through a study of Israel – a country that has repeatedly held together against enormous odds – Dickson and Baum show us the true meaning of "resilience" in their interviews and teach us how we can follow the example of these incredible personalities and this remarkable country.

William C. Daroff
Chief Executive Officer,
Conference of Presidents of Major American Jewish Organizations

These stories of remarkable men and women tell an essential story about Israel: how a people that lives under constant siege, moving from war to terrorist attacks to boycotts to delegitimization, has created one of the world's most successful societies. We owe a great debt to Michael Dickson and Dr. Naomi L. Baum for telling this story and telling it so movingly.

Yossi Klein Halevi
senior fellow, Shalom Hartman Institute; author,
Letters to My Palestinian Neighbor

ISResilience gives valuable voice to a wide range of diverse voices who share their Israeli experiences of dealing with adversity and overcoming it to build meaningful lives.

Einat Wilf
author

Israel and Israelis are not always given a fair representation, to say the least. This excellent book by Michael Dickson and Dr. Naomi Baum profiles some extraordinary Israelis who – by being both tough and sensitive – have much to teach us all. *ISResilience* is an insight into the real Israel. An inspirational and uplifting read!

MK Orit Farkash Hacohen
Minister of Strategic Affairs

ISRESILIENCE

What Israelis Can Teach the World

MICHAEL DICKSON
&
DR. NAOMI L. BAUM

gefen publishing house בית הוצאה לאור גפן Est. 1981
JERUSALEM ◆ NEW YORK

Excerpt from Yitzhak Ben-Zvi, *The Jewish Settlement in Peki'in* (Tel Aviv: Ahdut Ha'avodah, 1922) translated by Michael Dickson.
Excerpt from *Man's Search for Meaning* by Viktor E. Frankl, copyright © 1959, 1962, 1984, 1992 by Viktor E. Frankl, reprinted with permission from Beacon Press, Boston Massachusetts.
Excerpt from *The Case for Democracy* by Natan Sharansky, copyright © 2004, reprinted by permission of PublicAffairs, an imprint of Hachette Book Group, Inc.
Excerpt from *Fear No Evil: The Classic Memoir of One Man's Triumph over the Police State* by Natan Sharansky, copyright © 1998, reprinted by permission of Penguin Random House.
All interviewee photos graphically manipulated by Moran Reijzer; photo of Avigdor Kahalani courtesy of IDF Spokesperson's Unit; photo of Natan Sharansky by Ram Mandel (https://commons.wikimedia.org/wiki/File:Sharansky.jpg); photo of Noam Gershony by robbiesaurus (https://www.flickr.com/photos/30595457@N00/6128353846, https://creativecommons.org/licenses/by-sa/2.0/); photo of Margalit Zinati by Michael Dickson; photo of Chief Rabbi Israel Meir Lau by Wini (https://commons.wikimedia.org/wiki/File:%D7%94%D7%A8%D7%91_%D7%9C%D7%90%D7%95.JPG); photo of Tal Brody by Michael Dickson; photo of Sherri Mandel by Debbie Cooper; those unspecified provided by interviewee.
Photo of Michael Dickson by Jared Bernstein.

Cover design: Moran Reijzer
Cover illustration: Moran Reijzer
Typesetting: Optume Technologies

ISBN: 978-965-7023-46-4

1 3 5 7 9 8 6 4 2

Gefen Publishing House Ltd.
6 Hatzvi Street
Jerusalem 9438614,
Israel
972-2-538-0247
orders@gefenpublishing.com

Gefen Books
c/o Baker & Taylor Publisher Services
30 Amberwood Parkway
Ashland, Ohio 44805
516-593-1234
orders@gefenpublishing.com

www.gefenpublishing.com

Printed in Israel
Library of Congress Control Number: 2020912331

Contents

Michael Dickson

"I always think of Israel as a plucky little country."
Diana, Princess of Wales, to Shimon Peres,
Kensington Palace, January 1986

"We're fine."

As I write this, I'm responding to a flood of messages coming from friends and family abroad, as a long-range rocket has been fired from Gaza into Israel.

"We're fine."

It happened at 5:18 a.m.; the Red Alert sirens woke my eldest daughter first. We hurried to wake our four other sleeping children.

"We're fine."

Hundreds of thousands of Israelis were also awakened at the crack of dawn to the sound of the siren propelling them to rush their kids into bomb shelters, as I did, praying that the rocket fired from Gaza was not heading for our home.

"We're fine."

One family was not as lucky as ours was today. Their home was totally devastated by the rocket, sending seven people to hospital; it was a miracle that they even escaped alive. Cars were blasted with shrapnel, which also hit four dogs, who lay in a pool of their blood and debris on the street outside.

We're not fine.

How could we be? On the one hand, within hours of the rocket attack, schools opened, people went to work, and a normal day resumed. On the other, the conversation both in the playground and at the water cooler revolved around the attack. Yes, we are physically fine (with the exception of those injured). But mentally? That's another story.

Picture the scene. It's the morning of Remembrance Day – a solemn day when ceremonies are held and a moment's silence is observed for fallen soldiers. My family is eating at the breakfast table. My daughter turns to her sister and says, "Now remember, the siren that will sound today is the one where we stand and remember, not the one where we run to the bomb shelter, so don't be scared." She should know – her own birthday party was rudely interrupted by a rocket alert siren as she and her friends were jumping up and down on an inflatable castle, causing them to race for the nearest shelter. The wailing alarm warned all to run for cover, as rockets thankfully were intercepted above by the missile-defense system, leaving a plume of smoke in the blue sky. Meanwhile, we sang "Happy Birthday" underground, amid reinforced concrete, in a bid to soothe the nerves of the rattled kids.

My point is that the topic of my children's breakfast-table conversation, as matter-of-fact as it was, belies the stress behind the scenes. After a decade of life in Israel, my young children had known wars, kidnappings, rocket attacks, stabbing rampages, and violent acts of terror.

A tiny country in a hostile neighborhood, facing off against the rockets, the bullets, and the bombs, you could be forgiven for thinking Israel should be a national basket case. With each conflict able to turn into an existential war at any point, you might argue that Israel's mere existence is miraculous. Israel, however, does not just exist, it thrives. The idea behind exploring Israeli resilience comes from years of witnessing stressful situations unfold, of watching Israelis – both in regular, day-to-day life and in times of extreme crisis – continue on and flourish.

Are Israelis unaffected detrimentally by the threats, the rockets, and the terror attacks, the volatility of regional adversarial regimes, the ongoing potential for conflict to intensify? Categorically not. The high number of cases of post-traumatic stress disorder (PTSD) in the region of southern Israel that borders Gaza, whose citizens have suffered tens of thousands of rocket attacks in recent years, is well documented. Israel's military is a citizen army in which service is mandatory – an experience that has the potential to shape and scar both those who serve and their families. Geographically, Israel sits on a tiny sliver of land, giving national events a local relevance and impact. When the chips are down, everyone feels it.

The fact is, behind the eyes of every Israeli is a knowledge that today's reality could change at any minute. However strong the military is, you are never fully secure. However humdrum the daily routine, it can be upturned in a heartbeat. Your sons and daughters will likely serve as soldiers, inspiring in parents a combination of pride and anxiety. In such a small country, joy and grieving are collective acts in the face of national moments of pride and catastrophe. The gap between the personal, the familial, the local, and the national not only feels small but actually is small. Anyone who has lived in Israel for even a few years knows someone whose life has been affected by war or terrorism. But as seen in the immediate shift into normalcy following the aforementioned rocket attack, Israelis have developed the capacity to move on. To compartmentalize, but not to ignore. To grieve, but not to crumble. To take a hardship and build upon it – and often, in doing so, to beat the odds and skyrocket to success.

Resilience. I've seen it from driving on the roads of Israel to walking through the corridors of the powerful and famous. There's a steel to the spirit, a mettle that is just waiting to be tested. It's the resolve to carry on, the courage to continue, and the determination to succeed.

It's ISResilience. And the journey exploring what creates and sustains it was truly fascinating.

Naomi L. Baum

"Israel is this little pit bull surrounded by her enemies, and yet, it is strong enough to not only hold its own, but to flourish."
Howie Mandel, *Times of Israel*, July 26, 2013

September 1, 2000. I am patting myself on the back and feeling awfully proud that I have been accepted as a fellow in the ninth cohort of the Mandel School for Educational Leadership. I have been eagerly look-ing forward to the two-year fellowship, after working around the clock for more than eighteen years, most recently as director of the school psychology center in a neighboring regional center and director of the Education Department at a local teacher's college.

Who knew that on September 9, 2000, all hell would break loose with roadside shootings, suicide bombers, and random terrorist attacks that went from bad to worse in days? My dream of two years of peace-ful academic endeavors literally went up in smoke, as the psychological stress of the people around me, both where I lived and where I studied, was sent into the stratosphere.

How could I sit by and do nothing? To a certain degree, my hands were tied. By committing to the fellowship, I had agreed to leave all employment. I certainly wanted my replacement at the psychological services center to succeed and didn't want to undermine her. Yet how could I sit quietly and watch the suffering of so many children and adults, as they dealt with their very real fears – and often with sudden and traumatic loss? I morphed that feeling of helplessness into the creation of the Building Resilience Intervention (BRI), an innovative project that became the cornerstone of my work for the next two decades.

Resilience, the central concept of the BRI, focuses on the strengths we all have and how we can increase them. In a situation where terror is rampant and we feel helpless, we can actively choose to focus on coping, on strengths, on the cup that is half full. Taking these concepts into the community and introducing the BRI into work with teachers, childcare workers, first responders, parents, medical staff, and more has been the gratifying result of the initial two-year fellowship that gave me the time and resources to develop my knowledge and skills in the field of resilience and trauma.

As director of the Resilience Unit at Metiv – The Israel Psychotrauma Center, I was called upon to bring my knowledge and programs to disaster areas all over the world, including Haiti after the earthquake; Mexico in the wake of kidnappings; Biloxi, Mississippi, after Hurricane Katrina; and more. In each unique location, I was humbled by the mental health needs of the local population and their willingness to learn from our experiences and practices. While appreciating that cultures and languages may be quite different from our own, I have come to recognize that human feelings are universal. Sad is sad all over the world. Fear is fear no matter if you live in Port au Prince or Jerusalem. Trying to tease out the secrets of resilience – whether on my home turf in Israel or in Kathmandu, Nepal – has been an exhilarating professional journey.

On the personal side of things, a diagnosis of stage III breast cancer in 2010 brought me face to face with the fragility of life. All of the many skills related to resilience I had spent the last ten years teaching came to my aid as I met my cancer head on. Along with this came a very personal knowledge of how resilience can assist in a wide variety of challenging life circumstances. Working with women dealing with cancer has once again been a humbling experience, as I find that I learn more from them at each encounter.

Our book, *ISResilience*, shares with you some of the secrets we have learned from the remarkable Israelis we have met about their resilient approach to life. We are excited to have you join us on this journey and hopeful that, at book's end, you will share with us some of *your* secrets to resilience. We all have them. We invite you to open your hearts to learn, paying attention to what resonates with you as you read through the book. We look forward to hearing from you – you can contact us via the website: www.isresilience.com.

The Israeli Sabra – Resilience Personified

"I always enjoy coming to Israel. Israelis are warm, they're energetic people. Forthright. Very smart. I always like smart people. They're nice people, you know. Aggressive, and I respect that aggressiveness because you need it in their situation."

Robert De Niro, Presidential Conference, Jerusalem, June 19, 2013

The Prickly Pear

National symbols can provide a shortcut for understanding national character. The English are identified with the rose. The French are represented by the fleur-de-lis. Holland is associated with the tulip. Israelis have the cactus.

To be more precise, Israelis are often referred to as Sabras. A sabra is a cactus plant, and like the prickly pear, Sabras are known for their thorny exterior and their soft, sweet interior. Israelis are, by and large, proud of this description. In his book *The Sabra: The Creation of the New Jew*, sociologist Oz Almog explores the idea that the generation of Israelis born to the pioneers of the nascent, reborn State of Israel were both tough and self-assured, a product of nurture rather than nature. Presumably, the DNA of the inhabitants of the modern state was not so different from that of their immigrant parents or their Israeli forebears who remained in the land for millennia, even as so many were dispersed abroad. Yet the net result was a sea change.

Israelis have needed to be tough. Located in the most dangerous of regions, Israel is a tiny country, just nine miles wide at its narrowest point. The world's only Jewish country, it has historically been surrounded by hostile states, with some bent on Israel's destruction. More than three thousand years old and just several decades young, Israel is an amalgam of the ancient and the modern. The challenges that the reborn State of Israel has faced since its inception in 1948 are enormous. These include conventional war, terrorism, the absorption of millions of immigrants from different parts of the globe, and a concerted effort by regional enemies and their global allies to malign, sideline, and isolate the only truly free, democratic nation-state in the region.

Despite constant polls ranking Israelis among the "happiest" of world populations, life in Israel is insecure. Centuries of persecution have taught Israelis not to rely on others to rush to their defense. Nothing – not even ruling themselves independently – will give them complete security, and recent history has shown them that it never will. The modern State of Israel has held an outstretched arm of peace to enemies since its rebirth, and yet Israel is unable to fully trust the peace treaties it has already signed and the others that it so desperately seeks, in a region where one Middle Eastern dictator in the morning might be replaced by another in the afternoon. Meanwhile, events play out with a critical and too-often hypocritical world judging Israel's every action. It is a biting yet achingly true characterization of the very real threats continually faced by the Jewish state that the only people Israelis can truly depend on are themselves, something they have learned from experience.

Despite trying times, and against all odds, Israel has nevertheless prospered, and Israelis have demonstrated both a personal and national resilience that is recognized by all visitors to this tiny country. You often hear tourists to Israel bristle as their expectations of common courtesy and politeness brush up against the average Israeli's frankness and blunt manner. Get to know the Israeli people up close, however, and their warmness and hospitality abounds. Therein lies the contradiction. It is puzzling to tourists, as well as to those newcomers to Israel who have grown up abroad in more courteous and considerate societies. Adjectives used to describe Israelis include brash, skeptical, questioning, determined, stubborn, hot-headed, and combative, yet those pair with warm, loving, family oriented, forgiving, optimistic, and open.

When the chips are down and Israelis feel their collective back is up against the wall, both the exterior and interior characteristics of the Sabra take center stage. Outpourings of help, volunteerism, and caring for the less fortunate soar to unheard-of heights during times of trouble. The characteristics that manifest themselves on an individual level are a microcosm of what happens on the national level. Things do not always go Israel's way; far from it. Danger, including very real existential threats, is always just around the corner. Following each terror attack, border skirmish, or all-out war, Israel in general and Israelis in particular go through a grimly recurrent cycle of picking themselves up, dusting themselves off, and carrying on with life. That's called resilience.

Resilience Defined

The term *resilience*, or as it is known in Hebrew, *hosen*, refers to the ability to withstand difficulties, bounce back after troubles, and continue on, even in the face of gathering storm clouds. The concept includes within it two seemingly contradictory abilities: on the one hand to withstand and hang tough, and on the other hand to be spontaneous, to improvise, and to dare to attempt hitherto untried solutions to difficult problems. Psychologists have talked about "mental hardiness" or "coping" to characterize the essence of resilience, but while both ideas shed some light on the concept, the true definition is elusive. We seem to know what resilience is but have a hard time defining it.

The Oxford dictionary defines resilience as the capacity to recover quickly from difficulties and adds as a further clarification the word *toughness*. Resilience is this and much more. The source of the word *resilience* comes from the science of metallurgy, in which engineers measure how much stress or pressure various materials can withstand before breaking. The second Oxford definition, "the ability of a substance or object to spring back into shape; elasticity," relates to just that quality.

While the jury is out on the "real" definition of resilience, working definitions have developed out of necessity in planning interventions to help populations and individuals to recover in the aftermath of terror attacks, war, and natural disaster. Psychological literature has pointed the way to understanding what the essential elements of resilience are.

One of the conclusions of this research is that there are people who are born with internal characteristics that foster their resilience. People who are of above-average intelligence, good-looking, and were raised in intact families tend to be more resilient. Unfortunately, these are characteristics that are not within our control. On the other hand, even those who have grown up in adverse circumstances can find and foster resilience. In this book, we have preferred to focus on aspects of resilience that people can learn, grow from, impact, and possibly control, as well as lessons that we can all learn from some extraordinary Israelis who have overcome significant challenges.

The Three Keys

The Talmud (in *Taanit* 2a) teaches us that God holds the keys to childbirth, rain (which alludes to material sustenance), and reincarnation, but leaves the rest to us. To our minds, that means that resilience is in our hands. In the pages to follow, we will focus on those keys to resilience that we can control. What exactly are those keys? They include empathy, flexibility, and meaning. While this list is not exhaustive, these three keys, to our minds essential, will help us to analyze the outstanding people who have shared their stories with us and enable us to learn what we can take into our own lives in order to grow our resilience.

Key one: empathy. Empathy refers to the ability to be conversant in emotions, to identify one's own feelings and those of others, and to be open to a wide range of emotions. It includes the skills of self-awareness as well as sensitivity to others. A resilient person will not avoid a feeling, even if it is difficult or painful. Resilience demands that people feel a wide range of emotions, from sadness, loss, and pain to joy, happiness, and optimism. If people are afraid of pain or sadness, they tend to avoid it, shut it down, or become numb. This then interferes with their ability to feel other feelings as well. Israelis tend to be fairly open with their feelings. They show their joy and their pain. They certainly let you know why they are upset or frustrated. This empathy is an essential resilience key.

Key two: flexibility. Flexibility refers to the ability to approach life in a dynamic way. Sometimes we expect one thing and get another. Often, the road we have chosen appears blocked. Occasionally we are expecting a yes but receive a no. What do we do when that happens? How flexible are we? Can we change mid-course? Can we stop, review our options, and choose something else? Do we have a range of responses in our repertoire? Resilient people do. The famous Israeli ability to improvise stems from this flexibility in both thought and action.

Key three: meaning making. Viktor Frankl was a psychoanalyst and later the father of logotherapy, who survived the Holocaust by holding on to the idea that if you have some meaning in your life, you can withstand just about anything. He himself was living proof of this, surviving the horrors of the Shoah. Bringing the discussion of meaning to the table is imperative in our understanding of the nature of resilience. Why do bad things happen to good people? We may not have all the answers. We may actually have none of the answers. But encouraging discussion about why bad things happen, what we are to do with this, how we make peace with it, how we understand it, what message it has for us, and what meaning we make from it is essential in the building of resilience. Often, adults avoid this area of discussion or enquiry because they feel that they don't have the "right" answer. There is no "right" answer, and there rarely is one answer. Bringing the discussion of meaning out into the open is what is essential.

Ordinary Magic

Is resilience a character trait? Are you born resilient? Ingrid Schoon, a respected academic from University College, London, argues that resilience is not a personality characteristic. While you may be born physically strong, it is your environment, your upbringing, and the challenges you face that will help determine your mental capability to deal with what life throws at you, or in other words, your resilience. Resilience can be learned, and environments can be modified so that resilience can thrive. Anne Masten, a well-known psychologist who has spent her professional life researching resilient children, has called resilience "ordinary magic," a term that we embrace wholeheartedly.

Resilience is common enough to be considered ordinary. Yet the ability of people to bounce back from great adversity and continue on with their lives, often developing and thriving, is quite magical. While we have just said "bouncing back," what we really mean is "bouncing forward." This is a term that Frimet Walsh, a noted family therapist, coined to describe a resilient response. Bouncing forward carries with it the understanding that trauma and challenging life situations change people. When they return to their lives, they are not exactly the same people they were before, and they usually don't pick up exactly where they left off. Ask anybody who has recovered from cancer, survived a terrorist attack, gone through a war, and they will tell you that they are different people than they were before. This added value often takes the form of greater perspective, new relationships, deeper beliefs, life changes, and more.

Are some people more naturally resilient than others? Do you know a resilient personality when you see one? Resilient people are able to withstand very difficult and often traumatic situations. They don't crumble; sometimes they show great strength and leadership that they didn't know they had. The resilience test comes in the weeks and months following a crisis or trauma. In the first hours and days after a potentially traumatizing event, the adrenaline flows, and there may be a lot of support from the community. Resilience, though, is built for the long term; it's how people cope day in and day out when a lousy situation goes on for a while. Social support and community support are absolutely critical and probably some of the most important aspects that support resilience.

The Israeli Character

In this book, we set out to meet resilient Israelis and understand where their inner strength comes from. Our journey has taken us the length and breadth of Israel, meeting people from all walks of life. This adventure was at turns inspiring and emotional, deeply affecting and uplifting, often at the very same moment. It gave us a deeper understanding that Israel as a collective and Israelis as individuals have become particularly adept at turning a bad situation into an advantageous one – or, as the saying goes, turning lemons into lemonade.

Any Israeli could have given testimony for this book. Israelis routinely carry on with their day-to-day lives not just when things are calm and peaceful but when rockets are launched at them, through stabbing intifadas, during official conflicts and wars and unofficial waves of gruesome terrorism. And they don't just survive – they thrive. Imbued in the DNA of this nation is the understanding that survival isn't optional – it's a necessity. Two national mottos in Hebrew symbolize the hard-headed, deep-seated refusal to give up under any circumstance: "*Am Yisrael chai*" (the Jewish nation lives) and "*Ein li eretz acheret*" (I don't have any other land). As Golda Meir is said to have remarked of Israel's prowess in an ongoing conflict: "We Jews have a secret weapon in our struggle…we have no place to go."

Have Israelis developed resilience and the capacity to survive in a manner that is distinct and different from other peoples? Is there something unique in the way Israelis cope? We met and engaged with some notable Israelis to examine their personal resilience. We also explored whether personal resilience plays out nationwide, and if there is such a thing as national resilience.

Some of the people we interviewed are easily recognizable; their acts of bravery, success, and achievement are well known. Others are living out their daily lives with little public recognition, yet have overcome unimaginable adversity. Our journey took us to meet with Israelis young and old, male and female, black and white, Jewish and Arab – people with vastly different backgrounds and socioeconomic circumstances. As we observed, talked with them, and explored their personal resilience, we began to extrapolate the keys to resilience in order to learn just how an individual can identify and strengthen his or her own powers of resilience. We reflected on how these personal stories can be a window to understanding the complexity of Israeli resilience nationwide and how all of us as individuals can apply these lessons to our personal lives.

Our hope is that you will not only enjoy reading these stories, but will actually be able to apply some of the lessons to your own lives, developing your own "keys to resilience." The cactus, tough yet soft enough to be flexible, combined with a lot of feeling and a good dose of empathy as well, is an apt characterization of resilience from the Israeli perspective. Add to that a generous measure of living a life filled with meaning, and you get the essence of Israeli resilience. This is reflected in all of the stories you will meet in this book.

Against All Odds

"If you tell yourself, 'I will win,' then you'll win."

Avigdor Kahalani

Valley of Tears

Here were the odds: Syrians, more than 1,200 tanks; Israelis, 170 tanks. How did Avigdor Kahalani, a twenty-nine-year-old lieutenant-colonel, overcome this disparity and lead his beleaguered battalion to victory, quashing the Syrian tank invasion in its tracks? That is precisely what happened in the middle of the Yom Kippur War in October 1973, at a place that would later become known as the Valley of Tears. Even today the rusting skeletons of burnt Syrian tanks remain as a gruesome reminder of an epic battle.

Forty-five years after the campaign that would define his career, Kahalani reflects on his character and what led him to this moment of extreme bravery. In doing so, he quotes a line from Shaul Tchernichovsky's famous Hebrew poetry:

A human being is nothing but a little plot of land.
A human being is nothing but the view of his native landscape.

Kahalani is, in his own words, an image of the homeland he grew up in. He was born in British-ruled Mandatory Palestine in 1944 and lived a simple life in a strife-filled region. A mere ten meters separated the Jewish neighborhood in Nes Ziona that he called home from the adjacent Arab village. Relations were tense. Gunshots would ring out every evening as night fell, targeting the unarmed citizens of Nes Ziona. Life was full of contradictions. On the one hand, young Avigdor feared that an Arab would kidnap him some night. At the same time, his best friend and playmate was an Arab neighbor boy named Mahmoud.

Kahalani's Yemenite parents immigrated as infants to pre-state Israel together with their parents. At the turn of the last century, before his grandparents immigrated, there were approximately thirty thousand Jews in Yemen. Today, after a century of persecution and resulting rescue attempts bringing them to safety in Israel, there are no more than thirty. Avigdor's mother washed floors to earn money for the family. Never having attended school, she could neither read nor write. His father completed the fifth grade before being forced to leave school in order to work and help support the family. Irrespective of their lack of formal education, the home they made together with their four children was a warm and loving one. Avigdor's father would return home from work at four in the afternoon, only to head back out, this time accompanied by his son, to work the nearby fields in order to earn more money for their growing family.

Traditions were strong in the Kahalani family. Father and son would attend the neighborhood synagogue together every Friday night and Shabbat, but there were flourishes of modernity too. Young Avigdor was allowed to ride his bicycle on the Sabbath, a practice frowned upon by some more religious Jews in the neighborhood. Unlike his parents, Avigdor, growing up in the nascent State of Israel, did get an elementary as well as a high school education, which was not mandatory at the time. His parents did not have the money to pay tuition for high school, however the Ort School that he attended allowed him to work while studying in order to pay for his education. Graduating high school in the early 1960s, Kahalani was crystal clear about his future. He wanted to be a combat soldier.

Toughness and Tenacity

To his great satisfaction, Kahalani was immediately drafted into the Armored Corps in 1962. Ambitious Avigdor quickly began climbing the ranks, becoming a tank commander and following that, a platoon commander. The journey was not a smooth one, however. Kahalani was kicked out of the Bahad 1 officers' training course as he was training to become a platoon commander. As a tank commander, he excelled, and his superiors could not understand how their number one commander had been asked to leave the officers' training. This provoked an unusual internal IDF argument, whereupon it was decided that Kahalani should return to the second half of the officers' training course, which consisted of specialized training in the Armored Corps. He did well there but could not get the rank of second lieutenant because he had never completed the first level of training and thus had not received an officer's pin. The army offered Avigdor the rank of "acting officer" and said that if he returned to Bahad 1 to complete the first part of the training, he would then get the full rank. He refused what he perceived as a downgrade and remained a platoon commander without rank for nine months. In the end it was the army, not Kahalani, who backed down, and he was awarded the full officer's rank, without ever completing officers' training.

In 1967, during the waning hours of the Six-Day War, Kahalani's army career – and his life – nearly came to an end. In some of the final fighting of the conflict, twenty-three-year-old Kahalani's Magach M48 tank suffered a direct hit and caught fire. Avigdor was rushed to the hospital, the sole survivor of the four-man crew. Sixty percent of his body was burned, and he required seventeen operations, including twelve plastic surgeries. Avigdor lay in a hospital bed for a full year. Even after being discharged from the hospital, he continued to bleed from the burn wounds, but nothing would stop young Avigdor.

Despite his life-threatening injury and his incomplete healing, Kahalani continued to fixate on the goal of serving his country. Knowing that his health profile would gain him an immediate dismissal from the army, he finessed his way back by lying and saying that his medical record was lost in the war. Surprisingly, he was assigned a new profile of 97 (out of 100), paving his way back to the Armored Corps. Just a year after flames had ravaged his body and taken the lives of his crew, Kahalani readied himself for the toughest test of his young life – getting back into a tank. Acutely aware that he had suffered a traumatic event, Kahalani worried that the trauma might come to haunt him, and he feared freezing in the line of duty.

While post-traumatic stress disorder was not a well-known entity back in 1968, Kahalani was familiar with combat stress and knew enough about the freeze response that might threaten his future functioning. He made a conscious decision not to let this hinder him. In the end, he in fact functioned very well under fire, while it was his tank that froze and refused to move.

On Yom Kippur, October 6, 1973, the holiest day on the Jewish calendar, Kahalani was twenty-nine years old. On that day, Egypt and Syria launched a surprise military assault on two fronts against Israel. Israelis went from fasting and praying in synagogues nationwide to heading out to fight a war in which the stakes were survival itself. While the Syrians and Egyptians had planned the attack for nine months, the IDF was caught totally off guard. On the northern front, Syrian forces overran the Israeli defenses within twenty-four hours, penetrating deep into Israeli territory. Over the next two days, Israeli forces were able to impede the Syrian advance at great cost in men and machinery, but the enemy was intent on advancing.

It was the fourth day of fighting, and the IDF knew it was imperative to head off a fresh Syrian advance in the Golan Heights, which, if successful, would have allowed the invading army to advance deep into the heartland of Israel. Israel could not afford to lose the strategic advantage afforded them by Mount Bental and the surrounding Golan Heights. The man tasked to counter the Syrian attack was Avigdor Kahalani.

What ensued was one of the most significant tank battles ever to take place in the annals of military warfare. Leading up to the battle, Kahalani pulled together tanks and soldiers from several armored corps units that had been decimated in the previous days of fighting. As the battle began, Kahalani directed it from the roof of his tank, unprotected. He did this in order to maintain a line of vision between himself and his soldiers. They knocked off Syrian tank after tank, under heavy, unceasing mortar fire, eventually turning the tide of the war and regaining momentum. The IDF was then able to push the Syrians back over the 1967 border, creating a major turning point in the war. With tanks on fire as far as the eye could see and casualties in the hundreds, the battlefield became known as the Valley of Tears.

Driven by Meaning

Avigdor Kahalani today is a kindly man in his seventies with a warm smile, father to three children and grandfather to seven. His final rank in the Israel Defense Forces was brigadier-general, and he became one of Israel's most decorated soldiers, having received the Distinguished

Service Medal, the Medal of Valor, and the Presidential Medal of Distinction. Had he not lied about his medical records and forced his way back into the army from a debilitating injury, the course of the military campaign might have been very different.

His heroic battle was an act of bravery by any estimation. Kahalani reflects that his courage stems from resilience: "I have medals of honor for bravery, but it's a matter of place and time and constellation. You could say that I succeeded against all odds. In Hebrew, the word *gever* [man] is derived from the word *l'hitgaber* [overcome] and the word *gevurah* [bravery]. If I had any kind of bravery, it was overcoming my injuries and returning to my tank, not because I stopped the Syrians in their tracks. I overcame my fears: that's where my bravery was." He overcame those fears via sheer force of will – mind over matter.

On the national level, Kahalani sees mandatory military service as a benefit for the personal development of Israelis, calling it "the greatest blessing a citizen could have." His view is that anyone who serves in the IDF will thereby become more mature, more responsible, more patriotic, and a better friend. Most of all, he feels that army service imbues young adults with a sense of leadership. To prove his point, he quotes the Bible: "Look upon me, and do likewise," said Gideon (Judges 7:17). Like Gideon, IDF commanders lead by example. The rallying cry of the IDF commander is *"Acharai!"* (After me!), unlike other armies' commanders who stay in the rear and direct the battle from there. As a result, more commanders are killed in battle in the IDF than in other militaries, because they lead from the front.

Kahalani compares a military commander to a stage actor on Israel's famed Habima Theater stage. "An actor, even if he has a fever, gets up on the stage and continues to act. A commander needs to be an example and a symbol, no matter what. Sure, he is also afraid, but he needs to overcome his fears."

Avigdor Kahalani is certain that what carried him through the difficult hours and days of his life is a sense of duty and a positive attitude. His way of thinking is always centered around the meaning with which his life has been imbued and the path that he has chosen: service to people and to country is a guiding beacon for him. From a young age, Kahalani knew he wanted to be a combat soldier. He never gave up, even against all odds, when he suffered burns on more than half of his body. He was driven. Driven by purpose, driven by duty, and driven by meaning.

For Kahalani, purpose in life lies at the root of his resilience. There was no finer or clearer purpose than serving his country. While it would have been very easy and even honorable for him to retire from active duty after his devastating injury, Kahalani would not even consider that route. He was a man with a mission. He would not let anything stand in his way, even a life-threatening injury.

Finding meaning and purpose in our lives can enrich us and guide us when times are tough. For many of us, this is not as simple as it was for Kahalani. Often the search for meaning and purpose is circuitous and may take us down some roads that prove to be dead ends. That is fine. The essence is that we are looking, searching, and journeying. Some of us find our raison d'être more easily than others. The key is never giving up. Finding one's life's purpose – or perhaps identifying even more than one driving force in our lives – is an important piece in the mosaic of resilience. Avigdor Kahalani's purposeful focus helped him overcome terrible injuries and subsequent fears and propelled him into a life well lived.

Thirty years since his retirement from the IDF, Kahalani feels blessed that he was imbued with a sense of duty and a positive attitude. Losing, he says, was simply not an option. He has chosen to spend his retirement educating thousands of twelfth-graders at the site of his most famous battle. Every week he meets groups of high school students who are on the threshold of induction into compulsory military service and shares with them his life's lessons. Looking across the vista on the Golan Heights, Kahalani reminds the next generation of Israel's citizens and soldiers of the words inscribed on the gravestone of John F. Kennedy, taken from the president's 1961 inaugural address. "Ask not what your country can do for you – ask what you can do for your country." As he retells his story, the students and their teachers often shed tears. Avigdor Kahalani reminds those gathered that they hold Israel's future in their hands, as he holds aloft the nation's flag, overlooking the Valley of Tears.

David Beats Goliath

"The drug of freedom is universally potent."

Natan Sharansky,
The Case for Democracy

A Giant Mind

Religion was nonexistent in the Ukrainian city of Donetsk, part of the militantly atheist Soviet Union of the 1950s and '60s. For young Anatoly Shcharansky, that meant no Jewish traditions and no knowledge of Jewish history. He was born in 1948, the same year that the Jewish homeland of Israel was reborn, but Israel was also taboo in the USSR, as it sealed its borders to the democratic world in a quest to have complete dominion over the minds and souls of its citizens. The Soviet Union prevented any contact with the West to all its citizens, and its Iron Curtain policy curtailed movement, including the freedom to leave.

Sharansky remembers a small sculpture in his childhood home of Donatello's David with his foot on Goliath's head. His aunt had seen it at the open-air market and bought the sculpture thinking that his parents might like it because of its Jewish theme. With their almost nonexistent sense of Jewish identity, that association was lost on the young Shcharansky children. Anatoly's older brother reacted to the statue by telling his mother that she ought to make pants for the naked David. In hindsight, there could scarcely be a better role model for the diminutive Sharansky than tiny David defeating the giant Goliath. One cannot help but think about the parallel between little Anatoly Shcharansky and the superpower Soviet Union, which he would eventually help to bring down.

As we sit in his large, bright office in Jerusalem, with an Israeli flag and a life-sized portrait of human rights activist Andrei Sakharov as a backdrop, it is hard to imagine that the man in front of us once languished for more than nine years incarcerated in the Gulag of the former Soviet Union. This Prisoner of Zion (who Hebraized and simplified his name to Natan Sharansky long before his arrival in Israel) is charming, articulate, and warm. We meet in his office, that of the director general of the Jewish Agency (he has since moved on to the Institute of the Study of Global Antisemitism and Policy), but growing up in Donetsk, the only thing Jewish about Sharansky was that his father told him he was a Jew. More specifically, his father made sure that young Anatoly knew that the only way a Jew could get ahead was by being the best in whatever he chose to do. That resounding message would lead Sharansky to become an outstanding mathematician as well as a world-class chess player.

The arc of Natan Sharansky's life is as remarkable as is the fact that he brought the Soviet regime to its knees from his solitary prison cell. It was his mother who taught young Anatoly chess at a very young age. She told him it was important that he learn how to play, because in chess, unlike in the society in which they lived, one could think freely. Her son followed his mother's advice and became a chess prodigy. For

Sharansky, height became consequential in the chess arena as well; the taller his opponent, the more driven he was to beat his adversary quickly.

While these messages may have been nuanced rather than overt, there were strong undercurrents in the family household laying the foundations for the dissident free thinker that Sharansky would become in the early 1970s. His nascent interest in Israel and all things Jewish began to develop after the Six-Day War in June 1967. He became involved in the Soviet dissident movement, aligning himself with Sakharov, and as he did so, Sharansky's Jewish identity began to take shape.

Surviving the Gulag

In 1973, Sharansky applied for permission to leave for Israel. His application was refused due to "security reasons." This spurred him to become a spokesman and leader for the "refuseniks," those Jews who were forbidden to leave the Soviet Union for Israel, sometimes for months and often for years. He also represented the Moscow Helsinki Group, which scrutinized Soviet compliance with human rights. During this time, Sharansky had contact with many Westerners, including politicians, reporters, and American Jews who came to teach and support the refuseniks. On July 4, 1974, on the eve of her departure to Israel, he married his twenty-four-year-old fiancée Natalia Stieglitz (who later changed her name to Avital) in a private Jewish ceremony, itself an act of rebellion. Less than twenty-four hours later, Avital left, with her husband reassuring her that they would most definitely meet up again in no more than three to six months. That was not to be. Twelve long years of separation ensued before they would be reunited.

Sharansky was arrested by the KGB (the Soviet secret police) in 1977 and was falsely accused of being a spy for the CIA. After a six

month "investigation," he was brought to trial and accused of espio-
nage and high treason. Found guilty in the Soviet court, Sharansky was
sentenced to thirteen years of imprisonment and forced labor. His cap-
tivity would include stretches inside the infamous Lefortovo, Vladimir,
and Chistopol Prisons, where he spent much time in solitary confinement as well as detention in the notorious Perm-36 Gulag. Just prior to
receiving his sentence, Sharansky addressed his accusers: "To the court
I have nothing to say – to my wife and the Jewish people I say, 'Next
year in Jerusalem.'"

In trying to extrapolate from Sharansky's life experiences some
of what contributed to his resilience, a feeling of control or agency is
prominent. At the very beginning of his incarceration in Lefortovo, he
decided that no one could or would impact his own self-esteem. He
would grant no one that amount of control over him, ever. "The only
person who can demean me," Sharansky relates to us in his spacious
Jewish Agency office, "is myself, by doing something that I would later
be ashamed of." In Sharansky's memoir, *Fear No Evil*, he writes: "I
decided it was best to treat my captors like the weather. A storm can
cause you problems, and sometimes those problems can be humiliating. But the storm itself doesn't humiliate you." Once he realized this,
he "repeated this principle over and over," like a mantra, until it was an
integral part of him: "*Nothing they do can humiliate me.*"

Defiance in the face of isolation, intimidation, and torture became
the theme of Sharansky's long detention in the Gulag. A sense of humor
also became an essential survival tool for Sharansky, aiding his ability
to detach himself from the reality of Soviet detention. In line with his
coping mechanism of taking charge, Natan would enjoy telling his captors funny anti-Soviet jokes and watching them attempt not to burst
into laughter, for doing so would betray a disloyalty to the regime.
Again asserting self-control, Sharansky undertook hunger strikes to
stand up for his rights and those of the other inmates.

Sharansky turned into the icon of the movement to grant freedom to Soviet Jewry, and his wife became the campaigner-in-chief, teaming up with legions of activists the world over who rallied for the cause and targeted global pressure on Soviet leader Mikhail Gorbachev. Avital traveled around the world and met with political leaders and heads of state, while Jews and human rights leaders around the world united around the effort. On February 11, 1986, Mikhail Gorbachev ordered that Anatoly Shcharansky be freed. He arrived in Israel that same day.

In exploring the roots of his personal resilience and the resilience of Israelis, Sharansky shares with us a very tight conceptual model of what makes Israel and the Jewish people unique. According to Sharansky, the two concepts that characterize Israel and the Jewish people are freedom and identity. To make his point, he says that Europe today holds freedom as an ideal, but has given up on identity, adopting the anti-nationalist idea expressed in John Lennon's "Imagine." Europe, with its common currency, passport, and open borders, has to an extent erased the notion of national identity. At the other end of the spectrum are the radical Islamists who have a very strong identity but have trampled the concept of freedom.

Central to the character of Israel and the Jewish people is the marriage of identity with freedom. This, says Sharansky, is the secret of how the Jews have continued to live and flourish outside their homeland for thousands of years in the diaspora. That, together with optimism. The inveterate optimist, Sharansky quotes a study showing that when asked to say whether today is better than tomorrow, 75 percent of Americans agree that today is better. In contrast, 75 percent of Israelis think that tomorrow will be better than today. Positivity is a core part of Sharansky's own personality, reflecting his analysis of optimistic Israel. He readily smiles, laughs, and always looks at the bright side of things. That upbeat optimism is all the more exceptional when considering the depths from which Sharansky has emerged. Yet transitioning from life in solitary confinement to life as a family man in Israel was not as difficult as one might think, according to Natan. Because he felt free on the inside and never adopted the mentality of a prisoner, it was not so hard for him to adjust.

A Woman with a Mission

When he talks about his wife Avital, Natan gets a special look in his eye, and his voice takes on a certain softness. He shared with us Avital's well-known dedication to gaining his freedom and reiterated how her simplicity, straightforwardness, and reserved nature won the leaders of the free world over to her cause. She maintained a determined posture and a single-minded focus over the course of thirteen years, never wavering for a moment. Convinced that shining a light on the plight of her husband would result in his freedom, she traveled the world tirelessly, making her case for her husband, including – famously – to US president Ronald Reagan. Yet she never let the publicity or fame confuse her or lure her back into the public eye once Natan achieved his freedom.

From the moment he arrived in Israel, despite his well-earned celebrity status, his wife Avital insisted on leading a private family life away from the spotlight of fame. In fact, she was so adamant about this that she would actually prevent people in the street from taking pictures of her husband and was fiercely protective of both him and their two daughters. Today, Sharansky is certain that this allowed them to raise their children in a normal environment and gave him the ability to live a balanced life. In trying to understand her great success, Natan is sure that her spiritual convictions gave her the confidence and were at the root of her resilience, allowing her to keep fighting during the long years of his imprisonment. She was a woman with a mission.

Avital's outspoken activism, coupled with her husband's brave stand, inspired Jews and people of good faith around the world to rally to the cause of freedom for the three million Soviet Jews. Sitting with Sharansky, the authors recall how we joined demonstrations and campaigned to support our brothers and sisters who were suffering under the regime. One of us (Naomi) was tapped along with her husband to infiltrate the Soviet Union, smuggling prayer books, Jewish history books, and books about Israel to refuseniks, along with vitamins and jeans that could be sold on the black market so that the refuseniks would have a bit of food, after losing their jobs.

You Are with Me

Does spirituality or religious belief aid his own resilience? Sharansky, who has avoided labels such as "religious" or "secular," has an attachment to his tiny, well-worn book of Psalms, which he whips out of his shirt pocket to display with a broad smile. This small leather-covered book was a gift from Avital, given to him just days before his arrest. The book was confiscated on his arrival to the Gulag, and it took three long years of fighting with the Soviet authorities for it to be returned to him in prison. The day his Psalms were returned to him was also the day Sharansky received the heartbreaking news of his father's death. The confluence of these two events led him to an in-depth study of the book, in which he found solace, joining Jews who have for generations found comfort in Psalms during times of great sorrow. He painstakingly copied each one of the 150 Psalms and then began translating them into Russian. When later on in his prison life, the Psalms were confiscated once again, Sharansky went on hunger strikes and spent more than 186 days in solitary confinement in his fight to get the Psalms back. In the end, he won the battle, and the Psalms were returned to him.

One of the first psalms that Sharansky read in prison was Psalm 23: "Though I walk through the valley of the shadow of death, I will fear no evil, for You are with me." Whether the "You" symbolized God – as the Psalmist had intended – or Avital or the legions of supporters who were rallying to Sharansky's side in Israel and worldwide, it mattered not. The idea of support, even from afar, gave Sharansky strength to withstand the worst of KGB incarceration. Indeed, the miniature book of Psalms with the tiny letters held within it a message he felt was being channeled forward three thousand years directly to him from its author King David, whose statue had adorned the mantelpiece in his childhood home. The book had become imbued with a feeling of spiritual connection and protection.

On February 11, 1986, the eve of his liberation, before alighting the plane that was to take him to Berlin and then on to Israel, Sharansky asked for his book of Psalms. He was told that he had already received everything that was allowed, and he would not receive anything more. Immediately, he dropped to the snowy ground, flat on his back, shouting and screaming, instigating his final one-man demonstration on Soviet soil. Sharansky refused to budge until the treasured book was safely returned to his hand. On his flight to freedom, he turned to Psalm 30: "I will extol You, oh Lord, for You have raised me up and have not let my enemies rejoice over me…. Oh Lord, You have brought me up from the abyss."

Sharansky was able to endure incarceration, solitary confinement, and isolation. The factors contributing to his resilience included his optimism, humor, and the knowledge that he had dedicated support from his wife and his supporters in the West. Sharansky embodied all the keys of resilience we outlined in the introduction: his fight against the Soviets was imbued with meaning; he was a man whose mission was crystal clear, and he never wavered; he knew what he was fighting for, and all of his deprivations were for a higher purpose. All of these elements together with his unique personality forged a battle for freedom that the world will never forget.

Standing on the Glienicke Bridge, which linked East and West Germany, the crossing point between Communist suppression and the free West, Sharansky's captors gave a final instruction to their prisoner: Walk in a straight line across the bridge. In his inimitable way, Sharansky zigzagged his way to the waiting Americans on the other side. Once again, David had beaten Goliath.

Journey to the Promised Land

"For me, resilience is the emotional resources plus the social support that allow you to cope with injury, conflict, distress, and pain. And laughter. Laughter is part of resilience."

Shula Mola

A Grueling Exodus

Shula Mola and Mequnante Rahamim welcome us into their modest living room at their third-floor walk-up in a Jerusalem neighborhood that is on the brink of becoming up-and-coming. When offered something to drink, we immediately request, "Ethiopian coffee, of course!" They both smile and laugh, and Shula whips out the frying pan and measures green coffee beans into it. Within minutes, the aroma of the roasting beverage fills the air. Little did we realize that making Ethiopian coffee was such a labor-intensive endeavor, and if we had, we probably would have settled for an instant coffee. However, the wait and the pride in Shula and Mequnante's eyes as we savor the strong, bitter coffee is well worth it.

We sit on matching gray sofas in their small living room. Settling down to our conversation, Shula takes over, and Mequnante sits nearby, closely listening as his wife tells her story. Shula is completing her doctorate in communications and directs an organization for Ethiopian *olim* (new residents of Israel). Mequnante is a clinical social worker at Metiv – The Israel Psychotrauma Center – where he heads up a project to develop treatment protocols and modalities for Ethiopians in Israel. This is the first time he is witnessing his wife retell her journey from start to finish. While he has facilitated for many of his clients the retelling of their own personal exodus, surprisingly, he has never heard a complete version of his wife's arduous trek to seek a new life in Israel. This is indicative of the reticence that the Ethiopian community has displayed in sharing their traumatic journeys to Israel, reminiscent in some ways of Holocaust survivors who were not eager to share their stories until many years had passed.

Shula is a lively, articulate forty-something mother of four. She arrived in Israel at the age of twelve after a harrowing voyage from Africa, which she proceeds to relate in great detail. She has a captive audience and appears to enjoy relating her story, even if some of the moments are quite painful. In hundreds of scattered villages in the north and northwest of Ethiopia lived the Beta Israel, Jews who had been separated from global Jewish communities for a thousand years. Over the centuries, some had been forcibly converted to Christianity, but many tens of thousands continued to practice Jewish ritual, omitting many of the more "modern" rabbinic customs and practices that were simply unknown to them in villages where Jewish history stood still and existence was relatively basic. Aside from material constraints, life was not easy: over the years, Ethiopian Jews faced persecution from Christians, Muslims, and later communists.

Ethiopia in the 1970s was racked by civil war and revolution as a government inspired by Marxism was swept to power. Toward the end of that decade, the Israeli government extended the Law of Return – which gives Jews the right to citizenship in the world's only Jewish country – to apply to Ethiopian Jews. Great efforts were made to help them escape to Israel from Ethiopia, which did not have diplomatic relations with the Jewish state and which banned emigration. The first refugees from the Tigray area walked the entire journey to Israel by foot with little external assistance. Mass immigration reached a peak in the early 1980s with the clandestine operations bringing huge numbers of people from Gondar, through the Sudan, with Mossad agents waiting there to assist them to flee by plane. Escape was perilous – with the danger of robbery, rape, and disease awaiting them – and over four thousand people perished along the way. In the 1980s and 1990s, larger numbers of immigrants were brought to Israel, most notably around eight thousand as part of Operation Moses (November 21, 1984–January 5, 1985) and later over fourteen thousand in Operation Solomon (May 24–25, 1991). Today, there are approximately 150,000 Israeli citizens of Ethiopian origin.

Shula's life began in the village of Doro Wuha, a name that means "water of the chickens." Jews in Ethiopia often settled near bodies of water that could be used for purification ceremonies. Her community was so close to a river that the chickens would walk down to take a drink, hence the name of the village. One of three children, she grew up like most other Ethiopian Jews in a very rural society. Her mother, recently divorced, saw the move to Israel as a way to improve her unsatisfactory situation in the village. Despite the fact that her grandfather felt this was not a good time to make the trip, Shula's mother insisted and joined a small group of people setting out for Israel via the Sudan.

It was to be a difficult and sometimes tragic journey. Along the way, people stole their jewelry and household items, insisting that they would not need them where they were going. There wasn't enough food to go around; Shula remembers this but does not remember actually feeling hungry. She does remember carrying her baby brother on her back for many hours, giving her mother, who was in a weakened state, a break from the burden. They walked barefoot, at night, over rocks and brush. Shula can remember that her feet were bruised but does not remember a feeling of pain. The dominant emotion that she does remember is fear. Fear when highway bandits robbed them at gunpoint, and fear at the border with Sudan when the soldiers did not allow them entry. After enough *baksheesh* (bribes), they were allowed to pass through, all except for one old man who was too exhausted to move and stayed behind.

The season was summer. Heavy rains fell at night, followed by days of searing sunshine. Malaria was rampant. Shula's little brother became ill, and her mother herself was in a very weakened state. At this point, the group pooled their money to rent some trucks. They piled into the rickety vehicles, but after about thirty minutes, one of them broke down. They decided to turn around and return to the village from which they had set out. By then there was no food, and they had to beg from the villagers for some sacks of rice. Meanwhile, Shula's baby brother was getting sicker and sicker. They were at the mercy of the Sudanese, and rumors were rampant. One rumor circulating was that the Sudanese were planning to abandon them in the desert. Another rumor was that the bread had camel milk in it, which was not kosher. Starving but strictly adherent to their religion, the adults refrained and only the children ate it. A pervasive sense of fear accompanied these weeks.

Dream Meets Reality

What kept Shula going and occupied her thoughts more than anything else was Jerusalem. She spent her days and nights dreaming of the shimmering city. In her twelve-year-old mind, the goal of this lengthy and treacherous journey that she, her mother, and brothers had undertaken, along with all the other people from her village, was to reach Jerusalem. She was certain that there she would find the Beit Hamikdash, the Holy Temple, resplendent in all its glory. She pictured the Kohanim (priests), all of them dark-skinned, wearing white robes and bringing sacrifices. These thoughts got her through the long days and the even longer nights.

Shula's journey took a total of four months. The final stop was Khartoum, where the group boarded a plane to France arranged for them by the Israeli authorities, spending one night in a hotel in Paris before taking off from there to Israel. When they arrived at the hotel in France, they were afraid to sleep on the sheets, they were so clean and white. They had no idea what to do with the toilets, and when they were told what they were for, they were appalled that such a sparkling, clean, and beautiful room would be used for such a base purpose! Arriving in Israel, they were immediately given Hebrew names with little regard to the Ethiopian names they came with. Shula recalls being astounded by all the white people around her. She had no idea that in Jerusalem (and she was certain this was Jerusalem, rather than the airport) there would be so many *farangim* (their word for white folks). She had seen only a very few white people in her twelve years. She was also surprised by the immodest way the women were dressed, in tight pants and tank tops. This did not reconcile well with her fantasies about Jerusalem and service in the Holy Temple.

Upon arrival in Israel, Shula and her family were taken to a hostel in the southern city of Kiryat Gat. Adulation at their arrival soon gave way to reality. The journey had taken its toll. Her brothers and mother were immediately hospitalized, her mother for a month and her younger brother for six months. Shula's first weeks in Israel were spent in the hospital tending to sick family members. When asked how she made the journey from Kiryat Gat to the hospital, she shrugs off the question, not remembering it as a difficulty. At twelve years old, Shula was taking care of everybody and everything. Having made her way from Africa to the Middle East, now nothing was too hard for her.

After less than a year, she enrolled in a secondary school with a dorm and moved out of the family apartment. In school she excelled, and though she did very well academically, she has very mixed feelings about the school and its staff. Her feeling of being patronized, of being put down and minimized, is very strong. In the same way that she had never interacted with white people, they were unaware of black Jews. Her customs and practice of Judaism were often not recognized as legitimate or of value, and she was expected to adapt to Talmudic Judaism, without a murmur. Ethiopian culture was viewed as primitive and was looked down upon.

It took more than a year after arriving in Israel before Shula finally reached Jerusalem. The opportunity came via a school trip, and her excitement and anticipation were palpable. A disappointment lay in store for her. No-one had told her that the Second Temple had been destroyed. When she saw the Western Wall for the first time – a symbol of devotion for so many since it was liberated from foreign rule in 1967 – she was crushed. The Wall, the remnant of the retaining wall of the Second Temple, is considered a holy place for Jews and a site of pilgrimage and prayer, but for Shula it was a poor excuse for what she had dreamed of on her long journey to Israel. She had imagined the majesty of the Temple as it once was, gleaming and gold. The large stones representing its remains held no magic for her.

The Boy Who Loved School

As Shula winds down her story and Mequnante begins his, the contrast between the couple is remarkable. Shula is outgoing, lively, and some might even say brash. Undoubtedly her chutzpah and her intelligence has gotten her through many a tough spot. Mequnante, on the other hand, is a gentle, soft-spoken man, whose exterior demeanor belies his inner strength.

Mequnante begins his story describing village life in Ethiopia, as the tenth of eleven children. He was a shepherd along with his older brother at the age of six or seven and desperately wanted to go to school. His father said that only one of the boys could go to school, and Mequnante insisted it would be him. When his father did not agree, citing the brother's age as a reason to send him, Mequnante made sure that several of the goats were lost, so that his father would soon realize that he had chosen the wrong son to be the shepherd. His father acknowledged his mistake, and Mequnante and his brother switched places. Thus began Mequnante's quest for education, which continues to this day, when he is pursuing an advanced degree in social work at the Hebrew University of Jerusalem.

Mequnante's journey from Ethiopia is in some ways similar to Shula's, but in many aspects quite different. He left on his own, at age thirteen, without his family. He actually left surreptitiously, without notifying his parents or siblings, not wanting any of them to get into trouble with the authorities for aiding and abetting his departure. Mequnante joined up with a group of Jews making their way to Israel via the Sudan. His group, like Shula's, was plagued by bandits and robbers, by starvation, by trickery and thievery, and by disease. Unlike Shula, he spent close to three years in a refugee camp in the Sudan, taking on the identity of a Sudanese Arab, before escaping and arriving in Israel at the age of sixteen. There he was reunited with a brother who had come to Israel seventeen years earlier. He enrolled in an agricultural high school and spent his days as a high school student and his nights working in a slaughterhouse in order to be able to send money back home for his family to come to Israel. Mequnante tells the story in a matter-of-fact way, but considering how most sixteen-year-olds behave, he is clearly extraordinary.

Mequnante talks about the great responsibility he felt then and still feels for his entire family. Shula and Mequnante are the in-between generation, young enough to adapt to a new country and learn its language and mores, yet old enough to shoulder responsibilities far beyond their years that normally belong to the family elders. Due to their inability to learn the language and adapt to the culture, the elders have lost an element of their previous status within the family and community; they look to Mequnante and his generation for guidance and leadership. Mequnante's family eventually arrived in Israel a few years later. All arrived except for one brother, who was lost along the way. His loss is an open wound until this day.

The Fire Inside

Both Shula and Mequnante went on to serve their country in the IDF and then pursue higher education. What kept them going against all odds? How were they able to adapt to life in modern Israel, a country so different from the one they left? Aside from the obvious differences of lifestyle (starting with electricity, running water, and indoor plumbing), the move from rural Ethiopia to urban Israel was a major culture shock, which at times resulted in the questioning of the validity of their religious Jewish practice and more. Add to that economic distress and a general breakdown of family structure and traditional society, and it is remarkable that so many Ethiopians like Shula and Mequnante have succeeded. What is the secret of their success?

Mequnante is certain that his ability to withstand hardship and emerge stronger for it comes from the education he received from his mother. When he talks about her, his eyes light up. He talks about how as a young child he walked twelve kilometers (well over seven miles) to school every day and consciously hid the fact that he was a Jew. These early experiences served him in good stead on both the long trek through the Sudan and the even longer journey upon arrival in Israel.

Shula's sources of resilience were twofold. The first source of Shula's resilience is herself. She tells us that she was once invited to a group interview and was asked to bring a personal item that reflected something important about her or her life. She arrived at the interview with just herself, and when her turn came she pointed to her legs, saying that these legs of hers reflected something central and important about her. These were the legs that carried her through the Sudan. These were the legs that supported her with her sick baby brother on her back. These were the legs that went back and forth from their home in Kiryat Gat to the hospital where her mother and brothers were hospitalized, when she was only twelve years old. These legs have served her well. Shula's belief in herself, her confidence in who she is and what she can do gives her the resilience to carry on in the face of many challenges.

The second source of her resilience was Shula and Mequnante's dream of Jerusalem and the Holy Temple. This vision drove them forward and kept them going from making her way through the wilderness to long after they arrived in Israel. Even once they learned that the Temple was no longer there, this dream gave meaning to their lives; it had taught them to aim high. Though no longer physically there, perhaps, even to this day, the fire of the holy sacrifices in the Temple is burning: it is the fire burning inside of Shula and Mequnante themselves.

Olympic Resilience

*"I'm not the most talented, I'm not
the strongest, not the most athletic,
not the smartest and I don't have the
best tactics. I think the advantage
that I have over my rivals is that I
take things in proportion."*

Noam Gershony

We Feel You

After a tense final round, the medal is placed around the champion's
neck. He shakes hands with the official and looks down at the heavy gold
medal, bearing the words "XXX Olympiad London 2012," cradling it
in his hand as he shakes his head in disbelief. A bouquet of flowers is
thrust into his arms. He holds the flowers aloft in one hand and the
medal in the other. The crowd roars out a cheer. He exhales deeply as
the stadium announcer's voice comes across the public address system:
"Please stand for the national anthem of Israel." "Hatikvah" strikes up
as the blue and white flag climbs the flagpole, framed on either side
by the American stars and stripes, at a slightly lower perch. He looks
down and begins to cry, sobbing and shaking and unable to sing as the
music continues. Regaining composure, he joins in for the final words
of the anthem, the strings now accompanied by a brass section: *"lihiyot*

am chofshi b'artzenu, Eretz Tziyon v'Yerushalayim" (to be a free people in our country, the Land of Zion and Jerusalem).

The Israeli TV sports announcer chokes up as he reports from the scene. As pictures of their champion are beamed into houses all across Israel, the television commentator says:

> It's impossible not to be with him, crying with him right now...on the winner's podium, with "Hatikvah" playing, tears in his eyes. When you look back to six years ago, at what he has overcome and his journey to get here, there is only one thing to say: *kol hakavod* [all strength to you], Noam. We are with you. We are here for you. We feel you. We love you.

As Noam Gershony moves his wheelchair down from the podium toward the cheering crowd, someone drapes an Israeli flag around his shoulders. Noam looks up at the audience and reflects; the thought crosses his mind that he is Israel's first Paralympic gold medalist. This is followed immediately by a second thought. "By all rights, I should not even be alive." That's because, by all rights, you don't fall from an Apache helicopter and live to tell the tale. You don't, that is, unless you are Noam Gershony.

Falling out of the Sky

July 20, 2006, three weeks after Israeli soldier Gilad Schalit had been kidnapped by Hamas terrorists utilizing underground tunnels and eight days since Lebanese terrorist organization Hezbollah abducted three soldiers at Israel's northern border, Noam's fateful day began. These events had precipitated reciprocal attacks by the Israeli Air Force which had escalated, as the IDF entered Lebanon to fight Hezbollah in what later became known as the Second Lebanon War. With attack helicopters deployed over the Gaza Strip and in southern Lebanon, Lieutenant Noam Gershony, an IDF Apache pilot, was very busy. This was the day that he fell from the sky.

On the morning of the 20th, Noam was assigned to a formation of two Apache helicopters and had flown to the Gaza Strip to attack Hamas targets. He completed the mission successfully. Later in the early evening, he and his copilots were briefed on the escalating situation in the north. Ground troops were about to enter Lebanon, and his squadron was tasked with providing air support. The mission started off uneventfully, but around eleven p.m., two Apache helicopters flying at six thousand feet collided and plummeted to the earth. Miraculously, one helicopter managed a safe emergency landing, but the second, the one that Noam was piloting, was more severely damaged. One of their own missiles had fired in the collision, causing damage to the main rotor. As the helicopter went into a free fall, spinning out of control, the tail rotor fell off. The helicopter crash-landed within a minute. Hearing a loud noise and rushing to the crash site to help, local residents found copilot Major Ran Kochba, thrown several meters outside the ruined helicopter, with his helmet still on. He was dead. Noam was still strapped into his seat in the cockpit, partially conscious, mumbling and bleeding profusely. He had lost a lot of blood and was having trouble breathing. The impact of the crash had smashed his lower jaw, which collapsed into his throat, leaving him no airway. The initial report from the scene: two pilots are dead.

But he was still alive. Within minutes of the crash, the helicopter of the Combat Search and Rescue (CSAR) extraction unit, also known as Unit 669, arrived on the scene. With unbelievable luck, the rescue team included Dr. Yoav Paz, a chest surgeon, on board. Dr. Paz was able to stabilize Noam, and they whisked him away toward Rambam Hospital in Haifa, a thirty-minute trip. On the way, Noam's condition worsened, necessitating an emergency landing on the rooftop of

Ziv Hospital in Safed, where Dr. Paz managed to stabilize Noam once again, before taking off to Rambam Hospital, where Gershony would remain for many long months of treatment and rehabilitation.

Noam lay unconscious for a week. When he woke, he had no memory of the crash. He felt pain and was unable to move his arms or legs. The doctors had repaired his smashed jaw and glued it shut, so he couldn't speak. An alphabetical table was brought to him so that Noam could point to letters, but since both his arms were broken, he could not use that either. His injuries were extensive. Two broken arms and two broken legs. A broken pelvis, vertebrae, jaw, left elbow, and left shoulder rounded out the list of damage. A couple of days passed, and Noam's family and the doctors slowly broke the news of what had happened. When Noam was told that he had been in a serious crash, he assumed it was a car wreck, not a helicopter accident. In a cruel twist of fate, in addition to having to absorb the details of the crash and his copilot's death, Noam was informed that separately, another helicopter had crashed due to a rare malfunction, resulting in the death of his twenty-three-year-old friend, Lieutenant Tom Farkash.

Noam expected to rehabilitate quickly and return to flying, since he had always been physically fit and into sports such as soccer, basketball, volleyball, and tennis. At the very least, he thought to himself, knowing that he wouldn't be able to attend the funeral of his friend Tom, he hoped to be there for the memorial service held traditionally at the end of the thirty-day mourning period. Now, doctors were telling him that the only way for his back to heal would be to lie in bed for two months. "That bed was like a jail cell," Noam says. His jaw was wired shut for two and a half months, and he was fed liquids through a straw. He lost sixteen kilograms (over thirty-five pounds), dropping to a skeletal forty-six kilograms (101 pounds).

Initially, Noam's attitude was positive and upbeat, but after weeks of the monotony of the hospital, stuck in bed, and in pain, Noam's mind began to wander, and he began to ask himself what he calls "dangerous questions." Why had this happened to him? Was he being punished? What if he had followed his original plan and become an infantry soldier instead of attending flight school? His parents worried about his mental state, but Noam refused psychological help. Two unlikely visits helped lift Noam's spirits. The bereaved parents of his copilot Ran and the bereaved parents of his friend Tom helped him return to the land of the living. His friends visited and played him a song titled "A Million Stars," written and sung by Tom's sister, Amit Farkash, in memory of her fallen brother; it had become an anthem of the Second Lebanon War. Those visits caused Noam to make a decision: "I will never get depressed about my new physical or mental status again, because I am alive."

Stemming from a sense of gratitude that his life had been spared and a feeling of debt to his two buddies who were no longer alive, Gershony had reached a turning point and decided with new determination to make the most of his life. From the moment they were notified that Noam was being medevaced to the hospital on life support and for the six months that he remained there, his parents, brother, sister, or best friend were by his side morning, noon, and night. Slowly it was dawning on him that rehabilitation in his case would not mean returning to his former life. The spinal cord injury he suffered resulted in paralysis of the left leg, and while the right leg moved, due to an open fracture on the ankle, he could not put weight on that foot. It became clear to Noam that he would never fly an Apache again. More than that, he would leave the hospital in a wheelchair, not as he had hoped, on his own two feet. He was beginning to realize that it was time to focus on what he could do to compensate for the abilities he had lost.

A New Focus

This new focus led him, upon leaving the hospital, to visit Beit Halochem, a sports rehabilitation and recreation center serving disabled veterans and their families. Noam tried everything, including swimming, wheelchair basketball, shooting, and more. In the end, it was wheelchair tennis that he enjoyed the most, feeling that it was the closest to being an able-bodied sport. He practiced every day and began to compete in Israel and abroad. In the winter of 2010, he was sent to Prague, where he handily won a tournament.

By September 2011, Gershony had qualified for the US Open Wheelchair Championship finals, beating one of the top players, David Wagner, the first time they played each other. Now Noam had a goal: the 2012 Paralympic Games, to be held in London the following year. The Tennis Masters Series in Belgium followed; there Noam became the first Israeli player ever to qualify for the Quad Singles finals. In January 2012, Noam won first place in Australian Open events for wheelchair tennis, again beating David Wagner, who was seeded second in the world. That was the year that he would achieve success in the Pensacola Open and the Japan Open Tennis Championships, as well as winning first place in Quad Singles in the French Open tournament. Now, he was ready for the Olympics.

London was uncharacteristically bathed in sunshine for much of the summer, and excitement was building as the much-anticipated 2012 Olympic and Paralympic Games began, but Noam Gershony's Olympic journey could scarcely have gotten off to a worse start. Upon landing, with just two days until the competition began, Noam discovered that his special wheelchair – designed specifically for his body and his needs and the one he had used in all his competitions – had been broken in transit. It was unusable. Then the draw was announced, and Noam had been pitched against one of his best friends, a British athlete who was in top form. That match began badly. Gershony lost the first set of the first match of his first Olympics. It looked like he would fall at the first hurdle. He gritted his teeth and won the following sets 6-3, 6-3. Success followed in the next round and then again in the semi-finals. Now Gershony was facing his biggest challenge since recovering from his near-fatal accident. The pressure was immense: he carried the hopes of a nation on his shoulders.

"My service in the Air Force and my training in flight school prepared me for pressure, and playing in the Olympics is pure pressure. The first time I ever actually felt paralyzed was in the Olympic final." Faced with this one-time opportunity, Gershony thought the difference between winning gold and winning silver looked vast. At the start of this, the biggest and most highly anticipated match of his life, Noam found it almost impossible to move the wheels of his wheelchair. His opponent once again was the favorite, the experienced and talented David Wagner. This was Wagner's third Paralympic Games, and he had previously won the bronze and silver medals. Within three minutes, Gershony had lost two games. Noam did not lose his concentration and ended the first set with a win. At one point during the second set, Gershony heard screaming and cheering coming from his family and friends. His opponent was approaching the net to shake hands. Noam had won the gold.

The sense of his life being a rollercoaster was crystal clear to Gershony at that moment. "I had gone from flying an Apache helicopter to being told I was disabled and confined to a chair. My military service had meaning. I took out Hamas and Hezbollah outposts; I saved lives and eliminated threats. Then I was disabled. And all of a sudden, I find myself at the Olympics, hearing 'Hatikvah' and seeing the Israeli flag. It was hard to understand how I got there. I saw my friends and family who had been with me through it all. I thought of the friends that I had lost. I'm a proud Israeli and a proud Jew. I was so proud and humbled to be able to bring honor to Israel." Gershony was selected to be his nation's flag bearer at the closing ceremony of the Summer Paralympics.

A Positive Outlook

When asked to define what underpins his resilience and positive mental attitude, Gershony is clear that while events are beyond our control, people can control and influence their perspective and outlook. Gershony, now in his thirties, is wise beyond his years. He continues: "My advice is to – on a daily basis – find the thing that will remind you how good your life is. Turn everything that happens to you into a positive." Even when he is dealt a bad hand, Gershony maintains he can twist the circumstances to convince himself to focus on the positives. Reflecting on Israelis' ability to maintain resilience, he credits "resourcefulness. We don't take things for granted. We want to improve. We always ask questions. We always ask: Why do things this way, and not the other way? We don't just accept things the way they are."

This is flexibility, one of the keys of resilience. Noam personifies that flexibility in his optimistic approach. While he had moments when his optimism failed him, his flexibility helped him to restore it. He was able to refocus and gain perspective, aided by family and friends, and most particularly the parents of the two friends he lost in combat. The combination of flexibility, perspective taking, and optimism is a winning one for Noam Gershony.

Funny, charming, and good-looking with an infectiously positive attitude, Gershony doesn't let anything hold him back. He not only scuba dives, seat-skis, and water-skis, he also teaches disabled children how to ski and volunteers teaching mathematics to underprivileged children as well. Noam travels the globe speaking to many thousands of people as a motivational speaker. "I have stage fright!" Noam laughs, "I never thought I would become a pilot, I never dreamed I would be a Paralympic gold medalist, and I never imagined that I would become a public speaker." Gershony is still in good shape and continues to play tennis for enjoyment, but rarely competitively, choosing to end his professional career at its peak. The journey from Lebanon to London provided a sense of closure, as that gold medal was placed around the neck of the man who fell to earth, survived, and became an Olympic champion.

CHAPTER 5

The Two-Thousand-Year-Old Woman

*"They say I'm two-thousand years old.
I was born here, my parents were born
here. And we have always been here."*

Margalit Zinati

Continuity after Calamity

It is an event so cataclysmic that to this day, Jews everywhere refrain from eating for twenty-five hours, from the eve of the Ninth of Av until sunset the next day. An entire tract of biblical lamentations was written detailing the destruction of the Jewish Temple in Jerusalem and the desolation that was wrought in its wake. The Temple was destroyed and the people of the capital were starved, raped, and murdered. Blood flowed in the streets of Jerusalem as the holy site was set afire. The site of the Holy of Holies, built on the Foundation Stone at the fulcrum where Heaven and Earth are said to meet, was ransacked, and the golden Menorah, symbol of the Jewish people, was stolen, never to be seen again.

A bas-relief on the Arch of Titus in Rome depicts Jewish prisoners of war laboring under that golden candelabra, an enduring commemoration of how, in the year 70 CE, indigenous Jewish self-rule was

49

crushed by the Romans, and the Temple's spoils were plundered in a procession led by Emperor Titus himself. Hundreds of thousands of Jews living in Israel, then referred to as the Kingdom of Judea, were murdered or exiled and dispersed around the world, leaving only a tiny population of Jews in the Holy Land. The surviving Jews who remained in Israel escaped Jerusalem and Judea, moving to the Galilee region in the north of the country. They never left Zion. Among their number were the ancestors of Margalit Zinati, who serves as a living bridge between Israel's present and its past. She has lived in Peki'in from birth, a town located right next to a village named, appropriately enough, Hosen (meaning "Resilience").

Margalit Zinati draws her lineage back to an ancient Jewish family that has lived continuously in the same place since the days of the Second Temple. Throughout her life, she has dedicated herself to preserving the ancient synagogue in Peki'in and to conveying the local history and her family's story to future generations. Margalit has thus become a symbol of the Jews' eternal connection to Peki'in and to the Land of Israel, unbroken and unextinguished after two thousand years of diaspora.

Zinati, who wishes those she meets both "*Shalom aleichem*" (in Hebrew) and "*A-salaam aleikum*" (in Arabic), can trace her family back to the priests who worked in the Temple in Jerusalem. Her priestly ancestors escaped the carnage wrought by the Romans by making the arduous trek to Peki'in on foot. Once there, they became farmers and worked the land. Peki'in is located in the north of Israel, not far from Meron, where the famed second-century sage and kabbalist Rabbi Shimon Bar Yochai hid in a cave with his son. They were wanted for violating Roman edicts prohibiting Torah study, Sabbath observance, and *brit milah* (Jewish circumcision). The Roman leaders, intent on wiping out Jewish practice and the Jewish people, sentenced many of the leading rabbis to death, including Rabbi Shimon Bar Yochai.

Legend tells that a carob tree grew up miraculously right next to the cave where he and his son were hiding and provided them with food, and a spring appeared to give them water to drink as well as a mikveh (ritual bath) in which to immerse themselves. It was there, according to tradition, that Rabbi Shimon Bar Yochai wrote the *Zohar*, the foundational book of the Jewish mystical tradition. The site is considered holy by many, and the nearby natural spring and ancient carob tree can be visited even today.

Visiting Zinati, one needs to listen carefully, as she talks in Hebrew with an Arabic accent. Her deeply lined face reflects the many years she has walked this earth and all she has seen and experienced. Zinati speaks of the town's synagogue, whose building included two ancient stones brought from the Temple itself by her ancestors. One stone depicts the seven-branched Temple Menorah, the lulav and etrog used on the Sukkot festival (Tabernacles), and the shofar (ram's horn), as mentioned in the Bible. On the other side facing it is a stone featuring an illustration of the Nicanor Gate, one of the seven gates of the Temple courtyard. In today's synagogue, the stones are situated opposite each other, but originally, they were placed face down as a way to acknowledge the devastation of the destruction of the Temple. Only when the modern-day State of Israel gained its independence were the stones once again placed upright, says Margalit, to symbolize that Israel would last forever. "The people of Israel never left their homeland," Zinati declares, "and I hope that they will never leave. I am the keeper of the flame. I'm here, keeping the embers of Jewish presence in Peki'in alive."

Coexistence and Conflict

In the eleventh century, Arabs joined the Jewish residents of Peki'in, who were followed by Christians in the twelfth century and Druze in the eighteenth century. Peki'in became a model of coexistence. The second-largest Greek Orthodox Church in Israel was built there in 1894. Zinati speaks fondly of the Jewish festival of Simchat Torah, the holiday on which Jews rejoice in the completion of the Torah reading cycle. This Jewish holiday became a special celebration for everyone. Local Christians, Druze, and Muslims would wish each other *chag sameach* (happy holiday) and dance with the Jews and their Torah.

The communities lived together. During Passover, the local Jews would provide those of other faiths with matzah, and as the holiday ended, the non-Jews would bring pita (pocket bread) to their Jewish neighbors. Weddings, like the holidays, were celebrated by all. Nowadays, Peki'in is populated by several thousand Druze. Margalit is the only remaining Jew in Peki'in. Over the centuries, Israel was occupied and reoccupied by different rulers, yet the Zinati family persevered in the town of Peki'in. The Jews of Peki'in are mentioned by Rabbi Moses Basola, a traveler who arrived in Peki'in during Passover in 1522. He published a book about his travels, leaving a record that substantiates Margalit's family story.

First the Romans, then the Byzantines, the Arabs, the Crusaders, the Mamluks, the Ottomans, and then the British all took a turn controlling this special piece of land. The various rulers all had an impact on the local residents. Zinati's family, like their Jewish neighbors, became Mustarabim – Jews heavily influenced by Arab culture – and began taking on Druze modes of dress and speaking Arabic. However, the Jews of Peki'in maintained an unwavering commitment to Jewish rites and rituals.

The town hosted a seminal visit in 1922, when Zionist leader and future president of Israel Yitzhak Ben-Zvi arrived in Peki'in. Ben-Zvi became a patron of the town and later was instrumental in the Israeli government's interest in investing in and maintaining the heritage sites of Peki'in. Ben-Zvi was so impressed with his visit to Peki'in that he wrote a book about his visit (*The Jewish Settlement in Peki'in*) in 1922. He wrote:

> Like an ancient legend, and like an echo rising up from the depths of centuries, awareness of the remnants of the Jewish peasant farmers rings in our ears.... Peki'in is not beyond the rivers of Kush, but here among us.

Ben-Zvi arranged for the renovation of the cemetery and synagogue and inspired a reawakening among the local Jews. Margalit credits Ben-Zvi for reminding her family of their Jewish roots following decades of Arab influence, and she proudly holds aloft the modern-day 100-shekel bill with a picture of President Ben-Zvi on one side and an illustration of the door and window of Peki'in's synagogue on the other.

While coexistence was often the order of the day, Peki'in has known more difficult times. In 1936, the Arab Revolt led by Grand Mufti Haj Amin al-Husseini began. Hundreds of Jews were killed and injured throughout the land. Husseini, who later became infamous for meeting with and professing friendship for Hitler, was eager to put an end to Jewish immigration in British-mandated Palestine. It took three years to crush the violent protests, but the net result was the British caving in to the violence and the creation of the White Paper of 1939 drastically limiting the number of Jews allowed to immigrate legally to British Mandate Palestine. During this time, the Jews of Peki'in found themselves, like many of their brothers and sisters across the country, in the crosshairs of violent Arab attacks. Margalit recalls when her father was nearly murdered. He was about to be doused in kerosene and set alight in public by the attackers when a Muslim neighbor intervened and saved his life. Most Jews fled the town during the violence of those years. After quiet returned to the village, the Zinati family were the only Jewish family who came back.

Keeper of the Flame

With no children of her own, Margalit cared for her parents, and after they passed away, her primary concern was preserving the Jewish roots of her hometown. She faithfully takes the keys to the synagogue, each and every day, opens it up, cleans it, and ensures its upkeep. She personally welcomes all visitors to the site of the synagogue, right next to the one-bedroom home she was raised in. In 2018, on the seventieth anniversary of the creation of the modern state, Margalit Zinati was fittingly honored. The "keeper of the flame" was chosen to light one of the Independence Day torches at the prestigious national ceremony in Jerusalem. Despite her advanced years, she has played a daily role in personally hosting groups at the Beit Zinati (House of Zinati) Visitors' Center in Peki'in, a charming and fascinating off-the-beaten-track place to visit.

It took almost two thousand years for the Jewish commonwealth to be reestablished in the Land of Israel in May 1948. The Menorah, whose theft from the Holy of Holies in the year 70 CE is celebrated on the Arch of Titus, was chosen as the official symbol of the modern State of Israel. Peki'in is a testament to continuous, uninterrupted Jewish presence in the Land of Israel from time immemorial. Whereas today, Jews are so often described in terms of where they were exiled to or where their family was living most recently, or by whether they are Ashkenazi or Sefardi/Mizrachi, Margalit Zinati and her family demonstrate that these are modern, artificial constructs and that all Jews trace their roots back to the place that her family never left: the Land of Israel. The story of the Jewish people in Israel persevering from the time of the destruction of the Temple until now is one of sustained determination, overcoming hardship and persecution in order to survive and thrive.

Jews are the People of the Book, and Jewish survival has been perpetuated by their ability to tell their story. No one is more personally emblematic of that story than Margalit Zinati. Margalit still regales spellbound audiences who visit the town of Peki'in with stories of the glory of days past. She no longer has any living relatives, so the many thousands and even tens of thousands who have met her will carry Zinati's torch as they tell future generations about the two-thousand-year-old woman.

From the Ashes

"We have no choice! We are not fighting for status, prestige, or ego. We are fighting for our lives. We are fighting for our country. We have no other country! This is it. We have no choice."

Rabbi Israel Meir Lau

Where They Don't Kill Jews

Sitting in Rabbi Israel Meir Lau's formal living room, it is hard to imagine this venerable elder, immaculately dressed in a black satin frock coat, sporting a long white beard and twinkling eyes, as an eight-year-old orphan and three-year veteran of Buchenwald concentration camp. As he shares with us his bone-chilling stories of seeing his father murdered, being torn from his mother's arms at age five, and getting tossed into a cattle car with his sixteen-year-old brother, it is unfathomable that someone so young could have experienced such horrors and not only lived to tell the tale, but gone on to become one of the foremost spiritual leaders of Israel today.

When asked to reflect about how the Holocaust shaped him and affected the State of Israel today, Rabbi Lau replies that this is a redundant question. The devastating attempted genocide murdered over a third of the world's Jewish population. Despite some political opposition from many quarters, that this had been allowed by the nations to occur was an important part of the moral case for the rebirth of an independent Jewish country. For Rabbi Lau, it is clear that the Holocaust loomed large as an independent Israel was reestablished in 1948. It is not purely because of the Holocaust that there is an Israel, but had there been an Israel at the time, the Holocaust could not have taken place. Indeed, it was this thought – that Israel is a place where Jews are not killed – that kept him going as a child surviving the Holocaust.

Sitting in a relaxed setting on a sofa in his Tel Aviv home, Rabbi Lau shares with us his incredible biography. While he has probably told his story thousands of times and has written extensively about it, most notably in his autobiography, *From the Ashes*, retelling it does not fail to stir him and bring very real tears to his eyes. We ask him about his arrival as one of the first postwar immigrants to the Promised Land. Listening to him vividly retell how his ship, carrying orphan refugees, landed on the shores of British Mandate Palestine in 1945, one can picture the scene of his entry.

He tells us how his brother had gone off to find their belongings as they neared the shore, and the man whom he was with told him that the men rowing their boats out to the large ship to bring passengers to shore were Arabs. He scared the eight-year-old Lau, who – even at this young age – had more than a lifetime's experience of horror and fear, joking that the reason the Arabs wore *sharwal* (wide pants that drooped down in the middle) was to hide the Jewish children they kidnapped. Yisrael started screaming and bawling, telling his brother that he would not get off the ship. It took several long minutes for Naphtali, Yisrael's nineteen-year-old brother, to understand what had happened when he left his brother's side, and longer until he was able to calm his brother down and explain that the man was just teasing him, and that in fact the Arabs would not kidnap him.

But to little Yisrael, or Lulek, as he was known in Yiddish, this was no joking matter. He was a boy carrying an unbearable weight on his shoulders. He knew no Hebrew and nothing about Israel. He was unschooled and unlettered, having spent his childhood years in the ghetto of Piotrków, forced into slave labor at the age of six in the Hortensia Glass Factory and then in the inconceivable horrors of Nazi concentration camps. The only thing he knew was what his brother Naphtali – also known as Tulek – had told him: *Israel is the place where they don't kill Jews.* Unimaginable! There was actually a place in this world where they didn't kill Jews? Eight-year-old Lulek could not even conjure up what that might look like. His brother Naphtali had become his guardian and sole support on that awful day in late 1944 when the ghetto was liquidated. At the train station, on a crowded platform filled with Nazis, their dogs, and frightened Jews, his mother made the split-second decision to push him to Naphtali's group with the men, realizing that the women and children would meet with certain death.

After spending several months in a forced labor camp, they were transported to Buchenwald, arriving in mid-winter, at the outskirts of Weimar, cradle of German culture, the birthplace of Goethe and Schiller. Understanding that Lulek's only chance to survive the death camp was to pretend he was Polish, his brother Naphtali was able to procure for him the letter *P* and sewed it onto his uniform in place of the *J* for Jew. Within days, he was transferred to Block 8, where Russian prisoners were held. Better food and easier work ensured that seven-year-old Lulek would have a chance at survival. The men of the block adopted him, and though the separation from Naphtali was excruciating, his brother was insistent and gave him no choice. He explained to Lulek that he must pretend that he was not Jewish, and the youngster immediately agreed, understanding innately that his life depended on this.

Despite the separation, Naphtali would drag himself up to the fence separating him from his younger brother every few days to make sure he was okay. Never for a moment did he forget his mother's charge to him that day on the platform when she pushed Lulek into Naphtali's arms, saying "Tulek, take care of Lulek." Nor did he forget his father's charge to make sure the family's rabbinic lineage would be perpetuated. Meanwhile, the Nazis assigned to Naphtali the most indescribably horrible job of carting bodies from the gas chambers to the crematoria.

Naphtali became what the inmates referred to as a Musselmann, one who is on the verge of starving to death. Few survived. As rumors ran rampant, with prisoners fearing that the Germans would kill them all before the Americans or Russians could liberate them, an emaciated Naphtali dragged himself over to the fence by Block 8 once more and called to Lulek, who ran out to see his beloved brother. With tears in his eyes, Naphtali told him that if they should ever be separated, and if the war should one day be over, he, Lulek, should go to Eretz Yisrael (the Land of Israel). Lulek had no idea what that was. He knew no Hebrew. He hardly remembered a thing about Jewish practice. The one thing he knew was how to survive. His brother made him repeat the words over and over: Eretz Yisrael, the Land of Israel, Eretz Yisrael. Lulek had only one question for his brother. "*Czemu?*" he asked in Polish. "Why?" Why had his brother told him to go to Eretz Yisrael, and only to Eretz Yisrael? *Because there, they don't kill Jews.*

The Unbroken Chain

Some seventy-five years later, in the living room of his stately Tel Aviv home, Rabbi Lau repeats the phrase: *Here, they don't kill Jews.* Luckily, he was not, in the end, separated from Naphtali. He goes on to describe the trials and travails of coming to Israel in July 1945 as an eight-year-old orphan and Holocaust survivor. He highlights the wonderful care he received from his aunt and uncle, who had moved to Kiryat Motzkin, a suburb of Haifa, before World War II. Yisrael Meir's uncle explained to him that he had been saved in order to realize his destiny: to follow in the footsteps of his esteemed rabbinic family, succeeding his late father to become the thirty-eighth generation in an unbroken family chain of rabbis. This is exactly what he did, immersing himself in Torah study in various yeshivot (institutions of higher Torah learning). In each yeshiva he found a mentor, someone who knew his father, Rabbi Moshe Chaim Lau, the last chief rabbi of their Polish town of Piotrków Trybunalski, who was murdered in the Treblinka extermination camp. Yisrael Meir Lau, in winning fashion and with inestimable charisma, was able to make bonds and bring out the best in people, who wished to help this young orphan with the most incredible life experiences to pursue his dream of perpetuating the esteemed line of rabbinic and spiritual leaders.

Naphtali, Rabbi Lau's older brother, took his father's charge most seriously to make sure that the rabbinic dynasty of their family would continue. Rabbi Lau relates that in 1993, when he was appointed chief rabbi of Israel, he and his brother went to the Western Wall to offer up thanks to the Almighty. His brother then turned to the new chief rabbi and said to him that only now did he feel he had been relieved of a great weight. For the last fifty years, he had been walking around with the burden that his father had placed on him on that fateful day in 1942. Now that Lulek had become the chief rabbi of Israel, he could rest easy.

In considering the path he has chosen to take, Rabbi Lau most vehemently states that he has chosen life, he has chosen ambition and opportunity to fuel his achievements. Yes, life dealt him unimaginably difficult blows, but giving in to them would have given victory to the Nazis. His conscious response to fear, deprivation, and feeling alone in the world was to seek out every opportunity, to relish every kind word or response, and to use his great gifts to make his mark on the world.

Rabbi Lau notes that his father was a renowned public speaker, and often over the course of the years, people who had the opportunity to hear his *derashot* (Torah discourses) would come over to Rabbi Lau to tell him how powerful they were and what an impact they had made. Rabbi Lau has continued in that tradition and is a powerful charismatic orator, with a very simple message: The Jewish people must continue. Jewish tradition is at the very heart of our lives here in Israel, the country in the world *where they don't kill Jews.*

Rabbi Lau's ability to rise from the ashes and achieve all that he has accomplished in his lifetime is remarkable. In considering what contributed to Rabbi Lau's resilience in the face of the devastation and loss he experienced at such a young age, one cannot overlook his early beginnings and the very strong bonds he had with his parents – and particularly with his mother – during the first five years of his life. Rabbi Lau tells how his mother made sure to bring his favorite honey cookies with them to the hiding place where they were escaping the Gestapo, in order to make sure the four-year-old Lulek wouldn't make any noise at the wrong moment. Her ability to be in tune with her son and to understand his needs despite her own worries and anxiety is indicative of masterful parenting. Studies show that early attachment is key in later psychological development, and solid, stable attachment to parental figures helps form a strong core in youngsters. If parenting is inadequate, if children are abused or neglected, this may have far-reaching implications for their future ability to cope and weather the challenges of life. Although he lost them at far too young an age, little Lulek was fortunate indeed to be born to the parents he had.

Not only did his mother and father lay the foundation for Yisrael Lau's resilience, but also his brother Naphtali was a key player. His brother kept him close, protecting him under extraordinary conditions, and did not give up on him for a moment, even though his own life undoubtedly would have been simpler without the burden of being the guardian of a child. His brother Naphtali stood in for mother and father, sheltering the young Lulek as best he could.

Bringing Out the Best in Others

Trying to picture the seven-year-old Yisrael Meir Lau in the Buchenwald death camp, in the special block Naphtali was able to get him into that was reserved for non-Jewish Russian and Polish political prisoners, one can only imagine that he had a lot of presence and charm, even then. Studies bear out that children who are winning, who are able to communicate and to attach themselves to adults in their environment – to find mentors and protectors – are more successful in life. Lulek found love and protection from one Russian prisoner in particular, who not only gave him larger food portions, but also covered Lulek's body with his own, when during the final battle before liberation, bullets whizzed overhead from all directions. Until this day, Rabbi Lau is certain that the Russian prisoner Feodor Mikhailichenko is the one who saved his life. Seventy years later, Rabbi Lau made a special visit to Rostov, Russia, to pay his respects at the grave of his rescuer.

Upon arriving in Israel, the eight-year-old was fortunate to reconnect with his aunt and uncle, who brought him into their family and treated him as a beloved son. These wonderful people, who were barely making ends meet as it was, unhesitatingly provided him with all his material and emotional needs during his first years in Israel. One can only imagine that this was not an easy task. As Yisrael Meir Lau grew up, he left his aunt and uncle's home to attend a yeshiva in Jerusalem. The rabbis and teachers he met were also charmed by him and taken by his personal story and his personality. He felt cared for and appreciated the special interest that the adults he met took in him. Everywhere he went, he seemed to bring out the best in people.

Having witnessed unspeakable horrors, Rabbi Lau built upon those tragic foundations to marry Chaya Ita Frankel, the daughter of Rabbi Yitzchak Yedidya Frankel, chief rabbi of Tel Aviv-Jaffa, and to create a home and raise a family of his own – three sons and five daughters. He was able to dedicate his life to serving his communities, as chief rabbi of the coastal city of Netanya and then of Tel Aviv, and subsequently chief rabbi of all of Israel. Rabbi Lau became a well-known leader in Israel and on the global scene, meeting with world leaders and winning both the Israel Prize and the French Legion of Honor, the former recognizing his contribution to the State of Israel and the latter acclaiming his work building bridges between different religions.

In January 2020, a historic event took place. Forty-seven global leaders, among them presidents, prime ministers, and members of royal families, gathered together at Yad Vashem World Holocaust Remembrance Center in Jerusalem to commemorate the seventy-fifth anniversary of the liberation of Auschwitz concentration camp. It was an extraordinary spectacle, and many moving speeches were given, but perhaps the most poignant moment belonged to the man representing the Holocaust survivors at the state ceremony, Rabbi Lau. He addressed the audience in his rabbinic garb, speaking forcefully, yet with quiet restraint. "I cannot forgive, because I'm not authorized to forgive. My parents, before they went away, before they were *taken* away, they did not ask me to forgive. They asked me to continue the chain, so the Jewish chain will be unbroken, unbroken forever. That's what they said. My mother…[said], 'Remember that you are a Jew, wherever you go, remember you are a part of a rabbinic chain…' She didn't speak about forgiveness. What else do you ask me? To forget. Forget? How can I forget? How can I forget the beatings, the freezing, the starvation?… I do remember the sufferings. I do remember the tortures. I do remember the victims. And I can never forget."

Rabbi Israel Meir Lau is a man with a mission. It was ever thus. At a young age, he was commanded to survive in order to get to Israel. Soon afterwards, the raison d'être instilled in him from childhood was to carry on the family rabbinic tradition. Having a sense of mission kept him alive during the Holocaust and guided all his steps during his formative years. This mission has been a beacon to him his entire life – a strong and clear purpose that was an essential part of Rabbi Lau's resilient climb from the ashes of the Holocaust to the Chief Rabbinate of the modern State of Israel. Now in his eighties – impressive, energetic, and forward-looking – he has as keen a sense of loss as ever, but he can now say to his younger self: mission accomplished.

Glass Ceilings

"Stay focused. When the door was closed on me, I found other doors."

Gadeer Kamal-Mreeh

Bridging Realities

The phone rang, and Gadeer Kamal-Mreeh answered it. It was a short conversation but enough to bring her to tears. The voice on the other end of the line was Sheikh Muafak Tarif, spiritual leader of the Israeli Druze community. He congratulated her on becoming Israel's first female Druze member of Knesset and told her how proud he was of her. To understand Gadeer's tears, it is important to understand the barriers she broke, the community from which she had come, and the obstacles that were in her way along the road to reaching the Knesset, Israel's parliament.

It is hard to imagine that any of this was actually so difficult, when we meet Gadeer (pronounced "Ra-deer") at her parliamentary office inside Israel's Knesset. A gold sign sits on a teak desk with the words "Boss Lady" imprinted on it. She is dressed in pressed slim jeans and a silk blouse, and her office is adorned with an Israeli flag proudly standing in the corner. Gadeer Kamal-Mreeh has blazed her own trail to arrive at the place where she is today.

Gadeer was born and raised in Dalyat al-Karmel, a Druze village established in the seventeenth century that has grown into a town located south of the city of Haifa. This is where her parents and grandparents were born as well. Her father, a builder, imbued in her the message that if you want to succeed, you will succeed. He told her that she could achieve anything she wanted and that the sky was the limit. As a child, Gadeer had a dream and a direction. She knew that someday she would be a TV journalist and used to practice with a microphone looking into the mirror, pretending that she was on prime time. While she was determined to reach her goal, the journey toward her aspirational objective was anything but straight or clear. Gadeer's community, the Druze community of Israel, which numbers approximately 140,000, is situated at a particularly special and sensitive part of Israeli society. The Arabic-speaking Druze are a unique ethnoreligious minority in Israel. Their religion dates back to the tenth century when they broke away from mainstream Islam. Although their rituals and beliefs are kept secret, it is known that Druze believers recognize the prophets of Islam, Christianity, and Judaism. Their most revered prophet is Jethro, the father-in-law of Moses.

While hundreds of thousands of Druze live in Lebanon and Syria, and some in Jordan as well, they disavow greater Arab nationalism, and their loyalty lies with the country in which they reside. Interestingly, the Druze have their own five-colored flag, each color symbolizing one of their prophets, yet their respect for the blue-and-white national flag of Israel, emblazoned with a Star of David, is total. Gadeer explains that to the Druze, land is secondary, and loyalty to their country of birth is of primary importance. As far back as 1948, the Druze community has shown this loyalty, fighting bravely and falling alongside their Jewish countrymen in the War of Independence. Druze were accepted as full citizens from the inception of the modern State of Israel. In 1956, the mandatory military conscription law was passed, and Druze males have been drafted into the IDF ever since, unlike their Muslim counterparts, who are exempted from the draft but can choose to volunteer. Historically, many Druze have achieved high-ranking positions in the army.

Gadeer maintains that the experience of being a minority community in Israel has positive elements and that other minorities could learn a lot from the Druze experience. She says that from an early stage in the creation of the modern State of Israel, the Druze leadership understood the similarity between Druze and Jews and their mutual interests. They recognized that the democracy that would be established in 1948 would be good for their community, and they understood the importance of serving in the army to defend the country they call their own.

For Gadeer this dual identity, Israeli and Druze, is something to cherish, and she feels that her community has been successful in bridging the two realities. She makes the intricacies of melding various identities sound so easy and matter-of-fact. "On the one hand," she says, "we have our own religious identity, and on the other we live in the big, wide world. We are conservative and liberal. We are West and East. We have our own flag, but we know that our flag is the Israeli one. I am an anchorwoman, a journalist, a member of Knesset, and a simple Druze woman who can learn from her mother-in-law how to cook traditional dishes – all these factors enrich us and enrich my identity."

In fact, while balancing these diverse facets of life is a beautiful thing, it is also a daily challenge, and one that is even harder for women than men. Women often face more difficulties on the road to success, and Druze women are no exception. Women in the Druze community are expected to be modest and private people, whose focus is on the home and family. Gadeer's mother was a traditional Druze homemaker, dedicating all her time and energy to her family. Gadeer has tremendous respect for her mother and the standards that she set. Looking at her own life, Gadeer is always trying to find a balance between career and family, like so many others of her generation.

Breaking Through

Soon after starting out in her journalistic career, Gadeer was given the opportunity to anchor a television show, an Arabic-language program about social issues. The show was a success, as was Gadeer, and in 2017 she was offered a new and exciting opportunity that would thrust her into the public spotlight. She was chosen to anchor the prime-time Hebrew-language evening news on Israel national television. While Gadeer was thrilled with this high-profile, breakthrough position, what followed was pushback from her community. Religious leaders lobbied her parents, saying that this role was not appropriate for a Druze woman because it was so visible and furthermore required long hours away from home. Gadeer felt isolated and lonely, censured by many in her community for the choice she was making. Gadeer recalls being stopped in the street and strongly admonished by a neighbor. The easy option at this point would have been to pull back and take another path, but she was not deterred. In fact, her biggest fans were her mother, father, and husband, who bolstered her flagging confidence and supported her throughout.

There is more to reading the evening news than just sitting facing the camera in the news studio wearing TV makeup. Gadeer's day began early and required her to be fully up to speed on the intricacies of Middle East politics and Israeli society. She needed to be on top of things in a country where news breaks around the clock and where war can begin and regimes can fall by the end of a day. Soon, she recognized a subtle shift in the perception of her by her own community. Slowly, her new on-air presence became respected and embraced. Since that time, Gadeer credits her community and in particular her family for giving her the strength and support she needs to succeed. As she notes, "It takes a village to raise a child," and she is very fortunate to have that village helping her on a daily basis.

Another challenge Gadeer has had to contend with is geography. Living in the periphery of Israel means that everything from education to local resources to distances from the main population centers is more demanding than living in Tel Aviv or Jerusalem, where her TV studio was located. It often takes upward of two hours to reach her office in the Knesset, and of course the return trip awaits her at the end of the day.

Gadeer's husband, a successful businessman in medical technology, is also Druze, and also from Dalyat al Carmel. She met him in an online chat room, and as fate would have it, they are distant relatives, even though they had never met before. When they married, Gadeer was in her early twenties. They have two young boys. Her husband is very supportive, helpful, and always encouraging. She depends on her extended family not only for babysitting, but primarily to share the burden and the joy of raising her two sons. When asked directly about what is at the core of her personal resilience and inner strength, she points unhesitatingly to her very strong sense of belonging, starting with the inner circle of her family and moving on to the community. Without question, these rings of support are the basis of her inner steel to push on and succeed.

Who among us has achieved our life's dream and ambition by age thirty? Gadeer certainly had, but what came next was even more interesting and perhaps surprising. She was approached by former chief of staff of the Israel Defense Forces Lieutenant-General (Res.) Binyamin ("Benny") Gantz, who asked her to join him on the slate for his new political party, aptly named Israel Resilience. Gadeer initially refused. In fact, she refused three times before she agreed to join. While used to pushing the limits, she is also always careful to check and see if she is still working within acceptable communal boundaries. Although hesitant to put her name into the political ring, she ended up receiving a tremendous amount of support from the Druze community, an indication of how she had become a local celebrity and also how Druze society has progressed in their acceptance of women being active professionals outside the home. In politically turbulent times, the party did well, and Gadeer was swept into the Israeli parliament in 2019, becoming one of the youngest of the new members of Knesset at age thirty-four.

A Bridge to Positivity

When Gadeer talks about her place in the world, she states that she is a minority within a minority. She is an Israeli citizen, but she is not a Jew. She speaks Arabic, but she is not Muslim. As a consequence of this, she says proudly, "I can be a bridge – I can be the positive face of Israel not only in the region but also in the whole wide world." And indeed she can.

It might seem that Gadeer's life and surging career have been without setbacks. To the contrary. She experienced racism and sexism in the workplace. She acknowledges that when she started out as a television news reporter, she experienced a feeling of being different and an outsider. She is, however, at pains to stress that this has been the exception rather than the rule and prefers not to dwell on this part of her career. Gadeer overflows with positivity. She looks back without rancor and is determined to make a difference in her political career for her community, to ensure that the Druze people maintain a cherished position in Israeli society and that they are given everything they deserve.

In considering the sources of resilience in her life, she emphasizes that her family has always played a significant role in supporting her and helping her along her sometimes thorny path. In recent years, her community has as well come to her support, and if in earlier years this wasn't always the case, she now feels that they are firmly in her court. If we consider what else has helped her along her road, there is no question that a feeling of mission and purpose drives Gadeer and has helped shape who she is and how she approaches obstacles. She believes in what she is doing, wholeheartedly, and that sincerity is both very believable and very winning. The meaning that her hard work brings into her life is significant and plays an important role in her personal resilience, her ability to withstand the hardships of her career, including travel, long hours away from her children, and the stresses of politics.

She clearly also has ambition. With rising prominence, at only age thirty-six, she is setting her sights high and is definitely one to watch on the Israeli and international scene. Following the March 2020 election, Gadeer acted on her principles and decided not to enter the government coalition together with her leader Benny Gantz, instead joining the opposition with Yair Lapid's Yesh Atid Party (formerly allied with Gantz's Blue and White). The criticism she faced when choosing her career path, placing work outside the home as a value in addition to family and community, has dissipated. The rebukes she confronted are now just distant memories. Everybody wants to take credit for her success, but it is Gadeer Kamal Mreeh herself who has blazed her own trail, shattering the double-glazed glass ceiling to become Israel's first-ever female Druze MK.

CHAPTER 8

Lessons from the Sports Field

"We are on the map and we are here to stay."
Tal Brody, FIBA European Champions Cup, 1977

Path of Meaning

Imagine that you have to choose between two mutually exclusive paths. The first path is one that you have been toiling toward unceasingly for the last twelve years. It entails following a strict regimen of basketball practice and drill. This path is the fulfillment of your dreams. You have been chosen in the first round of the NBA draft to join the Baltimore Bullets and offered a salary in the millions of dollars. The second path is a year playing with a virtually unknown team in a small, war-torn country in the Middle East. This particular dilemma doesn't seem so difficult. It should be a no-brainer.

This was the choice that loomed on Tal Brody's horizon back in the summer of 1966, but as he tells the story, the choice for him was an easy one. And once he made his decision, Brody never looked back. Fifty years after coming to Israel, the 187-centimeter-tall (6 ft. 2 in.) Brody with his familiar smile is a celebrity in the Jewish state.

75

He reminisces on a life that began in Trenton, New Jersey, filled with achievements, awards, and recognition. This was a life replete with meaning and fulfillment, both personally and professionally. Sitting with the youthful-looking septuagenarian as he shares his life story, one cannot help but marvel at the honesty and straightforwardness that come shining through. More than any government leader, politician, diplomat, negotiator, or celebrity, it was basketball superstar Tal Brody who really and truly put Israel "on the map." Instantly recognizable among Israelis, Brody has become something of a national treasure.

Joining the Maccabi Tel Aviv team for one year, before planning to return to the United States to take up his offer with the Baltimore Bullets, Tal fell in love with Israel and stayed. Following that, only a short two-year hiatus interrupted more than fifty years of life in Israel. In 1968, Brody once again faced a dilemma of near-epic proportions. Receiving a draft notice from the US Army, he debated with himself whether to complete the aliyah immigration process he had begun in order to stay in Israel, or to return and serve his country of birth. Once again, according to Tal, he was faced with deciding between doing the "right" thing and doing what you really "want" to do. Choosing to answer the call, he returned to America and was drafted into the army for a two-year stint. After several grueling months training to be an infantry soldier, he was plucked out of his unit and certain deployment to Vietnam to join the Army basketball team, where he spent the remainder of his career with the armed forces playing ball and winning championships.

Upon completion of his US military service, Brody received a letter from Moshe Dayan, then defense minister of Israel, beseeching him to return to Maccabi Tel Aviv to raise the level of basketball in Israel. He was deeply touched by the letter and decided to come back to Israel, thus changing the trajectory of his life. Since then, Tal has spent half a century on and off the court, in business, as a family man with a wife and three children, and currently as a goodwill ambassador for Israel. In that capacity he represents the country overseas, often using basketball as a way to connect to people and share his love of his country.

Facing Great Odds

Dr. Fred Price, Brody's high school basketball coach, has remained his inspiration since Brody trained with him when he was in his teens. Price was not only a coach but also an exemplary educator, and the lessons that he taught young Tal have accompanied him for a lifetime. These are lessons Tal remembers and relates to even today, many decades after originally learning them:

- Look at the cup as half full.
- The people you meet going up the ladder are the same ones you will meet coming down.
- Expect difficulties. Consider them challenges.
- Don't sweat the small stuff. Keep your eye on the big picture.
- Persevere and you will win.

These are just some of the memorable phrases that run like a playlist in Tal's mind, looping continually and helping him through many a rough spot.

If anyone personifies perseverance in the face of great odds, it is Tal. The year was 1977. Israel had made it to the Euroleague Basketball Semi-Finals for the first time in history. The mood in Israel was somber, in the wake of the great losses incurred during the Yom Kippur War, less than four years earlier. A sense of the fragility of life was once again in the forefront of the Israeli psyche. On a fateful evening in April, all eyes were on the court in diplomatically neutral Virton, Belgium, where Maccabi Tel Aviv was meeting the Soviet Red Army team, CSKA, who had won four European Championships in as many years and had not lost a game for the past number of seasons. The odds were heavily against Maccabi. Yet aside from a few Soviet KGB agents, the enthusiastic crowd consisted of hundreds of Israeli supporters. The blue and white flag dominated the arena, and the language heard courtside was Hebrew. The stadium collectively held its breath as the final basket sunk through the net propelled by Captain Tal Brody, bringing in victory at the final buzzer with an upset win of 91 to 79.

In the seconds after the surprising turnaround, a reporter caught sight of the jubilant Brody and stuck a microphone under his nose. Brody's response, broadcast on live TV to a euphoric nation, was to become iconic: "We are on the map, and we are here to stay." In those few short words, Tal Brody encapsulated the sentiments of the Maccabi fans and underscored the tenaciousness and perseverance of the entire nation. The phrase has since taken on a life of its own, becoming emblematic of a generation of Israelis and symbolizing a confidence that their little country, always punching above its weight but hitherto existentially endangered, was here to stay.

The High Road

Choosing between the moral imperative and the temptations of ego and fame, Tal has always chosen the high road and counsels young people he meets both in the sport arena and in daily life to do the same. Aside from that momentous decision to come to Israel and leave fame and fortune behind, he was faced with a moral dilemma one week before the European Cup Finals, in 1977, as the team was getting ready to fly to Belgrade. Tal received word that his father had suffered a heart attack and was in the intensive care unit. Without wavering or hesitating, he made his way to the airport and flew off to the United States, not knowing whether he would eventually make it to the finals, but knowing that he was doing the right thing. He found his father recuperating, and at his urging, Tal made a quick U-turn and returned to

John F. Kennedy Airport only to discover that the ticket arranged for by his team had not arrived at the Yugoslav ticketing desk at the airport. Demanding to see the person in charge, Brody found himself facing a startled Yugoslav ticket officer who remembered Brody from a game he had played in Ljubljana the previous season. The official allowed Tal to board the plane without a ticket. For Tal this was a vindication that he had indeed done the right thing and was thus being rewarded. He arrived in Belgrade just in time for the final game.

Exploring the resilient fiber that runs through Tal Brody, one clearly can see that meaning and meaning-making are critical features of resilience. Victor Frankl characterized this best when he talked about how a person can withstand the most difficult trials if he has a purpose in life. Frankl was, of course, referencing his experiences as a concentration camp inmate during the Holocaust, where he witnessed people on both sides of the divide. There were those who gave up and perished, and others who hung on tenaciously with the fire of purpose burning in their hearts and minds. Even in situations that are not life and death, finding meaning contributes to feeling one's life has been well lived and to having the ability to meet day-to-day challenges and overcome obstacles.

Tal Brody exemplifies this kind of meaning when he talks about how meaningful it was for him playing for the Israeli team. According to Brody, the Israeli basketball team has had a huge impact on the Jewish communities wherever they have played, whether it be in Los Angeles, Paris, or Peru. The sense that the "shtetl Jew" has shed his shadow and can now stand tall and win on the professional basketball court has been a source of great pride to Tal, and he feels the generations of Jews cheering on the sidelines.

Life can be full of ups and downs, and Tal's life has been no exception. While he is reticent to delve into the rough times he encountered, he is eager to share the keys to his personal resilience. For example, what helped him make that fateful decision to leave the NBA, without second-guessing himself and wondering whether he was doing the right thing? What helped him adapt to his new country, language, and culture? What helped him weather the vagaries of business? Brody cites three key factors: a basic optimism, an ability to keep perspective and focus on the larger picture, and flexibility. Humor, he adds, doesn't hurt either. When asked about Israeli resilience from a national perspective, he unhesitatingly points to the ability of Israelis to come together in a crisis to open their hearts and their homes for strangers and to give freely of themselves. This is a perfect example of the concept of social support and how it is critical for the building and maintenance of resilience.

For Tal Brody, resilience is a way of life. It is something you work at, something you practice, and something you do. Resilience doesn't happen automatically or all by itself. Setting goals and then developing a steady practice are things Tal understands very well, and he does practice what he preaches. It is that outlook and perspective that gave him the confidence to make the right decisions on his path in life. The confidence, indeed, to declare just eighteen years after its reestablishment that a small Middle-Eastern country was now well and truly "on the map."

CHAPTER 9

Determination and Discovery

"Don't blame others. It all depends on you!"
Dr. Amit Goffer

Hitting the Brakes

When Dr. Amit Goffer's wife bought him a new pair of pants at the local mall, the last thing he expected to receive along with the clothes was a winning raffle ticket. The prize was a new quad bike, colloquially known as a *tractaron*. It was a win as surprising as it was unwanted. Goffer simply had no use for an all-terrain vehicle (ATV), and he decided not to redeem the prize.

His children were less than pleased with this decision. In an effort to make it up to them, Dr. Goffer, a successful CEO of a magnetic resonance imaging (MRI) company, took them out for a day of riding on ATVs. If they couldn't own one, at least they could rent a couple of them for the day and enjoy the ride. His son was in one vehicle, and Amit rode behind him together with his daughter on a second ATV. Approaching a steep downward slope, Goffer hit the brakes, and his vehicle bumped into something, causing him to fly through

81

the branches of a tree at literally breakneck speed before crashing to the ground. On impact he could feel nothing. He could not move his arms or legs and immediately knew that he had broken his neck. In an instant, he had become a quadriplegic.

Nearly twenty years later, we are sitting in the living room of his modern, suburban home near the Jezreel Valley in the north of Israel. Sunshine is peeking out of gray skies after the season's first rains. Toys are scattered around the room, a reminder of Dr. Goffer's grandchildren who regularly visit. His desk is covered with papers attesting to the multiple projects he is involved with. Seated in his wheelchair using a specially customized mouse, Goffer logs on to a CNN breaking news item showcasing the innovation of his latest company.

Amit Goffer has been to hell and back, but, in doing so, he has changed the lives of paraplegics around the world. His current success is the result not only of his intelligence and ingenuity but also of his resolve and resilience at a pivotal moment of his recovery from this life-altering accident. Turning a tragedy that could easily have led to a downward spiral into a challenge to be met, Goffer chose to be spurred forward by his accident rather than set back. As a result, his innovations have transformed the world of paraplegics.

At Eye Level

Long before his life-changing injury, Amit Goffer was an outstanding student who excelled in innovation. While service in the Israel Defense Forces is mandatory, a few exceptional students are selected for a special track that includes academic studies prior to their service. Goffer was just such a student. After graduating from the Technion–Israel Institute of Technology in electrical engineering, Amit served for five years in the IDF, becoming a captain in the Israeli Air Force. The Israeli army was, in his words, "a unique University of Life. You go through a process in the army which is very positive, and it has an impact on the rest of your life – the people, the sense of contribution, and the fact that you are working for your country." During his army stint, he was in charge of several defense projects, most of them too secret to discuss till this day, so many years later. The amount of responsibility given to him at a young age taught him how to think out of the box. That is only one of the many contributions he ascribes to his army experience. He underscores the contribution of army service to his own personal development as well as that of so many Israeli youngsters.

Goffer served in the IDF after the Yom Kippur War of October 1973. He and his peers experienced the stark contrast between the lightning Israeli defeat of its enemies in only six days back in 1967 and the great losses suffered by Israel after a surprise simultaneous attack by Syria and Egypt on Yom Kippur, the holiest day of the year. At one point, while working on secret experiments at an isolated IDF base, Goffer complained to his superior, Yair Shamir, the son of former prime minister Yitzchak Shamir, raising his voice as he listed what was wrong with his equipment and issuing a list of demands needed for his research. Instead of dismissing the rantings of his subordinate or punishing him for behavior that was unacceptable, Shamir listened patiently and then made sure that Goffer received everything that he needed.

Having a supportive community around you helps build resilience, and Goffer cites the environment that was created in his unit by his commanding officer. "He cared about the mission, above all. The fact that someone more junior than him was yelling at a commanding officer was not important. Ours is a different kind of army." Goffer compares the IDF to other military organizations, highlighting the ability to question authority – not taking anything as a given – and the critical and analytical thinking that is characteristic of Israelis. Goffer summarizes, "We have a different kind of approach."

Following his army service, Goffer, by then married with three children, began working at Raphael Defense Systems. Subsequently he began his postdoctoral work at Drexel University in Philadelphia. While at Drexel, he had two advisors, one American and the other Israeli. Goffer learned from both of his advisors, albeit in different ways. While working with his older American advisor, Goffer was acutely aware of the "pecking order." In contrast, his Israeli advisor encouraged him to feel confident about his abilities and urged Goffer to see him and other professors and professionals "*b'govah einayim*," a Hebrew expression that means "at eye level." Understanding the importance of not being intimidated by higher-ups or letting them restrain his creativity would become critical to Amit's future endeavors.

The Only Way Up

Reflecting on the immediate days, weeks, and months following his accident, Amit acknowledges he felt that he had fallen into a deep chasm. "The way I saw it then," he says, "I was in a very deep hole… I was in deep depression. I wished I hadn't survived the accident. So many people don't survive such accidents, and I wondered why I did." Goffer had overcome medical challenges in the past, having fully recovered from life-threatening leukemia a decade earlier. Now he would need to dig his way out of an even harsher circumstance.

Drawing on his own inner resilience, he came to the conclusion that "I knew I couldn't fall any deeper. The only way was up. I had to climb out of the hole toward the light." In Greek mythology, while overcome by his grief, Orpheus ventures to the Underworld to bring his beloved Eurydice back to life. Amit references Orpheus when crediting his wife as being the one to bring him back from his personal abyss. His children also motivated him to recover: "I refused to give up the role of being a father." The tremendous support of his family and the meaning and purpose derived from his important role in his family's life helped him climb out of the depths.

The support and goodwill of friends added another layer of community that helped his ascent toward the light. Goffer remembers one particular friend, Aaron, who encouraged him to leave the house for the first time. "Although my friends' positive reactions felt like a hug, my thoughts were not directed at them but were focused on myself. When you go outside, you carry much emotional baggage with you. You worry about things, such as *will I embarrass myself?*" Getting to Aaron's house required navigating a dirt road. Aaron had engaged a tractor to smooth out the road so that Amit could get to his house by wheelchair. When heavy rains fell and the road flooded, Aaron once again used a tractor to restore its accessibility for his friend. This gesture touched Goffer deeply, and he recalls it to this day with a smile, even though it happened so many years ago.

After reaching a plateau in his physical rehabilitation, confined to a wheelchair but with his depression lifting, Goffer began to ponder why the sole solution for paralyzed people was the wheelchair. It had been created in the 1700s, and since then virtually no progress had been made in helping paraplegics move around. There must be, he thought, a way to help paraplegics walk again. His innovative, entrepreneurial mind began to whir, its personal, professional, and business sides coming together synergistically in his search for a solution. As former Israeli president Shimon Peres commented: "When you have two alternatives, the first thing you have to do is to look for the third that you didn't think about, that doesn't exist." A wearable robotic exoskeleton that would literally put disabled people back on their feet was the innovative idea Amit came up with. The desire to bring his vision to life combined with the need to return to his previous functioning kept him going. Reflecting on this invention, Goffer notes that the injury brought something superhuman out of him.

With the help of government and private funding, he was able to create the exoskeleton. Clinical trials were held at Tel Hashomer Hospital, where Goffer himself had undergone rehabilitation. ReWalk,

Goffer's product, has helped many paraplegics get back on their feet. Ironically, due to the extent of his injuries, Dr. Goffer himself cannot use the ReWalk exoskeleton and is still confined to a wheelchair. When asked how he feels seeing people walk again using his invention, Amit points to a photo of himself on the day in New York when ReWalk filed for an initial public offering (IPO) on Nasdaq to raise $58 million at a company value of $250–300 million. The inventor is pictured sitting in his wheelchair, surrounded by several "ReWalkers" who are all standing upright thanks to Goffer's robotic exoskeleton. They have their hands placed symbolically on Amit's torso in a gesture honoring the man who has given their mobility back to them. "Entrepreneurs talk about the thrill of an exit. I love money as much as anyone else, but what I have received from the ReWalkers and their families is something that no exit can compete with."

Choosing to Smile

Is ingenuity inherent in Israeli society? Goffer believes it is, and feels that he himself personifies this trait that is a product of ancient Judaism and modern chutzpah. Having been taught that each Israeli soldier has "the baton of the chief of staff in his bag," meaning that anyone can assume greatness, Goffer contends that this education begins young. Appreciation for nonconformity and creativity are also part of the Israeli educational process. In contrast, he recalls that when he and his family lived in America, the parents were invited to school around Thanksgiving and saw pictures of turkeys that the kids had painted. All of the turkeys were brown except for one, which was all the colors of the rainbow. The name on that painting was Yuval Goffer, Amit's son, a demonstration of Israeli individuality that made his father proud.

In analyzing Dr. Goffer's resilience, several factors come into play. Without a doubt, support from family and friends was key in his recovery. Without them, he would not have made it back from the abyss. They are in fact what brought him back to life, but what helped him thrive? In looking back, his advice to anyone grappling with the aftermath of an accident, illness, or major setback is not to assign blame, whether it is to doctors, others involved, or anyone else. He advises getting help; remembering that even though you're suffering, the people around you are suffering too; seeing the glass as half full; and setting a goal. Remind yourself that you are in charge – the path you choose is in your hands, and, as he says, "it is up to you whether you have a smile or a frown. So smile." His native intelligence, skill, and ability to think out of the box provided him with the tools to continue to create. This creative urge has powered the drive he has discovered to make the lives of paraplegics better. His life has meaning. His creativity has a purpose. His resilience thrives.

Amit recalls receiving acclaim after being the keynote speaker at a conference in London, only to attend a reception afterwards where the cocktail tables were out of reach and the guest of honor sat in his wheelchair at "ass-level" while other guests shifted awkwardly around him. "Being a grown-up at the height of a child is a humiliating experience. There is a loss of dignity and self-esteem." Despite the fact that ReWalk was not helpful to him personally, Goffer would not give up and continued his work to help himself and others stand upright again. His most recent invention – the UpNRide – resembles a specially customized scooter, a two-wheeled robotic device with supports to help paralyzed users get up and moving. This time Goffer was able to benefit. With UpNRide, Goffer was moving upright and outdoors, after two decades of being confined to a wheelchair. In 2015, Goffer unveiled UpNRide at the huge Rehacare Trade Fair in Dusseldorf, Germany. Following his presentation, Dr. Amit Goffer enjoyed lunch with his colleagues and hosts, this time eating at tall reception tables. Amit's invention, pioneered in the aftermath of tragedy, had restored him back to "eye level."

CHAPTER 10

Against the Stream

*"When you believe in your cause, nothing
can stop you."*

Yoseph Haddad

In the Spotlight

The studio lights were bearing down on the guests at Newzroom Afrika,
the twenty-four-hour news channel based in Johannesburg, South
Africa. Four guests sat opposite the host, Lindi Sirame, as Muhammed
Desai, cofounder of BDS South Africa, the local branch of the anti-Israel Boycott, Divestment, and Sanctions campaign, turned the conversation to the ongoing COVID-19 pandemic. "In Israel, you have
the Israeli Ministry of Health that issues notices to its population,
which includes Palestinians, but they only issue them in Hebrew, not
in Arabic." Immediately a strident voice countered, "That is a lie. Stop
the lying." The person behind that voice knew of what he spoke. "I live
in Israel," he said. "Moreover, I think the audience should know who I
am. I am an Israeli Arab, and I received the coronavirus instructions in
Arabic. So, number one, stop lying. And number two, ask me – I will
tell you the truth."

Yoseph, spelled in phonetic English as it would be in Hebrew but pronounced the Arabic way ("Youseff"), is a sharply good-looking and youthful man, polished and determined to take the offensive. Not allowing false accusations about his country to go unchallenged, he regularly writes and broadcasts in Hebrew, English, and Arabic, with many of his social media posts going viral. The bravery and sincerity of this young Israeli Arab is met with a warm embrace by people of goodwill across Israel and around the world. However, not everyone is happy with Yoseph, and his outspoken activism is not without risk. Yoseph is constantly attacked for his views and has even received death threats from extremists.

Dueling Perspectives

Arab citizens of Israel make up just over 20 percent of the country's population. Among them there is a diversity of opinions, just as in any community. The majority define themselves as Arab Israelis, some consider their identity just Arab, some call themselves Palestinian. Around three-quarters of Israel's Arab citizens are Sunni Muslims, with the remainder being Bedouins, Christian Arabs, Druze, and Circassian. Druze Arabic-speakers live distinctly from the larger Arab populations, as do the Circassian community. Whereas America is often described as a melting pot, Israel sees itself more as a mosaic: the different parts do not always overlap, but they do form together to create a greater whole.

Polls show that a majority of Arab citizens of Israel are proud of their nationality, but the situation is complex indeed. The voice heard in the media and the picture painted in public is largely represented by the Arab parties in the Knesset, which tend to verge toward more extreme positions. In fact, they are often at odds with their electorate, many of whom would like them to join a government and wield political influence, something that has not happened yet in the modern State of Israel. While Arab citizens tend to agree that life in Israel is good and comparatively much better than in other Middle Eastern countries, some have difficulty grappling with the reality of being a minority in a Jewish country. Parts of the community support Palestinian nationalistic goals, which call for the destruction and dismantling of the State of Israel, although this is a minority view. While considered by some a potential fifth column during the first decade of Israel's existence, Israeli Arabs have made giant steps forward integrating into all the professions and businesses. The quest for equality, as in any country but especially sensitive with Middle Eastern geopolitics at play in the background, is something that society continues to grapple with.

Yoseph's activism is not always well received in his community. There are those who think that that he goes too far and that he should be ostracized for going against the stream. This does not seem to bother this outspoken man and certainly does not slow him down. Where does Yoseph come from, and how did he come to this unusual place where only a small number of Israeli Arabs have publicly dared to tread?

Yoseph grew up in Nazareth, the largest city in northern Israel and a predominantly Arab town, comprised of both Muslims and Christians. The second of four children, Yoseph has two sisters and one brother. His parents taught their children to be open-minded, to explore and question the world around them but, above all, to be good people, contributing to the world. Yoseph recalls that his parents strongly encouraged the children to integrate into Israeli society. Yoseph's perfect English and unaccented Hebrew is such because while Arabic was spoken in the family home for five days each week, the remaining two days were split with one day only Hebrew spoken and the other day, only English. If the children did not approach their parents in the language of the day, they would not receive an answer! This interesting arrangement resulted in trilingual offspring, with everyone being fluent in each of Israel's three main languages Arabic, Hebrew, and English.

Yoseph was born in Haifa, and the family moved to Nazareth when he was a youngster. Most of his extended family and friends lived in Haifa, populated by a mix of Jews, Muslims, Christians and others, so as a youngster, Yoseph would often take the bus to Haifa to play soccer with children from all different backgrounds. After completing high school, Yoseph, like most eighteen-year-olds, was faced with big decisions about his future. Jewish Israelis are subject to a universal draft into the Israel Defense Forces. Arabs and Bedouins are exempt from this mandatory service due to the sensitivities of both their communities and the realities of Israeli army service. However, they can volunteer to serve if they so wish. Only a few take that route, but Yoseph, who has never taken the easy way out, decided to volunteer for IDF service in a combat unit. And if he had any shred of doubt about serving in Israel's army, a horrific act was about to affirm why taking that step was the right thing to do.

Coexistence under Attack

The Maxim restaurant in Haifa is more than just an eatery. Jointly owned by Arab and Jewish proprietors, and overlooking the sea, it is a symbol of the city and its ethos of tolerance and coexistence. On October 4, 2003, that very symbolism made it a target. Two days before Yom Kippur, a twenty-eight-year-old woman entered the restaurant, which was bustling with people. A law student – on the verge of qualifying as an attorney – from Jenin (a city in the Palestinian Authority, not far from Haifa), she had been recruited by Palestinian Islamic Jihad terrorists. She detonated the powerful bomb belt that she was wearing, and the results of the attack were devastating. Twenty-one innocent people were murdered, and over sixty people were injured. Reports from first-responders at the scene told of a macabre aftermath. The casualties mirrored the diversity of the clientele. Five members of a single Jewish family – the Zer-Avivs – were killed in the attack. The

Arab head waiter, Hana Francis; waiter Sharbal Matar, twenty-three; and cook Osama Najar, twenty-eight, were killed. Another five members of one family – the Almogs – also died. Ten-year-old Oran Almog survived, but in addition to losing two of his grandparents, his father, his brother, and his cousin, he also lost his sight in the blast.

The Maxim restaurant bombing took place just as Yoseph Haddad was about to begin his IDF service. The response to Yoseph's decision to enlist in the IDF was mixed. It simply was not a usual decision to take for someone from his community. Some of his friends were so upset with his decision that they ended their friendship with him immediately. A handful of them have never spoken to him again. Yet others supported him, although this was a step that they themselves would never take. Years later, many of Yoseph's friends have shared with him in confidence that they wished they had followed his example, and if they could do it over again, they too would have enlisted. This underlies Yoseph's contention that he in fact represents the unspoken majority of the Arab Israeli community, not the minority view, as the media would have you believe. Yoseph's parents were most supportive of his decision, although his mother was understandably worried about his safety. The Maxim attack affirmed to Yoseph what he had already decided, that serving in defense of his people – Arab and Jewish – and his country was what he needed to do.

Overcoming Injury

Yoseph's army service took him to the frontline of the fight against terrorism. He drafted into the Golani infantry brigade. His comrades, hailing from a variety of places and backgrounds, welcomed him with open arms. He went on to become a commander in the brigade and served on Israel's borders in the north and south of the country. Throughout his IDF service, Yoseph had no doubts about the rectitude of what he was doing. Even as he found himself, an Arab, fighting for the Jewish state inside the Arab country of Lebanon during the 2006 Second Lebanon War, he felt certain about his role.

The summer of 2006 was very hot indeed. The enemy was not Lebanon or the Lebanese people, but rather the terrorists of Hezbollah. They had been responsible for launching volley after volley of rocket and missile attacks on communities in northern Israel during that conflict, which injured over 1,350 civilians and killed 44. Yoseph's brigade was among those tasked with finding IDF soldiers who had been kidnapped and taking out Hezbollah's rocket-launching capability. Nearly half of those killed by Hezbollah rockets were Arab citizens of Israel, including two babies from Yoseph's hometown, Nazareth. For him, this war was personal.

One of the fiercest battles of the war took place in Bint Jbeil, a large town in southern Lebanon with a population of around twenty thousand. Hezbollah had turned it into a stronghold, embedding their fighters among families, homes, and businesses to create a human shield around them. As a combat soldier in the city, Yoseph recalls being approached by a Lebanese man who entreated him in Arabic, "We welcome you. Please, please, beat Hezbollah." The irony of a Lebanese Arab making this plea to an Israeli Arab soldier was not lost on Yoseph. During the conflict, he lost many friends in battle, as well as his deputy commander, Major Roi Klein, who heroically jumped on a grenade to save the lives of his soldiers.

As the war was winding down, just two days before a cease-fire was declared, Hezbollah fired an anti-tank missile toward the position that Yoseph and his fellow soldiers were defending. The missile hit a wall close to Yoseph, causing him to be thrown several meters. His first thought was, "What will I tell my mother?" He knew immediately that he had been badly injured. His mom would indeed have cause to worry: Yoseph's foot had been severed. He was evacuated to a helicopter by his comrades, still under fire, and taken to the Galilee Medical

Center in Nahariya. Several surgeries later, Yoseph woke and raised his head to discover his foot had been successfully reattached.

Grueling months of recovery and rehabilitation ensued. Yoseph kept his focus on his goal of resuming the active life he had prior to his injury and was able to maintain his high spirits, even when the medical prognosis he received was disappointing. He was told he was lucky to have his foot back, and while his doctor thought he would walk again, they expected that he would limp. Yoseph turned to the doctor and said, "You watch! I will play soccer again!" Competitive and determined, Yoseph set about trying to prove the doctors wrong. He worked hard at rehabilitation, advancing more quickly than expected. One year after the injury, Yoseph went for his final checkup. He entered the doctor's office with a soccer ball, with which he then proceeded to demonstrate his considerable soccer skills right there in the office. He had achieved his goal. Not only does he walk without a limp, nowadays, Yoseph runs ten kilometers (six miles) every week.

Creating an Outlet

Following his military service, Yoseph moved to Canada, where he worked for a couple of years before returning to Israel as COO of a marketing research company based in Tel Aviv. It was a well-paid job with great benefits, including something prized by working Tel Avivians in Israel's busy urban business center: a parking space. After five years, he decided to give this all up and establish a nonprofit organization. He quit his job and cofounded Together We Vouch for Each Other, which has a board comprised of Christian, Jewish, Muslim, and Druze Israelis. The focus of his organization is to encourage full Arab integration and participation in Israeli society, all the while being a vocal opponent to misinformation about his country. All this has given his life a sense of purpose that working in business could not. As the organization grows, more people from diverse backgrounds are joining the movement. It is hard not to be won over by Yoseph's charisma and dynamism, but most of all, his conviction and passion for the cause. He is confident that he and his organization best represent the Arab consensus within Israel.

A self-appointed ambassador for Israel, Yoseph has no problem talking about societal problems and where Israel needs to improve. Israel is not perfect, he contends, but no country is, and dialogue is healthy. He states that he is not there just to criticize, but rather to help be part of the solution to problems that trouble him as a citizen. His organization is committed to playing its part in the Jewish and democratic state of Israel within which its members are proud to live. He sees his role as demolishing the narrative of extremists on both sides of the spectrum. To extremist Jews who claim Arabs do not want to be part of the Jewish state, he serves as an example of an Arab who served his country in uniform. To the Arab extremists, he is showing that the majority of Jews want Arab citizens to be equal and to share a positive role in society. "If both extremes are against us, I must be on the right path," he says with a smile and a twinkle in his eye.

"Until recently," he says, "most Israeli Arabs who thought like me didn't dare speak out. What our organization has done is to say to those people: Don't be afraid. We've got your back. Together we can make a change." The response has been immense. He and his cause have garnered tens of thousands of followers on social media. While some of the public responses to him are fiercely critical, the private messages are generally supportive. It is hard for the Arab community to praise Yoseph's message. Even his sister, Yoseph says, is careful about how encouraging she can be to his posts, publicly. Each time she sees his work on social media, she begins typing, "Brother, I am so proud of you," but before her comment has been fully typed, she often deletes it for fear that extremists may curse and threaten her. This is something that Yoseph fully understands. "When I speak one on one with someone from the Arab community, they often say, 'Keep doing what you're doing.' But if that same person is with other Arabs, he changes the way he talks. Even in a group where most people think the same thing, they're afraid to say it out loud."

Yoseph has embarked on extensive speaking tours around the world, talking with groups of students on campuses abroad as well as groups of students visiting Israel, presenting a side of Israel that few are familiar with. He shares the experience of growing up in the Arab community of Israel, living alongside Jews. Many university campuses have long been hotbeds for anti-Israel activism, led by radical, often antisemitic groups. Yoseph's voice is credible, as evidenced by a speaking engagement that he took part in at Harvard University. Yoseph asked the moderator not to introduce him in any way before he began his presentation. Twenty-five minutes into it, a student from the political science department derided Israel, saying critically: "This is the exact type of presentation I would expect from an Israeli Jew." With his most Arabic-sounding accent, Yoseph replied: "Actually, my name is Youseff Haddad, and I am an Arab Israeli." The questioner was stunned. It was unimaginable to him that the passion for Israel given voice to came from not only an Israeli citizen, but an Arab one at that. This is why, contends Yoseph, his engagement with the public is so important.

Yoseph Haddad is well aware of the complexities and the disputes that populate his world, but he is fiercely proud to be an Israeli. There has been a lot of discussion in the media about "Hatikvah," Israel's national anthem, and how it is problematic for the non-Jewish citizens of Israel, beginning, as it does, with the words, "As long as in the heart within, the Jewish soul yearns…" When asked about this, Yoseph answers immediately. "Do I have a problem with the 'Hatikvah'? Yes. Do I sing the 'Hatikvah'? Yes. Do I change one word in the 'Hatikvah'? Yes." He has no wish for the country to change the words, it is just something that he does for himself. Instead of saying "Jewish soul," he changes it to "Israeli soul."

He illustrates this with a story. He was once at a ceremony for wounded IDF veterans in Canada. Prior to addressing the audience, Yoseph and three Jewish veterans were on stage as first the Canadian national anthem and then the Israeli national anthem were sung. One of the IDF vets turned to him and asked him if he would sing the Israeli anthem. He replied in the affirmative and noted that he would just change that one word from Jewish to Israeli. They went onstage and the ceremony began. Following a rendition of "Oh, Canada," Joseph began to sing the "Hatikvah" along with the other vets. When he got to the word he was about to change, he heard all three of his Jewish comrades do exactly the same thing alongside him, and a tear came to his eyes. When their presentation was finished and they exited the stage, Yoseph had the chance to ask them why they too changed the word, and the others replied, "We are brothers. We couldn't let you sing alone."

Finding Your Voice

Yoseph is someone who clearly chooses to swim against the stream and is willing to fight uphill battles for things he passionately believes in, even if his beliefs are unpopular with many and often garner responses that would scare a more timid individual. What gives Yoseph this strength to speak out loudly and clearly for his beliefs? What helped him bounce back from his injury? What is the secret to Yoseph's personal resilience?

A dose of good old Israeli chutzpah as one of the keys to his own resilience. He speaks his mind, is articulate, and is not willing to step down. This is a quintessential Israeli characteristic that he seems to have an adequate measure of. He is impatient. This too is an aspect of chutzpah. He wants things to happen now and is not willing to wait.

He will go out and fight for what he wants and not worry about the consequences. On deeper reflection about the characteristics of resilience that underlie Yoseph's life choices and actions, the importance of community and meaning are ever present. The encouragement he has received for standing up and speaking out has strengthened him through the more difficult moments that he has encountered. Surrounding oneself with a supportive, sympathetic, and encouraging environment is an important aspect in building personal resilience.

Aside from finding community and support, an additional feature of Yoseph's resilience is the meaning with which his life is imbued. Yoseph has often chosen to forge his own unique, nonconformist path for things that he very much believes in. This belief gives him strength and propels him to stand up and brave the storm that he often attracts like a lightning rod. Thus, community and meaning seem to be key in Yoseph's life at this juncture. He is young, and the future is promising. It will be interesting to keep an eye on this maverick as he makes his way in the world. And what makes him brave enough to persistently go against the stream? "If a Hezbollah rocket didn't stop me, nothing will."

CHAPTER 11

Loss and Life

"Resilience is about becoming, not overcoming."

Sherri Mandell

The Unimaginable

The day dawned bright and clear on May 8, 2001, with no hint of the life-shattering tragedy that would rip apart Sherri Mandell's well-ordered life and family just a few hours later. Her eldest son Koby, five weeks short of his fourteenth birthday, had decided to play hooky from school and went off with a classmate for a hike in the nearby wadi, a canyon that was a mere ten-minute walk from his house. The trail winding through the wadi is literally in the backyard of Tekoa, a small village located south of Jerusalem and east of Hebron that the Mandells call home. It is a beautiful expanse of Judean desert scenery. This canyon has it all: earth tones, jagged rocks, cliffs, and caves that were inhabited by monks in the second and third century CE seeking solitude and a place to connect to God. It is a favorite place for hiking and communing with nature. It is a quiet, peaceful place, where people go to escape the pressures of everyday life, to find silence and solace. That sunny morning in May, however, the canyon turned into a place of horror.

Koby and his friend, Yosef Ishran, were brutally murdered by Palestinian terrorists: first kidnapped and bound, the boys were then stabbed and stoned to death. A local sheep rancher graphically described how the terrorists left the boys' mutilated bodies to be found by the search parties who went out looking when the hour got late and the boys had not returned home.

Sherri, an articulate and lively fifty-something, greets us in her house in the village of Tekoa with a ready smile and an easy laugh. It is the better part of two decades since that fateful day, and Koby would have been in his early thirties by now. Sherri easily recalls the horrors of the first few days and weeks after Koby's death; the memories of the aftermath of his murder are still palpable. She vividly recalls a searing pain so sharp that she thought she was going to die. She *wanted* to die. She also remembers the words that picked her up and propelled her forward. Her husband Seth, a rabbi and educator, said to her, "We have three children who need us. We will not ruin their lives." Those words, along with the togetherness that they were able to find amidst the grief both within the family and their community, allowed them to rise and not only return to the living, but to go on and create the Koby Mandell Foundation, an organization that helps bereaved families and has created therapeutic healing programs for thousands of children and adults. Taking their personal tragedy and turning their grief into an organization that provides services for a hitherto overlooked element in society has given meaning and purpose to Sherri's life and helped her deal with the death of her beloved eldest son.

Journey of Healing

Returning to those early days and months after the murder, the daily visits from her good friend Shira, who also happened to be a grief counselor, were perhaps the most important part of her healing. Shira not only massaged her weekly, but reassured her that it was okay to cry and mourn, comparing her situation to that of a baby who would need to relearn how to walk. When Sherri was ready to come out of her cocoon of grief and to begin walking, Shira was right by her side to walk with her. Along with the daily visits from her friend, the feeling of solidarity, of being one with her husband, Seth, further supported her during this dark time. According to Sherri, she and Seth have very different personalities and different ways of being in the world. Yet after Koby's death, she felt that they were together, in her words, "one body with two heads." This feeling gave her the strength to carry on.

Shira not only visited on a daily basis, she also guided Sherri in her responses to her grieving children and to life events. When grappling with how to deal with the constant flow of tears, Sherri tried Shira's suggestion that she give the kids a clock and tell them to time her, stopping her after one minute. The kids, then aged twelve, eleven, and six, readily agreed and became the timekeepers for their mom's tears. This unique intervention allowed Sherri to cry when she needed to, yet provided a boundary both for herself and for her kids, who soon realized that Mom would cry, and then Mom would stop.

Another suggestion of Shira's became a very powerful mechanism for the family to remember Koby in an active and meaningful way. As his fourteenth birthday neared, a mere five weeks after the murder, Shira encouraged Sherri and Seth to commemorate the day by doing something special. The family decided to give alms to fourteen beggars in Jerusalem, as giving charity was something that Koby loved to do. The situation became almost comical, as they had trouble finding enough needy people to distribute money to. They had to actually chase some of them down, leading to slapstick scenes filled with healing laughter. The family continued this tradition for many years, each year adding another person in need to equal the number of years Koby would have been. As they neared Koby's thirtieth birthday, they wondered whether they would find the requisite thirty beggars, or perhaps it was indeed time to lay this custom to rest.

Laughter has been a constant theme of healing in the Mandell house. Both Seth and Sherri are naturally funny and laugh a lot, and Koby was a funny kid himself who always loved a good laugh. The theme of laughter has become one of the ways the Koby Foundation has supported its activities, creating evenings of laughter called Comedy with Koby. These evenings bring laughter and good times to the world and have helped the foundation reach its annual fundraising goals.

Looking back over the years since Koby's death, Sherri shares that the infusion of spirituality into her life has been one of the great surprises. By her own admission, she had never been a very spiritual person, not interested in past lives, reincarnation, or the life of the soul. However, after Koby's death, she was literally "hit on the head" with it, in the form of birds that kept bumping into her, dying on her doorstep, flying into her house and car, all of them as if coming with a message from Koby saying, "I am here." This element of spirituality has found a warm place in Sherri's heart, as she went on to study pastoral counseling, continue with Torah study, and combine both of these in the writing of two books: *The Blessing of a Broken Heart* and *The Road to Resilience: From Chaos to Celebration*.

When considering her own resilience, Sherri says that she is not resilient by nature. At the time of Koby's death, she felt fragile and on the brink of either insanity or death. Yet with the support of family, friends, and community, and by identifying a spiritual link to Koby, she returned to life. Since that time, she has found ways to reach out to others dealing with the death of a loved one, to provide support, advice, and a shining example of how to continue.

Grief and Gratitude

The culture of bereavement in Israel is pervasive. The term "family of grief" is an inclusive one. Anyone who has lost a family member in war, during army service, or in a terror attack "joins" this family and is embraced by them. There is public acknowledgement of this grief and loss on both the national and community levels. This manifests itself most prominently when public ceremonies occur on Israel's Memorial Day, commemorated one day before Israel's Independence Day. The juxtaposition of these two days, while perhaps jarring, underscores how Israelis honor the sacrifices that have been made to ensure its some-times tenuous existence. Families of the bereaved are invited to special ceremonies and visited by dignitaries, including the top brass of the military and national leaders. Parents and siblings are interviewed on radio and television, and there is government support to help the families memorialize their loved ones in a variety of ways, ranging from books published in the deceased's memory to a hiking trail carved out of the wilderness and named for the deceased.

Transitioning from the depths of sadness brought on by Memorial Day to the excitement and pure joy of celebrating the actual creation and existence of the modern State of Israel can be challenging. How does one move from grief to joy instantaneously? The radio in Israel mirrors that difficult transition. During Memorial Day, sad songs are played all day long. In the late afternoon, as the sun begins its descent, the music begins to change its beat, and minor key subtly changes to major. By the eve of Independence Day, it is full-out merriment and joy. Honoring those who have sacrificed their lives, acknowledging the tremendous sacrifice and sharing the grief of the families leads the way into thanksgiving for the country we have. This is the core of Israeli resilience.

In Israel, children meet death at a much earlier age than in other countries of the West. It is not unusual to see a child attending a funeral in Israel, and schools hold memorial services for the victims of the Holocaust as well as for soldiers and terror victims. Indeed, even the youngest of children are exposed to these losses when the special sirens sound and the entire country stands still for a moment of silence in honor of the fallen. This embrace of bereaved victims of terror and soldiers who have found death on the battlefield or in training is at the very core of Israeli society. It impacts the way that Israelis deal with civilian deaths as well. Funerals are generally large and well attended. Visiting the bereaved is part of the fabric of life: yearly memorial services are held to commemorate grandparents or parents who are long gone. Death is very much a part of life in Israel.

The presence of death in Israel introduces one more face in the mosaic that has created Israeli resilience. By necessity, death is present, and because Israelis tend to be straightforward, it is not skirted around. Learning how to live life to the fullest while not forgetting about the deceased is at the heart of a resilient approach. It involves understanding that there may be moments of unbearable pain, accepting them, and then allowing them to make way for the inevitable moments of joy and happiness. Incorporating loss into life leads the way for that special brand of Israeli resilience.

While Sherri has described the very important role that social support played in her life, learning how to live alongside the grief and to find meaning in Koby's death came from the creation of the Koby Mandell Foundation. Without the daily visits of her friend and the strong togetherness with her husband, Sherri would have floundered, but this sense of mission gave Sherri's loss a direction and purpose and filled her days and nights with creative activity. Memorializing Koby in an active way that kept his name on the lips of many, not allowing him to be forgotten, was part of the healing process. Taking the pain of the loss and turning it into a creative endeavor helping first hundreds and by now thousands to heal from their own personal grief has brought a feeling of comfort to Sherri and her husband. Summer camps for kids, healing retreats for bereaved mothers and widows, and spiritual support groups are just a few of the activities that the Koby Mandell Foundation has promoted. For Sherri, knowing that much good has come out of the horror of her son's death allows her to continue living life to the fullest.

Sherri has touched death and returned to the living. She felt that each time she was at the edge of this bottomless pit, she was called back to life – by her children, by her friends, and by her community. When she advises people who have experienced a tragic loss, she tells them, reaching out from her own experience, "You will survive." She characterizes grief as a wild animal. It can come at you without warning and hit you when you are down. But you need to know that you will survive. In her final words of wisdom to us, she shares, "When you know death, you know life." This is an apt phrase from the mouth of a bereaved mother, born in the United States and now a full-fledged Israeli. This is the epitome of Israeli resilience.

CHAPTER 12

The Mayor of Rocket County

*"You always have to see the cup as half full.
I am a lucky guy."*

Gadi Yarkoni

Tell the World

The Palais des Nations in Geneva, Switzerland, is an imposing, historic building, housing the second-largest United Nations presence (after their headquarters in New York). Among other bodies, it is the base for the UN Human Rights Council, making the city a center for global human rights organizations, including the Red Cross. In a committee room overlooking Lake Geneva, three committee members sit in dark suits. Across from them sits an Israeli kibbutznik. It is the winter of 2015, the temperature that day dropping to 2°C (36°F). Yet, incongruously, the Israeli wears shorts with his work shirt. He looks like the typical kibbutznik that he is, but that is not why he is wearing shorts. He is wearing shorts because his legs were blown off six months earlier, the stumps are still healing, and he finds long pants uncomfortable. He has temporary prosthetics on both legs and uses a walker to ambulate. He is still in significant pain and has not completed his rehabilitation.

Half a year earlier, Gadi Yarkoni lost both his legs when a rocket landed between them. Israel was – to all intents and purposes – at war. It was the seventh and final week of Operation Protective Edge, a defensive military campaign launched by Israel in Gaza to counter a sustained rocket barrage toward Israel, which lost sixty-six soldiers and six civilians as the conflict played out. Earlier that day, a terrorist rocket had hit the power line carrying electricity to Kibbutz Nirim, where Yarkoni had been born and raised and was now part of the kibbutz management. He and two colleagues went out to fix the line. Gadi was unlucky – an hour before a ceasefire took hold, Hamas fired the rocket that exploded where he stood, less than fifteen seconds after the warning sirens sounded. There was nowhere to run. Yet Gadi considers himself lucky – he lost both his legs, but his colleagues – the kibbutz security coordinator Ze'ev Etzion and his deputy, Shahar Melamed – lost their lives in the attack.

When he was asked to fly to Geneva to give testimony to the United Nations Independent Commission of Inquiry on the 2014 Gaza Conflict, Gadi Yarkoni overcame initial hesitation and – accompanied by his wife – made the trip. Official Israel boycotted the commission, citing the bias of the controversial committee known for being steered by many human rights–abusing countries and for its relentless, disproportionate focus on Israel. Yet despite the pain and discomfort, Gadi's motivation in flying there was to articulate to the UN officials the unbearable reality of civilians living under fire – including Yarkoni's wife, his three daughters, his neighbors, and friends. He also wanted to make sure that the committee understood something that is so obvious to him: that the Israel Defense Forces are a moral fighting force, and that while there is sadly unintended collateral damage in war, the focus of IDF firepower is directed toward taking out terrorists, while the Hamas aim their weapons at civilians. If there had been no terror, there would have been no conflict.

Up for a Challenge

Several years after these events, we meet in the office of now mayor Gadi Yarkoni. The unpretentious office of the head of the Eshkol Regional Council is a modest building that is built of reinforced concrete to protect it from missile attacks. The regional council covers a triangular area of southern Israel between Ashkelon and Beersheba, with a border adjacent to both Egypt and the Gaza Strip. The latter has been run by Hamas since 2007, when an internal Palestinian conflict with the Fatah-run Palestinian Authority ignited a civil war between Gazans that saw hundreds killed.

Yarkoni experiences a certain amount of discomfort talking about his personal story and the attention he has received in recent years since his injury. While the limelight is no longer new to him, he feels more at ease when the focus of the discussion is on leadership, development, and working with the local population to create infrastructure, economic security, and quality of life. The region he oversees has been under continual rocket fire for two decades. There is the constant worry that terrorists are once again burrowing below residential homes as they seek to build more terror tunnels in order to kidnap and kill. PTSD cases are common in the children of this area. It is a physical and mental war of attrition. In some years, the rocket attacks are sporadic, but at times there are severe escalations: children stay home from school, and workplaces are shut down. When the situation will flare up again is anyone's guess. It is this reality that is wreaking havoc with the quality of life that Yarkoni is trying so hard to improve.

Despite this situation, Yarkoni exudes optimism and defiance when discussing life in his region surrounding Gaza, and even when he reflects on his injuries. That may be because the rocket attack that took his legs was not Yarkoni's first setback. Beginning back in 1985 when he was drafted into the IDF and was unable to serve as a combat soldier, Gadi has learned to deal with disappointments and setbacks of a physical nature. When he was diagnosed with glaucoma at age twenty-four and lost vision in one eye completely, with only limited vision in the remaining eye, Gadi had to make a life course correction and move from agricultural work in the fields that he loved so much to a different kind of employment where his remaining eyesight would be protected. Although schooling had never come easy for him, he decided that now was the time to make the maximal effort to study and prepare himself for a new career. In order to do that, he needed to complete his high school matriculation exams and get accepted to a college.

With much determination and hard work, Yarkoni successfully completed a college degree at Ruppin College, and upon return to the kibbutz took up various leadership positions, including director general of the kibbutz, a position he held for ten years. When he suffered a massive heart attack at age forty-two, his response was not to reduce his workload and take the easy path. To the contrary. Gadi added a neighboring kibbutz, Kisufim, to his work responsibilities, as he became the director of that kibbutz as well. He ran both kibbutzim, something virtually unheard of, for the next four years until the fateful day of his injury.

Gadi was not the only one giving testimony at the UN hearing in Geneva. Others included Gila Tragerman, the mother of four-year-old Daniel, who was killed in his home on Kibbutz Nahal Oz as a result of rocket fire, and Haim Yellin, then head of the Eshkol Regional Council. A longtime friend of Gadi's, he shared that he would be stepping down from his position in order to run for the Knesset, Israel's parliament, thus vacating this senior position. Gadi, who had never considered local politics before, began to think about whether this was a challenge he was up for. After consulting with his wife and some close friends, he decided to run and won, beating two other contenders to win 51 percent of the vote in the mayoral election. Currently Gadi is in his second term as council head, with no signs of stepping down or giving up the mantle.

A Lucky Guy

As Gadi tells his story, he shares about the fifteen days he was suspended between life and death. An unintended result of being intubated and put in a drug-induced coma immediately after his injury was that he missed the deep mourning the kibbutz members experienced for those they had lost, and he was not there with them to experience their great sense of disheartenment and loss of hope. This difficult period of time passed him by almost completely as he struggled for his life. When he awoke and was told by his wife about the death of his two friends, he knew that while it was important to remember them, it was even more important to carry on with more energy, more enthusiasm, and more spirit than ever before. As he began to heal in the rehab unit of Tel Hashomer Hospital, he continued to work, even though there were people replacing him in the day-to-day operations of the kibbutz. It is clear that being in control is an important feature of Gadi's leadership and likely a key feature of his ability to bounce back. He wants to know what is going on. He wants to be on the inside, to be part of the decision-making process, to be a mover and shaker, for all the right reasons.

When he heard that the position of head of council would soon be vacated, he began to see himself in that position in order to continue the momentum of his professional development. Till this day, he believes this is the antidote to sinking into depression, despair, and anxiety. He himself has never suffered symptoms of post-traumatic stress since his injury and the loss of his good friends who were standing right next to him. He does not – thankfully – appear to be wracked by "survivor's guilt," a common post-traumatic feeling experienced by those who live while others die. He clearly sees himself as a survivor, rather than a victim. He is sympathetic to others who suffer and maintains that what helps him, and the way he helps to encourage others, is focusing on the cup being half full. To that end, he remarked more than once how lucky he was that his amputations were both below the knee. Many would not see that as "luck," but Yarkoni expresses it with such sincerity that you believe him. No matter that he has two prosthetics. No matter that he still suffers from pain. He is a lucky guy, and he believes this with all his heart. He is alive to enjoy his family, his community, and his life.

When asked what else helped him heal aside from his innate optimism and his drive to lead and to create, he talks about his family and gets a bit misty-eyed. His wife, three children, two sisters, and parents showered him with constant visits during his long rehabilitation, despite the distances (a good two-hour trip in each direction). He notes that his family has become much closer since his injury, for which he is very thankful.

How do you build resilience in the population of the south of Israel that has been under rocket attacks for twenty years? How do you blunt the psychological impact of the constant yet unpredictable red alert sirens, the never-ending sounds of rocket fire, and the resulting carnage from attacks? Gadi seems incredibly resilient, and we can learn from him two important principles: optimism and activity. Gadi doesn't sit still and doesn't wait for things to happen. He is clearly in the driver's seat. He is in charge; he controls, initiates, and directs. Much of this is inborn or imbibed from a very early age from his parents and other people who influenced Gadi, as well as from the generation of kibbutzniks he represents. When looking at the younger generation, whose entire childhood has been spent in the shadow of rocket attacks, we often see a different story, a more nuanced and complicated one.

For example, the percentage of children and young adults who have grown up in the area bordering Gaza and suffer from post-traumatic stress symptoms is exceptionally high. The levels of anxiety reported by parents and children alike is similarly extreme. This is not surprising, despite the existence of resilience centers for treatment and the proliferation of "safe rooms" and shelters in most houses and community buildings. The sheer number of rockets that has fallen over the last twenty years erodes feelings of security and safety and makes resilience hard to come by.

Gadi Yarkoni is a shining light in this often troubled setting and works hard at keeping up morale for the entire community. His emphasis on economic development and growth, his dynamism, and his enthusiastic optimism are magnetic. This is not only central to his being, but explains in large part how he has overcome the challenges that life has dealt him. He believes that in order to live in this part of Israel, one must be convinced that the current situation will not go on forever, and that the rocket fire will cease one day. Peace may be elusive, yet his hope that the citizens of both Israel and Gaza will be able to coexist, without warfare, reigns strong. The mayor of rocket county is an eternal optimist.

CHAPTER 13

The Climb

*"In the airless void, the only thing that stands
between you and death is yourself: your wits,
your preparation, your mental and physical
strength."*

Nadav Ben Yehuda,
AIPAC Policy Conference, 2013

Pushing the Limits

It was a high-altitude engagement. They had met as students, and Nadav
introduced Lena to climbing, which she grew to love. The mountaintop marriage proposal had been in the planning for quite some time.
Any major climb takes meticulous months of organizing, but in addition to preparing for change of weather or potential injury, Nadav
needed to prepare for Lena's answer. At the summit of Kilimanjaro,
there was just enough oxygen to say a yes or no. Demonstrating clearly
his thoroughness of character, Nadav had brought two rings with him
up the mountain. One was his mother's and one his grandmother's.
Neither of them were actually for his potential fiancée to keep, but they
were of different sizes, and Nadav assumed that at least one of the rings
would work for the proposal, before choosing the perfect ring for her
back home. Fortunately, Lena said yes, and Nadav removed her glove,
baring her hand to the -20°C (-4°F) cold just long enough to put the

117

ring on. Due to inclement weather conditions, they were unable to communicate their happy news to friends and family for a few days. To the blissful ignorance of the outside world, the climbers were engaged!

Everyone has peaks and troughs in life, but few get to experience the highest of highs as Nadav Ben Yehuda has. He is the Israeli who has climbed the most mountains above eight thousand meters (twenty-six thousand feet), and he is the first Israeli to climb Annapurna I, the deadliest mountain on the planet. He also made the first Israeli winter ascent of the highest mountain in Europe, and holds the record as the Israeli champion of Skyscrapers Stair Climbing. Nadav's story is all about pushing the limits of human potential and moving forward despite setbacks, meeting challenges head on.

Nadav is tall and engaging, with a deep voice and a kind face. Appropriately enough, he was born to a family living on a mountain – in Jerusalem. Later his family moved to the city of Rehovot in the central plains of Israel, south of Tel Aviv. He is the oldest child in his family, followed by two sisters and two brothers. His parents met on Kibbutz Merom Golan in northern Israel. Nadav, their firstborn, always had an outdoorsy kibbutz spirit and a strong connection to nature. Whenever Nadav's parents had some savings to spare, rather than buy furniture or appliances, they took the family to travel abroad. Thus, young Nadav traveled in several remote places, exposing him to landscapes and terrain that looked very different from his native Israel.

Nadav recalls seeing his first "real" mountain in Chamonix, France, when he was about eight years old. Nadav stood on tiptoe to peer out of the cable car window. While everyone else's eyes were on Mont Blanc, "the white lady," Nadav was transfixed by the glacier below. From his tiptoe perch, he managed to make out dots that looked like tiny pixels in a picture. They were in fact mountain climbers. His mind was afire to know not simply why they climb, but rather practically how they climb. The sense of challenge and direct connection to nature fascinated him and led to his eventual lifelong devotion to ice climbing.

Nadav began his own climbing career during his teens. He started by going down, rather than up, utilizing ropes as a method of transport. He practiced rappelling, canyoneering, caving, and river crossing, then started rock climbing, eventually focusing on alpine, mixed, and ice climbing, in addition to high-altitude mountaineering. Those ropes would become central to his life. Nadav enlisted for his mandatory IDF service, which was an intensive one, serving in the Sayeret Golani special forces unit as a combat soldier, acting operations officer, and combat team commander. Nadav continues to do reserve duty in the Special Forces Alpinist Unit. Looking back on his service, Nadav notes that when the army wants to train you, you carry someone on your back; when they want to teach you a lesson, you carry someone on your back; in order to receive a reward, you carry someone on your back. Looking out for one another and extracting your comrade from danger is a lesson well learned and a value that would become a tenet of Nadav Ben Yehuda's life.

Living on the Edge

Nadav says he believes in love at first sight. This was true of his wife Lena, and this is true of mountains as well. He falls in love with mountains the first time he sees them. His relationship with climbing, on the other hand, he defines as a love-hate one. You embark on a journey that you really are looking forward to, and you have chosen to do, but the cost is great. First there is the actual financial cost, which is substantial. Add to that a mental cost, a physical cost, a medical cost, and a cost to family life, and you can begin to understand the complex nature of this profession. Nadav Ben Yehuda has experienced and endured all of these costs, multiple times.

Nadav's entire life is about mountains. His wall is adorned with a giant map. He places a pin in it to select his next climb and then begins to research. With a vocation such as ice climbing, preparation and training are key, but the only real way to do this is on the ice – and Israel does not have a single glacier to train on. This requires several months a year of training abroad, and every mountain, icefall, or crag that he climbs is also a preparation for the next one. There are no shortcuts to climbing. You must take into account the risks as well as your skill level and ability to make the climb. Mental preparation – visualization, as Ben Yehuda terms it – is critical. You have to think and even dream about the mountain so much so that when you eventually get there, it feels like déjà vu. Photos and intelligence gathered by other climbers play an important part here. Despite the intensive days, weeks, and months of planning, the actual terrain is never exactly what one had imagined. Unlike rock climbing, the face of an icy mountain changes on a daily basis, and the surprises involved are part of the project. Once the climb begins, Nadav describes his single-minded concentration as he enters a state of mental hardiness that allows him to focus solely on his mission, shielding thoughts of family, friends, sea-level concerns or luxuries, and of the perils involved in a "safe zone" within his mind.

In 2016, Nadav became the first Israeli to ascend the deadliest mountain in the world, Annapurna I (8,091 meters or 26,545 feet) – which has a more than 30 percent death rate for those attempting the climb. He climbed for almost seventy days. The night after this exhausting climb, Nadav recalls falling asleep, enveloped in his hotel room bed in Kathmandu, only to wake up hours later with feverish nightmares of dangerous, life-threatening scenarios. After closing off his consciousness to these thoughts for over two months, he was suddenly beset by them. Fear, says Nadav, is an important part of climbing: "If I meet a person who is not afraid of a climb, I am immediately afraid of them."

Most people live out their lives within a safe zone. Nadav lives within a danger zone, literally on the edge. The truth is, he says confidently, that he is not a risk taker, and when it comes to climbing, he works relentlessly to minimize, mitigate, and avoid dangers. There is a spectrum between making conservative choices and taking risks. Nadav does not view himself nor what he does as extreme. He does not gamble, drink coffee or alcohol, eat salt or sweets, smoke, or do drugs – all to keep his body and mind oriented to his goals. Nadav looks at things scientifically and assesses the likelihood of potential for danger. He is not reckless. He is literally, as goes the Hebrew phrase for a science nerd, a "good boy from Jerusalem." Nevertheless, in climbing, as in life, there is always an element of the unknown. You cannot predict every eventuality or be 100 percent confident about everything. Being at peace with that fact allows you to live outside your comfort zone and to take on new challenges with confidence.

In a life of shifting ice fields, instability is a constant. It is the predictable unpredictability that prevents Nadav from having a clear timeline of upcoming climbs. There are so many variables to consider. A country might close its borders, permits may be withheld, or a cardinal serac (a column of glacial ice) may break on one particular mountain. As a result, Nadav has learned to be flexible, but once he has decided on an objective, he fully commits. That commitment is imperative, as there will always be good excuses to be found for not attempting a given climb.

The Moment of Truth

Nadav started eyeing the highest mountain in the world a few years before attempting to climb it. Preparation was hard and lengthy. Mount Everest (8,848 meters or 29,029 feet) was a challenge he wanted to take on, but Nadav did not see it as an end in itself – he wanted to climb in the world of the eight-thousanders, the nickname for the fourteen mountains above eight thousand meters (26,427 feet). Climbing Everest takes months. In preparation, you have to acclimatize in different altitudes for the low oxygen levels and to understand the intrinsic logistics needed for this vast Himalayan ascent. In addition to heavy high-altitude climbing gear on your body, such as a down suit, crampons, ice axes, and a helmet, the equipment list goes on and on. Even if you get your own preparation right, you are still in the hands of much larger and uncontrollable forces, such as glacial movements, avalanche risk, and meteorological states, all making it very clear that reaching a summit is never guaranteed.

The year 2012 was a controversial time for Everest, which experienced one of the busiest seasons in its history. This prompted fears that commercialization would lead to inexperienced climbers attempting a climb that they were not ready for. In addition to committed climbers like Nadav, there are those adventurers or attempted record breakers who see Everest as something to check off a bucket list. Climbing Everest is an expensive undertaking. Just the cost for the permit alone is between $11,000 and $18,000 (and constantly rising) per climber, and that is before the additional costs for logistics, gear, insurance, and the climb itself; which can run into additional tens of thousands of dollars. It is also dangerous. Toward the summit of Mount Everest lie more than two hundred dead bodies. Without proper training, posing for that precious photo at the summit could be one of the most expensive and dangerous selfies you ever take. Plenty do, however, bear the expense and take the risk.

One such person was a Turkish climber whom Nadav met on his way to the mountain. Despite having no climbing experience at all, he wanted to be the first person in the world to scale Mount Everest, as the first mountain in his life, while holding a bicycle. Later on, he would be arrested for attempting this stunt; a showman at heart, he had threatened to set himself and the camp on fire with cans of kerosene if anyone touched his bike. In the end, both he and his bicycle were removed from the mountain by the authorities, an action he accused of being a Nepali government conspiracy against him. As Nadav would later find out, this did not deter the Turkish climber from reattempting the climb, with serious repercussions for Nadav as well.

It happened as Nadav was just about three hundred meters (a thousand feet) below the summit. He had already encountered two dead bodies on the last part of the climb, and his apprehension of the consequences of too many inexperienced climbers on the mountain was being confirmed before his eyes. Then he saw another body that at first glance appeared to be dead. It was the Turk he had met on the way to the mountain. He was in a very bad way, but still alive. He had no oxygen equipment and was injured and unable to speak. He was a total mess, with no backpack, gloves, or ice axes. In Nadav's words, it looked like "he was waiting for the end." Nadav was furious that someone would place himself and other climbers at a significantly higher risk due to his lack of preparedness for the climb. As a result, Nadav now needed to make an instantaneous decision, one that would prove fateful: climb up and become the youngest Israeli to reach the summit of Mount Everest, or give up when he was so close to the top in order to help a stranger in distress, while imperiling his own life, too.

This was no dilemma for Nadav. There was no doubt in his mind about what he needed to do. Nadav decided to abort his own climb just about three hundred meters short of the summit in order to try to lower the injured person down the mountain alive. Nadav attached him to his own harness between his legs via a short-rope, loading both their weights on the rope systems, using his legs to traverse horizontally and his hands to control the vertical descent, while maneuvering with the additional gravitational pull of the injured man. On the way down, Nadav's own oxygen system broke, and he needed to constantly remove his gloves in temperatures of tens of degrees below zero so he could operate the systems. Not long after, his right hand completely froze and ceased to function. It took eight hours for Nadav and the Turk – who was flitting in and out of consciousness – to get to the highest camp. Periodically assisted by other climbers along the way, the descent continued to a lower glacier at an elevation where a helicopter could land.

Nadav himself was severely injured during the descent, leaving him with orthopedic disorders, injuries to his feet, hands, and face, and drastic weight loss throughout the climb and rescue (nineteen kilograms, nearly forty-two pounds). The helicopter brought them to safety, and medical care was at hand. When Nadav was finally seen by doctors, they wanted to immediately amputate four of the fingers from his right hand. He flatly refused, insisting on fighting for his hand; his fingers, while not perfect, remain quite functional today. Both Nadav and the person he saved survived, and over time, recovered, relatively. Looking back, Nadav explains that the decision he made whether to reach the summit or save a life was instantaneous. Subsequent to that first decision there were a series of additional decisions, each one life threatening, with the need to constantly assess whether by making the dangerous descent together, they would survive or whether it would kill one or both of them.

This event attracted a lot of attention from the international media, and for the first time, Nadav found himself unwillingly in the spotlight. Since the person that Nadav, the Israeli, had saved was Turkish, and those two countries were diplomatically at odds, the media gave the coverage a geopolitical slant. They posed for photos with their flags, and the Turk thanked Nadav in multiple interviews and videos for saving his life. He called Nadav's mother to thank her, telling her they now have family in Turkey too. However, later on, pressure got to him, and the man Nadav saved changed his story. He subsequently claimed that he was never rescued at all, particularly by an "Israeli soldier," and that he was a victim of an Israeli conspiracy against him as a Turkish national. He began to rail against the Jewish state, defaming Israel with some of the worst allegations made by anti-Israel organizations. This was difficult for Nadav, who loves Turkey and the Turkish people. While the world saw an act of humanity, which not only cost Nadav reaching the summit, but more importantly severely endangered his life, no one expected it to become politicized. Up until that moment, Nadav's experience within the climbing community was one in which borders did not exist. Nadav has friends from many countries that do not maintain diplomatic relations with Israel, and this has never been a problem.

Two months after the life-threatening rescue, while Nadav was still undergoing intensive rehabilitation, he received a phone call from the office of the president of Israel, Shimon Peres. He was to be awarded the Israel Presidential Medal of Honor. He also received an honorary medal from the president of Florida International University. In the following years, he was given the Best Athlete in the Alpine Climbing Field award by the Israeli Federation for Non-Olympic Competitive Sports and was chosen by *Forbes* magazine as one of the most influential people under the age of thirty.

Despite the unsought adulation, recovery was tough, and Nadav's fingers were still blackened from frostbite for months later. He had frostbite in four fingers on his right hand and several toes, and he had damaged sensation and mobility in his left hand. Many medical procedures ensued. With the support of his family and doctors, he recuperated and slowly returned to climbing, but Nadav did not return to the Himalayas for sixteen months, a frustratingly long time for him to be away from his passion. When he finally did return to the big mountains, it was to the eighth highest mountain in the world, Manaslu, Nepal, which means "mountain of the spirit." It was cathartic for him get back into thin air.

Back in the Saddle

The story picks up again in 2014, when Nadav Ben Yehuda was returning home from Tibet, having concluded an eight-thousand-meter climb. He was contacted by the Israeli Ministry of Foreign Affairs. There had been a severe snowstorm caused by a massive cyclone in the Indian Ocean during the busy trekking season in Nepal, which is one of the destinations that young Israelis enjoy visiting as part of their post-army trips. The Israeli embassy in Kathmandu had been alerted about Israeli trekkers who were trapped on a mountain pass. The stranded Israeli trekkers had written a note in Hebrew, which they attached to a mule led by a local porter who managed to descend the mountain pass to a nearby village. The message was then communicated to the embassy.

Israeli search and rescue teams flew out to Nepal to help find the survivors of the blizzard. Due to high altitudes they would experience during the rescue attempts, the teams would need time to acclimatize to the heights, whereas Nadav was already acclimatized. He was asked to join the search and rescue efforts, and immediately agreed to embark on various missions across the great Himalayan ranges of Everest, Langtang, and Annapurna. A year later, in late April 2015, Nadav joined the embassy of Nepal in Israel to coordinate rescue missions and humanitarian support, while assisting Israel's Foreign Ministry to trace missing Israeli citizens immediately following the massive earthquakes in Nepal.

There is an innate loneliness to mountaineering. However much support one might have, it is your individual hands and feet that make their way from crag to dangerous crag. Nadav is fortunate to have teams and the operations center of logistics, meteorology, and rescues managed by Lena, who is a very important partner in his achievements. The perseverance and stamina needed to continue comes from both inner reserves and also from knowing that there are a lot of people willing you on, from thousands of feet below you or thousands of miles away.

There is also great comfort and strength in knowing that if you are in danger, those people would come to your aid.

Following the snowstorm rescue effort, Nadav was asked by an American tourist why there were so many Israelis in Kathmandu assisting with the search effort. In response, he showed him the front page of one of the most popular Hebrew news websites, reporting on another rescue effort happening at the same time in Peru. A handful of Israelis were missing following a rafting accident – it was being reported as a major disaster. The story had been front-page news for several days. Whereas in many countries of the world, a few lost tourists might be considered a minor story, in Israel, this merits headline news, because each Israeli is a "brother" or "sister." The ethos drawn from the Talmudic proverb that "all Israel is responsible one for the other" is something learned early in life and engraved on the hearts of even the toughest Israelis.

In 2018, Nadav attempted Kangchenjunga, the third highest and one of the most difficult mountains in the world, soaring at 8,586 meters (28,110 feet), located in the Himalayas, between Nepal and India. It was his second try at the climb. One year earlier, Nadav had climbed to 8,150 meters, the highest point achieved for several years on Kangchenjunga. Following that, it was time for the next challenge: he set out to climb another eight-thousander in a bid to see how quickly he could make it from sea level to summit without the use of supplemental oxygen or any pre-acclimatization. He managed that potentially months-long climb in just fourteen days, and then decided to go back to Kangchenjunga for a second attempt in the next season of 2018.

This time, Nadav reached the highest point among any of the few climbers who did not use supplemental oxygen. But about 140 meters below the summit, due to changing conditions, Nadav decided to turn back, a difficult decision to make on one of the hardest mountain faces in the world. It was on this descent that disaster struck, and he fell.

He was so badly injured that he stayed above eight thousand meters at temperatures of tens of degrees below zero, still without an oxygen system, for an additional twenty-four hours, unable to climb down, relentlessly trying to move himself a few centimeters at a time. Fellow climbers who had lost contact with him transmitted multiple times via voice communicators that Nadav had perished, and they decided to descend the mountain. Nadav was left for dead in the "death zone."

But he survived and managed to get himself down the mountain with the help of friends from all over the world, as part of a complicated and formidable multi-day extraction – and now he is recovering. With a broken and necrotic body, Nadav has undergone multiple operations, including amputation surgeries, and now walks with crutches. This is a marked improvement from when he was confined first to an isolated ICU bed and then to a wheelchair, for more than a year. But life is stronger than anything, and Nadav keeps moving forward. During his recovery, Nadav was appointed a Goodwill Ambassador by the government of Nepal, promoting links between the two countries he considers his home: Israel and Nepal. While he plans his way back to the mountains and rehabilitates his body, Nadav spends his time also developing his mind and his curiosity: in addition to his past two bachelor degrees, he completed an MPH in emergency and disaster management at Tel Aviv University, and is studying for an MSc in extreme medicine at Exeter University. He is working on his PhD proposal in medical sciences and lectures about his fields of expertise around the world.

Several years after Nadav's mountaintop proposal to Lena, there is a newcomer on the scene. Newborn baby Adam is cooing and gurgling as he heads off for an afternoon nap, while we continue the interview. It is clear that Nadav is besotted with his son. Yet minutes later he is once again consumed with talking about his previous expeditions. This is the restless life of a climber: when you are in the mountains, you want to be back with your family, and when you are at home, you want to be back in the mountains. Nadav underscores that those are different types of love, both filling his heart with happiness and fulfillment. Even when you are feeling low, you set your sights high, and the sky is not the limit.

Nadav is used to working under conditions in which the next step you take can literally be the difference between life and death. Most of us do not crave these challenges, nor do we find ourselves in a freezing, high-altitude environment with a paucity of breathable air. But climbing, like life, is predicated on a series of consequences and decisions, and there is much to learn from Nadav's story. The consequences, we have no control over; but when it comes to the decisions, we do have total control. Flexibility, one of the keys to resilience, is a vital coping mechanism for unknown terrain – whether on a mountain or in our daily lives. It allows us to make clear-eyed decisions, as it did for Nadav on the day he set aside his goal to reach Everest's summit and instead chose to save a life.

CHAPTER 14

National Resilience

"What Israelis can teach the world is that life goes on, despite terrible things. And I think that's a wonderful message."

Colonel (Res.) Miri Eisin

A Time of Terror

During the late 1990s and early 2000s, Israel was suffering an ongoing period of terror attacks that were overwhelming in their sheer number, their gruesomeness, and the toll they took on human life. The number of Israelis murdered and maimed by terrorists reached a peak in 2002, with over double the fatalities of the previous year. The terrorists' methods and targets were myriad: snipers, roadside bombs, suicide terrorists, shootings, vehicle rammings, and stabbings took place on civilian roads, in restaurants, buses, shopping malls, discotheques, and even an ice cream parlor and pizzeria. Israelis girded themselves on a daily basis for the next breaking news report telling of where the latest carnage had taken place. As always, the conflict made headlines on news networks the world over. That year, for the first time, the internationally recognized public face of the Israel Defense Forces was a woman. In

2002, Colonel Miri Eisin was thrust from her behind-the-scenes role into the glare of the media limelight as the new IDF Spokesperson to the international media.

Colonel Eisin was ready for the challenge. Born in the United States, she moved with her parents to Israel when she was a child. Eisin's English was fluent, and she spoke in clear, empathetic tones. After graduating high school in 1980, she joined the IDF and was accepted into officers' training in the Intelligence Corps. Eisin served for more than twenty years in the Military Intelligence Directorate of the IDF in a variety of field and research positions, across the tenure of several different generals. Positions she held included deputy head of combat intelligence and personal assistant to the director of military intelligence.

This allowed her the privilege of being the proverbial fly on the wall to important matters of state and privy to many critical military discussions. As adjunct to the chief of staff, Eisin sat in Israeli government cabinet meetings chaired by successive prime ministers. Miri is one of a small cohort of people who can summon twenty-five years of insider's knowledge as to how decisions are made in the Israeli cabinet relating to military assessments and national readiness planning. Retiring as a full colonel, Eisin is also one of the tiny group of Israeli women to achieve that rank in the military (fewer than 2 percent of colonels are female).

Having previously been a military spokesperson, Eisin entered her new role in government in 2002 as the prime minister's foreign media advisor following a particularly brutal and symbolically painful terror attack, the Seder night massacre at the Park Hotel. The beachfront promenade of Netanya, a seaside town thirty minutes north of Tel Aviv, is typically a serene place on a spring evening, with both local residents and tourists out strolling alongside the sea. On that particular night, few were walking the boardwalk, as it was the first night of Passover.

When it comes to observing the Jewish calendar, there are two dates during the year that the vast majority of Israelis commemorate dutifully, whether they are religious or not. They are the Yom Kippur fast and the Passover Seder. On the night of March 27, 2002, hundreds of guests were gathered to observe the holiday by partaking in their Seder meal in the large dining room at the hotel, looking forward to a night spent celebrating together with their family members, young and old.

Abdel-Basset Odeh had other plans. The twenty-five-year-old Palestinian terrorist affiliated with Hamas disguised himself as a woman and walked into the hotel carrying a powerful bomb inside a suitcase. Managing to avoid detection by the security guard, he detonated the explosive, turning the traditional holiday feast into a scene of carnage. In an instant, twenty-eight people were killed by the blast and over 140 were injured, many seriously. Two more people subsequently died of their injuries. It was later discovered that Hamas had planned to use both cyanide and chlorine nerve agents during this attack, as well, but fortunately for some unknown reason they did not make it to the bomber. The majority of those murdered were over the age of seventy; they included survivors of the Holocaust, family patriarchs and matriarchs, and young children. The oldest victim was ninety years old.

Even for a nation that had become accustomed to terror attacks, the ensuing images were stomach churning. The symbolism of the massacre taking place at Passover was a gut-punch to Jews worldwide. Within days, the IDF responded to the bloodshed with Operation Defensive Shield – the largest military operation in the West Bank since the Six-Day War in 1967. The goal was to root out terror cells and put an end to the heinous attacks. The operation lasted over a month, beginning with placing Palestinian Authority leader Yasser Arafat under siege while Israeli forces confiscated enormous quantities of weapons and arrested terrorist leaders.

The Public Face of Israel

Against this backdrop, Colonel Miri Eisin made a move that few have, leaving the anonymity of her role in military intelligence to become the new public face of Israel to the world. TV news broadcasts have rarely been willing to give Israel the benefit of the doubt, and Eisin, new to the job, found herself on the receiving end of many a hostile interview. She represented Israel's position with poise and a no-nonsense manner, yet was able to show concern and empathy toward unintended Palestinian casualties during the campaign. Eisin went on to consistently represent Israel's point of view to CNN, the BBC, the Associated Press, and multiple other networks.

When her husband, a lieutenant colonel at the time, was accepted to the Wexner program at Harvard University, Miri left together with their three children under the age of five to live in Boston for the duration of the school year. While there, she addressed a wide variety of audiences on issues relating to Israel, security, and public diplomacy. By the time Eisin returned to Israel, events had rocked Israeli politics. In January 2006, Prime Minister Ariel Sharon, who led the evacuation of Israeli communities from Gaza a year earlier, suffered a sudden, debilitating stroke. His successor was the former mayor of Jerusalem, Ehud Olmert.

The mettle of the new prime minister was tested early. On June 25, 2006, a group of terrorists from Gaza, comprising members of the Izz ad-Din al-Qassam Brigades, Popular Resistance Committees, and Army of Islam, crossed into Israel via an underground tunnel and attacked an IDF post. They killed two Israeli soldiers, wounded another two, and kidnapped a young IDF corporal by the name of Gilad Schalit. Within weeks, tensions rose to the north of Israel, as well. Following the unilateral withdrawal of forces from Southern Lebanon in 2000, Israel's northern border had remained relatively quiet for years, but inside Lebanon, the Hezbollah terrorist organization was growing stronger by the day. Steadily, they became part of Lebanon's political scene, yet all the while, with significant funding from both Syria and Iran, they invested heavily in rockets pointed toward Israel and a complex infrastructure of bunkers, anti-tank and anti-ship missiles. On July 12, 2006, Hezbollah carried out a cross-border attack, ambushing two IDF patrol vehicles inside the Israeli border. They killed two soldiers and injured two more, while taking two others – Ehud Goldwasser and Eldad Regev – hostage.

The IDF retaliated with a large campaign, which carried through the summer of 2006, later becoming known as the Second Lebanon War. In the new internet era, where social media was beginning to take hold and cable news was 24/7, Prime Minister Olmert needed urgent help with Israel's public relations and the image Israel presented to the world. He requested that Eisin become his personal international media advisor. She was initially reluctant, but with an abiding sense of duty, she agreed to do this on an interim basis. After several months, she was asked by the prime minister to continue. The first female in this position, Eisin was a reassuring TV presence, calm, clear, and eloquent, strong, yet sympathetic. Reflecting on her performance during the conflict, Eisin stated, "I don't expect to win the media war, but I don't intend to lose. We have managed to hold our own with our messages."

Most official spokespeople have been men, many of whom stood before television cameras in uniform. Eisin gave the government line but also showed heart for casualties on the "other side," for instance, Lebanese who found themselves in the firing line due to Hezbollah fighters deliberately embedding themselves in communities in order to utilize them as human shields. She was also unflappable. Despite constantly being tested by TV news anchors who oftentimes would rage at Israel via its spokesperson, Miri maintained her cool. Frequently the framing of the story being told abroad was that Israel – rather than

Hezbollah or Hamas – was the aggressor. This made Eisin even more determined to portray her country on visual media in empathetic terms and not as overly bellicose or hardline. The result often had audiences questioning the tone of the questioner rather than that of the person answering the questions.

The aftermath of the Second Lebanon War saw international criticism of Israel as well as a flurry of diplomatic activity aimed at bringing the conflict to a halt. Eisin continued by the prime minister's side serving as the voice of Olmert's administration to the world media as he headed to Maryland for the 2007 Annapolis Peace Conference with the Palestinians, hosted by President George W. Bush. Since becoming Israel's spokesperson in war and in peace negotiations, Eisin has extensively lectured on issues relating to her previous work in the IDF and on the skill involved in crafting and framing Israel's message. Given her unique background, she is perfectly placed to reflect on issues related to Israelis' internal sense of resilience in the face of a never-ending and multifaceted conflict.

Shaped by Service

While Miri Eisin's personal resilience is huge, her perspective on the national character of Israel – and resilience as a characteristic of the national psyche – is unique and powerful.

One of the facts of life for those living in Israel is that military service is compulsory. A narrow sliver of land in a neighborhood of rogue regimes and terror groups and always under threat, Israel requires most of its eighteen-year old citizens, both male and female, to enlist. Eisin contends that this service will likely be the most significant thing that people do in their lives and speaks to a sense of service to a greater cause, of which Israelis are overwhelmingly proud. While for the majority, this is a hugely positive experience, for some it can take a toll, whether via physical or emotional injury.

Speaking as both an IDF colonel and as a mother, Eisin talks of the unwritten contract between the state and its parents. Parents understand that this service may require exposing their children to unsafe environments, but are reassured that the country promises to do everything it can to bring their offspring back home safely. You can see it on the faces of parents on the child's conscription day: a mixture of pride and concern. That demonstrates the fraught and complex nature of this unwritten contract, to which both sides are, for the most part, willing partners. Parents are expected to do everything they can to support and facilitate their children going to the army. Eisin puts it this way: "As a mother, I want my kid to be safe. As a citizen, I want my country to be safe." It is an intensely sensitive topic, but Israelis take it as a given – part of the socialization of Israeli society. In a very real sense, it is not just the eighteen-year-old "kids" who are enlisting; the parents of those "kids" are being drafted too. In recent decades, parents have become more involved, and the military has become more understanding that they need to give responses to parental concerns.

As a colonel, Miri Eisin's sense is that the IDF is a place that gives young adults the chance to do things that are amazing at that period of life. It provides them with the kind of responsibility or authority that few other countries offer people of that age. It is, she says, part of the reason that Israel has been termed a "start-up nation." Conscription age, somewhere between eighteen and twenty, comes at a time when brains are developing and capabilities are being honed, but in most places, this is also the age when formal education ends, even while brain development continues. So, at a stage when most countries send young people to college or out into the workforce, Israel is putting them into a very stressful environment but giving them authority and responsibility as well as a framework and a purpose. It was that sense of service that attracted Eisin to remain inside a structure that she feels gives people a variety of ways to serve and allows people within it to be innovative and to create change.

Eisin also considers it important that Israelis are exposed to responsibility and authority at a relatively young age. She contends that the phrase "young adults" does not really exist in Israel, because at the age of consent, Israelis are thrust into a strict hierarchy for a number of years. When they are released from the army, they are already several years older than those who are just starting out in most other countries.

On the flip side, while their peers elsewhere are deciding for themselves what to do and making active choices about their future, Israelis are being told what to do. They are assigned a position, and although they can express a preference, it is not always accommodated. They have someone, usually only a year or two older than them, telling them what to do day in, day out. The military has its own set of priorities, and it is the military that decides how and where to utilize the skill set of each conscript, whether the individual is happy about that choice or not. This combination of being given real responsibility in an environment that puts a value on innovation and flexibility means that the students walking onto university campuses following their IDF service are older and of a different caliber compared to first-year students around the world. The army experience teaches the importance of both flexibility and of meaning, two key components for building resilience.

The Survivor Mentality

Our discussion with Eisin takes place just prior to Holocaust Memorial Day, and in her mind, the Holocaust looms large in the collective memory of the nation. Internationally, Holocaust Memorial Day is observed on January 27 – the anniversary of the liberation of Auschwitz – but in Israel, Yom Hashoah is on the date of the Warsaw Ghetto Uprising to celebrate defiance in the face of tyranny while commemorating the victims of tyranny's slaughter. The Israeli psyche is heavily influenced by a feeling of post-traumatic stress. Not only have Israelis experienced gargantuan traumas in their recent history, but there is a constant feeling that their backs are against the wall, prompting them to say, "We will survive because history has taught us that we *must* survive." Eisin notes an interesting contrast. She remarks that Israelis give a large amount of freedom to their children, as if to counter the fact that the region is a dangerous one. Israel is a child-friendly society and there is a low rate of street crime, allowing Israeli children to freely ride the bus and go out independently day and night. Their resilience and strength is built by having a greater level of personal freedom at a relatively young age.

Israelis also feel they belong to a community – whether on a national scale or locally via their city, kibbutz, village, school, or synagogue. Beyond work and family, that sense of community gives citizens cohesiveness, resilience, and a sense of being "in it together." As a result, they also feel the pain of loss of each and every soldier, and each and every terror victim, whether they knew them personally or not. The nation grieves together too. Citing the 2014 Hamas kidnapping of three Israeli teens that gripped the national psyche of Israelis for weeks, Eisin points to the way that kidnapping affected the collective. These were everyone's kids. When someone in the community gets hurt, everyone hurts.

Israelis are also notably thick-skinned; their tough exterior has become something of a national characteristic. Eisin cites the fact that modern-day Israel is a *kibbutz galuyot* of identities – using the biblical term for "the ingathering of the exiles." For millennia, this was the prayer of Jews around the globe, dispersed in an ongoing exile from Israel, longing to reunite once more with the smaller number of Jews who never left the Holy Land and with the land itself. An early piece of legislation passed by Israel's parliament following the reestablishment of the modern Jewish state was the Law of Return, giving Jews worldwide the automatic right to obtain Israeli citizenship. Today, Israel's Jewish population is a polyglot of languages, cultures, and birthplaces from Russia to Ethiopia, from Iraq to Australia, and everything in between.

Among the many who immigrated to modern Israel, a large number were from nondemocratic countries where they faced great adversity. This is something that plays into the Israeli national character but also makes it all the more interesting that there was never any doubt in 1948 that Israel would be a liberal democracy. That Israel has been able to absorb and bring together such a tapestry of peoples is a modern-day miracle. While challenges abound, that unity – which is prevalent around so many issues of national identity and security – builds into an essential resilience firewall.

Returning to her personal resilience, Miri is no longer part of the rough-and-tumble that went along with representing official Israel, but she reflects on her time in front of the cameras. There are particular tensions between the type of job she was in – both in the military and as a government representative – that are often harder for a working mother than for her male counterparts. The job took its toll on family life. Eisin admits that she often considered resigning, but she could not say no to the prime minister and to her country.

While representing her country to ABC, Fox, MSNBC, and others during the Second Lebanon War, Eisin was mother to three children under the age of seven. She recalls returning home from a particularly grueling day at the office, and, as frequently happened, work spilled over into home life, and she was speaking on the phone to the prime minister in the evening. Yael, Eisin's then six-year-old daughter, wanted her mother's attention, but Miri gestured her away so she could finish the conversation with the Israeli premier. Aware that she could not make a noise due to the importance of the person on the other end of the phone line, but unable to suppress her need for attention, Yael silently sobbed. Seeing that made it clear to Eisin that it was time to leave her job and move on.

Now in civilian life for over a decade, Israel's spokesperson has cultivated her own voice. In her current, "unofficial" capacity, she remains connected to the security establishment and is briefed regularly on public diplomacy. Yet with the freedom and balance that being a freelancer gives her, she feels that she is a better representative of the country she loves than when she was doing so as an official. She also has a clear perspective on Israel's national character: "When I think about resilience," she says, "I think that what Israelis can teach the world is that life goes on, despite the terrible things that happen. That's a wonderful message – it's a survivor's message, not a victim's message. The day after a terror attack is a regular day when you send your kids back to school. We take a deep breath and carry on. That's resilience."

Afterword

*"Everything can be taken from a man, but one thing: the last of the
human's human freedoms – to choose one's attitude in any given set of
circumstances, to choose one's own way."*
Viktor E. Frankl, *Man's Search for Meaning*

Given the very real danger of regional instability coupled with ongoing
and constant threats of destruction by its neighbors, by any rational
analysis, Israel should not exist at all, let alone be a thriving powerhouse
of a country. Yet as we rediscovered via the personalities we met on this
journey, Israel defies reason, logic, and historical precedent, and these
amazing Israelis embody the wonder that their country represents.

Even in peacetime – or to give it the Hebrew vernacular, *shigrah*
(routine) – Israelis are under great stress. The threat to Israel's existence
is ever present and often manifests itself without warning. One does
not need to dwell on history to see this in action: terror attacks are
unfortunately far too commonplace in modern-day Israel. Yet life goes
on, and people are not just living day to day but making long-term
plans as well.

Is resilience a product of nature or nurture? Is an Israeli child born more resilient than, say, a Mexican, an American, or anyone else? That is a good question that we are not prepared to weigh in on. If you have come this far in the book, you will have learned that Israelis come in every shape, size, and background, as evidenced by the range of people we interviewed. But environment does matter. Israel has a paucity of oil and natural gas, a deficit of neighboring allies, and innumerable national challenges to face, but Israelis do seem to have an innate resilience that is actively honed by the society they grow up in. The key is in the keys.

You will have noticed a thread that flows through the personal stories of each and every one of the people we profile in this book. They all embody and exemplify one of the ISResilience keys that we outlined at the beginning of this journey:

Empathy. It is the interpersonal skills, the inner strength, and the community of support that allowed Israel Meir Lau to survive the Nazis, arriving on the shores of Israel as a child orphan refugee and becoming the spiritual leader of Israel. It is the emotional heart of Sherri Mandell and her ability to share her feelings both in written and spoken word that transforms unbearable grief into a promise to ease the pain of others. It is Yoseph Haddad's sympathy for the sensitivities of others while overcoming personal death threats as he expresses his voice as an Arab citizen of the Jewish State of Israel. It is Miri Eisin's compassionate voice as she overcame the odds to break through barriers, becoming a colonel in the Israel Defense Forces and representing her nation to the world.

Flexibility. It is the motivation of Noam Gershony to change his direction mid-course, dedicating himself to a new goal after falling from the sky, beating death, and finally emerging an Olympic hero. It is the guts that Nadav Ben Yehuda demonstrates when forgoing reaching the peak of Mount Everest in order to save a life. It is overcoming a profound disability, the result of a freak accident with the potential to ruin your life, and using that as a jumping-off point to pioneer technology helping paraplegics walk again, as did Dr. Amit Goffer. It is Tal Brody giving up the opportunity to play in the NBA, in order to take a tiny country to basketball glory and in doing so, putting it on the sports map of the world to stay.

Meaning-making. It is the persistence of Brigadier-General Avigdor Kahalani moving forward after sustaining burns over 90 percent of his body, leading his troops to victory in battle and going on to live a life of service. It is the single-mindedness of Gadi Yarkoni to recover from having limbs blown off and win high office in order to better the life of his community. It is the grit and determination of Gadeer Kamal Mreeh to refuse to have others in her community define what a woman could achieve. It is the perseverance of the Zinati family, holding on to their traditions and identity at all cost, embodied in the last Jew in her town, Margalit. It is the relentless focus on the goal of reaching Jerusalem that led Shula Mola and Mequnante Rahamim to walk barefoot from Ethiopia, through the desert to the Promised Land. It is the fortitude and willpower of Natan Sharansky to survive years of solitude in the Soviet Gulag and emerge a human rights icon because he stood his ground for what is right.

These three keys: empathy, flexibility, and meaning are not exclusive. All of our interviewees express all of these keys to a greater or lesser degree. Each one of them exhibited the flexible and adaptive approach to life that is so integral to a resilient outlook. Flexibility means not only the ability to change direction mid-course. It also refers to the ability to touch the trauma, experience the pain and sadness, talk about the loss, yet be able in the next moment to experience joy, happiness, and excitement. This particular skill to move back and forth among a myriad of often conflicting and strong emotions is characteristic of each one of our interviewees and may be the single most important component of resilience.

Often there are additional factors that play into the resilient approach to life exhibited by the people we interviewed. Yet focusing on these three keys can provide a window for us into understanding the nature of resilience and help us to reflect on how these keys play out in our own lives.

Our interviewees are inspiring people who shed light on each one of the keys to resilience by the exemplary way they have lived their lives. Were they born that way? Were they raised that way? The answer to both those questions is most probably yes. But one thing is for certain. They all adopted a resilient mindset, which gave them the strength they needed to move forward and succeed. This resilient mindset is characteristic of Israeli society at large. Israelis are inculcated with a can-do attitude, expecting success, with no challenge too great to overcome. Israel's greatest natural resource is its people, as we have shown over the course of this book.

So what can you take from this book? Resilience can be a part of your life as well. Each one of us faces setbacks and adversity. We all have the ability to turn lemons into lemonade. The question is, how? The next time you are challenged, when an obstacle is placed in your path, when you are feeling lost or overcome by the circumstances you are confronting, recall the three keys to staying strong and moving ahead – empathy, flexibility, and meaning-making – and remember the people that embody ISResilience.

About the Authors

Michael Dickson

Michael Dickson is Executive Director of StandWithUs-Israel, an international educational nonprofit dedicated to supporting Israel and fighting antisemitism around the world. Michael regularly addresses audiences and broadcasts on issues pertaining to Israel and public diplomacy. He is an accomplished writer, with many published articles and TV appearances. Michael has addressed audiences in global forums, including at the UN, in the Knesset, and in Europe, America, Asia, and Africa. Michael is a Senior Fellow at the Center for International Communication of Bar-Ilan University, is an honorary member of Alpha Epsilon Pi, and in 2015 was appointed to the Spectrum Forum of leading Executive Directors in Israel under the age of forty. In 2016, he was listed as the fourteenth most influential Jew on Twitter and also named in the "30 Israelis Making a Difference" at a special event at the President's Residence. Michael was listed in the top thirty of the *Jewish News*-Jewish Agency Aliyah 100 list of British immigrants to Israel as one of the "flag bearers who shape the State of Israel and made a significant contribution." In 2019, he was awarded the Bonei Zion ("Builder of Zion") Prize, recognizing the achievements of outstanding Anglo immigrants and their contribution to the State of Israel, at a ceremony in the Tower of David, Jerusalem. In 2020, he was listed on the Global Jewish 100, "a celebration of people across the world who are moving Jewish culture forward, selected according to their accomplishments, influence, and impact." He lives in Israel with his wife and five children.

Dr. Naomi L. Baum

Naomi L. Baum, PhD, is a psychologist who consults both in Israel and
internationally in the field of trauma
and resilience. She received her MA
and PhD from Bryn Mawr College
and her BA from Bar-Ilan University.
Naomi created the Building Resilience
Intervention (BRI), an evidence-based
resilience model that has been applied
widely in Israel and abroad. She was
Director of the Resilience Unit at

Metiv – The Israel Psychotrauma Center for twelve years and directed
the International Course in Trauma and Resilience in cooperation with
the Rothberg School of the Hebrew University. She trained with the
Center for Mind-Body Medicine (CMBM) from 2004 to 2006 and is
a member of their international faculty. In 2015 Naomi developed a
multi-year post-trauma intervention in collaboration with Tevel b'Tze-
dek and helped to train staff and implement it in Nepal. She has worked
with CMBM in Sonoma County, California, in the wake of the forest
fires that swept that area. She is the author of professional articles on
resilience building and trauma as well as several books, including *My
Year of Kaddish: Mourning, Memory and Meaning*, published in April
2020; *Life Unexpected: A Trauma Psychologist Journeys through Breast
Cancer*; and *Free Yourself from Fear: The Seven Day Plan for Overcoming
Fear of (Recurrent) Cancer*. She is also a student and instructor of Qi
Gong, a meditative form of movement based on the principles of
Chinese medicine. She has been married to the same man for forty-five
years and is mother of seven and grandmother of twenty.

Acknowledgments

Writing this book has been a labor of love and a small testimony to the significance that Israel, our homeland, has in the lives of my family. We are blessed to live in this time and to be able to live in this place.

My love and thanks to my childhood sweetheart, my best friend, and my wife (all one and the same person), Deborah, and to our beautiful children Dalia, Yoav, Yael, Dan, and Ella.

I am overwhelmed by the number of people who have played such a significant role in my life and who have been kind enough to encourage the genesis of this book. So lucky am I that my fear is that I will forget to mention people. With that disclaimer, I will do my best.

To my parents, Ruth and Stuart Dickson, thank you for imbuing me with a sense of love for my heritage, for my people, for society in general, and for our homeland. To my parents-in-law, Diane and Paul Kutner, I cherish your advice and encouragement. I must also thank my ever-kvelling brother and sister, Jonathan and Rachel, for their support. May the memory of my grandparents Renee and Woolf Isenberg and Jenny and David Dickson be a blessing; I remember them always.

I am dedicating my writing to Leah Silverman, my sister-in-law, who has been the model of resilience as she continues to overcome the setback of injury.

My wholehearted thanks to my coauthor Dr. Naomi Baum for her wisdom and professional insight. One of the first people I interviewed for this book (a number of years ago!) was Naomi, due to her extensive experience in this field, and I am grateful to her for agreeing to join me on this journey of discovery of a people and a country that we both love. She has achieved so much in the field of resilience and has been a wonderful writing partner.

I am lucky that my job is also my passion: I am blessed to have been part of the StandWithUs leadership team for fourteen years. My admiration and respect go to StandWithUs CEO Roz Rothstein for her leadership as well as her faith in me, which allowed me to be in a position to shine a light on the real Israel. I extend my appreciation to Roz's fellow StandWithUs cofounders Jerry Rothstein and Esther Renzer for your vision, commitment, and consistent support.

Thanks to my stellar team in Jerusalem as well as colleagues internationally, both present and past. I am blessed to work with such an array of talent. Particular thanks to my right-hand woman Shany Lousky-Levy, to my talented Associate Director Tamir Oren, and to Ilana Sherrington-Hoffman and Charlotte Korchak (with whom I always love to engage on books we read and ideas we have), as well as to the talented Paul Gorbulski, Noam Koren, Noa Raman, and Avigail Messika for their help and encouragement. Thank you to the exceptional Moran Reijzer for the cover art and for all his wonderful graphic design. Thank you to the students, activists, and global staff of StandWithUs who touch lives every day in an enduring fight against antisemitism with their dedication to bring people worldwide closer to Israel.

There are leaders in the Jewish world whom I have come to appreciate so much; they include the wonderful Debbie and Naty Saidoff; Rita and Steve Emerson; Adam and Gila Milstein; the late Newton Becker, *z"l*; Dahlia and Art Bilger; Nancy and Harry Bloomfield; Loretta and Perry Cash; Haim and Helen Dayan; Barbara Diamond; Jonty Feldman; Sharon and Larry Finegold; Motti Gur; Janice and Steve Hefter; Larry Hochberg; Alan Howard; Marty and Susan Jannol; Andrew Kligerman; Bruce Lederman; Dina and Fred Leeds; Barak Lurie; Alon and Rosana Miller; Tamara Morgenstern; Janet and

David Polak; Larry Post; Barak Raviv; Sheri Ross; Susy Rubenstein; Janet Sasson; Faith Schames; Peggy Shapiro; Rhona Wacht; Sonya and Howard Waldow; Adrienne and Michael Wienir; Barry Wolfe; Joy Wolfe MBE; Sylvan Adams and Evelyn and Dr. Shmuel Katz (Shmuel, you are a mentor whom I so admire).

Many extraordinary and inspiring people have advised me during this project, and others have been kind enough to give feedback on this work: special thanks to Senator Joe Lieberman, Rabbi Lord Jonathan Sacks, Professor Gil Troy, Ambassador Gilad Erdan, Ambassador Ron Prosor, Minister Orit Farkash Hacohen, Yossi Klein Halevi, Isaac Herzog, Daniel Gordis, David Horovitz, Einat Wilf, Yael Eckstein, Yaakov Katz, William Daroff, Aviva Klompas, Arsen Ostrovsky, and Joe Hyams. Thanks also to Sheryl Sandberg, the coauthor of *Option B: Facing Adversity, Building Resilience, and Finding Joy*, for her leadership on this issue and for her encouragement.

It was important for us to publish with an Israeli publisher. Thank you to Ilan Greenfield, CEO of Gefen Publishing House, for believing in this book and including it in a family of incredible literature. Our thanks go to you and to the entire team in Jerusalem and New York, especially to Project Manager Daphne Abrahams and to Senior Editor Kezia Raffel Pride for wise and incisive input.

To the wonderful people who agreed to be interviewed for this book and in doing so share their life lessons for us all to learn from, thank you. There are so many more stories of ISResilience to be inspired by; I pledge to continue telling them.

Michael Dickson
Jerusalem, August 2020

It is always a great pleasure to reach the stage of acknowledgements. First, great thanks to my coauthor Michael Dickson for his vision, inspiration, and invitation to work with him on this book. It was an honor and a privilege to meet so many outstanding individuals and to get a chance to have some wonderful conversations with them. Working with Michael has led me to appreciate his sincerity and drive, his ability to connect with people, and above all, what a mensch he is. What a pleasure it has been. In addition, his support staff was more than helpful in arranging for the many interviews that form the backbone of this book. Thank you all.

Thanks to my life partner, Mike, for always being ready to listen, support, and be an all-around best friend, and to my kids, all seven of them, who are my most loving critics. Thanks to the folks at Gefen for the encouragement and hard work to make this the final product it is.

And finally, I second Michael's thanks to our interviewees, the wonderful people who not only made time for us in their busy lives, but opened their homes, their hearts, and their souls to our probing and sometimes difficult questions. They taught us so much, and I am humbled and grateful to be able to share some of what we experienced with you, the reader.

Naomi Baum
Jerusalem, August 2020

"In ReJesus, Alan and Michael successfully reinstate Jesus at the center of the spiritual life and mission of God's people. In an era overly focused on how to 'do church,' their message is clear; we must take a closer look at the life of Jesus. If you want to jump back into authentic, New Testament discipleship, then take their challenge to recalibrate the mission and work of the church around the story of Jesus. As only true practitioners can, they provide an abundance of practical insights and inspiration."

—Matt Smay, Missio Director of the Missional Church
Apprenticeship Practicum, co-author, *The Tangible Kingdom*

"Frost and Hirsch excavate the ruins of Western Christianity, digging through the accumulation of 2,000 years of dust in order to return the church to the sure foundation of Jesus Christ. This book is a challenging and helpful addition to the task of re-centering, re-founding, or, in their words, 're-Jesusing' Christianity. The Jesus-shaped church will look quite different from many of the modern variety, and Frost and Hirsch skillfully articulate both the need and the means to align the way of Jesus with the religion that bears his name."

—Mike Erre, Teaching Pastor at Rock Harbor Church in
Costa Mesa, California, author, *The Jesus of Suburbia*

"THIS is THE conversation to be had! While everyone is obsessed with reinventing the church—this puts not just the conversation, but the focus squarely back on where it belongs: Jesus! It's not the forms, the structures, the styles, the venues—it's the person of Jesus. I devoured every page of this book; I was completely engrossed in it. All true missional living starts and finishes with Jesus. When Jesus is at the core, not just of telling others about him but of creating a new life within us, we will be transformed and the church will be redefined. It will come not from ideas from without but from a person from within—Jesus! When Jesus is at the core, our faith and the church will always be alive to anyone, any time, any culture, and any place in the world. What Alan and Mike have done is write a book that answers the 'so what' of Jesus to his followers. The book is profound."

—Bob Roberts Jr., Senior Pastor of NorthWood Church
in Keller, Texas, author, *The Multiplying Church*

" 'The times, they are a-changing,' observed and sung by Dylan decades ago, continues to be the reality facing the church at the beginning of the 21st century. In response to our present challenges, Frost and Hirsch offer a fresh and provocative reading of the person of Jesus as the key for Christians to draw upon in living as contemporary disciples. They dig deep into the Jesus narrative for clues in understanding a wild Messiah—a ReJesus—and they discover key resources that are used to reclaim a radical call to discipleship. The reader will find their proposal to be openly invitational but should be prepared to be quite challenged."

—Craig Van Gelder, Professor of Congregational Mission,
Luther Seminary, author, *The Ministry of the Missional Church*

"Is the religion of Christianity the religion of Jesus? Is Jesus to be a model for our lives, or is he just a God-shaped security deposit? Frost and Hirsch recover God's call to become more like His Son and dare to place an earthy, narrative Christology at the center of all things missional."

—Sally Morgenthaler, author, *Worship Evangelism*, contributor, *An Emergent Manifesto of Hope*

"As Christendom dies a slow death, people scour the landscape of literature to find answers for how to redo church, re-engage faith, or reposition so that we can maintain our present status quo of reputation, resources, and rest. In *ReJesus*, Hirsch and Frost call us past these pathetic pursuits to a new world, or old world, in which leaders follow Jesus and let Jesus reform the church. Read, only if you're willing to rethink everything."

—Hugh Halter, Missio Director, Pastor of Adullam in Denver, Colorado, co-author of *The Tangible Kingdom*

"The themes of mission and personal and corporate renewal can be approached from a variety of perspectives. Many books on mission take a pragmatic approach, focusing on strategies; while those addressing renewal tend towards a nostalgic spiritualizing, drawing inspiration from previous revivalism the church. *ReJesus: A Wild Messiah for a Missional Church* represents a different approach. It draws together three key themes that are all too often compartmentalized: Christology, Missiology, and Ecclesiology. So many churches in the West are suffering from amnesia with regard to the Biblical narrative, or at best are guilty of a selective reading, resulting in a misrepresentation of Jesus to conform to our cultural assumptions and boundaries. Frost and Hirsch present us with a faithful portrayal of Jesus as fully human, as God intended us to be, by showing us what the God who dared to make us in his own image is really like. The authors present an untamed Jesus who makes scary, radical demands, while at the same time giving of himself to empower his followers with the courage and resources necessary to follow his leading. *ReJesus* reveals abundant evidence of extensive research, and dropped into the text are brief descriptions of individuals who embodied the challenges Frost and Hirsch present to the reader. In confronting such a gospel every seeker will find more than they bargained for! But the gospel was never a bargain, it is always a gracious gift—far too great and glorious for us to ever fully comprehend or exhaust its potential. In reading this book be prepared for a wild ride!"

—Eddie Gibbs, Senior Professor at Fuller Theological Seminary, author, *LeadershipNext*

"Frost and Hirsch have done it again. Reading *ReJesus* provoked, frustrated, and ultimately convicted me of my need to live more deeply in the way of Jesus. If you are looking for another book on simply bolstering church *as-we-know-it*, this is not for you. If you and your church want to be challenged to walk in the Way of Jesus, this book delivers."

—Ed Stetzer, blogger (www.edstetzer.com), author, *Planting Missional Churches*

"Alan Hirsch and Michael Frost continue to push the church into the future with their latest project, ReJesus. Herein they focus on what every Christian church must focus on—Jesus Christ—and they develop a Christ-centered strategy for missional ecclesiology. This is a timely and relevant book and deserves a wide readership."

—Tony Jones, national coordinator of Emergent Village, doctoral fellow in practical theology at Princeton Theological Seminary, author, *The New Christians: Dispatches from the Emergent Frontier*

"ReJesus calls to mind Jaroslav Pelikan's *Jesus Through the Centuries* and the stubborn fact we can never get outside our own culture(s) to a pure Jesus. That way is not open to those who confess the Incarnate One. In every age Christians are compelled to wrestle with the meaning of Jesus again. Colin Greene's *Christology in Cultural Perspective* reminds us of how we must continually wrestle with how to be faithful to Jesus in our day. Neibuhr's *Christ and Culture* shows how we continually shape Jesus out of our cultural imaginations. Yet, in all its eradicable shortcomings, the church is still the location where we're shaped by the revelation of God in Jesus Christ. We always wrestle with how to re-Jesus because we have no choice. May we do it with humility and a deep love for these clay vessels of history we call the church, for there is no other place in which Jesus is made present. This book is a contribution to that wrestling; like all such wrestling it is itself enmeshed in culture. I trust it encourages others to wrestle that we might all be more faithful followers of Jesus."

—Al Roxburgh, Vice President, Allelon Canada, co-author, *The Missional Leader*

"It is with such ease that the church veers off course. ReJesus draws us back to Jesus in all of his radical, passionate, and transformative beauty. Frost and Hirsch demonstrate by word and example that to be the church demands a fearless, intimate, and constant encounter with Christ. As individuals and as a community, we have no option but to heed their wisdom."

—Daniel M. Harrell, Associate Minister at Park Street Church in Boston, author, *Nature's Witness: How Evolution Can Inspire Faith*

"At this moment in history we are in the middle of an ecclesial and theological reformation that is at least as radical as, and likely more significant than, the Protestant Reformation of the 16th and 17th centuries. In this bold, compelling, and prophetic masterpiece, Hirsch and Frost articulate the beautiful vision of the Jesus-centered Kingdom that is driving this new Reformation. Hirsch and Frost brilliantly weave together insightful biblical exegesis, critical historical reflection, transforming spiritual discipleship, probing cultural analysis, and even a good bit of humor in ways that help readers get free from the deadening yoke of the Christian religion and rediscover the wild, untamed, life-giving Jesus of the Gospels. I hope everyone who professes faith in Christ will dare to read this book. They will not put it down unchanged."

—Greg Boyd, Senior Pastor of Woodland Hills Church in St. Paul, Minnesota, co-author, *The Jesus Legend*

"Calls for a fresh, radical following of Jesus Christ are not new. Reformers from Francis of Assisi to Mother Teresa have sounded the call; already in the New Testament the Apostle John says true Christians must 'walk as [Jesus] walked,' and Peter insists we must follow in Jesus' steps. What is new about the message of ReJesus is the creative interweaving of the themes of Jesus' example, God's mission, and the kingdom mission of the church—the 'reintegration,' as the authors put it, 'of the theological concepts of missio Dei, participatio Christi, and imago Dei.'

"The book is filled with images—visual, imaginative, conceptual, biographical— that evoke Jesus Christ and Jesus-like discipleship. The authors' eclectic mining of secondary sources also helps free Jesus from well-rooted stereotypes. I view this book as an enlargement of the foundation of the authors' provocative and prophetic earlier works, rather than a sequel to or restatement of them. I think the authors are correct: 'Christianity minus Christ equals Religion'—not authentic discipleship."

—Howard A. Snyder, Professor of Wesley Studies,
Tyndale Seminary, Toronto, author, *Radical Renewal*

"How horrific it is to think that we could be so passionately missional, but subtly drift from being entirely Jesus-centric in the process. Anyone in the missional conversation must never, ever forget about this subtle drift. ReJesus challenges us all in very theological, hopeful, and practical ways to never let that happen."

—Dan Kimball, Pastor of Vintage Faith Church in Santa
Cruz, California, author, *They Like Jesus But Not The Church*

"This books reads you; you don't read it. Over and over you will find yourself wrestling with yourself and with God. In the end you have more than a decision to make; you have a quest to pursue. What you do about that will define your life."

—Reggie McNeal, Leadership Network,
author, *Missional Renaissance*

RE
JESUS

MICHAEL FROST
& ALAN HIRSCH

A WILD Messiah
for a Missional Church

STRAND PUBLISHING
Sydney

Published jointly, 2009, in the United States by Hendrickson Publishers, Inc., P.O. Box 3473, Peabody, Massachusetts 01961-3473, and in Australia and New Zealand by Strand Publishing, Suites 12–13, Fountain Plaza Business Centre, 148 The Entrance Road, Erina NSW 2250.

United States ISBN 978-1-59856-228-6
Australia ISBN 978-192-120-2919

Printed in the United States of America

Second Printing — February 2009

Hendrickson Publishers is strongly committed to environmentally responsible printing practices. The pages of this book were printed on 30% postconsumer waste recycled stock using only soy or vegetable content inks.

Library of Congress Cataloging-in-Publication Data

Frost, Michael, 1961–
    ReJesus : a wild Messiah for a missional church / Michael Frost and Alan Hirsch.
        p. cm.
    Includes bibliographical references and index.
    ISBN 978-1-59856-228-6 (alk. paper)
    1. Mission of the church. 2. Jesus Christ. 3. Christianity—21st century. 4. Postmodernism—Religious aspects—Christianity. I. Hirsch, Alan, 1959– II. Title.
    BV601.8.F76 2009
    270.8′3—dc22
                                2008034100

DEDICATIONS

Alan

To my various partners in the missional enterprise: Forge,
Church Resource Ministries (especially Sam Metcalf), *Missio*,
Shapevine, Church Planting Network (Exponential), and Christian
Associates. Also to Bob Roberts Jr. for his loving sponsorship,
and to my great friend and co conspirator, Michael Frost.

Michael

For Peter Horsley in gratitude for his partnership
in life, leadership, and the gospel.

Contents

Introduction: Read This Bit First

Jesus is the center of all, the object of all, whoever does not know him, knows nothing aright, either of the world or of himself.
—Blaise Pascal

> *The means to know God is Christ, whom no one may know unless they follow after him with their life.*
> —Hans Denck

On the morning of June 7, 1964, the recently consecrated wing of the Ku Klux Klan known as the White Knights gathered solemnly in the Boykin Methodist Church in the pine woods near Raleigh, Mississippi. Concerned about what they saw as a wave of blacks and communists hitting the streets of Mississippi, the Klan had marshaled their forces to plan a so-called counter-attack against the civil rights movement. Armed with rifles, pistols, and shot-guns and protected by men riding on horseback through the woods and by two Piper Cubs circling the property overhead, they bowed their heads as their Grand Chaplain ascended to the pulpit to read the following prayer:

> Oh God, our Heavenly Guide, as finite creatures of time and as dependent crea-
> tures of Thine, we acknowledge Thee as our sovereign Lord. Permit freedom
> and the joys thereof to forever reign throughout our land. May we as klansmen
> forever have the courage of our convictions that we may always stand for Thee
> and our great nation. May the sweet cup of brotherly fraternity ever be ours
> to enjoy and build within us that kindred spirit which will keep us unified and
> strong. Engender within us that wisdom kindred to honorable decisions and
> the Godly work. By the power of Thy infinite spirit and the energizing virtue
> therein, ever keep before us our oaths of secrecy and pledges of righteousness.
> Bless us now in this assembly that we may honor Thee in all things, we pray in
> the name of Christ, our blessed Savior. Amen.[1]

The congregation said their amens softly under their breaths. Later, Sam Bowers, the Imperial Wizard of the Ku Klux Klan of Mississippi, took to the pulpit and in overtly religious language declared what amounted to a holy war against the civil rights leadership, detailing a formal protocol for all Klan attacks on the "nigger-communist invasion of Mississippi."[2] Within the month, three civil rights workers were murdered execution-style in nearby Neshoba County.

The overtly Christian character of the Ku Klux Klan, its symbolism, and its language, will not be news to anyone—who can forget those burning crosses? But it's the specifically Christ-focused aspect of the Klan philosophy that continues to shock nearly half a century later. Praying in the name of Christ at the inauguration of what was effectively a racist death squad still jars, but there can be no denying that the KKK routinely called on Jesus to strengthen them in their quest. The devotion to Jesus of the Imperial Wizard, Sam Bowers, is well known. Ken Dean, the director of the Council of Human Relations in Mississippi in 1964, said of him, "The Imperial Wizard, in the most radical sense possible, is a believer in the sovereignty of God."[3] Indeed, more than that, Bowers believed that God's sovereignty is most supremely demonstrated in his raising of Jesus from the dead:

> There is one simple, and central, Empirical Fact, of manifested human history. That Empirical Fact, of course, is the Physical Resurrection of The Galilean . . . The genuineness of Faith is in the Omnipotent Power of God to perform the Miracle: The certainty of rational human knowledge is that the Resurrection did occur: As an Empirically manifested Fact.[4]

Charles Marsh, who in researching the civil rights movement in Mississippi began a correspondence with Bowers later in life, says of him: "Bowers as theologian is, in a most radical, perplexing, and bizarre sense, a believer in the Christ-centered shape of all reality."[5]

How distressing, then, to those of us who likewise seek to trust in the "Christ-centered shape of all reality," that we share such a faith with so reprehensible a set of characters as Sam Bowers and the KKK. How did followers of Jesus end up so far from the teaching and example of Jesus? How did Jesus followers like members of the Lutheran Church in Nazi Germany quote Jesus in one breath and incite racial vilification in the next? The same could be asked of the Crusaders or the Conquistadors or even the Rwandan death squads.

The KKK is, of course, an extreme example of a group adopting the image of Jesus in a way that seems foreign to us. But there are milder examples of this even within our own broad community of people who identify themselves as Christians. In 2005, while en route to a speaking tour of the United Kingdom, we decided to treat ourselves to a stopover in Rome. As one does when in the eternal city, we visited the Vatican and St. Peter's Basilica. It was every bit as beautiful as we had imagined. Everyone who sees St. Peter's agrees that it is a truly remarkable feat of human ingenuity, with perfectly designed shafts of natural light highlighting its artistic treasures, built on a scale designed to foster a feeling of spiritual awe. Like all tourists we wandered, mesmerized, our necks craned upwards to take in the sheer grandeur of the cathedral. Not looking where we were going, we accidentally bumped into each other, and there in the middle of the room that represented the heart of global Christianity for centuries, we reflected on what we were seeing and asked each other where Jesus was to be found in this place. Certainly, we agreed, the architecture of the basilica was stunning, and the sculpture, windows, and ceiling were beautiful. But both of us had the same nagging question bubbling around in our minds: Where is the poor, itinerant rabbi from Nazareth?

Similarly, on a recent speaking assignment in Moscow, Michael had the opportunity to wander through the Orthodox Cathedral of Christ the Savior. Constructed as recently as the 1990s, it is an astonishing feat of religious architecture. Situated on the banks of the Moskva River, a few blocks from the Kremlin, it replaced the original cathedral that had been destroyed by Stalin in 1931. It is constructed almost entirely of marble, and its gleaming golden domes or cupolas make it the tallest Orthodox church in the world. The white marble exterior is completely ringed by astonishing bronze relief statues of various saints and Christian heroes. Inside, the chapels are configured as an equal-sided cross measuring 85 meters wide, each replete with hundreds of gilt icons and frescoes. Wandering around the cavernous main chapel, which can hold up to ten thousand people, it is hard not to be amazed by the beauty of this house of worship. But if you look more closely, some disquieting features begin to emerge.

The original cathedral commemorated the so-called divine intercession that led to the Russian victory over Napoleon in 1812. In fact, Tchaikovsky's 1812 *Overture* debuted in the Cathedral of Christ the Savior in 1882. When Boris Yeltsin approved the rebuilding of the cathedral, it was designed to be as close a replica of the original as possible, including its deeply patriotic Russian themes. So, this great building manages to be both a religious space and a historical monument to the militaristic might of Russia. There are frescoes that deify historical figures and events. The two-story galleries surrounding the main church are devoted to the history of Russia and the war of 1812 specifically. In fact, the marble boards on the first floor commemorate the participants of that bloody war. The frescoes in the second-story gallery depict various historical events and personages that played a decisive role in the Orthodox church or in Russian history. Below the new church is a large hall for church assemblies, where the last Russian tsar and his family were glorified as saints in 2000. The face of Jesus therefore sits alongside an image of the incompetent Tsar Nicholas II, who oversaw the vicious Bloody Sunday massacre of unarmed, peaceful demonstrators in 1905.

As Michael left the cathedral and headed through the snow to the nearby Metro station he encountered an elderly woman kneeling on the frozen pavement, begging for loose change from disinterested passersby. While it was difficult to see the real Jesus in the cathedral frescoes, it wasn't hard to recall Jesus' words about what we do for the "least of these" being done as if for him. According to Jesus' own words, he should be identifiable in the ragged image of the suppliant pauper outside the cathedral far more than in the astonishing gilt iconography inside.

We open this book with these three vastly different stories—the 1964 massacre in Neshoba County, and our visits to the Vatican and the Russian Orthodox cathedral—to illustrate our concern with what has been promulgated in Jesus' name throughout history. In Mississippi, Rome, and Moscow, the name of Jesus has been invoked as central to movements that do not seem to be in accord with the Jesus we find in the pages of the Gospels. In the descriptions of the KKK's Bible-thumping reign of terror in Mississippi we are aghast that men could attempt to sanctify their actions with prayers to Jesus. In the Vatican, one of the archetypal buildings dedicated to the religion that was founded on Jesus Christ, we cannot locate the simple, hardy, revolutionary carpenter who is compellingly portrayed in the Gospels. At the Cathedral of Christ the Savior, the Jesus of the Gospels competes with tsars and generals for the affections of the devoted. All of these are unsettling insights that speak directly to the purpose of this book because they raise disturbing questions about the continuity between Jesus and the subsequent religion established in his name.

In saying this, we don't mean to equate the Catholic or Orthodox churches with the Ku Klux Klan. We simply mean to identify instances in which a group's depiction of the person of Jesus is incongruous to us. Indeed, the discontinuity between Jesus and the religion that bears his name that we found in Rome and Moscow is by no means limited to those churches or denominations. Both Catholic and Protestant groups, right up to our present time and including even the newer Christian church movements, have traded in the radical way of Jesus for the seemingly greater grandeur of such religious expressions.

These examples suggest questions that can be, indeed, should be, asked of all believers, churches, and denominations in any time and place:

- ⟿ What ongoing role does Jesus the Messiah play in shaping the ethos and self-understanding of the movement that originated in him?

- ⟿ How is the Christian religion, if we could legitimately call it that, informed and shaped by the Jesus that we meet in the Gospels?

- ⟿ How do we assess the continuity required between the life and example of Jesus and the subsequent religion called Christianity?

- ⟿ In how many ways do we domesticate the radical Revolutionary in order to sustain our religion and religiosity?

- ⟿ And perhaps most important of all, how can a rediscovery of Jesus renew our discipleship, the Christian community, and the ongoing mission of the church?

These are not insignificant questions because they take us to the core of what the church is all about. They take us to the defining center of the movement that takes its cue from Jesus. Rather than call this reformation, we will call this task refounding the church because it raises the issue of the church's true founder or foundation. And in our opinion, nothing is more important for the church in our day than the question of refounding Christianity. It has a distinct poignancy at the dawn of the twenty-first century as we collectively attempt to address Christianity's endemic and long-trended decline in the West. We seem a little lost, if truth be told, and no quick-fix church-growth solution can be found that can stop the hemorrhage. There is no doubt that we face a spiritual, theological, missional, and existential crisis in the West.

We must admit that both of us are somewhat obsessed with mission and what it means to be a missional people. But we both remain convinced that it is Christology that remains even more foundational and therefore the primary issue. We have elsewhere asserted that it is Christology (the exploration of the person, teachings, and impact of Jesus Christ) that determines missiology (our purpose and function in the world), which in turn determines our ecclesiology (the forms and functions of the church).[6] We have found

Follow Me—Becoming a Little Jesus

Following Jesus involves more than simply accepting him as your Savior via some prayer of commitment, no matter how sincere that prayer might be. In order to follow Jesus you must also emulate him, using his life as a pattern for your own. We call this emulation becoming a "little Jesus."

When we call ourselves little Jesuses, we aren't claiming to be able to walk on water or die for the sins of the world. No, being a little Jesus means that we adopt the values embodied in Jesus' life and teaching. Only Jesus was able to feed thousands with small amounts of bread and fish, but as little Jesuses we can embrace the values of hospitality and generosity. We might not be able to preach to the multitudes, but we can commit to speaking truth to lies. We can't die for anyone's sins, but we can embrace selflessness, sacrifice, and suffering.

We hope to see a conspiracy of little Jesuses unleashed all over the world, transforming their communities the way Jesus transformed his. To give concrete examples of what it means to emulate Jesus, throughout this book we will be giving thumbnail portraits of the little Jesuses who have inspired us.

no reason to revise our opinion on this, but over time we have only become even more convinced of the primacy of this formula. Both of us (together and apart) have written books about a distinctly missional form of discipleship and ecclesiology.[7] In writing this book, we feel we are now getting to the nub of the matter. We are going back to the founder and recalibrating the entire enterprise along christological lines.

The core task of this book therefore will be to explore the connection between the way of Jesus and the religion of Christianity. We will attempt to assess the Christian movement in the light of the biblical revelation of Jesus and to propose ways in which the church might reconfigure itself, indeed, recalibrate its mission, around the example and teaching of the radical rabbi from Nazareth. Where is the continuity? Why is what we experience as Christianity discontinuous with the way of Jesus? How consistent is our witness with his life and teachings? And can we move away from his prototypal spirituality without doing irreparable damage to the integrity of the faith? How far is too far?

Similarly, Jacques Ellul, the French theologian and philosopher, raises a disturbing historical problem for us to solve, a problem that he calls "the subversion of Christianity."

> The question that I want to sketch in this work is one that troubles me most deeply. As I now see it, it seems to be insoluble and assumes a serious character of historical oddness. It may be put very simply: How has it come about that the development of Christianity and the church has given birth to a society, a civilization, a culture that are completely opposite to what we read in the Bible, to what is indisputably the text of the law, the prophets, Jesus, and Paul? I say advisedly "completely opposite." There is not just contradiction on one point but on all points. On the one hand, Christianity has been accused of a whole list of faults, crimes, and deceptions that are nowhere to be found in the original text and inspiration. On the other hand, revelation has been progressively modeled and reinterpreted according to the practice of Christianity and the church. . . . This is not just deviation but radical and essential contradiction, or real subversion.[8]

And while this might seem to be an overstatement, Ellul proceeds to back up his conclusions with some unnerving scholarship. To our thinking, no one has yet answered his questions in a satisfactory way. Yet they cannot be avoided if we are to re-establish ourselves as an authentic church in the twenty-first century. Therefore, among other things, we have taken it upon ourselves to further develop his concerns and to continue to raise the questions first posed by Ellul.

But this quest is not limited to the realm of scholarship and philosophy. For example, at a more popular level, Erwin McManus takes up a similar theme in *The Barbarian Way*, in which he rails against the transformation of Christianity from a dangerous and revolutionary spiritual force into a "religious civilization." And rightly so. Is such a civilization, with its associated civil religion, what Jesus intended for the movement he started? Was it his intention to produce a domesticated religion with a fully fledged mediating priesthood, cumbersome rituals, and dense theologies, along with all the other trappings of religions with ambiguous connections to the surrounding society and culture? Is this what Jesus meant when he came pronouncing the arrival of the kingdom of God or the tearing of the veil in the temple at his death?[9]

So what's this book all about? It's all about Jesus, with direct implications for our discipleship, some radical challenges for our churches, and some suggested reformulations for our spirituality. In short, it's about re-Jesusing the church.[10]

It's All About Jesus

From the beginning, let us say that we believe that the only way we can truly authenticate ourselves as an expression of Christianity is to somehow measure ourselves against the life and teachings of Jesus Christ, our Lord. And it is to him that we must now return if we are going to faithfully negotiate the profound challenges of the twenty-first century. But surely this is what the church tries to do in every age and context? Surely all expressions of Christianity seek to call Jesus Lord and have a special place reserved for him in their life and theology. We would argue that while confessionally this might be true, the church throughout history struggles to concretely conform its life to the radical life and teachings of Jesus. We don't say this judgmentally, as we are well aware how difficult it is to live a life based fully on Jesus. It is no easy thing, because the way that Jesus sets for us to follow is inherently subversive against all attempts to control, and thus institutionalize, the revelation that he so powerfully ushers in. In other words, it's just plain hard to create a religion out of the way of Jesus.

So this book is dedicated to the recovery of the absolute centrality of the person of Jesus in defining who we are as well as what we do. As hard as it is to truly follow him, we assert that we must constantly return to Jesus to authenticate as well as legitimize ourselves as his people. We have no other Archimedean point by which to set our coordinates or any other touchstone by which we can assess the abiding validity of our faith and to see if we are authentically Christian. The love of Jesus, and our commitment to live in conformity to him, is in effect an inbuilt spiritual mechanism at the heart of the church's theology and experience that provides an instrument for our ongoing renewal. It seems to us that a constant, and continual, return to Jesus is absolutely essential for any movement that wishes to call itself by his name.

But it is hard to keep a clear vision of the true way of Jesus, particularly when you live within a culture that is far askew from that way. Missiologist David Bosch grew up as a proud racist Afrikaner near Kuruman in South Africa. Looking back with shame, he recounts how in 1948, the same year he entered teacher's college, the pro-apartheid National Party was swept into power. For Afrikaners like Bosch, "it was to us like a dream come true when the Nationalist Party won that victory. We had no reservations whatsoever."[11] It was during this very time that young David Bosch was sensing a strong call into the Christian ministry, seeing no conflict between his support for apartheid and his belief in the teaching of Jesus.

But Bosch is not the only well-meaning theologian to have been guilty of such dissonance. Early last century, the well-known historian Adolf von Harnack remarked, "There is something touching in the striving of every individual to approach this Jesus Christ from the perspective of his personality and individual interests and to find in Him none other than himself, or to receive at the very least a small part of Him."[12] By "something touching" Harnack means something sad or pathetic or pitiful. As a historian of dogma, he had seen too many agendas take Jesus captive, quoting him to justify all manner of beliefs and practices. He became convinced that the kernel of the gospel had been overlaid by the husks of metaphysical concepts alien to the teachings of Jesus. The primitive stories of Jesus had been corrupted by official church dogma, claimed Harnack.

Indeed, it's not hard to find examples to support his view. Those who want to find in Jesus merely a reformer of Judaism, or the last of the prophets, have managed to do so quite readily. Supporters of violence have characterized him as a revolutionary, while Tolstoy and his disciples saw him as a teacher of nonresistance. To New Age scholars, Jesus is the holy one of an esoteric order. To the enemies of the traditional social order, he was a warrior against the routine. And to racists, Jesus was an Aryan Galilean. In fact, after ten years in prison for his involvement in the deaths of the three civil rights workers, Sam Bowers returned to Mississippi to devote himself to a study of the life of Christ and was never, in forty years of research, convinced that Jesus was anything other than Bowers believed him to be when he ascended that pulpit in 1964.

Harnack believed that the only answer to the problem of losing the kernel of the gospel under the husks of foreign ideas was to emancipate the gospel by returning to its primitive form, freeing it from centuries of superstitious Catholicism. And in this he was right. Setting Jesus free from Nazis, racist Afrikaners, Klansmen, and the dogma of the church is essential, but even Harnack wasn't able to let Jesus be Jesus. As a leading Protestant liberal, he launched what would famously be called the "quest for the historical Jesus," believing sincerely that if only the real Jesus could be recovered, he would be the inspiration for a renewed Christianity. Today, twentieth-century German liberals like Harnack are often seen as falling into the very trap in which they accused others of being snared. Besotted by the liberal humanism of their time and unable to escape the rigors of the new science, history, they limited their rediscovery of Jesus to that of a purely human figure. Harnack's quest for an emancipated Jesus led him to one without such concepts as revelation, incarnation, miracle, and resurrection, which he considered unscientific. In the much-quoted judgment of the Catholic George Tyrrell, "The Christ that Harnack sees, looking back through nine centuries of Catholic darkness, is only the reflection of a liberal Protestant face, seen at the bottom of a deep well."[13]

Suffering Prophet

Martin Luther King Jr.

Like Jesus announcing the kingdom of God, Dr. Martin Luther King Jr. prophetically spoke to the possibility of a new American society—a society without racism, oppression, and violence. His iconic "I Have a Dream" speech, singing out his hope for America's future, echoes Isaiah 40, "I have a dream that every valley will be exalted . . ." and Amos 5:24, "No, no we are not satisfied, and we will not be satisfied until justice rolls down like waters and righteousness like a mighty stream. . . ." His uncompromising stance on non-violence even in the face of extreme provocation was influenced by the non-violent activism of Mahatma Gandi in India, and deliberately embodied the explicit teachings of Jesus to turn the other cheek and to love one's enemies. King's message of hope and justice inspired African-Americans to claim their place at America's table, rather like Jesus' message gave hope to the poor of his day. As a little Jesus, King transformed society, and his assassination in 1968 mirrors the sacrificial death of Jesus. King is one of the ten twentieth-century martyrs from around the world who are depicted in statues above the Great West Door in London's Westminster Abbey.

Surely the challenge for the church today is to be taken captive by the agenda of Jesus, rather than seeking to mold him to fit our agendas, no matter how noble they might be. We acknowledge that we can never truly claim to know him completely. We all bring our biases to the task. But we believe it is inherent in the faith to keep trying and to never give up on this holy quest. The challenge before us is to let Jesus be Jesus and to allow ourselves to be caught up in his extraordinary mission for the world.

Whether it is the grand ecclesiastical project of the institutional churches, epitomized by the ostentatious excess of the Vatican, or the tawdry grab for the hearts and minds of the aspirational middle class by prosperity-style Pentecostalism, the Christian movement has been subverted. Like a forgotten nativity scene in a shopping mall dominated by Santa Claus, reindeer, elves, Disney characters, tinsel, baubles, and fake snow, the biblical Jesus is hard to find. But Jesus is still calling us to come and join him in a far more reckless and exciting adventure than that of mere church attendance. When allowed to be as he appears in the pages of Scripture, Jesus will not lead us to hatred, violence, greed, excess, earthly power, or material wealth. Instead, he will call us to a genuinely biblical and existential faith that believes in him, not simply believing in belief, as in many expressions of evangelicalism. It requires an ongoing encounter with Jesus. This will raise issues in the *ways of knowing* that bring about true spiritual transformation, which we will explore later in this book.

And so it is all about Jesus for us, with some direct implications for our lives as followers of Jesus.

⟵ Direct Implications for Our Discipleship

Because this is a book about Jesus, it must also be a book that explores our living relationship with him. Therefore it should also be about discipleship—our experiencing the redemption he brings, being incorporated into his body, following in his way, becoming like him, and taking up his cause. And so any attempt to reJesus the church must also recover a real sense of the radical and revolutionary nature of what it means to follow Jesus in the current Western context. To be free in Jesus must somehow mean that the idols of our time come under some serious questioning. For instance, to be free in Jesus surely will mean liberation from the shackles of a predominant and omnipresent middle-class consumerism that weighs heavily on us. To be free in Jesus means allowing Jesus to be Jesus, and in doing so, allowing Jesus to challenge our religiosity or our self-righteousness or our greed or worse.

⟵ Radical Challenges for Our Churches

Following Jesus will also have implications for a religion constrained by degenerating institutional forms and expressions. And so this is also a book that will have direct implications for missional ecclesiology (our understanding and practice of church). We will explore the implications of the love and following of Jesus for the missional church at the dawn of what might prove to be the most missionally challenging century ever. And given that we are mainly concerned with how Jesus shapes our mission and our experience of church, we believe that if we don't deal with Christology, how can we ever get mission, or even, and perhaps especially, a right view of ecclesiology? How many so-called new movements has the Protestant church seen in recent memory? Whether it is Pentecostalism, church growth theory, the third-wave charismatic movement, the parachurch movement, rapid church multiplication, emerging church, simple church, or the passion movement, so many of them have been presented as new ways of doing church. From our perspective, this is putting the cart before the horse. Let's get our Christology right and then dare to place all our deeply held desires for how to do church at its service. Not vice versa.

Are we fundamentally aligned with Jesus' purposes and will for his community on earth? It's a good question, and one we must ask at this critical time in history. When we direct that question to our founder, we find the answer somewhat disturbing. The only means we have of proposing a viable answer is to compare the 'religion' of Jesus with the religion of Christianity to see if these coincide. How else are we to assess our authenticity? If we are to take him as the prototypal Christian, and if, apart from the uniquely messianic aspects of his work, we are to take his words and actions as exemplary and authoritative for all of his followers everywhere, then we are left no option but to make this dangerous comparison. In fact, it's dangerous because we believe such a comparison will reveal the church to be on the wrong side of Jesus' type of barbarian spirituality and religion, precisely because his form of spirituality can hardly be considered to be civil. It must be called subversive by all that is called civilized. It is what Ellul called "antireligion." Jesus undermines any status quo that is not built on the all-encompassing demands of the kingdom, and this must call into question much of our religious codes, institutions, and behavior.

⟵ Some Suggested Reformulations of Our Spirituality

And because this is a book about Jesus, it is also therefore a book exploring the nature of Christian spirituality and worship in our context. If Jesus is our center point, our guide, and the mediator between humanity and God, then we cannot bypass the implications that this will have for our spirituality.

It is true that Jesus is like God, but the greater truth, one closer to the revelation of God that Jesus ushers in, is that God is like Christ. As A. Michael Ramsey, the former Anglican archbishop, noted, "God is Christlike and in him is no unChristlikeness at all."[14] Or in the words of Jesus, "If you have seen me, you have seen the Father, I and the Father are one" (John 14:9, 1:14, 18). This has massive implications for us, especially for our understanding of God, but it does not exhaust the extent of the revelation we find in Jesus, because not only does Jesus redefine our concept of God but also he shows us the perfect expression of humanity as God intended it. In other words, he models for us what a true human being should be like. Therefore, focusing our discipleship on Jesus forces us to take seriously the implications of following him, of becoming like him. It sets the agenda for our spirituality. It acknowledges that Jesus as our model, our teacher, and our guide is normative for the Christian life. He is the standard by which we measure ourselves, the quality of our discipleship, and therefore our spirituality.

If the heart of Christian spirituality is to increasingly become like our founder, then an authentic comprehension of Jesus becomes critical. All too often the focal point of our corporate and individual life shifts from its true center in Jesus, resulting in various anomalies in our spirituality. A true Christian expression models itself on Jesus, and it is God's unambiguous aim to make us to be more like his Son. In fact, this is our eternal destiny: "to be conformed to the likeness of his Son" (Rom 8:29). In *The Forgotten Ways*, Alan calls this the "conspiracy of little Jesuses," and we believe it is fundamental to God's plan and purposes for his world.

If this worries us, if we think this would somehow upset the finely balanced ecology of our spirituality, then we can perhaps reframe the issue by posing it as a question: If Jesus is perfected humanity—the human image of God—how bad can we become if we became more like him? Would the world not be a better place if there were more little Jesuses around? It strikes us therefore as a matter of fundamental importance to our humanity, our spirituality, and our witness that we regularly get a truer perspective on the focal point and the defining center of our faith.

Finally, in doing this we hope that we can in some way restore Christology to the church at large, to make it applicable to the whole people of God. For far too long Christology has been the province of academic and professional Christians, who seem far more concerned with an examination of how the divine and human are related in Jesus' person than they are in the details of his life or the content of his teaching and vision. As theologians attempted to use speculative philosophy and ontology to explore the two natures of Christ, Christology became something of a complex science that in effect excludes the theologically uninitiated person. When the study of the remarkable

life and teachings of Jesus becomes the sole province of theologians and religious professionals, when it is done in abstract and divorced from our daily
concerns and from the missional context of the church, it will tend to degrade
the vitality of our Christianity. The system we have historically constructed to
try to probe the nature of Christ reaches Gnostic proportions and takes years
to comprehend in a meaningful way. Only few very smart people can do that,

Righteous Forgiveness

Born to sharecroppers in rural Mississippi, Fannie Lou Hamer rose
to prominence as an African-American woman in the Civil Rights
movement of the 1960s. Like others in the movement, Hamer was
deeply spiritual, and as a little Jesus, she stood up for the disenfran-
chised and forgave those who persecuted her. In 1962, the forty-four-
year-old Hamer attended a rally sponsored by the Student Nonviolent
Coordinating Committee (SNCC, an organization dedicated to fighting
for civil rights through civil disobedience) and, inspired, she and her
husband went to register to vote. Along the way, Hamer sang hymns,
including "Go Tell It on the Mountain" and "This Little Light of Mine."

Fannie Lou Hamer

For this, she and her husband were kicked out of their home, and Hamer
lost her job. However, her tenacity also attracted the attention of SNCC, and the organization
recruited her to be a field secretary. The following year, she was arrested with three other activists
on trumped-up charges, and she sustained a near fatal beating at the hands of the police. Hamer,
however, sang spirituals and refused to hate her tormenters. "It wouldn't solve any problem for
me to hate whites just because they hate me," she explained. For the next fifteen years until
her death, Hamer continued her work in the Civil Rights movement, including an organizational
role in the 1964 Mississippi Freedom Summer and as a seated delegate at the 1964 and 1968
Democratic National Conventions, always applying her belief in the biblical righteousness of the
cause. She was known for saying "I'm sick and tired of being sick and tired." She maintained
that it wasn't enough just to claim to be a Christian. "If you are not putting that claim to the test,
where the rubber meets the road, then it's high time to stop talking about being a Christian."

and the net effect is devastating for the church as an agency of Christ's kingdom. This is our concern, because the living link between Jesus and his people
must never be dissolved or placed beyond the reach of the average Christian.
To do this is to sever the church from its true source of life (John 7:38). Surely

any loss of a direct, grassroots comprehension of Jesus must be a major cause in the degeneration of Christianity in any time and any place?

Therefore, we propose a rediscovery of Christology that includes a pre-occupation with the example and teaching of Jesus for the purposes of emulation by his followers. Some will say that such emulation is arduous to achieve in general and impossible when it comes to the specifics of his redeeming death and resurrection, the miracles, and his judgment of the unrighteous. Surely, they argue, we cannot die for the sins of others or judge their deeds. And here's where we need a far richer Christology than we've been offered in the past. For us, Christology is the study and examination of the entire phenomenon of Jesus, including his person and work and teachings, for the purpose of determining in what ways the various elements of his life and activity can be emulated by sinful human beings. For example, we can't die for others, as Jesus did, but we can offer ourselves sacrificially in service of others. Paul compares husbands loving their wives with Jesus dying for our sins. A working Christology would help us understand Jesus better and provide the tools for appropriating his example into our lives.

So this is not primarily a book about renewal for its own sake, nor is it a book about Christology as a strictly theological discipline. Rather, it is an attempt to reinstate the central role of Jesus in the ongoing spiritual life of the faith and in the life and mission of God's people. More specifically, it is an attempt to recalibrate the mission of the church around the person and work of Jesus. This book then is a work of missional Christology, if there is such a thing. It is an attempt to revision and revitalize our vision of Jesus as master of history and Lord of the church against which, we are reminded, the gates of hell will not prevail (Matt 16:18). In short, it is about nothing less than reJesusing the church.

⟵ Notes

1. Don Whitehead, *Attack on Terror: The* FBI *against the* Ku Klux Klan *in Mississippi* (New York: Funk & Wagnalls, 1970), 4, cited in Charles Marsh, *God's Long Summer: Stories of Faith and Civil Rights* (Princeton, N.J.: Princeton University Press, 1997), 64.

2. Marsh, *God's Long Summer*, 65.

3. Ibid., 62.

4. Letters to Charles Marsh, cited in ibid., 62–63. Note Bowers's reference to Jesus as "The Galilean." Bowers used this term to distinguish Jesus as a non-Jewish descendent of Aryan colonists in ancient Galilee.

5. Ibid., 63.

6. Most recently, Alan Hirsch, *The Forgotten Ways: Reactivating the Missional Church* (Grand Rapids, Mich.: Brazos, 2006), 143ff.; Michael Frost and Alan Hirsch, *The Shaping of Things to Come: Innovation and Mission for the 21st-Century Church* (Peabody, Mass.: Hendrickson, 2003), 16ff.

7. Michael Frost, *Exiles* (Peabody, Mass.: Hendrickson, 2006). See also Alan Hirsch, Neil Cole, and Wolfgang Simson, *Igniting Primal Fires*, which explores Ephesians 4:11 ministry (forthcoming).

8. Jacques Ellul, *The Subversion of Christianity* (Grand Rapids, Mich.: Eerdmans, 1986), 3.

9. We think not. The idea of "one nation under God" is the calling of Israel, not that of the church. One church under God is more like it. And the church is called to live among the nations, bearing witness, influencing, but never dominating.

10. The Christian organization in England called rejesus has a wonderful interactive website (ReJesus.co.uk) exploring Jesus' "life, character, teachings, and followers." We recommend it as a great place to spend some time.

11. J. Kevin Livingston, "David Jacobus Bosch," *The International Bulletin of Missionary Research* 23/1 (January 1999): 26–32.

12. Adolf von Harnack, *The Essence of Christianity*, quoted in Alexander Mens, *Son of Man* (Torrance, Calif.: Oakwood, 1992), 5.

13. George Tyrrell, *Christianity at the Cross-Roads* (London: Allen & Unwin, 1963), 49.

14. A. Michael Ramsey, *God, Christ and the World: A Study in Contemporary Theology* (London: SCM, 1969), 99.

How Jesus Changes Everything

"Jesus is Lord" is a radical claim, one that is ultimately
rooted in questions of allegiance, of ultimate authority,
of the ultimate norm and standard for human life.
Instead, Christianity has often sought to ally Itself
comfortably with allegiance to other authorities,
be they political, economic, cultural, or ethnic.
—Lee Camp

In the same way the Church exists for nothing else but
to draw men into Christ, to make them little Christs.
If they are not doing that, all the cathedrals, clergy,
missions, sermons, even the Bible itself, are simply a
waste of time. God became man for no other purpose.
It is even doubtful, you know, whether the whole
universe was created for any other purpose. It says in
the Bible that the whole universe was made for Christ
and that everything is to be gathered together in Him.
—C. S. Lewis

Key to encountering the biblical Jesus is a step that many Christians seem to find painful, that is, our preparedness to read the Gospels in order to emulate Jesus. It appears that a good church upbringing will do many marvelous things for you, but one of the unfortunate things it also does is convince you that Jesus is to be worshipped but not followed. In his previous work, *Exiles*, Michael argued that the traditional Christian depiction of the porcelain-skinned Jesus has hindered our ability, indeed our desire, to actually be like him.[1] We readily acknowledge that none of us have within us the fortitude, the grace, the courage, and the imagination to actually be like Jesus. It is a lost cause. But it's a lost cause made worth it by the forgiveness and grace shown us in Jesus' death on our behalf. By dying for us to set us free from the penalty for our sinfulness, he doesn't nullify the call to good works and godly living. Rather, he elevates from an endless and hopeless attempt to impress God to a joyful adventure of enjoying Christ's presence by imitating him. The quest to emulate Jesus isn't folly. When it's embraced by those who know they are forgiven for all the ways they will fall short, it is a daring exploit!

Making this very point, M. Scott Peck in *Further Along the Road Less Traveled* recounted the episode when Baptist theologian Harvey Cox was addressing a convention of Christian healers—pastors, therapists, nurses, doctors—that Peck was attending. During his presentation, Cox retold the story from Luke 8 of Jesus raising Jairus's daughter from the dead. In the well-known story, as Jesus and his companions are heading for the home of Jairus's dying girl, a woman who has been hemorrhaging for years breaks from the crowd and touches Jesus' robe in the hope that she too will be healed. Jesus reels around and demands to know who touched him. The cowering woman sheepishly owns up, and Jesus, feeling compassionate for her having endured years of unspeakable suffering, heals her and continues on his way to the house where the young girl has since died. Thereupon Jesus promptly brings the child back to life.

Having related the story (no doubt in greater detail than we just did), Cox asked his audience of six hundred Christian healers and therapists to indicate which of the characters in the story they most strongly identified with. The bleeding woman? The anxious father? The curious crowd? Or Jesus? What Cox found was that around a hundred felt they could relate to the desperate woman; several hundred identified with Jairus, whose daughter was dying; the majority identified with the perplexed group standing by. And six—yes, six—people felt they could identify with Jesus.

Peck's point in recounting this experience was to point out that there is something seriously wrong with Christianity when only one in every hundred Christians can identify with Jesus. Here was a story about Jesus the healer, told to healers, but none of them identified with Jesus. Have we made him so divine, so otherworldly, that we cannot connect with him anymore? Peck suggests that this leads to the excuse that we can't really be expected to follow Jesus because we perceive ourselves way down here and Jesus way up there, beyond identification. Says Peck, "That is exactly what we're supposed to do! We're supposed to identify with Jesus, act like Jesus, be like Jesus. That is what Christianity is supposed to be about: the imitation of Christ."[2]

By making Christ seem otherworldly, even ethereal, the church has inadvertently put him out of reach to us as an example or a guide. Even though Jesus routinely called people to follow him, the church has often represented this following in purely metaphysical or mystical terms. We can follow Jesus "in our heart" but not necessarily with our actions. Even after the phenomenally successful *What Would Jesus Do* campaign, in which Christians were encouraged to ask themselves this question before every action, it seemed that Christians were more interested in asking the question than in doing what Jesus would do. We have sanitized and tamed Jesus by encasing him in abstract theology, and in doing so we have removed our motivation for discipleship. When Jesus is just true light of true light, and not flesh and blood, we are only ever called to adore him, not follow him.

In Charles Sheldon's popular novel *In His Steps*, one of the characters, Rev. Henry Maxwell, encounters a homeless man who challenges him to take seriously the imitation of Christ. The homeless man has difficulty understanding why, in his view, so many Christians ignore the poor:

I heard some people singing at a church prayer meeting the other night,

All for Jesus, all for Jesus,
All my being's ransomed powers,
All my thoughts, and all my doings,
All my days, and all my hours

and I kept wondering as I sat on the steps outside just what they meant by it. It seems to me there's an awful lot of trouble in the world that somehow wouldn't exist if all the people who sing such songs went and lived them out. I suppose I don't understand. But what would Jesus do? Is that what you mean by following his steps? It seems to me sometimes as if the people in the big churches had good clothes and nice houses to live in, and money to spend for luxuries, and could go away on summer vacations and all that, while the people outside the churches, thousands of them, I mean, die in tenements, and walk the streets for jobs, and never have a piano or a picture in the house, and grow up in misery and drunkenness and sin.[3]

This leads to many of the novel's characters asking, "What would Jesus do?" when faced with decisions of some importance. This has the effect of making the characters embrace more seriously the fact that Jesus lies at Christianity's core consciousness.

The difficulty for the church today is not in encouraging people to ask what Jesus would do, but in getting them to break out of their domesticated and sanitized ideas about Jesus in order to answer that question. Jesus was a wild man. He was a threat to the security of the religious establishment. He was baptized by a wild man. He inaugurated his ministry by spending time with

Practicing Dangerous Mercy

A single act of compassion altered the course of Sheila Cassidy's life. In 1975 while practicing medicine in Chile during the oppressive Pinochet regime, the young Australian provided medical care to one of the dictator's political opponents. Arrested and imprisoned by the Chilean secret police, Cassidy was tortured severely for information about anti-government forces. Her terrifying experience did not break the Roman Catholic, but instead proved to be the catalyst for a lifetime of human rights activism. Upon her release, Cassidy moved to the U.K., where she drew attention to human rights abuses in Chile by publicizing her story and writing a book, *Audacity to Believe*. She also spent a period of religious retreat in both a monastery and a convent before returning to her vocation as a doctor in 1980. Cassidy continued her human rights work to increase international opposition to the torture of political prisoners and also became active in the hospice movement, serving as the Medical Director of St. Luke's Hospice in Plymouth, England, for fifteen years. A true little Jesus, Sheila Cassidy emerged from her torture and imprisonment to a ministry deeply committed to life and peace.

Sheila Cassidy

the wild beasts of the wilderness. He was unfazed by a wild storm that lashed his boat on an excursion across a lake and with the wildness of the demoniacs of the Gaderenes. And while he ultimately brought peace to both those situations, in neither instance did Jesus appear overwhelmed or frightened by the circumstances. There was an untamed power within him. Even his storytelling, so often characterized by the church today as warm morality tales, was dangerous and subversive and mysterious. If your answer to the question "What would Jesus do?" is that he would be conventional, safe, respectable and refined, then we suspect you didn't find that answer in the Gospels.

As Terry Eagleton says, "[Jesus] is presented [in the Gospels] as homeless, propertyless, peripatetic, socially marginal, disdainful of kinfolk, without a trade or occupation, a friend of outcasts and pariahs, averse to material possessions, without fear for his own safety, a thorn in the side of the Establishment and a scourge of the rich and powerful."[4]

The process of reJesusing the church will begin with a rediscovery of the fierce and outrageous life of Jesus. Too many people have become turned off to the church because the object of our faith seems bland and insipid. It reminds us of the quip made by the archbishop who is reported to have said, "Everywhere Jesus went there was a riot. Everywhere I go they make me cups of tea!"

This was the experience of punk rocker, screenwriter, and novelist Nick Cave. Writing in an introduction to Mark's gospel, Cave talks about how as a younger man he found the Jesus presented to him in church as anemic and uninteresting. When he became interested in the Bible, he concentrated virtually all his attention on the Old Testament, drawn as he was to its violence and pervading sense of vengeance, perhaps not unsurprising for a punk. Later, an Anglican vicar in London suggested he read Mark instead, and Cave was astonished by the Jesus he discovered between its pages:

> The Christ that the church offers us, the bloodless, placid "Savior"—the man smiling benignly at a group of children, or calmly, serenely hanging from the cross—denies Christ his potent, creative sorrow or his boiling anger that confronts us so forcefully in Mark. Thus the church denies Christ his humanity, offering up a figure that we can perhaps "praise," but never relate to.[5]

Cave's introduction to Mark is beautifully written and deeply heartfelt. He writes about "that part of me that railed and hissed and spat at the world" initially taking pleasure in the "wonderful, terrible book," the Old Testament, before mellowing out in later life. "You no longer find comfort watching a whacked-out God tormenting a wretched humanity as you learn to forgive yourself and the world," he says somewhat unfairly of the Old Testament. Nonetheless, after all those blood-curdling stories he was well and truly ready to meet Jesus. And meet him he did, seeing Jesus in Mark with a fresh perspective many seasoned Christians often miss:

> The essential humanness of Mark's Christ provides us with a blueprint for our own lives, so that we have something we can aspire to, rather than revere, that can lift us free of the mundanity of our existences, rather than affirming the notion that we are lowly and unworthy. Merely to praise Jesus in his Perfectness, keeps us on our knees, with our heads pitifully bent. Clearly, this is not what Christ had in mind. Christ came as liberator. Christ understood that we as humans were for ever held to the ground by the pull of gravity—our ordinariness, our mundanity—and it was through his example that he gave our imaginations the freedom to rise and to fly. In short, to be Christ-like.[6]

Cave is no theologian and doesn't pretend to be, but he's on to something. Look at what happens to those Jesus encounters in the Gospels—the hemorrhaging woman, Jairus, the woman at the well, Mary Magdalene, Peter, Thomas—they are lifted up by him, transformed, strengthened, renewed. Jesus teaches them how to live, not just how to worship. Today, we need to accept Jesus as our guide, as well as our Savior. And only a Savior as human as the one portrayed in the Gospels could ever be our guide.

Long before Cave was writing this, another novelist was exploring the essential *humanity* of Jesus. The prodigious talent of Dorothy L. Sayers found in the story of Christ more than enough material to occupy her attention. Sayers, originally an advertising executive, is probably best remembered for her detective novels, set between the wars and featuring English aristocrat and amateur sleuth, Lord Peter Wimsey. While she might have preferred to be known for her magisterial translation of Dante's *Divine Comedy*, Christians seem to know her only for her 1941 radio play *The Man Born to Be King*, a dramatization of the life of Jesus. But the writing of that play was not the only time she turned her attention to Jesus. Her personal correspondence is littered with references to him, so much so, in fact, that it's not difficult to conclude that she was obsessed by Jesus. Her self-confessed quest was for a deep and proper understanding of his essence, his character and his mission, claiming as she did that such an understanding was "the difference between pseudo-Christianity and Christianity."[7]

For Sayers, an appreciation of the stained-glass Jesus was not enough to satisfy her. She needed to encounter the real Jesus. The "bloodless, placid Savior" that Nick Cave rebelled against repelled her every bit as much. In the introduction to the published version of *The Man Born to Be King* she discussed the importance of connecting with a flesh-and-blood Messiah:

> The writer of realistic Gospel plays . . . is brought up face to face with the "scandal of particularity." *Ecco homo*—not only Man-in-general and God-in-His-thusness, but also God-in-His-thisness, and *this* Man, *this* person, of a reasonable soul and human flesh subsisting, who walked and talked *then* and *there*, surrounded, not by human types, but by *those* individual people. The story of the life and murder and resurrection of God-in-Man is not only the symbol and epitome of the relations of God and man throughout time; it is also a series of events that took place at a particular point in time.[8]

While people like C. S. Lewis, who read *The Man Born to Be King* every Easter, appreciated Sayers's attempt to describe God in his *thisness*, not in his *thusness* (a great line), a good many churchgoers found her portrayal of

Jesus to be vulgar and unbecoming. Sayers's response to one caller, who telephoned to criticize her after the broadcast of her 1939 Advent play, He That Should Come, summed up her approach:

> If you mixed as much as I do with people to whom the Gospel story seems to be nothing but a pretty fairytale, you would know how much of their contemptuous indifference is due to one fact: that never for one moment have they seen it as a real thing, happening to a living people. Nor, indeed, are they fully convinced that Christians believe in its reality.[9]

You didn't want to cross Sayers when she was in full flight! But her assumption holds water. Until Martin Scorsese's The Last Temptation of Christ and Mel Gibson's gory The Passion of the Christ, all film versions of the life of Jesus portrayed him as unflappable and dignified. The crucified Christ was given a few spots of blood on his brow, his underarms were shaved, and his loincloth was fixed firmly in place. It seems that this was the church's favored version. Sayers's argument was that while the world saw a church that preferred a sanitized Savior, they had no choice but to conclude that the stories about him were myths and legends, not references to the historical incarnation of God in humankind. And while the central Christian story was merely a myth, it never laid any claim on the lives of believers or unbelievers alike. Like Robin Hood or the Knights of the Round Table, the Gospels might have taught a moral ethical code, but they didn't introduce us to this man, this person, who demanded to be the guide of my life. This Sayers called the "scandal of particularity," and it remains a scandal to this day.

But where is the scandalous Jesus in our churches today? Where is the Jesus who taunted the religious elite (Luke 20:32–36), who teased a Canaanite woman (Matt 15:21–28), who evaded arrest (John 7:32–36), who commended the faith of a pagan (Matt 8:5ff), who waited four days to resurrect Lazarus (John 9), who promised not peace but a sword (Matt 10:34ff)? To reJesus the church, we need to take Christians along on a journey of rediscovery, a pilgrimage toward Jesus, to see as Jesus saw. It will involve an embracing of this scandal of particularity.

⟿ Taken Captive by Jesus

So what does it mean, then, to be taken captive by the agenda of the flesh-and-blood Jesus? We will argue that a rediscovery of the biblical Jesus will radically reshape our view of God, the church, and the world. And further, we believe that by allowing Jesus to shape us in these three areas we are better equipped to reJesus the church communities of which we are part. Obviously, this will involve a preparedness on our parts to resist capturing Jesus for our ends or molding him to our theological or political agendas. And it will involve a thoroughgoing attempt to view reality as Jesus does; in effect, to see through his eyes.

Through the eyes of Jesus, we will see God differently, no longer as a distant father figure, but through the paradigm of the *missio Dei* to find the sent and sending God. Second, we will see the church differently, no longer as a religious institution but as a community of Jesus followers devoted to participating in his mission. We call this the *participatio Christi*. And third, through Jesus' eyes we will see the world afresh, not simply as fallen or depraved but as bearing the mark of the *imago Dei*—the image of God.

Those taken captive by the sight of Christ must be prepared for a reintegration of the theological concepts of *missio Dei*, *participatio Christi*, and *imago Dei*. These three concepts are foundational for a rediscovery of missional practice in our time. They are also foundational for us to reJesus the church in the West.

You Will See God Differently

When our imaginations are taken captive by Jesus, we will see God differently. Rather than seeing God as a loving but distant Father who calls us to himself and directs the affairs of history from on high, we will begin to see God as near, as integrally involved in our lives; in effect, as one who sends himself to us rather than waiting for us to come to him. The Latin phrase *missio Dei* is used to describe more the divine nature of God than simply the practical nature of Christian mission. In this respect the term is better translated as "the God of mission" rather than "the mission of God." First coined by Karl Hartenstein in the 1950s, the term gained real currency because it located the idea of mission with the doctrine of God, not with the doctrine of the church. We often speak of mission being a function of the church's work in this world, but Hartenstein was anxious that the church understand that mission belongs to and describes God's work. We, the church, become partners in what God is doing, but it is never our initiative alone. Those who are taken captive by Jesus see mission not merely as a practice preferred by God but as an aspect of his very character. He *is* mission. Core to understanding God's nature is the realization that God cannot *not* be about the business of mission. He inhabits mission as part of the very stuff of his personality. In effect, he is both the sent and sending God.

In John 5, Jesus heals a lame man on the Sabbath and incurs the wrath of the Jewish leaders for, as they saw it, flouting the law of Moses. In his own defense, Jesus appeals to an even higher law than that of Moses. In effect, he appeals to the doctrine of *missio Dei*, even though he never uses such a term, when he says, "My Father is still working, and I also am working" (John 5:17). In other words, you Pharisees might refuse to work on the Sabbath, but God is unceasing in his redemptive activity, no matter the day or the date. Naturally, the Pharisees are outraged, not only because he is apparently disregarding the Sabbath but because he is equating himself with Yahweh's missional work. But Jesus presses on, making an even more provocative claim: "Very truly I tell you, the Son can do nothing on his own, but only what he sees the Father doing; for whatever the Father does, the Son does likewise" (John 5:19).

Nothing could be more scandalous! Effectively, Jesus is claiming to be captive to the *missio Dei*, attending only to his Father's missional activity, irrespective of narrow interpretations of Hebrew law. This stunning claim, that he is not operating under his own steam or on the basis of his own strategy but entirely at the impulse of the sent and sending Father, is a challenge to us. If we claim to be Jesus followers, we ought to be committed to being similarly (if imperfectly) in league with the *missio Dei*.

Later, in John 8, after a lengthy discussion about his oneness with the Father and the meaning of his death, Jesus concludes, "The one who sent me is with me; he has not left me alone, for I always do what is pleasing to him" (John 8:29). Earlier he had referred to his being sent by the Father (John 8:16), but that could have been interpreted as him saying that he has the Father's backing in his dealings with people. By verse 29 he reiterates that he is not alone, but here he makes it clear that he is talking about the Father's personal presence with him at all times, including at that moment. Even though his followers might desert him, as many had done (John 6), he is claiming that he will never be deserted by his Father. Here we get a glimpse into the mystery of the relations between the Father and the Son, for the Father sends the Son and yet is present with the Son. The sending refers to the incarnation and the presence to the eternal relations. In other words, the Father is both sending and sent.[10]

But note how Jesus points out that the Father's presence relies on the Son's commitment to always do what is pleasing to the Father. In this way, Jesus reveals the primacy of the *missio Dei*—the missionary Father. All that exists, even the Son and the Spirit in their eternal, uncreated being, are dependent upon the Father as the source of all life. All life is an expression of the Father's life. To do what pleases God is not simply a matter of morality but of sharing in God's life and mission. It is another way of saying that Christ does

Imitatio Christi

Janani Luwum

Janani Luwum embraced his vocation as a little Jesus, imitating his Lord even to the point of death. The Anglican Church appointed him to be the archbishop of Uganda, Rwanda, Burundi, and Boga-Zaire in 1974, during the murderous regime of Idi Amin in Uganda. Seizing power in a 1971 coup, Amin and his squads were responsible for over 300,000 deaths. Amin destroyed the economy, while bestowing riches on himself and his friends. In 1976 Luwum convened a meeting with Catholic and Muslim leaders at which they passed a resolution deploring Amin's attrocities. In so doing, Luwum knew he had marked himself for death. He had consciously begun his *imitatio Christi*. Four days before his arrest, Luwum met with his bishops for the last time and shared with them the gospel passage in which Jesus calms the storm, comparing it with the political storm they were enduring and calling on them to rely on Jesus' calming presence. "They are going to kill me. I am not afraid," he confided. After an atrocious beating, including rape, the archbishop was shot dead. It was rumored that it was Amin himself who fired the fatal shots. His death was reported as a car accident. Luwum's humiliation and suffering embody the passion of Jesus. Like Martin Luther King Jr., Luwum is memorialized as a twentieth-century martyr at Westminster Abbey.

what he sees the Father doing and speaks what he hears from the Father. He is devoted to the mission of God. As such he is the model of all discipleship. The life Jesus is offering involves being taken up into the mission of the Father.

No one has helped us understand this concept more than the missiologist David Bosch. This is the same David Bosch who celebrated the election of the architects of apartheid to the South African parliament in the late 1940s and went on to become one of the most celebrated missiologists in the world. During that time, he underwent a series of experiences that transformed him from a bigoted Afrikaner to a deeply compassionate missionary who worked in a poor black community in the Transkei region of South Africa. Exhausted from the back-breaking labors of working with the poor, he eventually accepted a position in 1975 as the professor of missiology at UNISA (University of South Africa) Pretoria, where he served until his untimely death in a car accident in 1992. What he discovered about the mission of Jesus can be summed up in the following statement:

> Mission [is] understood as being derived from the very nature of God. It [is] thus put in the context of the doctrine of the Trinity, not of ecclesiology or soteriology. The classical doctrine of the missio Dei as God the Father sending the Son, and God the Father and the Son sending the Spirit [is] expanded to include yet another "movement": Father, Son, and Holy Spirit sending the church into the world.[11]

This triune element to the *missio Dei* is not unique to the thinking of Bosch. In the 1930s, thinkers like Karl Barth and Karl Hartenstein were advocating a trinitarian base for a missional doctrine of God. When we see God as Jesus understood him, we see a God so devoted to his broken planet that he issues himself forth to redeem it. In the incarnation of Jesus, we hear the *missio Dei* presented to us in his teaching and embodied in his flesh. But further than that, the ministry of the Spirit continues to testify to God's character and his core missional orientation. Jacques Matthey writes in summary of those committed to the idea of *missio Dei*, "We have not separated the Father from the Son and the Spirit. This has consequences: we cannot limit the scope of Christ or the Spirit to inner-church circles."[12] In effect, you can't keep the Trinity locked up in church. God escapes the stained-glass crypt and sends himself out throughout the world: Father, Son, and Spirit.

But this doesn't mean that the church is not involved. Far from it. As Bosch said earlier, the cycle continues with the triune God sending the church into the world. It is essential that we recapture the importance and role of the church within the overall frame of *missio Dei*, without reverting to an old ecclesiocentric approach. We will return to this discussion soon.

Nonetheless, part of the process to reJesus the church will involve a dismantling of its much-loved temple theology. While Jesus embodies the fact that the Trinity is both sent and sending, his followers very often seem to prefer a deity who reveals himself in sacred buildings, liturgies, and sacramental practices. So-called temple theology locates God as a withdrawn deity calling recalcitrants back to his temple/church/cathedral to be reunited with him. But an encounter with the Jesus of the Gospels flies in the face of this idea. While we do find Jesus revering the Jerusalem temple as "my Father's house" (Luke 2:49), we don't think he is saying that his Father lives in that building. Rather, he is acknowledging that within the Jewish system of his time, the temple was seen as a physical embodiment of God's presence in Israel. What he then does is to equate his own person as such an embodiment by saying, "I am able to destroy the temple of God and to build it in three days" (Matt 26:61). We know he was speaking of his own body and its impending death and resurrection. But this is not only a comment on his certainty of being resurrected. It is a comment on where the physical presence of God is located. Rather than being seen in the temple, Jesus sees it in himself. He is the temple. He is the physical embodiment of God.

The instance of Jesus' physical death is depicted as a moment of great wildness. In contrast to being a solemn moment in which Jesus tenderly resigns himself to death, Matthew describes it as a time of great horror! An earthquake is unleashed beneath the city. The curtain of the temple is vandalized by God, torn in two from top to bottom. Graves burst open and the dead rise to wander through the city as a foretaste of the final resurrection yet to come. It's like a scene from *The Night of the Living Dead*! Everything about Jesus is wild, even his death. And the symbolism is unmistakable. Something has shifted in the spiritual realm. A cosmic tsunami has been unleashed. Through Jesus' death God has entered into our world for good. God will now no longer dwell in temples, but in the hearts of those who serve God.

This is picked up again by Paul, when he refers to the church as the body of Christ. The triune God doesn't reside in a temple or any other building. Rather, the physical embodiment of the Trinity is in the people of God, the followers of Christ. The *missio Dei* describes the impulse that saw the Father send his Son into the world to enflesh him. It is also the impulse that sees the Father, the Son, and Spirit send us into the world as his ambassadors, his representatives, enfleshing him here on earth. This leads us to our second aspect of being shaped by Jesus.

You Will See the Church Differently

Through Jesus' eyes, the church is the sent people of God. A church is not a building or an organization. It is an organic collective of believers, centered on Jesus and sent out into the world to serve others in his name. When we are taken captive by the Nazarene carpenter, we can no longer see ourselves as participants in a similar system to the one he came to subvert. Not only does Jesus undermine temple theology by becoming the temple himself, but also he undermines the sacrificial system by dispensing with sin without reference to ceremonial washings, rituals, or liturgies ("Go in peace, your sins are forgiven"). As noted earlier, he also plays fast and loose with the legalism of Sabbath keeping. In fact, he subverts the whole religious system. So why would he do that simply to replace it with a Christian religious system? He doesn't! He is antireligious, offering his followers direct access to the Father, forgiveness in his name, and the indwelling of the Holy Spirit. Therefore, to be reJesused is to come to the recognition that the church as the New Testament defines it is not a religious institution but rather a dynamic community of believers who participate in the way of Jesus and his work in this world.

As we said earlier, God's mission in this world is his and his alone. The glory of God, not the church, is the ultimate goal of mission. Our role as the church, however, is a humble participation in his grand scheme—the kingdom of God. We neither determine our own agenda nor merely imitate his but rather participate in the marvelous plan of God according to his call and guidance. Again, Bosch addresses this superbly:

> Mission takes place where the church, in its total involvement with the world, bears its testimony in the form of a servant, with reference to unbelief, exploitation, discrimination and violence, but also with reference to salvation, healing, liberation, reconciliation and righteousness . . . Looked at from this perspective mission is, quite simply, the participation of Christians in the liberating mission of Jesus, wagering on a future that verifiable experience seems to belie. It is the good news of God's love, incarnated in the witness of a community, for the sake of the world.[13]

The participation of Christians in the liberating mission of Jesus is referred to by the Latin term *participati Christi*. As Bosch suggests, this can never be boiled down simply to evangelistic preaching or social justice. As soon as someone can tell you the one thing you need to be doing in order to participate in the mission of Jesus, you can be sure they're not telling you the whole story. Mission involves everything Jesus is about in the world. And this cannot be limited to merely religious concerns. The liberating mission of Jesus is unfolding all around us. As Robert McAfee Brown once said about the meaning of life, it is "our task to create foretastes of [the Kingdom of God] on this planet—living glimpses of what life is meant to be, which include art and music and poetry and shared laughter and picnics and politics and moral outrage and special privileges for children only and wonder and humor and endless love."[14]

In both Luke and Mark's gospels we find the report of an incident where the disciple John notifies Jesus of a stranger who is performing exorcisms in his name: "We saw someone casting out demons in your name, and we tried to stop him, because he does not follow with us" (Luke 9:49). At that time there were many charlatans and magicians willing to perform various acts of sorcery for a fee. For example, when Philip, Peter, and John visit Samaria (Acts 8), they encounter one of Scripture's most beguiling characters, Simon the sorcerer, who had held all of Samaria in his sway with his magical powers. Even after his conversion and baptism, he still offers the disciples cash in return for the even greater magic they can perform. Back in Luke 9, John has discovered an unknown exorcist, using the name of Jesus to perform the miraculous, and he has asked him to cease and desist. But Jesus' response is staggering: "Do not stop him; for whoever is not against you is for you" (Luke 9:50). Jesus is suggesting that rather than running around drawing lines of demarcation between those who are in the community of Christ and those who are not, we are simply to bless all those who participate with us in the work of Jesus. This is how robust Jesus' view of the kingdom was. It couldn't be contained within borders. It was a living thing, a wild thing, and it was bursting out everywhere. It is one of our greatest mistakes to equate the church with the kingdom of God. The kingdom is much broader than the church—it is cosmic in scope. The church is perhaps the primary agent of the kingdom but must not be equated fully with it. We need to be able to see the kingdom activity wherever it expresses itself and join with God in it. Jesus shows us how to see God working in the strangest of places.

In Matthew 13:24–30, Jesus offers us an illustration or metaphor to make better sense of this:

> "The kingdom of heaven may be compared to someone who sowed good seed in his field; but while everyone was asleep, an enemy came and sowed weeds among the wheat, and then went away. So when the plants came up and bore grain, then the weeds appeared as well. And the slaves of the householder came and said to him, 'Master, did you not sow good seed in your field? Where, then, did the weeds come from?' He answered, 'An enemy has done this.' The slaves said to him, 'Then do you want us to go and gather them?'
>
> But he replied, 'No; for in gathering the weeds you would uproot the wheat along with them. Let both of them grow together until the harvest; and at harvest time I will tell the reapers, Collect the weeds first and bind them in bundles to be burned, but gather the wheat into my barn.'"

It will be impossible to separate the wheat from the weeds, so allow them to grow up together and leave it to God to sort out in the end. In other words, John, if some guy you don't know is driving out demons in my name, don't stop him. My kingdom is no respecter of our arbitrary lines of distinction.

How much does the church today need to be reJesused in order to appreciate this! Conservative Christians won't even acknowledge that the rock star, Bono, is on the side of the angels in his fight against global poverty. Certain denominations have demonized others. Some churches won't work with certain other churches as a matter of principle. And yet whoever is not against you is for you, says Jesus. He is teaching John to appreciate all others who serve in Christ's name. In effect, he demands that we abandon our painstaking attempts to weed the field, pulling out each wild plant by hand. Instead, he says, tend to the wheat. Participate in the growth of the kingdom—the wheat—and leave the business of weeding the field to God and his angels.

This isn't to say that such participation is a solo venture for individual Christians. Rather, it ought to be seen as a communal commitment. In this respect, the doctrine of *corpus Christi* (the body of Christ) should be acknowledged. God calls together bodies of believers to participate in his mission. Or, as John Eldridge puts it,

> God is calling together little communities of the heart, to fight for one another and for the hearts of those who have not yet been set free. The camaraderie, that intimacy, that incredible impact by a few stout-hearted souls—that *is* available. It is the Christian life as Jesus gave it to us. It is completely normal.[15]

Interestingly, the term Jesus, and more often Paul, employed to describe a gathering of Christians (since there was literally no such collective noun at the time) was the Greek term *ecclesia*. Today we translate it into the old Anglo-Saxon term "church." But that term today has come to refer more to places of Christian worship or to the institutional aspect of the Christian community. It has strayed a long way from Paul's original usage. Remember, Paul didn't invent the term *ecclesia*. It was already part of the vernacular of his time. He takes this pre-existing term and invests it with a new, distinctly Christian meaning. But it would be helpful to recall in what ways the term *ecclesia* was employed by Paul's non-Christian contemporaries in order to get closer to the original raw material Paul uses in developing his unique ecclesiology.

Most dictionaries will tell you that *ecclesia* literally means "the gathering of the called-out ones." It comes from two words, *ek*, meaning "out," and *kaleo*, meaning "to call." But in its original usage an *ecclesia* was not just an assembly or a gathering, as many suppose. If that's all Paul wanted to convey, he could have used *agora* and *panegyris* as well as *heorte*, *koinon*, *thiasos*, *synagoge*, and *synago*, all of which refer to an assembly. The word *ecclesia* had a political aspect to it. In fact, it wasn't a religious term, and neither was its use limited to a religious gathering. In Paul's time, an *ecclesia* was a gathering of the elders of a community. In smaller villages and towns across Judea, local elders would gather regularly to discuss and deliberate over a variety of social and political dilemmas facing the community. Neighborhood disputes, arguments over estates of deceased persons, communal responses to natural disasters—these were the kinds of things the council of elders would consider. Today, this might be similar to a meeting in the local town hall of a group of community leaders. In other words, an *ecclesia* was a gathering of wise community leaders, brought together by their common vision for the harmony and well-being of the wider community.

It was more than a body of unseen lawmakers who exercised authority and ran the offices of government through a vast bureaucratic system. It was a community within a community whose function was to add value to that community. It brought wisdom to the village. It helped the village be a better village. And of course, being the elders of that village meant that the leaders were required to live with the ramifications of their decisions. They were in the village, and their destiny was as connected to the prosperity and peace of that community as anyone. How interesting that Paul takes this term and Christianizes it for his fledgling communities. Of course, he adds to it the idea of the *ecclesia* being a body, striving for unity and diversity (1 Cor 12:12–31). He calls us a family, a household, with all the attendant expectations of an ancient Hebrew family—devotion, loyalty, affection (Gal 6:9–11). He refers to the *ecclesia* as a bride, emphasizing our duty to holiness and fidelity (Eph 5:22–32), and as an army, presupposing discipline and focus (Eph 6:10–13). There's more to Paul's idea of the church than just a gathering. But isn't it interesting that the base, raw material he uses to develop his vision for us is that of a group of elders adding value to the village, bringing wisdom, and connecting our destiny with that of the community? We think that to be the sent people of God implies that we will have our neighborhood's best interests at heart. We think Christians should see themselves as sent by Jesus into the villages of which they're part, to add value, to bring wisdom, to foster a better village. In short, to participate with the work of Christ all around us.

When Michael was planting the faith community of which he is currently part, smallboatbigsea, he was given a prophetic word from a woman at a meeting he was attending. She told him that a day would come when, if smallboatbigsea was taken away from its neighborhood, the whole community would grieve for its loss. For him, it's a cherished word. Those ancient villages in Judea would have grieved had all their wise, godly elders been suddenly taken away. They wouldn't have known how to be good, true, noble, and peaceful without their input. Is it not possible that Paul imagined a similar appreciation toward his churches? Did he choose *ecclesia*, of all the terms he might have used, because it contained this element of community service and value adding? If so then, to be sent to participate in the unfurling of the kingdom in our communities will necessarily mean the bringing of wisdom, peace, and grace to our villages.

You Will See the World Differently

We recognize that each person is created in the image of God and thus possesses the inherent dignity and value that accompanies it. We recognize also that God has been, and continues to be, at work within them, leading them on a unique and sacred journey. In our previous book together, *The Shaping of Things to Come*, we wrote about the importance of prevenient grace, the confidence that God goes before us, prevening (preparing) our participation in his work. More than that, though, God has already touched every person, leaving his unique fingerprints on that person's soul. The Latin term for this is *imago Dei*, the image of God.

To say that we are all made in the image of God is to acknowledge that there are certain, special qualities of human nature that allow God to be made manifest in us. It is a statement about God's love for humans but also a statement about the uniqueness and beauty of humans. A belief in the *imago Dei* is not a denial of the inherent sinfulness of all people. To deny such is not only heretical, it's just plain ignorant. The human race continues to give myriad examples of our depravity and potential for evil. Rather, it recognizes that God's image is so indelibly stamped on our nature that not even the fall can completely erase it. We, of all creation, are the creatures through whom God's plans and purposes can be made known. In other words, when Christians acknowledge the image of God in us, we can see ourselves as participants or partners with God.

But further, we can see even the unbeliever as bearing the mark of God, and such a mark in even the so-called lowest person must be respected and acknowledged. In other words, if humans are to love God, then humans must love other humans, as each is an expression of God. Jesus pointed this out with his parable of the sheep and the goats (Matt 25:31–46). The regular refrain from the king in the story, "I tell you the truth, whatever you did/did not do for one of the least of these, you did/did not do for me" powerfully illustrates the doctrine of *imago Dei*. Why feed the hungry or clothe the naked or visit the imprisoned or tend to the sick? Because even these, the least of these in fact, bear the image of the king.

The Bible does not claim that animals, though created by God, bear his image in the same way humans do. Humans are self-conscious, with the capacity for spiritual and moral reflection and growth. We differ from all other creatures because of our rational structure—our capacity for deliberation and free decision making. This freedom gives the human a centeredness and completeness that allows the possibility for self-actualization and participation in a sacred reality. However, as previously noted, the freedom that marks the *imago Dei* in human nature is the same freedom that manifests itself in estrangement from God, as the story of the fall exemplifies. According to this story, humans can, in their freedom, choose to deny or repress their spiritual and moral likeness to God. The ability and desire to love one's self and others, and therefore God, can be neglected, even resisted.

The vision Jesus brings is one where the believer learns to identify and tease out that image in others. When Jesus acknowledges the serene faith of a pagan centurion (Matt 8:10), the persistent faith of a Canaanite woman (Matt 15:28), and the desperate faith of the thief on the cross (Luke 23:43), he is finding the *imago Dei* in the least likely people—foreigners and criminals. Romans, Canaanites, thieves, adulteresses (John 8), and Samaritans (John 4) were seen by the Jewish establishment as being on a par with dogs. As we mentioned, animals are not seen in Scripture as bearing the image of God, so to disregard the *imago Dei* in certain peoples is to treat them like animals. You never see Jesus doing that. Lepers, prostitutes, tax collectors, children, demoniacs—they were treated with great grace and respect by him. Even the hemorrhaging woman whose issue of blood made her perennially unclean is paraded by Jesus before the ogling crowd, her faith acknowledged by the Savior of the world for all to see. This was the scandalous Jesus at his most untamed.

If we reJesus the church, we will lead it toward a greater respect for the unbeliever, a greater grace for those who, though they don't attend church services, are nonetheless marked by God's image. It will lead to a greater respect for people in general. This is illustrated in Willa Cather's marvelous novel about Christian mission, *Death Comes for the Archbishop*. Set in the wild Arizona territories at the turn of the twentieth century, the book portrays the life stories of two Catholic missionaries, bringing the gospel to a melting pot of frontier families, Mexican settlers, and Native Americans. At one point, one of the priests, Father Vaillant, describes an experience that encapsulates his missionary call. It is one of the best descriptions of the missionary vocation:

Down near Tucson, a Pima Indian convert once asked me to go off into the desert with him, as he had something to show me. He took me into a place so wild that a man less accustomed to these things might have mistrusted and feared for his life. We descended into a terrifying canyon of black rock, and there in the depths of a cave, he showed me a golden chalice, vestments and cruets, all the paraphernalia for celebrating Mass. His ancestors had hidden these sacred objects there when the mission was sacked by Apaches, he did not know how many generations ago. The secret had been handed down in his family, and I was the first priest who had ever come to restore to God his own. To me, that is the situation in a parable. The Faith, in that wild frontier, is like a buried treasure, they guard it, but they do not know how to use it to their soul's salvation. A word, a prayer, a service, is all that is needed to free these souls in bondage. I confess I am covetous of that mission. I desire to be the man who restores these lost children to God. It will be the greatest happiness of my life.[16]

Father Vaillant's testimony is anchored in a belief in the *imago Dei*. The buried church supplies are symbolic of the image of God buried deep in the souls of all people. The missionary task is not to bring God to them but to uncover the *imago Dei* and assist people to use this knowledge for the salvation of their souls. Vaillant assumes that the gospel is buried deep in the soil of all people and it is his job, through "a word, a prayer, a service" to unearth this treasure and "restore to God his own."

Marked by Jesus

Put simply, to undertake the reJesus project one must first be committed to being marked by Jesus, to submit oneself to being shaped and changed to reflect more and more the lifestyle and teaching of Jesus. This idea is wonderfully portrayed by the much-loved novelist and short-story writer Flannery O'Connor. This devout Christian saw her function as a writer in part to shake the spiritual cataracts from her secular readers' eyes and open their vision to an incarnational faith and an awareness of the operation of grace in the everyday world. Within virtually every story she wrote was embedded the presence of grace, waiting to be accepted or rejected by her characters and her readers. She died before the age of forty, having spent the last decade of her short life suffering from the effects of lupus, the debilitating disease that was to claim her. One of the last stories she wrote was completed in a hospital bed in defiance of her doctor's orders not to push her failing body any further. "Parker's Back" is considered to be the crowning achievement of her

Christian vision as a writer because it marvelously illustrates the fact that the complete, most fulfilled human being is the one who incarnates Jesus in his or her life. It seems somehow fitting that O'Connor died writing it.

Obadiah Elihue Parker (that name is foreboding in itself) is a tragicomic country hick, a good-for-nothing who drifts from job to job and place to place. His only overriding interest seems to be the collection of tattoos that adorn nearly every inch of his skin, with the exception of his back. Inspired by a tattooed man he saw at a county fair when he was fourteen, OE has spent more than a decade covering the front of his body with a variety of images, trying to emulate what he remembered as the symphony of colorful images on that tattooed man. And yet with each new tattoo, his dissatisfaction grows. Whereas his hero's pictures looked harmonized and integrated, OE saw his own designs as haphazard and messy. In OE Parker, O'Connor has created the typical human, striving for redemption and yearning to be something beautiful. And yet each new attempt to correct the overall effect of his tattoos leads to even greater disappointment.

When we meet Parker, he has married the daughter of a fundamentalist preacher, a dour young woman named Sarah Ruth who would only marry him in the county clerk's office because she believed church buildings to be idolatrous. Sarah Ruth, outwardly religious and deeply pious, becomes the ironic foil for her heathen husband's search for redemption. She represents that kind of Christian that Dorothy L. Sayers identified as preferring to take Jesus in fairytale form, not straight from the Gospels. She has rules for everything, having learned all her life how to judge and find wanting every experience and every person.

Sarah Ruth, as one might imagine, despises Parker's tattoos. But more than that, she seems displeased with everything he does. In voicing her dissatisfaction as clearly and as often as she does, she reinforces Parker's disappointment with himself. He desires more than anything to do just one thing that would please her. In a sense, his quest for redemption becomes located in his focus on pleasing the unpleasable Sarah Ruth. For a man who has only ever performed menial jobs, who has no money and very few prospects, it's not surprising that in his simplistic way, he decides that the only thing he could do to please her is to get the right tattoo in the middle of his back.

He visualized having a tattoo put there that Sarah Ruth would not be able to resist—a religious subject. He thought of an open book with "HOLY BIBLE" tattooed under it and an actual verse printed on the page. This seemed just the thing for a while; then he began to hear her say, "Ain't I got a real Bible? What you think I want to read the same verse over and over for when I can read all of it?" He needed something better.[17]

Brow-beaten and anxious about choosing wrongly, he ends up in a tattooist's parlor leafing through a catalogue of religious images before being stopped by the piercing gaze of a Byzantine icon of the face of Christ. O'Connor describes how Parker felt he "were being brought back to life by a subtle power" as the image of Jesus takes hold of him. He decides there and then that the most pleasing thing he could do was to have his whole back tattooed with this face of Christ. The symbolism of "Parker's Back" isn't restrained. O'Connor is obviously depicting a man being marked by Jesus, inscribed with the express image of God. Albeit in a secular way, she is none-theless describing Parker's baptism, his initiation into the family of Jesus. As surely as any catechumen is being marked by Jesus at baptism, OE Parker is equally denoted as belonging to him. Where none of the other of his slapdash collection of tattoos can satisfy him, his whole back now bears the unified, single image of God.

But as you might expect, not even this painful act of sacrifice can win Sarah Ruth's approval. When he returns home and reveals the Byzantine Christ across his back, she is initially confused. "It ain't nobody I know," she says tellingly. The irony is bitter. The devout Christian woman cannot recog-nize the face of Jesus, while the recalcitrant heathen is stained by it forever.

"It's him," Parker said.

"Him who?"

"God!" Parker cried.

"God? God don't look like that!"

"What do you know how he looks?" Parker moaned. "You ain't seen him."

"He don't *look*," Sarah Ruth said. "He's spirit. No man shall see his face . . .

"Idolatry," Sarah Ruth screamed. "Idolatry . . . I don't want no idolater in this house!" And she grabbed up the broom and began to thrash him across the shoulders with it . . . and large welts . . . formed on the face of the tattooed Christ. Then he staggered and made for the door . . .[18]

Sarah Ruth can neither understand nor appreciate the incarnation. For her, God is a spirit, and no one can see his face. The idea that God has taken on human flesh and walked among us is beyond her comprehension and her spirituality. She prefers her Deity far beyond and distant. It is even less likely that she could comprehend the idea that her husband has chosen to incarnate God in his own body. The welts she leaves across the tattooed Jesus' face mirror the beatings that the real Jesus bore in his passion. The story ends most poignantly. Still gripping the broom and filled with rage, Sarah Ruth looks out toward a pecan tree in her yard: "her eyes hardened still more. There he was—who called himself Obadiah Elihue—leaning against the tree, crying like a baby."[19]

In this, the closing line of the story, O'Connor reminds us of Parker's full name. Obadiah, "servant of the Lord," Elihue, "God is he." Hanging on a tree, beaten by one who doesn't recognize his identity, bearing the hatred and condemnation of the woman who watches him, Parker is an embodiment of the incarnation. He is the suffering servant, the crucified one, and perhaps O'Connor is hinting that he has finally stepped into his name, living up to his calling at birth to be marked by God.

We confess that this calling is ours as well. Like Father Vaillant in *Death Comes for the Archbishop* and OE Parker, we too feel marked by Jesus and, as a result we see God, the church, and our world differently. We see God as the *missio Dei*, the church as the *participati Christi*, and the world as the *imago Dei*. And we echo Father Vaillant when he says, "I confess I am covetous of that mission. I desire to be the man who restores these lost children to God. It will be the greatest happiness of my life."

⟵ Notes

1. Frost, *Exiles*, 28–49.

2. M. Scott Peck, *Further Along the Road Less Traveled: The Unending Journey Toward Spiritual Growth* (New York: Simon and Schuster, 1993), 210.

3. Charles Sheldon, *In His Steps* (1896; repr., Peabody, Mass.: Hendrickson, 2004), 9. Originally published in 1896, this book was translated into twenty-one languages by 1935. It was the basis of the global campaign to take Jesus as guide and model that became known as the WWJD (What Would Jesus Do?) movement.

4. Terry Eagleton, "Was Jesus Christ a Revolutionary?" *New Internationalist*, May 1, 2008, 24.

5. Nick Cave, *The Gospel According to Mark with an Introduction by Nick Cave* (Melbourne: Text, 1998), xi.

6. Ibid.

7. Quoted in Laura Simmons, *Creed Without Chaos: Exploring Theology in the Writings of Dorothy Sayers* (Grand Rapids, Mich.: Baker, 2005), 78.

8. Dorothy L. Sayers, *The Man Born to Be King* (London: Victor Gollancz, 1955), 21.

9. Simmons, *Creed Without Chaos*, 79.

10. See Augustine In John 35.5; 36.8; 40.6; Chrysostom In John 53.2.

11. David Jacobus Bosch, *Transforming Mission: Paradigm Shifts in Theology of Mission* (American Society of Missiology 16; Maryknoll, N.Y.: Orbis, 1991), 390.

12. Jacques Matthey, "Congress 'Mission Dei' God's Mission Today: Summary and Conclusions (Reflector's Report)," (50th Anniversary of the World Mission Conference, August 16–21, 2002), 3.1. Cited 25 September 2008. Online: http://www.wcc-coe.org/wcc/what/mission/willingen.html.

13. Bosch, *Transforming Mission*, 519.

14. Robert McAfee Brown, quoted in "The Meaning of Life," *Life*, December 1988. Cited 25 September 2008. Online: http://www.maryellenmark.com/text/magazines/life/905W-000–037.html.

15. John Eldridge, *Wild at Heart* (Nashville: Thomas Nelson, 2006), 34.

16. Willa Cather, *Death Comes for the Archbishop* (1927; repr., New York: Vintage, 1990), 206–7.

17. Flannery O'Connor, "Parker's Back," *The Complete Stories of Flannery O'Connor* (New York: Noonday, 1992), 519.

18. Ibid., 529.

19. Ibid., 530.

ReJesus and Personal ReNewal

My mission is to introduce Christianity into Christendom.
—Søren Kierkegaard

We have to admit that there is an immeasurable distance between all that we read in the Bible and the practice of the church and of Christians. This is why I can speak validly of perversion or subversion, for, as I shall show, practice has been the total opposite of what is required of us.
—Jacques Ellul

We believe it is not possible to be following the biblical Jesus and not end up being molded by the *missio Dei, participati Christi,* and *imago Dei.* When taken captive by Jesus, we cannot help but see God, the church, and the world very differently. They are fundamental elements of a Jesus-shaped people. So, taking them as our starting point, let us now look more deeply into the nature and dynamic of the lifestyle and faith that Jesus taught and exemplified. We do this not so much to outline the contours of his teaching—so many books have done a better job of that than we can possibly accomplish—but rather to try and find its spiritual centers, to touch the wild and primal energy that radiates out of Jesus. In doing so, we believe we can begin to understand why it is that his people historically have obscured the dynamic of his message in various ways. And so from the broad framework we have explored so far, let us turn our attention to an exploration of connection between Jesus, the disciple, and the community of disciples, that is, the church. We use the term "disciple" deliberately because it emphasizes the kind of relationship that is decisive for the maintenance of a living connection with Jesus. For what is a church if not a community of disciples, of people devoted to following Jesus? If the New Testament is our guide in these matters, then discipleship should be the defining quality of the Christian life. And if this is the case, then we can never move from the more primal commitment that is involved in becoming his follower in the first place.

And yet, the ethos of discipleship and the presence of the wild Messiah are not readily associated with church and Christianity of our day. Far from it, our expressions of church range generally from what we might call high church, where Jesus tends to be relegated to some place in the outer echelons of the cosmos, to the more prevalent contemporary seeker-sensitive model where the radical message of Jesus is easily trivialized into some form of spiritual accessory in a consumerist paradise. From the fundamentalist co-option of Jesus as a religious fanatic to the liberal reduction of him into a schmaltzy moralist, it is probably fair to say that we have largely lost touch with our loving, wildly passionate, dangerous, radically merciful, and always surprising Redeemer-Lord. This is the Jesus so powerfully portrayed in the Gospels. The loss of the presence and power of *this* radical Jesus must surely account for a significant part of the spiritual bankruptcy of the church in the West. And therefore the importance of reJesus for spirituality and mission cannot be underestimated.

⟵ Rebooting to Jesus

If it is not already clear, let us state it emphatically: We believe that Christology is the key to the renewal of the church in every age and in every possible situation it might find itself. The church must always return to Jesus in order to renew itself. When, for whatever reason, the church gets stuck or loses its way in the world, it needs to recover its primal identity in its founder. It is not good enough to return to the founder of whatever denomination or organization we find ourselves in, although revitalization of that kind is not without merit. For Salvationists to rediscover the fire and fight within William Booth or for Methodists to have a re-encounter with John Wesley's passion and theology is valuable. But, when there is something fundamentally wrong in the basic equation of the faith, then it is time to recover a vital and active sense of Jesus: who he is, what he has done for us, the way of life he laid down for us to follow. His passions and concerns must become ours. In other words, as stated earlier, Christology must determine missiology (our purpose and function in this world), which in turn must determine ecclesiology (the cultural forms and expressions of the church).

Putting aside the issue of how missiology must inform ecclesiology (as that is dealt with in our previous books, specifically *The Shaping of Things to Come* and *The Forgotten Ways*), we believe that Christology is the singularly most important factor in shaping our mission in the world and the forms of *ecclesia* and ministry that result from that engagement. There must be a constant return to Jesus in order to ascertain that we are in the Way. It is no good just revamping our missiology or inventing new cultural forms of *ecclesia* unless we have first and foremost related them to Christology. This has become the misguided task of many so-called church renewal projects currently underway. Some such projects maintain that we need to get our theology and preaching right and renewal will flow from there. Others insist on Spirit-filled worship or alternative worship or church planting or a postmodernized approach to the faith. We are skeptical. Whenever these strategies are not anchored directly in a biblical Christology, they are doomed to limited effectiveness.

So, allow us to portray it this way:

Before there is any consideration given to the particular aspects of ecclesiology, such as leadership, evangelism, or worship, there ought to be a thoroughgoing attempt to reconnect the church with Jesus; that is, to reJesus the church as the first order of business. So much is bound up with this recovery of a radical New Testament Christology. The church's mission as well as its experience of community can be revitalized only by a renewed encounter with Jesus the Lord. And this is not something that is casual and intermittent. It requires a constant attention to the Lord of the church. As Wilhelm Visser T'Hooft once put it, "It belongs to the very life of the people of God that it must accept again and again to have its life renewed by a new confrontation with its Lord and his holy will."[1]

Think of it like a form of recalibration. When a machine gets jammed, the only way to kick-start it is to reset it to its original formulation. It's like a computer. When things go haywire and all else fails, we reboot it. By rebooting a computer, we restore its original operational settings, thus allowing it to function properly again. The software is back in sync with the

Resisting Evil

Dietrich Bonhoeffer

As a little Jesus, Dietrich Bonhoeffer refused to bend his knee to the Nazis, the empire of his time. His public resistance in 1933 to Hitler's policy to merge all Protestant churches into a pro-Nazi Protestant Reich Church put him at risk from the beginning. Bonhoeffer claimed defiantly that the church is not an organ of the state, but is subject only to Jesus and his mission. In 1939, faced with being drafted into the German army, he accepted an offer to teach at Union Seminary in New York. He returned home barely a month later, however, convinced that he would never have a voice in Germany after the war if he didn't stand with his people during it. He found an opportunity to resist Hitler through his brother-in-law Hans von Dohnanyi, an officer in the military intelligence agency Abwehr and a key figure in the covert resistance movement. Von Dohnanyi arranged for Bonhoeffer to travel to the Vatican and to Switzerland, where he helped a group of Jews cross the border, as well as to Sweden, where he met with British bishop George Bell to try to secure Allied support for a planned coup against Hitler. When the money used to smuggle the Jews across the border into Switzerland was traced to Bonhoeffer, the Nazis arrested him in 1943. While he was in prison, a group of Abwehr officers, including von Dohnanyi, attempted to assassinate Hitler but failed. The Nazis tied Bonhoeffer to this plot as well, and in 1945, a month before the surrender of the Germans, he was executed by hanging. Bonhoeffer's writings have inspired millions, but his courage in resisting evil and in paying the ultimate cost for his fidelity to the gospel is his greatest and most enduring legacy.

hardware again. This is precisely the image that we wish to convey—that by rebooting the church to Jesus, it will recover itself and become fully operational again.

The Bible describes Jesus as Alpha and Omega (Rev 1:8; 21:6; 22:13). It also describes him as founder and perfecter of faith (Heb 12:2). Surely these divine titles (functions?) must say something about the ongoing role of Jesus in the life of the disciple and in the life of the Christian community. If Jesus is as he claims, the Beginning and the End, then surely this must indicate that Christology claims central place in our self-understanding. If he is founder and perfecter, then he not only sets the primary template for authentic faith but also works at helping us bring it into mature expression.

We want to address this in two primary dimensions. First, the reJesus project for individual followers of Jesus is the reJesusing of personal discipleship. Second, in the next chapter, we will explore the impact of reJesus for the renewal of the church as an organization. This chapter is individually oriented; the next chapter is communal in focus.

↞The Capturing of Our Imaginations

Ignatius of Loyola, the founder of the Jesuits (one of the most significant Catholic missionary orders), developed a set of spiritual exercises for the initiation of new Jesuit candidates. The novel, and perhaps the most significant, aspect of the exercises was the requirement of the novitiate, as well as the established member, to activate their imaginations in order to encounter Jesus more directly. We will return to what this entailed in a later chapter, but for now it's enough to highlight why engaging Jesus through activating our imagination is an important thing to do.

Ask yourself what stimuli provoke your imagination on any given day. In other words, what stuff, coming at you from the world in which you live, most arouses or inspires you and your worldview? Television? Movies? Video games, sports, novels, business, the Internet? And yet these are not benign or valueless entertainments. They are owned or controlled by powerful forces in our society. They collectively contribute to a collective imagination that shapes us all: consumerist, materialist, individualist. In *Exiles*, Michael explored the way in which our post-Christian culture is not dissimilar to the empires into which the Old Testament exiles, Daniel, Esther, and Joseph, were repatriated. Our current empire is no more friendly to our faith than Babylon was to, say, Daniel's faith. Like all empires, our society seeks to maintain control over us in a variety of ways. These ways include

↞   the threat of violence (having a powerful army helps)

↞   the dominance of the economic system

↞   the capturing of the imagination of the people by various means (e.g., the ubiquitous use of Caesar's image throughout the empire on coins, artifacts, and statues)

On the last point, how is the ubiquity of Caesar's image any different from the intrusive and all-pervasive nature of the tools employed by our current empire for manipulating our imaginations? It, like all pervasive systems, seeks to claim our total allegiance by dominating our imaginations. Brian Walsh and Sylvia Keesmaat deal with this issue in their commentary of Paul's letter to the Colossians. They suggest that in order to overcome the ubiquitous and dominating claims of the Roman Empire, the Colossian Christians organized their lives and their thinking around a christological center. They cultivated an alternative imagination to the dominant imagination around about them and in so doing structured their lives around Jesus.[2] As we saw in chapter 1, this reorientation around Jesus changes everything.

One of the most urgent reasons why we need to re-envision ourselves around Jesus is that our imaginations so easily become captive to the dominant forces in our culture, whether those forces are economic, political, religious, or ideological. Furthermore, as we have already observed, our perceptions of Jesus readily become domesticated through familiarity, fear of change, spiritual indolence, or whatever keeps us from engaging Jesus as living Lord. Idolatry still has its lure, and in modern democratic societies and in the globalized, market-based economic system within which we all live it seems to have become almost totally pervasive and yet more subtle at the same time. There seems to be little ideological or religious alternative to the domination of the free-market-based consumption other than the reactionary responses of Islam. The Western church seems to have almost totally capitulated to the economic ideology of our day. Says Tom Sine,

> This imagery of the good life and a better future, that pervades Western society, is born of the Enlightenment and the rise of modernity. Essentially, the storytellers of the Enlightenment took the vertical quest for God's kingdom, which had been a centerpiece of European culture, and turned it on its side. It became the horizontal pursuit of western progress, technological mastery and economic growth.
>
> This vision of a better future is called the Western Dream or the American Dream, and now it is the driving myth behind the new imperial global economic order. In fact, as we will see, marketers of the new global order called McWorld, and the merchants of "cool" are seeking to influence people everywhere on this planet to live into this dream. And they are having stunning success.[3]

Furthermore, Walsh and Keesmaat state, "The messages are all telling the same story. . . . economic growth is the driving force of history, consumer choice is what makes us human, and greed is normal. If we live in an empire, it is an empire of global consumerism."[4] And the empire has a plan for our lives.

Into this profoundly religious empire, made up of the idolatrous lure of money, sexuality, competing ideologies and visions, comes an alternative vision of reality in the form of Jesus. The WWJD campaign invited us to imagine how Jesus would respond to the cultural and religious issues of our day. However, this question tended to become captive to a religious pietism that limited the issue to private morality and then further trivialized into an international campaign that focused almost entirely on the sexual ethics of young adult Christians. This is unfortunate, because WWJD has in it the capacity to become a global movement that takes the claims that Jesus makes over all of life seriously indeed. We would like to relaunch the campaign but this time keeping the broader issues in mind as well. What would Jesus do in the consumptive world in which we live? How would he respond to the environmental crisis? What would Jesus do with the banal depravities of reality television? What would Jesus do with our money and resources in a world of poverty and in need of grace and mercy? As we shall see in a later chapter, the lordship of Jesus cannot be limited to personal piety and must extend to all issues common to human experience. WWJD must extend to the issues of economics, environment, and politics if we are to truly unlock the world-renewing power inherent in the question.

Our imagination is such a powerful force. Jesus pointed out, "For where your treasure is, there your heart will be also" (Matt 6:21). In other words, the things that capture our imaginations (our treasures), whether they are wealth or sex or power, drag our hearts (our actions, our priorities) along with them. This is why he insisted that we store ourselves "treasures in heaven" (Matt 6:20). If we allow Jesus to capture our imaginations, our actions and priorities will mirror his lifestyle and teaching. The church needs an alternative imagination to that of the empire in which it finds itself.

In this respect, Walter Brueggemann comments on the role of the preacher as the source of an alternative, Christ-centered imagination. If the church needs to be continually reJesused, then those who give voice to the church's public speech ought to be committed to drenching the church's collective imaginations in the gospel. Says Brueggemann,

> The event of preaching is an event of transformed imagination . . . Because finally church people are like other people; we are not changed by new rules. The

deep places in our lives—places of resistance and embrace are reached only by stories, by images, metaphors and phrases that line out the world differently apart from our fear and hurt.[5]

We've heard too many sermons about how to be better citizens. Too much preaching is concerned with the fostering of a capitulation to the mores and values of a post-Christian empire rather than a call to allow our imaginations to be overtaken by Jesus and focused on treasures in heaven.

⟜The Conspiracy of Little Jesuses

Often the wake-up call to embrace an alternate imagination has to be made in a stark and uncompromising fashion. The 2005 film V *for Vendetta* is set in a totalitarian Britain in the not-too-distant future. The English have handed their imaginations (so to speak) over to a dictator whose empire is every bit as controlling as Caesar's. In fact, it resembles the Orwellian Britain of the novel 1984. A revolutionary in a mask, calling himself only V, embarks upon a program of civil unrest to shake people out of their stupor. In one scene, he takes over a British television studio and broadcasts an incendiary call to arms, concluding in the following manner:

. . . the truth is, there is something terribly wrong with this country, isn't there? Cruelty and injustice, intolerance and oppression. And where once you had the freedom to object, to think and speak as you saw fit, you now have censors and systems of surveillance coercing your conformity and soliciting your submission. How did this happen? Who's to blame? Well certainly there are those more responsible than others, and they will be held accountable, but again truth be told, if you're looking for the guilty, you need only look into a mirror. I know why you did it. I know you were afraid. Who wouldn't be? War, terror, disease. There were a myriad of problems which conspired to corrupt your reason and rob you of your common sense. Fear got the best of you, and in your panic you turned to the now high chancellor, Adam Sutler. He promised you order, he promised you peace, and all he demanded in return was your silent, obedient consent. Last night I sought to end that silence. Last night I destroyed the Old Bailey, to remind this country of what it has forgotten. More than four hundred years ago a great citizen wished to embed the fifth of November forever in our memory. His hope was to remind the world that fairness, justice, and freedom are more than words, they are perspectives. So if you've seen nothing, if the crimes of this government remain unknown to you then I would suggest you allow the fifth of November to pass unmarked. But if you see what I see, if you feel as I feel, and if you would seek as I seek, then I ask you to stand beside me one year from tonight, outside the gates of Parliament, and together we shall give them a fifth of November that shall never, ever be forgot.[6]

The film climaxes after V's death, with thousands and thousands of Britons, all wearing Guy Fawkes masks, marching on the Houses of Parliament in an unstoppable wave of resistance. V has duplicated himself in the lives of others. He has catalyzed a movement for change, for revolution. In this respect, V epitomizes what we've been talking about. He captures the imaginations of those who were previously held captive to the empire. He fashions a grand conspiracy in which hundreds of thousands of little Vs stand irresistibly against the totalitarian regime.

As mentioned earlier, Alan coined the phrase "the conspiracy of little Jesuses" to describe this same idea as portrayed in V for Vendetta. Jesus takes captive the imaginations of his followers and then replicates himself in them. In fact, we can sum up the task of discipleship as the lifelong project of literally becoming like him, of becoming a little Jesus. But the whole process of becoming more like him moves quickly beyond the individual to the group and from there to a movement. Even a superficial reading of the New Testament indicates that it was Jesus' strategic intention to create a movement consisting of Christlike people inhabiting every possible nook and cranny of culture and society—hence the idea of a mass conspiracy.[7]

Whether one talks about becoming a little Jesus or uses that wonderful old phrase "imitation (or following) of Christ," the essential function is clear—the modeling ourselves upon his life lies at the center of our spirituality. Says Kierkegaard,

> To be truly redeemed by Christ is, therefore, to impose on oneself the task of imitating him; As man Jesus is my model because as God he is my Redeemer; Christianity can be defined as a faith together with a corresponding way of life, *imitation of Christ*.[8]

The climactic scene in V for Vendetta, with countless Vs streaming out of side streets, leaping over barricades, and flowing like a torrent toward Parliament, represents the power that resides in such a conspiracy of imitation. Kierkegaard also said, "Unlike the admirer who stands simply aloof, the follower of Christ strives to be what he admires. Without this essential condition all attempts to be a Christian are fruitless."[9] This is the conspiracy of little Jesuses.

David Bosch rightly noted, "Discipleship is determined by the relation to Christ himself not by mere conformity to impersonal commands."[10] He said this when commenting on how preachers have used the Great Commission (Matt 28:18–20) to pressgang Christians into missionary service. Many well-intentioned church leaders have simplistically presented the words of Jesus, "Go therefore and make disciples of all nations," as some remote order barked by a stern sergeant-major. If Jesus said it, we should do it! But Bosch points out that missionary service that is motivated by blind obedience to an impersonal order from Jesus is built on a flimsy foundation. If our commitment to mission is only based on Jesus' "order" in Matthew 28, it makes mission an obligation for us rather than an act of love and grace. It's not unlike a woman who complains that her husband never brings her flowers. When the guilty husband rushes out and buys her a bouquet and presents it to her, she is still dissatisfied, because it wasn't that she wanted flowers in particular. What she wanted was for him to be motivated by his devotion for her so as to buy a gift. When we engage in mission only because we feel guilty that we haven't pleased Jesus and his order in the so-called Great Commission, we satisfy neither Jesus nor our own sense of calling. Rather, says Bosch, mission emerges from a deep, rich relationship with Jesus. The woman whose husband never brings her flowers doesn't want flowers. She wants him and his devotion. What Jesus is saying to his disciples in Matthew 28 is that little Jesuses will be naturally and normally about the business of making disciples, not to satisfy Jesus' demands but out of complete devotion for him. To paraphrase Bosch, the Great Commission is not a commission in the ordinary sense of the word, but rather a creative statement about the new order of things. Or as Garrett Green was noted for saying, "God is the one who conquers not by force, but by capturing the imagination of his fallen creatures."

However difficult it is to remain open to God, it is vital that this relationship must take the form of a direct and unmediated relationship with Jesus. It must involve a constantly renewed, up-to-date experience with our Lord. The loss of covenantal relationship results in a religion other than the one Jesus started. Even though it might take the forms of Christian faith, it will lack the reality of it.

That discipleship is foundational to Christianity and its mission therefore goes without saying. If we fail here, we will fail everywhere.[11] But the critical role of discipleship in the mission of the church once again highlights the role of the radical Jesus in the life of faith. And this bond cannot primarily merely involve a cerebral, objective, indirect understanding of Jesus and the Christian faith. This substitution of thinking about Jesus for existential encounter with Jesus is a constant temptation for the follower. This is partly because a living relationship with the Lord of the universe is a risky, disturbing, and demanding experience. We never get the better of him, and it is a whole lot easier, and less costly, to think than to do. It is not good enough that we just follow his teachings or a religious code developed in his wake. Discipleship requires a direct and unmediated relationship with the Lord, and the loss of this immediacy is catastrophic to the movement that claims his name.

Dallas Willard rightly bemoans the fact that for quite a while now the churches in the Western world have not made discipleship a condition of being a Christian.

> One is not required to be, or to intend to be, a disciple in order to become a Christian, and one may remain a Christian without any signs of progress toward or in discipleship. Contemporary Western churches do not require following Christ in his example, spirit, and teachings as a condition of membership—either of entering into or continuing in fellowship of a denomination or a local church. . . . So far as the visible Christian institutions of our day are concerned, discipleship clearly is optional. . . . Churches are therefore filled with "undiscipled disciples." "Most problems in contemporary churches can be explained by the fact that members have not yet decided to follow Christ."[12]

This living link between Jesus, discipleship, and authentic Christianity was highlighted by Dietrich Bonhoeffer when he says,

> Discipleship means adherence to Christ and, because Christ is the object of that adherence, it must take the form of discipleship. An abstract theology, a doctrinal system, a general religious knowledge of the subject of grace or the forgiveness of sins, render discipleship superfluous, and in fact exclude any idea of discipleship whatsoever, and are essentially inimical to the whole conception of following Christ. . . . *Christianity without the living Christ is inevitably Christianity without discipleship, and Christianity without discipleship is always Christianity without Christ.* [italics added][13]

The last sentence of this quote highlights the issue for us. At stake at the heart of discipleship is nothing less than the embodiment and transmission of the gospel. Who wants a Christianity without Christ? Well, if we are to avoid the ever-encroaching possibility of this form of spiritual deception, we had better be sure we keep our focus on disciple making as a key task. It is embodiment (our willingness to embody and live out Jesus' life and message) that creates spiritual authority. It also gives much needed credibility to our witness. And in the credibility of the message laid down through our lives lies the foundation for its authentic transmission from generation to generation and from culture to culture. Embodiment and (trans)mission therefore go together and all are bound inextricably to our relationship with Jesus.

Critic of Religiosity

Søren Kierkegaard

Like Jesus attacking Pharisaism, Søren Kierkegaard came out swinging against every phoney form of institutionalized Christianity. "An apostle proclaims the truth, an auditor is responsible for discovering counterfeits," wrote this nineteenth-century Danish philosopher and theologian. He saw it as his mission to be an auditor of Christendom, an institution he charged with sanitizing Jesus and making light of his message. Denmark's state church, he wrote, was "just about as genuine as tea made from a bit of paper which once lay in a drawer beside another bit of paper which had once been used to wrap up a few dried tea leaves from which tea had already been made three times." One of the fathers of existentialism, this remarkably complex and intelligent man underwent a profound spiritual transformation at the age of thirty-five and thereafter sought to apply some of his existentialist ideas to Christianity and thus reintroduce his nation to Jesus. Individuals, not the state, Kierkegaard argued, needed to make a "leap of faith" in order to enter into authentic Christianity. As a little Jesus, he hoped that his brutal attacks against the banality of institutional religion would anger Danish Christians enough to make them re-examine their relationship to Jesus.

The difficulty that we face in this issue of embodiment and transmission is that it is directly related to the credibility of the gospel. Our witness is a vital link in giving the claims of Jesus credibility in the eyes of non-Christian people. We are not allowed off the ethical hook by admitting that while our practice is poor, the beauty, purity, and truth of the Bible are nonetheless un-diminished. The Bible, claims Jacques Ellul, insists on the unity of the two:

> We have to understand this. No recognizable revelation exists apart from the life and witness of those who bear it. The life of Christians is what gives testimony to God and to the meaning of this revelation. "See how they love one another"—this is where the approach to the Revealed God begins. "If you devour one another, you do not have the love of God in you," etc. There is no pure truth of God or Jesus Christ to which we can return, washing our hands of what we ourselves do. If Christians are not conformed in their lives to their truth, there is [effectively] no truth. This is why the accusers of the eighteenth and nineteenth centuries

were right to infer the falsity of revelation itself from the practice of the church. This makes us see that in not being what Christ demands we render all revelation false, illusory, ideological, imaginary, and non-salvific. We are thus forced to *be* Christians or to recognize the falsity of what we believe. This is undeniable proof of the need for correct practice.[14]

Whether we like it or not, we carry the burden of having to live out the truth in such a way as to establish its viability among those who are watching. Shane Claiborne, author of *The Irresistible Revolution*, once surveyed a group of people who identified themselves as "strong followers of Jesus" and asked them, "Did Jesus spend time with the poor?" Around 80 percent replied in the affirmative, leaving a disturbing 20 percent of so-called strong followers of Jesus who think Jesus didn't spend time with the poor. That this could be the case should remind us of the levels of Christian ignorance about our founder and Lord. But the more disturbing fact is that Claiborne asked the same group, "Do you spend time with the poor?" Only 2 percent replied that they did. There is for many an almost complete disconnect between our beliefs about Jesus and our actions. This disconnection lies at the nub of the problem facing the church. Søren Kierkegaard expressed it this way: "Christ is the Truth inasmuch as He is the way. He who does not follow in the way also abandons the truth. We possess Christ's truth only by imitating him, not by speculating about him."[15]

But beyond issues relating to the mission of Jesus' people, the whole matter of the leadership and ministry of the church is also directly bound to discipleship. This is no small matter, and focused effort here must yield exponential results in terms of spirituality, ministry, and mission, because Jesus is thus made manifest in the life of his people.

Face Time with Jesus

Why the church tends to so easily lose this central focus on discipleship is a bit of a historical puzzle because it forms such a strategically significant part of our task as his people in the world. Perhaps it is because it is an essentially simple act that we tend to lose focus. Modeling ourselves on a hero comes naturally to us. We do it unconsciously all the time. This task of integrating life with our message has a long history of reflection and practice, even though it has seldom, if ever, been widely accepted by the majority of believers in the Western Christendom church. One of the particularly christocentric ways of seeing this process is called conformation (Rom 8:29; 2 Cor 3:18).

The Bible understands Christian formation in a way that is largely unfamiliar to us. In the New Testament, Jesus does not disciple people by generating information, developing programs, or implementing plans. Rather, Jesus' discipleship always involves a deeply personal process of being drawn into becoming more like the image, or form, of Jesus. The great German theologian Dietrich Bonhoeffer latched onto this idea and made it central to his understanding of discipleship and ethics. He said, "It comes only as formation into his likeness, as conformation with the unique form of Him who was made man, was crucified, and rose again."[16] For him, *conformation* was the way Jesus continues to incarnate himself in the world through his people: "The way in which the form of Jesus Christ takes form in our world is the concrete, obedient, con-formation of human beings to the form of the biblical Christ, the man whose existence for others is the world's true reality."[17] But he too pointed out that this cannot be a matter of abstract theologizing or merely developing discipleship programs or the like, but rather by the way of obedience to Jesus and his commands.

The image of Jesus to which we are called to conform to is not some sort of religious nut concerned with other-worldly religious matters as if the human issues don't matter. No, if the pattern is Jesus as we encounter him in the Gospels, then it means being drawn into the pattern of true humanity because Jesus models for us what it means to be a human being in the fullest sense. In Jesus, God has given us the archetype of what it means to be truly human. Now we must become more authentically human in the way that Jesus has set out for us, using Jesus' life as a model. It was never meant to be a matter of becoming a religious person but rather the forming of Christ in every person and in the life of the community of disciples.[18]

This idea of conformation focuses attention on the direct link with Jesus and his people. The loss of this relationship and this consciousness must surely lead to the decline in the spiritual keenness of the Christian. Conversely, the rekindling of our relationship with Jesus must surely lead to a renewal of the spirit. Surely the true disciple is the person who acknowledges Christ as a present reality in his or her life. This is what trusting Jesus is all about. It requires that we draw near to Jesus, live under his lordship, trust his saving work on our behalf, and in a concentrated act of worshipful and responsive love, conform our lives to his. Participating in the life of God "does not take place through ecstasy or any religious *tour de force* (feat of strength) but through Jesus

Christ. The saints are those who penetrate into the existence of Christ, who lift themselves not by their 'bootstraps', but by Christ's humanity into Christ's divinity."[19]

In trying to convey this need for immediacy between believer and Jesus, Kierkegaard coined a rather strange term, *contemporaneousness*. Although a cumbersome term, it is a useful one because it highlights the need for unmediated closeness between Jesus and his followers. He notes that for the believer, Jesus must be a "living reality, seen through the eyes of faith, and contemporaneous with each generation. His reality must be such that it transcends both time and space."[20] In Kierkegaard's thinking, therefore, contemporaneousness is a conscious effort by the believer to reach beyond the church's entire two-thousand-year tradition and, free of inherited presuppositions, encounter Jesus, seeing him with the eyes not of the first Christians but of the first eyewitnesses (crucifiers as well as disciples), and there, "in the painful tension of that dilemma; make his own choice as to whether Jesus is the God-Man who has an absolute claim to his life or a madman who should be avoided at all costs."[21] If Kierkegaard is right, then it is impossible to avoid this rather direct appointment with Jesus if we are to be saved and to truly follow him. A Christian must be a person who has engaged, and is engaging, Jesus directly. And it is only through the lifelong imitation of Christ, not just one encounter, that genuine contemporaneousness is fully achieved.

Without laboring the point, let us reinforce our conviction that such contemporaneousness is not simply a matter of getting one's theology right (whatever *right* might mean). Biblical faith cannot be reduced to believing in a set of doctrines, and neither can discipleship be seen in these terms. Faith, as Luther (re)discovered, is more like the supreme gamble in which we stake our lives upon a conviction. It can't be reduced to belief in a set of propositions. It is a profoundly existential act in which we are fully and personally involved. Contemporaneousness cannot be attained by speculation but only by the active presence of Christ in my own existence. There is much more to being a disciple than believing and trusting Jesus at the outset; Christianity also involves a well-defined way of existence, a way of life that can be summed up in the phrase "the imitation of Christ." When we choose this way, we take it upon ourselves to be his constant companion, his follower, his contemporary. All the aspects of our discipleship (worship, ritual, prayer, mission, theologizing) are in one sense or another directed toward the achievement of contemporaneousness. Christ's whole life in all its aspects must supply the norm for the life of the following Christian and thus for the life of the whole church.[22]

⟵ The Who? And the What?

So what can we use as our flashlight as we travel along this path towards Jesus? There are core truths about Jesus that provide the broad contours of the faith he set for us to journey toward. Understanding these enable us to repeatedly touch base with the elemental aspects that make Jesus and his way so special. They can provide the compass, if you will, that we can consult to see if we (individual followers and/or community of faith) are consistent with the wild and untamable Lord of the church.

Jesus' Life and Teaching	Implications for Disciple/Church	Examples of How These Could Be Lived Out
Ushers in the kingdom of God and focuses it around his own person (e.g., Mark 1:14–15; Luke 11:20)	Living under the King (see later chapter on existential monotheism, ch. 5). The kingdom of God is central and extends in and beyond the church to his entire cosmos. We are agents of the kingdom in all spheres of life common to human being. Jesus is Lord/King! We can live and work wherever we are, and we can expect the kingdom to already be there.	When we are at work, we invite Jesus to accompany us there. We look for opportunities to enact Jesus' qualities while we are working. We look for ways to mirror the work of God even through the most mundane and everyday activities.
Demands direct and active faith/trust in God (e.g., Mark 1:14–15, Matt 17:20)	Requires a radical openness to the sovereign and miraculous intervention of God in us. Faith as trust demands a distinct form of spiritual openness on our behalf. We should expect God to be involved in all aspects of our lives.	We refuse to give up when a situation seems hopeless; we have faith in God to work in the situation, somehow. We must not give in to our fears.
Mediates the grace and mercy of God (e.g., Matt 12:7)	Openness to receive as well as impart grace/mercy to others. The measure we give will be the measure we receive. We can be generous with both our resources and our time. God is merciful; we must try to find ways to be like God in daily life.	We refuse to rule out the unlikely agents of grace in our midst. Whether someone is uneducated, elderly, divorced, an ex-convict, disabled, or even just needy or annoying, we humbly accept their gifts to us as if they were from God.
Offers forgiveness of sins (e.g., Matt 9:2; Luke 7:47)	Repentance and forgiveness are a way of life (70x7). Radical openness to a holy God will require that we be constantly aware of our sinfulness and the possibility of radical evil that lurks in the human soul. Also, we must be a forgiving people (Matt 6:15).	We examine ourselves carefully for any bitterness or lack of forgiveness toward others. We place ourselves in relationships of accountability. We are open to the rebuke of the loving friend. We confess our limitations regularly.
Demonstrates the love of God for his world (e.g., John 3:16; 14:21)	Demands our primary love for God and a secondary love for others in his name. We need to know we are a loved people, and this should be expressed towards others. This love should include but extend beyond our family members to embrace even our enemies. We should be known as a people of love.	Our loves shows God's love. We show love to our family members and do so reflecting on the way it is an outpouring of the love we have received from God. We practice hospitality to the stranger. We create spaces in which others can grow and find grace.

Jesus' Life and Teaching	Implications for Disciple/Church	Examples of How These Could Be Lived Out
Heals the sick and casts out demons (e.g., Mark 1:23ff.; Luke 11:20)	Healing ministry should be part of the church's service in the world. These are signs of the kingdom's presence (John 14:12). We live in a wounded world: we should actively look for opportunities to heal people in body, psyches, and relationships.	We look for opportunities to pray for people, comfort people, reconcile with people. We must not shrink back from prayer for the sick or from engaging in spiritual warfare when necessary.
Calls all to follow and imitate him (e.g., Matt 4:19; 8:22)	He is the image of the human. Not only Savior but also God's pattern for authentic human life. This requires a following after, an imitation of Jesus . . . discipleship. It also involves a willingness to go against the flow and to stand with Jesus and his cause in the world. Even to the point of suffering and martyrdom. It will also mean we are more "attractive" to sinners and outcasts (as Jesus was).	We look for opportunities to disciple other Christians. We volunteer at a soup kitchen and sit down and talk with the clients, even if their appearance and actions make us uncomfortable.
Radicalizes the current standards of holiness (e.g., the Sermon on the Mount) (e.g., Matt 5–8)	Jesus sets a challenging ethical and moral code for the disciple/church to follow. The Sermon on the Mount is the most used discipleship text in the history of the church. This not only describes but prescribes the life of discipleship. We should make it a basic reference text and seek to live it out.	We practice hospitality, generosity, humility, and justice. We believe our faith brings not just personal salvation but a motivation for changing the world to reflect the justice and peace of God.
Introduces a distinctly non-religious (even anti-religious) way of loving and worshiping God (e.g., Matt 21; John 4:20ff)	Real countercultural forces are unleashed in the gospel. We therefore should be willing at times to go against the flow and status quo. People should be able to see that we are followers of Jesus—not that we are religious. Religious people can be off-putting to many non-Christians.	We challenge our faith community to join a secular group doing work that Jesus would approve of, even if we disagree with some of the other views the group holds.
Shows love and compassion for the poor and oppressed (e.g., Luke 4:18–19; 7:22–23)	We must serve the marginalized and downtrodden in Jesus' name. And this will mean we sometimes stand in direct opposition to systems and lifestyles that engender oppression—be they political, social, or religious systems.	We work with a group that helps HIV/AIDS victims, even though some of our Christian friends think this isn't a cause Christians should be involved with.
Befriends the outcast and misfit (e.g., Matt 9:9–12; Luke 19:10)	We should refuse to exclude people from fellowship based on cultural preferences. Also, we should be hanging around a lot more "freaks" than we ordinarily do. There is something we have to learn from the margins of society that we cannot learn from the center.	We make a point of welcoming visitors to our church who do not appear to fit in. We collect "freaks" and outcasts and look for what they can teach us about Jesus.
Follows the pattern of God's redemption (e.g., Luke 15:4–32)	We must act redemptively because God is a redeemer. We restore what has been lost or broken. Mission involves the redemption of broken people and lost culture. We don't judge, we redeem.	We aim at restoration and beauty, creativity and grace, hospitality and generosity. We live, love, play, and suffer, better than anyone else, for God is our Redeemer.

Jesus' Life and Teaching	Implications for Disciple/Church	Examples of How These Could Be Lived Out
Proclaims (as well as lives) the good news of the kingdom (e.g., Matt 5:13–16)	We should proclaim (as well as live) the good news of Jesus. In a sense we are (and must become) good news. (We *are* salt/light.) Love, forgiveness, mercy, compassion, righteous anger . . . these are the marks of a disciple.	We socialize with unbelievers. We pray with them. We model an alternate reality by our alternate lifestyle. We are always ready to give an answer for the hope within us. We acknowledge the ministry of the gifted evangelists among us.
Presents an existential call to the whole person (e.g., Matt 22:37–40)	We must respond with all that we are, not just believe with our heads or our bodies. The love of God engages heart, head, mind, will, body, etc. We cannot compartmentalize our lives in ways that divide our total devotion to God.	We see that pleasures are from God. But we direct them towards God, acknowledging that God gave them to us in the first place. We engage intellectually, emotionally, and bodily in the life God has given us.
Offers new beginnings (e.g., John 3:1–7; Luke 7:38–50)	We must be born again. We are the people of the new start! We must offer new starts to others. Give people a go. Learn to actively forgive.	We remember that we have received forgiveness and that others need it as well. We tell others of Jesus' gift of a new start and a life with God.
Hates hypocrisy (e.g., Matt 23:28ff.; Luke 12:1)	In Jesus' teaching, self-righteousness is abhorred! Mentioned far more than sexual sin, this is unacceptable sin of the spirit for disciples of Jesus. We have been forgiven much; we must be willing to offer the same grace to others.	We listen humbly when others point out our faults. We remember not to put sexual sins higher on the scale of sin than the more "spiritual" sins of hypocrisy and pride, since Jesus said more about these than about sexual sin.
Is coming again (e.g., Luke 11; Matt 25:1–13)	An adoring and expectant longing for his presence and return (like a betrothed virgin awaiting the bridegroom). He completes us. He also comes in judgment on unrighteousness. It's going to be a big day!	We hold on to a sense of Jesus' return and our need to live urgently. Seize the day! "Live as if Jesus died yesterday, was raised today, and is coming tomorrow" (Luther).
Lays down life for friends (e.g., John 15:13)	Calls us to self-sacrificial lifestyle. We are called to be servants to a lost and broken world (Matt 23:11–12).	We decide to give up a luxury— perhaps cable TV, dinners out, or cell phone games—and give the money to a good cause.
Brings salvation (e.g., Luke 1:76–77; 19:9)	We need to be saved. This is not only a decision, it is a lifelong process (Phil 2:12). Also, we are the messengers of salvation. Salvation in the Hebrew mind has connotations of healing and wholeness. We need to apply salvation holistically.	We hold on to the idea of salvation as a process in which we are involved on a daily basis.

We don't believe this list is exhaustive, nor do we think that it is even an adequate summary of the faith that has captured the hearts and imaginations of hundreds of millions over two thousand years of history. In fact, we suggest that readers might wish to compile a list of the central ideas and implications of Jesus and his teaching for themselves. It's a great exercise to remind the disciple of the essentials of the faith.

Following Missional Jesus

Scot McKnight, biblical scholar and blogger, has done something similar with his blog series called "Missional Jesus." He draws no conclusions as to how we ought to live as followers, but we believe that it should be reasonably clear how Jesus acted and affected those around him—readers can draw their own conclusions. Here is our summary/excerpting of the series.[23]

Bible Text Examined	Subject of Blog Entry
Luke 4:16–30	• Missional Jesus publicly announces the centrality of himself to the mission of God (4:21). • Missional Jesus sees his own mission in Isaiah 61:1–2, that means his mission involves justice for the poor, prisoners, the blind, and the oppressed. • The mission of Jesus is a Jubilee mission (4:19). • The mission of Jesus creates disturbances and rejection (4:24). • Homies reject Jesus (4:24–29). • The mission of Jesus will extend beyond the normal boundaries.
Luke 5:1–11	• Missional Jesus is a preacher of the word (5:1–3). • Encountering the missional Jesus brings bewilderment, wonder, and awe—leading to repentance (5:5, 8, 9–10). • Missional Jesus shares his mission with those who are attached to him (5:10). • Those who participate in the mission of Jesus are called to enlist others in the mission of Jesus (5:11).
Luke 9:57–62	• Missional Jesus knows the cost to the body (9:58). • Missional Jesus knows the cost to the family life when it comes to sacred customs (9:59–60). • Missional Jesus knows the cost to the family life when it comes to simple social courtesies (9:61–62). • Missional Jesus wants all from his followers, he wants them to make that decision now, and he demands all because he knows the kingdom of God is worth it.
Matthew 4:23–25	• Overall, missional Jesus did what was good for others. • Missional Jesus taught in typical centers of religious education. • Missional Jesus preached—which means declared good news—about the kingdom of God. What is the kingdom of God? Kingdom for Jesus is the "society in which God's will is established and transforms all of life." • Missional Jesus healed. • Missional Jesus was attractive.
Matthew 7:12	• Missional Jesus accepts anyone who comes to him for healing. • Missional Jesus breaks down boundaries between Gentiles and Jews. • Missional Jesus heals Gentiles too. • Missional Jesus believes that what mattered was faith in God (through Jesus) and not ethnic heritage and religious association. • Missional Jesus lauds the perception of faith in him as faith in the One who is sent by God with authority.

Bible Text Examined	Subject of Blog Entry
Mark 12:29–31	• Missional Jesus confronts the evil at home in persons ravaged by evil spirits. • The evil world recognizes missional Jesus as a threat of power. • Missional Jesus' power is intimidating and awe-inspiring, but it doesn't mean everyone who perceives turns into a follower of Jesus. • Missional Jesus summons those released from evil to witness to the mercy he [the Lord] has shown them. • Missional Jesus knows his mission is a spiritual battle.
Matthew 9:32–34	• Missional Jesus attracts those who are possessed by evil—the way flames attract moths. • Missional Jesus, therefore, attracts folks who know that Jesus can heal them. • Missional Jesus can flat-out cure folks. • Missional Jesus is opposed by the religious authorities: to the degree that they call him demon-possessed.
Matthew 9:35–10:4	• Missional Jesus participates in the mission of God. • Missional Jesus therefore prays to God for "extenders" of his mission-working kingdom of God. • Missional Jesus prays because he is moved by oppression and the need for mercy on so many. • Missional Jesus specifically identifies 12 workers for the kingdom and appoints them as his personal representatives in the kingdom work. • Missional Jesus appoints his "extenders" to do what he has been doing in Matthew. They are therefore extenders of Jesus and not doers of their own mission. Missional work is Jesus work. • Not all of Jesus' "extenders" follow Jesus faithfully.
Matthew 10:5–8	• Missional Jesus has a targeted audience. They are Jews. • Missioners of the missional Jesus have one message: God's kingdom. • Missioners do what Jesus did and extend what Jesus did and say what Jesus said. They are to "be" Jesus in a new place in order to extend Jesus and his kingdom into new places.

What we can say is that without qualification, the Gospels present us with the most compelling portrait of a person who was so wonderfully human, and yet one who lifted us up beyond the merely human and has shown us the life of God (John 14:9). He is the God whom we love and who is worthy of adoration. We will not let go! And we refuse to subvert this life in the petty concerns of church polity or middle-class mediocrity. We will strive to do anything in our strength to assure that in his church, he is named as Lord.

Another voice singing from this same song-sheet is Irish songwriter Sinéad O'Connor, who in 2007 released her album *Theology*, an anthology of reflections on various Old Testament passages that cry out in anguish for a faith not stained by the church that bears God's name. Raised Catholic, the brunt of her attacks has invariably been borne by the church of her childhood, but the sting in her beautiful songs can be felt by any church or denomination that shuts Jesus out of its religious system. In her searing lament, "Out of the Depths," she captures the psalmist's brokenhearted cry for mercy. It begins with a paraphrase of Psalm 130:1:[24]

> Out of the depths I cry to you
> O LORD.

In her song she imagines this lament being sung for a God who is locked out of his own church. The song closes with the lines:

> And it's sad but true how the old saying goes
> If God lived on earth people would break his windows

What a line! To truly understand God we must see him as the humbled one, the attacked one. Jesus' windows were all broken by the time he ascended the gentle slope of Golgotha. Sinéad ends the song by breathlessly repeating several times the Old Testament line (Ps 130:6a):

> I long for you as watchmen long for the end of night.

This is our longing, too. Renewal will begin with each of us. But like the conspiracy of the little Jesuses, it will have consequences for the renewal of the church as a whole. And to that subject we now turn our attention.

⟶ Notes

1. Wilhelm Visser T'Hooft, *The Renewal of the Church* (London: SCM, 1956), 1.

2. Brian J. Walsh and Sylvia C. Keesmaat, *Colossians Remixed* (Downers Grove, Ill.: InterVarsity, 2004), ch. 2–3.

3. Tom Sine, *The New Conspirators* (Downers Grove, Ill.: InterVarsity, forthcoming).

4. Walsh and Keesmaat, *Colossians Remixed*, 85.

5. Walter Brueggemann, *Finally Comes the Poet* (Minneapolis: Augsburg Fortress, 1989), 23.

6. *V for Vendetta*, directed by James McTeigue (Burbank, Calif., Warner Bros., 2005).

7. Hirsch, *Forgotten Ways*, 113.

8. Louis K. Dupré, *Kierkegaard as Theologian: The Dialectic of Christian Existence* (London: Sheed & Ward, 1964), 171.

9. Ronald Grimsely, *Kierkegaard: A Biographical Introduction* (London: Studio Vista, 1973), 103.

10. Bosch, *Transforming Mission*, 67.

11. Hirsch, *Forgotten Ways*, 102.

12. Dallas Willard, *The Spirit of the Disciplines*, quoted in R. J. Foster and J. B. Smith, *Devotional Classics*, rev. ed. (San Francisco: HarperOne, 2005), 14.

13. Dietrich Bonhoeffer, quoted in John A. Phillips, *The Form of Christ in the World: A Study of Bonhoeffer's Christology* (London: Collins, 1967), 100.

14. Ellul, *Subversion of Christianity*, 6–7.

15. Søren Kierkegaard, *Training in Christianity*, quoted in Dupré, *Kierkegaard as Theologian*, 172.

16. J. A. Woelfel, *Bonhoeffer's Theology: Classical and Revolutionary* (Nashville: Abingdon, 1970), 254.

17. Ibid.

18. Ibid., 255, 256.

19. Romano Guardini, *The Lord* (London: Longmans, 1954), 447.

20. Vernard Eller, *Kierkegaard and Radical Discipleship: A New Perspective* (Princeton: Princeton University Press, 1968). Cited 25 September 2008. Online: http://www.hccentral.com/eller2/part12a.html.

21. Ibid., e-text.

22. Søren Kierkegaard, journals, November 26, 1834, quoted in David J. Gouwens, *Kierkegaard as Religious Thinker* (Cambridge: Cambridge University Press, 1996), 173.

23. Scot McKnight's "Missional Jesus" series can be found online at http://www.jesuscreed.org/?cat=39.

24. Sinéad O'Connor, "Out of the Depths," *Theology* (Koch Records, 2007).

Chapter Three

ReJesus for the Church and the Organization

*Christ's whole life in all its aspects must supply the
norm for the life of the following Christian and thus for
the life of the whole Church.*
—Søren Kierkegaard

*All religious institutional embeddedness—whether
in the form of temple worship, unjust social systems,
or repressive religious practices—is challenged
by the revelation of God in the life, death, and
resurrection of Jesus.*
—Gail O'Day

In Revelation 3:20, we hear these famous words of Jesus: "Listen! I am stand-ing at the door, knocking; if you hear my voice and open the door, I will come in to you and eat with you, and you with me." We generally interpret this to say that Jesus is standing at the door of our hearts and asking us to allow him to come in. Even though we can appreciate the sentiment, the verse itself has nothing to do with personal evangelism. The specific church in question in Rev-elation 3 is that in Laodicea, the famously lukewarm church that Jesus wanted to vomit out of his mouth. The image here is of Jesus standing outside of the church asking to come in. The question that should spring to our minds is, "What is he doing on the outside of the church when he is meant to be the Lord of that very church?" But of course, John's revelation of the seven messages to the seven churches is given to us as a warning that we not make the same er-rors. Jesus is outside the door of the church in Laodicea! How is this also true for many communities and organizations that claim the name Christian? The question we ask in introducing this chapter must be, is Jesus similarly outside the door of your church? Have we shut him out of the fellowship of the insiders? And what has been the result?

⟵ReJesusing Our Organizations

As is now clear, our basic assumption is that Jesus provides the primary template for us as individual followers but also for the church as the community that is in Christ and that walks in his way. As stated earlier, we believe that the church must constantly return to Jesus to find itself again, to recalibrate, to test whether we are indeed in the faith. The inference is that by and large the church as we currently experience it in the West has to varying degrees lost touch with the wild and dangerous message that it carries and is duty bound to live out and to pass on. As Jesus' disciples we are called to a Christlike life, and no matter how we configure it, that must surely mean that somehow our lives and our communities must be in significant congruence with the life, teachings, and mission of Jesus. The degree that we are living the life laid out by our Master is directly proportional to the degree that we can call ourselves authentic disciples.

This might well sound like idealism to some more pragmatically inclined readers, and perhaps rightly. They may well point out the fact that as things now stand, we have built and established a massive global religion comprising thousands of organizations with massive capital and resources. And there is no denying that such organizations do manage to help many people and bring many to faith. Therefore, they might consider it an indulgence on our part to be prattling on about the radical life of Jesus when, whether we like it or not, we are now obligated to maintain those religious organizations with their associated programs, paid professionals, ideologies, capital, buildings, and so on. Theirs is a call to pragmatism over radicalism, although, we suspect, in more honest moments many of them would probably admit that much that we do seems to have only an indirect correlation to the uncluttered, nonreligious, life-oriented faith so compellingly portrayed in the Gospels. These objectors might, in spite of their deepest spiritual intuitions, simply say that we have no choice but to continue to operate the services and maintain the system or else the whole edifice might crumble.

And others still might add the fact that along with the institution of the church we have long and complex histories that have shaped us, carried us, and landed us where we are today. They would suggest that we are indeed inheritors of a grand religious tradition with rich rituals that has evolved from the early Christian movement even though it is not really the same phenomenon now. For them, the church as we have it is their reality, and they can't, indeed they won't, go back to some simple, somewhat naïve, aesthetically bankrupt, primitive Jesus-like faith of biblical Christianity. Such people will no doubt believe that for good or ill, Christianity now exists, embedded, in its rituals, dogmas, priesthoods, cathedrals, and other religious accoutrements and that the idealism of a reJesus project has no place in the sensible Christian religion we now have.

And we must admit that there is substance to both these responses—the pragmatic and the traditionalist. The institution of the church (traditional and contemporary) is not without God, beauty, or blessing. And we recognize that deeply spiritual people have tirelessly worked for their advancement. We don't wish to suggest that it is worthless (and please forgive us if we have given this impression), but we cannot escape the question, "Is this really what Jesus intended for his movement?" And isn't all this paraphernalia the very thing that partly obscures our access to the vital faith that we all seek and long for? Does advancing in the kingdom of God boil down to this? Running programs and services and/or guiding the laity through liturgical complexities in order to help people get to the God they are all meant to access directly through Jesus anyhow? Was this what Jesus had in mind when he established the church (Matt 16:18–19)?[1] And, whatever happened to the doctrine of the priesthood of all believers that many within the Protestant movements are meant to adhere to (1 Pet 2:9)?

We are not insensitive to the fact that a great many people feel connected to Jesus via the stained-glass imagination of grand ecclesiastical traditions. Nor do we dispute that contemporary-style seeker churches have given many people new hope and led them into a real experience of Christian faith. It would be ignorant of us to do so. God is everywhere, and his grace is manifest wherever he so chooses.

However, whatever case can be made for the status quo, none of us can, or should, avoid the spiritual test of evaluating the validity of our preferred expression of church by cues offered by Jesus the Messiah. Unless we can validate who we are and what we do by lining ourselves up with the measure that Jesus laid down in his life and work, then what in God's name are we doing? And how can we legitimately call ourselves Christ-ian, unless what we are doing is built squarely on the rock of Jesus and takes its direct agenda (and direct cues for its organizations and lifestyle) from him? His *modus operandi*, his teaching, his critique of religion, his commitment to the way of the kingdom, must become our primary source of guidance. We believe that in order to find renewal (organizational, communal, and personal) we need to rediscover Jesus

Evangelistic Activism

Alan Walker

Alan Walker was an Australian evangelist and theologian born in 1911 who devoted his life to both social activism and evangelism. In the 1950s Alan Walker launched a three-year-long evangelistic tour across Australia and New Zealand, in which he preached to more than half the total populations of each country. Evangelistic rallies like this were relatively common in Australia at the time; by the early twentieth-century fundamentalist preachers from the United States had begun regular visits to the country to conduct similar evangelism circuits. But the scale of Walker's itinerary was unique in that he heralded the integration of evangelism and social activism in a day when the Protestant church generally saw the two realms as incompatible. He also had the moral courage to be an outspoken critic of the racist "White Australia" policy as early as 1938, when the church had been largely silent on the issue. As a pacifist during World War II, and the Vietnam War, he attracted the ire of the media but remained true to his convictions. After his last evangelical tour in 1958, he took over the leadership of the Methodist Central Mission in Sydney, Australia and developed it into one of the country's largest social justice agencies. He was expelled twice from South Africa for his anti-apartheid stance and was knighted by the Queen of England, befriended by Martin Luther King Jr., and dubbed "the conscience of the nation" by the Governor-General of Australia. Alan Walker embodies Jesus because his social activism was never at the expense of his evangelistic passion; "Let it never be forgotten that it is Christ we offer."

afresh even though this be a dangerous course of action because it calls into question so much of what we might build our various religious houses on. At the beginning of this new century, we have never needed so desperately to rediscover the original genius of the Christian experience and to allow it to strip away all the unnecessary and cumbersome paraphernalia of Christendom.

It has surprised us that in recent years even our secular culture has been demanding this project of reJesusing the church. A number of filmmakers (secular prophets of our time?) have recently depicted Christlike characters in conflict with the institutionalized church. Those church leaders who have dismissed these films as savage attacks on Christ have missed the point. Films such as *Jesus of Montreal*, *Chocolat*, and *As It Is in Heaven* are not attacks on Jesus. They are scathing critiques of institutional Christianity, but they all portray their messianic-like protagonists with great sympathy, even reverence.

The most allegorical of them, the Canadian film *Jesus of Montreal*, depicts an out-of-work actor, Daniel, who is commissioned to breathe new life into a church passion play but who enrages the religious authorities when he stages it in an all-too-real manner. As he researches and rehearses the story of Jesus (tellingly, under the gaze of a stone statue of Christ outside the church), Daniel's life begins to mirror that of Christ's. Like Jesus, he gathers around him a troupe of misfits and outcasts—a man who dubs porno films, an overlooked middle-aged actress, a model often reduced to exposing her breasts for casting agents. Like Jesus, Daniel molds this band into a proud, functional community of grace and forgiveness. Like Jesus, Daniel appeals to the common people. His play is soon the talk of Montreal, with hundreds of non-churchgoers lining up for tickets. And inevitably, like Jesus, he finds himself in serious conflict with religious leaders, who are so outraged by his earthy, passionate portrayal of Christ they decide to shut the play down, resulting in Daniel's tragic death.

Jesus of Montreal is more than a drama about an actor who becomes consumed by his role. It is an allegory in which Daniel is essentially a Christ figure right from the opening John-the-Baptist parallel scene. And while it offers us an agnostic retelling of Jesus' life, we wouldn't expect a secular filmmaker to do anything else. But if we're wise, we'll listen to the film's basic premise: if Jesus really did turn up in Montreal, the church would be his greatest enemy!

Likewise, in two other films, Christ figures turn up in small communities, offering hope to the marginalized but ending up in conflict with the church establishment. In *Chocolat*, a woman called Vianne transforms a dour French village with love and grace (and, of course, chocolate) and is nearly run out of town by the mayor, who is the overbearing power behind the meek priest. In *As It Is in Heaven*, an internationally famous symphony conductor retires to the small Swedish town of his childhood and is inveigled into directing the local Lutheran church choir. His methods are so radical that he transforms the rag-tag amateur singers into a world-standard choir, but in so doing he finds that the Lutheran minister has become his sworn enemy. Like Daniel, he too dies tragically but leaves behind a group of men and women who will never be the same.

We don't suggest that we should take our cue from filmmakers, but these movies have intuited something important and are popular precisely because they hit a nerve in their audiences. Even though they might prefer to depict decidedly nondivine Christ figures, they do speak to an audience that believes the real Christ was more about transforming a small band of followers than running a wealthy religious institution. These films, and many more besides, insist that a faithful, determined, loving, honest community of friends, inspired by an extraordinary visionary, can change its worlds. Daniel's acting troupe resolve to carry on his work by establishing an avant-garde actors' studio. Vianne's friends from the chocolate shop initiate a revolution that eventually sees the dismal village change into a vibrant colorful community. And in As It Is in Heaven, the conductor, also called Daniel, dies of a heart attack listening to his choir win a prestigious choral contest in Austria, knowing they have achieved a sense of harmony rarely accomplished by even the best choirs.

The message these films seem to be making was also expressed by anthropologist Margaret Mead, when she wrote, "Never doubt that a small group of thoughtful, committed citizens can change the world. Indeed, it is the only thing that ever has."[2] How different is this from the revolution forged by Jesus? We do well to remember Roland Allen's profound observation about missional movements and how they center on Jesus:

> The spontaneous expansion of the Church reduced to its element is a very simple thing. It asks for no elaborate organization, no large finances, no great numbers of paid missionaries. In its beginning it may be the work of one man and that of a man neither learned in the things of this world, nor rich in the wealth of this world. What is necessary is faith. What is needed is the kind of faith which uniting a man to Christ, sets him on fire.[3]

We feel that at this critical juncture of history, when the church is forced to find itself again by the sheer circumstance of the adaptive challenge of the twenty-first century, we must return to being that simple, uncluttered, passionate community of Christ, filled with the love of God that so imbued our spiritual ancestors. We must reignite our passion directly from Jesus' flame. This process of going back to our generative center will mean a process of rediscovering Jesus afresh. We need to reJesus our organizations.

⟵ Christianity Minus Christ Equals Religion

In order to get to the nub of the problem, let's reverse the way of looking at the process of reJesus: let us think about what happens when you take Jesus out of the experience of Christianity. To see this consider the following equation:

Christianity − Christ = Religion

It makes sense, doesn't it? Some statements have an immediate ring of truth about them, and for many Christians this is one of them. Of course, Christianity without the lifeblood, the vision, the love of the real Jesus is a soulless religious institution. If you have not already noticed, we tend to use the word "religion" in rather negative sense—as a set of inherited rituals, rules, and structures devoid of a vital spirituality. Mostly religion in this sense tends to be quite oppressive and controlling. And this is how we mean it here. The removal of Jesus from the faith does result in the rise of religious consciousness and institutional expression. A study in European church history will more than adequately prove this point. The Inquisition was not a freak of history but rather was the logical result of a highly coercive and controlling religion that had lost sight of its reason for existence—had lost contact with its founder. But how does this happen? How does a movement as vital as that of early Christianity find itself having drifted so far from its foundation? This is not so mysterious a matter. In fact, it can be readily explained by the sociology of religion. Sociologists recognize that the fading of the initial founding impulse of a movement is not unique to Christianity but is true of all religious expressions. Sociologists call this the *routinization of charisma* and say it accounts for the decline of religious organizations and people movements. What happens in the beginning of a movement is that the people encounter the divine in a profound and revelatory way, but with successive generations this encounter tends to fade like a photocopy of a photocopy of a photocopy. What begins as a revolutionary, life-transforming, confrontation with Jesus eventually subsides into a codified religion and is subsequently incorporated into normal social life.

And herein lies an irresolvable dilemma for all people of faith: Although genuine faith is born out of direct encounters with God, it cannot survive and prosper without some form of stability and order. Viewed positively, rituals, creeds, and organizations can help people structure their relationship with God. In fact, we believe this is what they initially were designed for. But unless the worshipper is very wary, the glory of the God encounter will slowly fade and the ritual, creeds, and rules intended to preserve the encounter will take its place. The crisis dawns when the outward forms of worship no longer match the inward experience and spiritual condition of the participants. At that point, decline becomes inevitable, authentic Christianity is subverted, and constant renewals become necessary . . . hence the need to reJesus.

It is, as O'Dea says, a dilemma born of the tragedy inherent in the human condition in a fallen world. But for the disciple, the simple truth must remain; one cannot bolt down, control, or even mediate the essential God encounter in rituals, priesthoods, and theological formulas. We all need to constantly engage the God who unnerves, destabilizes, and yet enthralls us. The same is true for our defining relationship with Jesus. It is like the story of the Israelites in the wilderness. They tried to store up the manna from heaven for another day. Religion can give into the same temptation to try to store up and rely on the souvenirs of a past spiritual experience. For how many years did the church rely on the system of holy Christian relics—a bone from Peter's finger, a wooden shard from the cross of Christ, cathedrals and sacred buildings, inherited rituals, even creedal formulas, more than it relied on a fresh, daily encounter with Jesus? We, like Israel, are called to be willing to collect the fresh manna every day—and we are to do this without becoming spiritual thrill seekers but rather lifelong worshipers. To do otherwise is to "outsource your encounter with Jesus" to a religious system of souvenirs, ritual, and religious paraphernalia. Said Maurice Friedman:

> Theophany *happens* to man, and he has his part in it as God has His. [Religious] forms and ideas result from it; but what is truly revealed in it is *not* a form or an idea but God. [Genuine] religious reality means this; it is the undiminished relation to God Himself. Man does not possess God; he meets Him.[4]

The more one replaces a fresh daily encounter with Jesus with religious forms, over time he is removed from his central place in the life of the church. The result of this removal (by whatever means) is the onset of dead religion in the place of a living faith.[5] And to be honest, much of what has gone under the name Christendom can readily be called religion and not Christianity as defined by the Bible. Centuries ago, Blaise Pascal uttered these incisive words about the spiritual condition of the Christianity of his day: "Christendom is a union of people who, by means of the sacraments, excuse themselves from their duty to love God."[6] And while religious people tend to be sincere, they do use religion to qualify the God experience–to soften it and control it. One of the functions of religion, sociologically speaking, includes that of avoiding God. All attempts to reduce the faith to intellectualism, or to condition our understanding of God, or to domesticate Jesus, or to diminish the call to lifelong discipleship will result in the loss of the God experience and the encroachment of some form of religion. Anglican missiologist John V. Taylor says, "We need not go all the way with Karl Barth in defining all religion as unbelief. But . . . it is plain that man uses religion as a way of escaping from God. This is true of Christianity as of any other religious system."[7] And it was yet another Anglican who rightly said, "Jesus was inaugurating a way of life which had no further need of the Temple."[8] Any attempt then to reconstruct a temple theology of church goes clean contrary to the work of Jesus. He is the new temple.

Martin Buber, the great articulator of dialogical Hebraic spirituality, says that what were originally the true forms of the God encounter soon deteriorate and then become obstacles or substitutes for God. We do very well to heed the warning he gives:

> The ur-danger of man is "religion" and mystic ecstasy. It may be that the forms by which man originally hallowed the world for God have become independent . . . then they eventually cease to embody the consecration of the lived, everyday life, and become instead the means of its separation from God. Life in the world and religious service then begin to run on unapproachably parallel lines. But the "god of this divine service" is no longer God, it is the mask, the real partner in the communion is no longer there, the worshipper gesticulates into the empty air. Or, it may be that the state of soul underlying the divine service that becomes independent, the devotion, the reaching-out, the absorption-in, the rapture; which was meant to be and intended for a verification, flowing from the fullness of life, becomes instead detached from life. Now the soul only wants to deal with God; it is as if she [the soul] desired to exercise her love for Him and for Him alone, and not on His world. Now, the soul thinks, the world has disappeared, and only she alone, the soul is left. What she now calls "God" is only a figment in herself, the dialogue which she thinks she is carrying on is only a monologue with divided roles, for the real partner in the communion is no longer there.[9]

As harsh as this might seem, the Hebrew Bible sustains a constant critique of its own religious forms. Psalm 50 is a classic example of a prophetic railing against the formulization of faith. The prophets were the guardians of the covenantal relationship between God and his people. They were obsessed with the call to faithfulness to God. And they insisted that true faithfulness toward God could not be fulfilled through religious ritual, but only with a heart given over to him. This basic challenge is repeated throughout the prophetic wrings. For instance, Isaiah cries, "The Lord said: Because these people draw near with their mouth and honor me with their lips, while their hearts are far from me, and their worship of me is a human commandment learned by rote . . ." (Isa 29:13, cf. Isa 58; Jer 7:3–16; Amos 5:21). It's not about sacrifice in itself that the prophet rails against; it is the loss of covenantal worship. It is the intent one brings to religious forms that gives them their true meaning.

↢Christianity as Antireligion

As we are thinking about the dangers of formulaic religion, it might be useful to take a look at the Pharisees. Most readers of the New Testament would agree that the Pharisees are often portrayed as the bad guys and not as a group of people we would want to join. Let's take a closer look at the Pharisees. What do we know about them?

Well, from the Bible and from historical research, we can say that

- ↢ They were very sincere in their belief system.

- ↢ They were an extremely zealous and passionate bunch—the commitment of a suicide bomber would probably be similar to the zeal of a good Pharisee.

- ↢ They were meticulous tithers and gave beyond what was required of them (mint, rue, and cumin were not listed in the things needed to be tithed).

- ↢ They upheld a strong moral code—they were very decent people.

- ↢ They believed in the authority of the full Hebrew Scriptures. And in this they opposed the Sadducees, the theological liberals of their day, who limited the canon to the first five books and then began diminishing their authority over matters of life and faith.

- ↢ They believed in miracles. They believed that God can and did break into the course of human affairs in the form of miraculous intervention. Against the theological liberalism of their day, they fiercely defended the doctrine of the resurrection (the primary miracle), which the Sadducees denied.

- ↢ They were the keepers of the tradition, and therefore the custodians of the identity of Israel. It is unlikely Israel would have survived the stormy intertestamental period without their presence and contribution.

- ↢ They were what we would call missional. Imbued with messianic causes, they went over land and sea to make just one convert.

- ↢ They prayed arduously and often with set prayers prescribed for all possible situations in life.

⟿ They were strongly messianic. They longed for Israel's (and the world's) redemption.

We would be wrong to characterize Pharisees as mean-spirited people with nothing but evil on their minds. Generally they were sincere and well-intentioned in all they did. As degenerate and in need of renewal as the Judaism of Jesus' time was, they were nonetheless exemplary religious people as far as religions go.

We might want to ask ourselves the question, "Which brand of contemporary Christianity most closely adopts this form of spirituality?" To which we must surely answer, "It is the Bible-believing Christians . . . the evangelicals!" And the most frightening aspect of this realization, as just noted, is that these were the people who were most responsible for putting Jesus on the cross. So herein lies the rub. They are us, or at least what we can become if we are not attentive to the dynamics involved in the slow erosion of faithfulness into religion. They are living mirrors of what can happen to all well-meaning and sincere people when they lose focus on the central issues of faith—the "weightier matters of the law" (Matt 23:23). The horror of this realization is complete when we remember that these fine, upright, devoted religious people—people not unlike us—were hell-bent on murdering Jesus.

But let's press this exercise even further. Remember that, theologically speaking, Jesus was a true Pharisee. He affirmed all the things on that list regarding the authority of the Bible, the reality of miracles, the resurrection, the need for an ardent holiness, and so on. The world of difference exists in how we inhabit the theology we adhere to—how we believe it. Divorced from love, humility, and mercy, it readily becomes a dead and/or oppressive religion. And here again Jesus is the key. Without the active love for, and presence of, the radical Jesus, Christianity easily degenerates into an oppressive religion. Make no mistake, the Christendom project is full of atrocities perpetrated in the name of religion; the Inquisition and the Crusades stand out, but they were not isolated incidents. One can even argue that it is partly from the snares of religion that Jesus came to save us. We do well to remember the judgment that came upon the legalistic moralism that the Judaism at the time of Jesus had degenerated into. The parables of judgment have ongoing validity to all religious people, not just the scribes and the Pharisees.

While teaching at a seminary in the American Bible Belt, Alan once posed the question, "What would we do with Jesus if he turned up at our churches?" One brave soul answered with heart-stopping honesty, "We would probably kill him!" And we all somehow knew that his answer was disturbingly true. But the disquieting question remains: what *would* your local church do if Jesus, the real, undiminished reforming revolutionary that we see portrayed in the Scriptures, came into the community? For most of our churches, we expect that sparks would fly! Why? Because Jesus and religion just don't mix. Jacques Ellul is absolutely right when he says that

> For the Romans nascent Christianity was not at all a new religion. It was 'antireligion.' . . . What the first Christian generations were putting on trial was not just the imperial religion, as is often said, but every religion in the known world.[10]

> Christianity claims not to be a religion that is superior to others, but to be an antireligion that refutes all the religions that attempt to link us with a divine universe. No doubt Christianity constantly becomes a religion . . . [however] the Christian religion itself is constantly called into question by the absolute that is revealed in Jesus Christ.[11]

In Jesus we have the undoing of all that we call religion. In the place of a mediating system with its temples, rituals, creeds, and priestly cultus, he opens up the God experience to all and shatters the oppressive religious system of the day (Matt 21:28–46; Luke 19:10–26; 23:45). That the advent of Jesus signaled the demise of the temple system is clear. Says N. T. Wright, "Jesus was inaugurating a way of life which had no further need of the Temple."[12] Even a cursory reading of Mark reveals that immediately after his Spirit baptism and ordeal in the desert, Jesus immediately begins confronting the forces that oppress human life—the demonic forces and the religious system. His attack on religion is relentless and cuts deep. In the ministry of Jesus, the kingdom of God breaks out among those whom the religious system had marginalized—the poor, the oppressed, the prostitutes—and the religious people find themselves under the judgment of God (e.g., Matt 23:13–39). And in Jesus' answer to the Samaritan woman we see Jesus delegitimizing all attempts to localize and thus mediate and control God through the operation of sacred spaces (John 4:20–24).[13] Furthermore, Jesus' parables of judgment all call into question any attempt to control God and people and are therefore undeviating condemnations of religion in all its forms. Taken as a whole, it is difficult to see Jesus fitting into any religious system. In him is the undoing of all religion.

And because of this, the religious people hated Jesus and constantly plotted to kill him . . . and eventually did, in cahoots with the politicians and the mob. And we would suggest that all religious people will likewise hate Jesus and seek to remove him from the equation because what he does is effectively invalidate the system that they have so deeply invested in. To reJesus the church, we must first look in the mirror and ask ourselves whether the strange and wonderful God-Man has invaded our life with purpose and freshness. If Christianity minus Christ equals religion, then Christianity plus Christ is the antidote to religion.

The Founder and the Found

Part of the basis to this claim comes from an understanding of the defining role that Jesus plays for the movement that sprang from his life and work. In all people-movements, including religious movements, there is a defining relationship between the originator and the subsequent movement that forms from the work and teachings of that person. In some rare cases, a movement might well evolve from the original template set by its founder, taking on a broader vision or a new philosophical base while still remaining essentially true to its original self (e.g., the women's movement as it has evolved from the original suffragettes to modern-day feminism). But we would suggest that this ought not to be the case for the church. The living link between the founder and the found is critical for the health of Christianity in particular, as we have already tried to articulate.

Max Weber, the famous sociologist, was one of the first to broker these insights when he described the role of the "charismatic leader" in the founding of a movement. The charismatic leader in his view is distinguished from other types of leaders by his or her capacity to inspire loyalty toward himself or herself. And the source of this authority exists apart from any status gained from membership in an established institution. He also noted that movements, particularly religious movements that survive beyond the first generation, are started by such an extraordinarily gifted (charismatic) person who in a crisis situation puts forward a radically alternative vision of the world and thus initiates an ensuing mission to change the world in order to fulfill that vision. This annunciation of a radical vision and mission subsequently attracts a set of followers who collectively experience various successes and encounters that further validate the charismatic's mission. And so we find that eventually a team of devoted followers emerges to further advance the radical message of the founder.[14]

The point we make in referring to Weber here is that he rightly understood the critical factors that made for significant people movements and
transformational organizations. For one, he clearly understood the role of

Radical Hospitality

Jean Vanier

By his mid-thirties, Jean Vanier, a native of Geneva, Switzerland, had
also lived in England, France, and Canada; served in the British Navy
and the Royal Canadian Navy; completed his doctorate in philosophy;
and become a dynamic young professor at the University of Toronto.
But it wasn't until 1964, when Vanier was thirty-six, that Vanier
discovered what would become his true life's work. After witnessing
the desperate situations of thousands of intellectually disabled people
in mental institutions, he bought an old house in Trosly-Breuil, France,
invited two men from such institutions to live with him, and established
a community with them. Naming the home L'Arche, which means "the
ark" in French, Vanier and the two men opened their home to others, gradually building a mutual
community in which people with mental disabilities and people without maintained a genuine
community. Since then, 130 other community homes have been formed in places all over the
world. Although he has become internationally regarded, Vanier still makes his home in the
original community of Trosly-Breuil. Jean Vanier is a little Jesus because he embodies the
Christlike motivation to live among, befriend, and serve those who are otherwise treated as
social outcasts in our world.

the founder as decisive, not only for the initiation of the religious movement
but also in defining the ongoing life of the organization that outlives him or
her. He also noted that in order to survive the loss of the founder, the movement has to somehow build the charisma of the founder into the life of the
organization.[15] He said, "The genuine charismatic situation quickly gives rise
to incipient institutions, which emerge from the cooling off of extraordinary
states or devotion and fever."[16] In fact, it was Weber who coined the phrase we
have already introduced: the routinization of charisma.

Thomas O'Dea refers to these catalyzing encounters that kick-start
movements and then fade with the passing of time. He points out how con-
secutive generations tend to construct religious systems to take the place of
the original encounter. He says, "Worship is the fundamental religious response [to such encounters] but in order to survive its charismatic moment

worship must become stabilized in established forms and procedures."[17] In fact, he argues that this is an unavoidable paradox for religious movements.[18] The ultimate and the sacred cannot be expressed in institutional structures without those structures taking on a life of their own and corrupting what they are meant to represent. Yet without some form of institutionalization, religious experiences of themselves will not sustain a religious movement.

And herein lies an irresolvable dilemma for religious organizations: although religious movements are born out of firsthand religious experiences, they cannot survive and prosper without some form of stability and order. The *charism* (the originating grace or gift) has to be diffused, ritualized, and mediated by the organization so that the initial gift of the founder can be made accessible through the organization itself. While O'Dea saw this process of institutionalization as inevitable and even necessary, he also saw that it was paradoxically the process that would dilute or possibly even obliterate the initial message and ethos of the founder. Yet this routinization of charisma has a tendency to snuff out the life it was meant to protect and enhance. The crisis inevitably dawns when the outward forms of worship no longer match the inward experience and spiritual condition of the participants. Decline becomes inevitable. Authentic Christianity is subverted and constant renewals become necessary . . . hence the need to reJesus.

Weber maintained that the process of institutionalization and renewal involved a constant return to the charismatic center in order to relegitimize, or in our language, refound, the subsequent movement. To remain true, all religious organizations require a form of renewal that requires a return to the original ethos and the power of the founder. And whether one applies this to a denomination or to Christianity as a whole, one can call this rediscovery of one's original message radical traditionalism because it involves going back to the organization's deepest tradition and reinterpreting it for a new context.

In fact, there is a certain way of thinking and acting within an organization that can be traced back to its founder. This is called the organization's foundational culture, and it is formed through three sources:

- The beliefs, values, and assumptions of its founders

- The validation of these beliefs through the learning experiences of the group

- The enhancement of these beliefs by the new beliefs, values, and assumptions brought by new group members.

But we can say categorically that the impact of the founder is the most important factor in determining the resultant culture of an organization or religion.[19] In relation to the church we can call this process refounding the church, or simply reJesus.

In the formation of Christianity we can clearly see all these forces at work. In the New Testament (even the word "new" implies a departure from, or at least a radical reinterpretation of, the "old") Jesus redefines the way people had previously understood and experienced the kingdom of God. As the true prophet of God, he totally radicalizes the kingdom by negating and bypassing the religious institution that has inadvertently begun to block its operations and activity (Matt 23:13ff.), and in so doing he opens up direct access for the people, for all who would draw near (e.g., Matt 11:28–30; 21:43; John 4:20–24). In doing these things, Jesus explicitly becomes the founder and initiator of a new covenant with the people of God. He initiated a way of engaging the God of Israel that later came to be called Christianity, the religion that takes its cue from him. We also know from the Gospels that Jesus spent significant and strategic time devoted to initiating his followers into the ways of the kingdom and to discipling and teaching them to recognize the dynamics of what it meant to be one of his followers. The basics of what it means to be a disciple are thus built into the system at its inception.

It was Peter Berger who alerted us to the fact that reality is in fact socially constructed. The social process is exactly how leaders get their ideas implemented. Their ideas are taught to the group, even imposed at times in the form of commands, as we can see in some aspects of Jesus' teaching. But they are generally passed on to the followers through a combination of socialization, through the charismatic power of the founder, and by acting, by doing, by living out confidence in the message.

They knew they were bound to his teaching and template. Any apostolic development of the teachings of Jesus are authentic only insofar that they refer directly to the person, and extend the work of, Jesus. They are all bound to the revelation of God given in and through Jesus. They have no authority to speculate beyond that. They can, however, interpret Jesus and his teachings and reapply them in fresh cultural ways. As such the whole movement grows and evolves, but the nascent ethos of the founder is maintained. This is exactly what Paul does. The most cogent example of apostolic imagination and practice was given to us by Paul who spent his best energies in establishing new ground for the gospel and in working out the redemptive significance of the Messiah, in terms of both his person (e.g., Ephesians and Colossians) and his work (e.g., Romans and Galatians). But he too is self-consciously bound by the revelation given in and through Jesus (Gal 1:8; Col 1:15–20; 1 Cor 3:11; 9:16–23). In a real sense his work always harks back to the Christ event to be true and authentic.

Early on, the original church had cause to recalibrate to Jesus. The original believers were largely Jews, and The Way was considered a sect under the broader umbrella of Judaism. As such, many of their expectations were colored by their Jewish nationalism. For instance, expectations of a restored Jewish kingdom were not met within a generation. In fact, rather than being liberated from foreign control, Jerusalem and the temple were brutally destroyed by the Romans, and Jews were scattered throughout the empire. The Jewish believers had cause to seriously rethink the bases of the faith. Their assumptions had to be radically reconsidered. Note the way that within a generation the Christian movement was already forced back to its founder to rediscover its original charism. Was it a Jewish renewal movement or something more? The Christian movement would have ample reason to do this again and again throughout history. It is what renewal of the faith, ministry, and mission of the church is all about.

And remember, we are talking here about both the founder and the found. Whatever sociological process we might use to understand the role of the founder of a movement, in order to be valid, his or her followers must somehow strive to embody the life, ideals, and reality of that founder. Likewise for the Christian movement, the founder must be able to be seen in the lives of the found. This is the process of embodiment, which is so essential to movements.[20] This is what it means for the church to have Jesus in its midst. This must surely partly be what it means to live "in Christ" and he in us. Observers should be able to encounter Jesus in and through the life and community of his followers. People observing us ought to be able to discern the elements of Jesus' way in our ways. If they cannot find authentic signals of the historical Jesus through the life of his people, then as far as we are concerned they have the full right to question our legitimacy.

Tony Campolo tells the story of a drunk who was miraculously converted at a Bowery mission in New York. Like all Campolo stories, it has a jokey punch line that betrays a far more serious and convicting point.

The drunk, Joe, was known throughout the Bowery as the worst kind of wino, a hopeless derelict of a man, living on borrowed time. But following his conversion, everything changed. Joe became the most caring person that anyone associated with the mission had ever known. He spent his days and nights hanging out at the hall, not balking at even the lowliest job. He mopped up vomit and urine and cleaned up drunks whatever their condition. He considered nothing too demeaning for him.

One evening, when the director of the mission was delivering his evening evangelistic message to the usual crowd of still and sullen men, their heads hung in penitence and exhaustion, there was one man who looked up, came down the aisle to the altar, and knelt to pray, crying out for God to help him to change. The repentant drunk kept shouting, "Oh God, make me like Joe! Make me like Joe! Make me like Joe!" The director of the mission leaned over and said to the man, "Son, I think it would be better if you prayed, 'Make me like Jesus!'" The man looked up at the director with a quizzical expression on his face and asked, "Is he like Joe?"[21]

The New Testament writers likewise call people to emulate their example, knowing that they had committed their lives to Jesus and that he indeed "lived in them." It takes either self-delusion, a lot of chutzpah, or a real commitment to the embodiment of Jesus' message to be able to say "follow me as I follow Christ." But Paul was never coy about calling people to follow his example. This might seem like arrogance to us, but, like the ex-drunk in Campolo's story, he was so given over to the example of Christ that he had become a living embodiment of Jesus. It was Jesus he was pointing to, but it is Jesus through the medium of his own life. He understood Jesus lived in him and he in Christ. It is out of this conviction that he could say,

Be imitators of me, as I am of Christ. (1 Cor 11:1)

Join in imitating me, and observe those who live according to the example you have in us. (Phil 3:17)

For you yourselves know how you ought to imitate us; we were not idle when we were with you . . . (2 Thess 3:7)

Note how in Philippians 3:17 he also directs his readers to observe others whose lives mirror that of Jesus. In effect, the found are to replicate the founder to outsiders and to each other.

But to push the point a little further, consider the difference between Christianity and Islam. In both cases, the founder sets the primary pattern for others to follow—they provide the authenticating human image of the spiritual person for their followers to emulate. There is in all religions some real expectation of continuity between the founder and the follower. So, when we

see a person or organization claiming to be Christian but acting in a gratu-
itously violent and unloving way, we can say that that person or organization
is clearly out of sync with the way of Jesus. We can say with some confidence
that one cannot follow Jesus and at the same time act in ways deeply inconsistent with his teachings. That is why violent fundamentalisms are aberra-
tions of Christianity as defined by Jesus. They distort the reality of love and
forgiveness that are embodied in the Messiah.

But in the case of Islam, the founder set an entirely different model
from that of Jesus. The Koran depicts Muhammed as a passionately spiritual
man who called people into the worship of *Allah*. And there are some great
spiritual insights in the Koran. However, the same Koran depicts Muhammad
as a man with a rigid morality, an assertive sexuality, a bad temper, and distinctly warlike tendencies. So following the logic, we can say that when Islam
acts similarly it is not entirely inconsistent with its founder at this point.

However, when Christianity is warlike and voracious, it betrays Jesus
in a significant way. This is why racism, the Crusades, the Inquisition, or the
Christian endorsement of unbridled capitalism of our day are such apostate
distortions of the faith—apostate because they run contrary to the faith expression, the initial pattern, that Jesus set for us to follow. The founder's influence must imbue the movement because we get our sense of place and our
ongoing identity from him.

The following chart will give the reader a feel of what we are saying here:
we ought to get a feel of what a religion stands for by examining the lives and
teachings of the founders (or key figures).[22]

ABRAHAM	KRISHNA	MOHAMMED	BUDDHA	JESUS
↓	↓	↓	↓	↓
JUDAISM	HINDUISM	ISLAM	BUDDHISM	CHRISTIANITY

⟵ Discerning the Inner Voice of the Organization

But beyond the role of the founder in the ongoing renewal of the church,
we must briefly return to the idea of radical traditionalism. Another useful
way of conceiving the renewal of organizations is to talk in terms of reforming, or even better, refounding the organization. Movement expert Steve Addison calls this discerning the inner voice of the organization.[23]

Drawing on the insights of organizational theorist Robert Quinn,[24] Addison says that rather than us finding a purpose, a purpose finds us. Quinn argues that every organization has an inner voice that constitutes its moral core. Following this cue, then, we can say that in various forms of organizational renewal, the goal is not so much to impose a purpose on its members but to help them rediscover it, to train them to listen for the inner voice of the organization. Still, we can be sure that any attempt to realign the organization with its inner voice will threaten the existing culture, whose central impulse is self-preservation. Nonetheless, as Quinn says, this "articulation of the inner voice of an organization is often the first step toward revitalizing a company and uncovering a vision filled with resonance."[25]

Similarly, in his study of religious orders, Lawrence Cada refers to the "founding charism" of an order to describe its unique vision of the world transformed by the gospel.[26] The use of the term *charism* (grace) implies that the purpose of an organization is a gift that lies at the heart of the organization—a divine bequest, unique to that particular organization. And the recovery of that gift means a "return to the sources."[27] Organizational renewal is about the discovery of an organization's true identity and mission. The authority to bring transformation to the church does not rest in the person of the leader or group but in God's calling. If this is so, then the key to the revitalization of religious organizations is to reappropriate, or recover, their founding charism.

But as mentioned earlier, this must not be the blind return to traditionalism but an innovative insight into how the founding charism is to be expressed in the contemporary world. This involves a rediscovery of the founder's vision matched with spectacular innovations that are as yet unheard of.[28] Addison suggests then that revitalization requires an innovative return to tradition.

While many people use the term "radical" to mean a departure from the traditional, it refers to a return to the root cause of a thing. Webster defines "radical" as "of or pertaining to the root or origin; reaching to the center, to the foundation, to the ultimate sources, to the principles, or the like; original; fundamental; thorough-going; unsparing; extreme; as in, 'radical evils': 'radical reform'; 'a radical party.'"

We have been called radicals in our time, but using this definition, aren't we all meant to be radicals in some form or another? We are hardly calling the church into new, uncharted territory. Rather, we advocate a return to our most fundamental cause. If that's radical, then we are radicals indeed!

Central to the organizational renewal process is the rediscovery of the organization's identity and at the same time the innovative interpretation of that identity in a changed world. Thus, there is both a continuity and discontinuity in the revitalization process, involving both a conservative dimension as well as a radical one. Addison illustrates by referring to Volkswagen's innovative reinterpretation of the Beetle to illustrate this process. This iconic motorcar ceased production in the late 1970s before being resurrected for the new millennium. The new Beetle that emerged definitely has continuity with the original one but was in some sense radically new. It was a great success and a powerful illustration of radical traditionalism involved in refounding organizations.

But we can also learn from educational psychology in this matter. Jean Piaget, the great educational psychologist, conducted much of his early research on the streets of Geneva, interviewing children and observing how they played structured games together. He noted that very small children unquestioningly played games according to the inherited rules. They slavishly obeyed the traditional rules of, say marbles, because their older siblings or their parents had taught them how to play that way. Piaget then noted that at a certain stage in the development of the child he or she wanted to throw these rules away. A rule-less game of marbles on the streets of Geneva last century was exactly as you'd expect it to be—chaos! Later in childhood, these same children, fed up with chaotic games that were always won by bullies or the most crafty, rediscovered the original rules of the game. Piaget noted how much more powerfully these rules worked in the lives of the older children. They were the same rules they were taught as tiny children. But the difference now was that they had discovered these rules as an antidote to disorder. They felt these rules were *their* rules. In a sense, this process of childhood development mirrors what we've been discussing.

What we are advocating is a radical traditionalism. The church needs to follow the same path as the children did with their games of marbles. ReJesus, the refounding of the church, means departing from a blind, slavish allegiance to religious rules inherited from our parents and forebears. It means walking into the turmoil of chaos and daring to trust that the at the end of the path will be not bedlam but a rediscovery of the way of Jesus, a rediscovery of the original rules that we can own ourselves with greater conviction and authenticity. Jesus, as our founder, is our guide on this path. His words and his example are the constants as we leave our old traditions and look to bring the church and the gospel into new contexts of traditional radicalism.

⟵ **Notes**

1. "And I tell you, you are Peter, and on this rock I will build my church, and the gates of Hades will not overcome it. I will give you the keys of the kingdom of heaven, and whatever you bind on earth will be bound in heaven, and whatever you loose on earth will be loosed in heaven."

2. This quote has appeared everywhere from fridge magnets to school blackboards. We found it online at http://www.quotationspage.com/quote/33522.html.

3. Roland Allen, *The Compulsion of the Spirit* (ed. David Paton and Charles H. Long; Grand Rapids, Mich.: Eerdmans, 1983), 47–48.

4. Maurice S. Friedman, *Martin Buber: The Life of Dialogue* (Chicago: University of Chicago Press, 1955; repr. New York: Harper's N.Y., 1960), 32. Cited 25 September 2008. Online: http://www.religion-online.org/showchapter.asp?title=459&C=377.

5. The word "religion" can be used in either a positive or a negative sense. We almost use it always in the negative.

6. From Abraham Heschel, *A Passion for Truth* (New York: Farrar, Straus and Giroux, 1973), 169–70.

7. John V. Taylor, *The Go-between God: The Holy Spirit and the Christian Mission* (London: SCM, 1972), 190.

8. N. T. Wright, quoted in Bruxy Cavey, *The End of Religion: An Introduction to the Subversive Spirituality of Jesus* (Ottawa: Agora, 2005), 62.

9. Martin Buber, *Mamre* (Melbourne: Melbourne University Press, 1946), 103–4.

10. Ellul, *Subversion of Christianity*, 55.

11. Ibid., 141.

12. Quoted in Cavey, *End of Religion*, 62.

13. He says to her, "Woman, believe me, the hour is coming when you will worship the Father neither on this mountain nor in Jerusalem. . . . But the hour is coming, and is now here, when the true worshipers will worship the Father in spirit and truth, for the Father seeks such as these to worship him. God is spirit, and those who worship him must worship in spirit and in truth."

14. Weber's ideas are widely discussed and freely available. See, for instance, H. H. Gerth and C. W. Mills, *From Max Weber: Essays in Sociology* (New York: Oxford University Press, 1958), 262ff.

15. See the work of Ichak Adizes, *Corporate Life Cycles* (Englewood Cliffs, N.J.: Prentice Hall, 1988).

16. Quoted in H. B. Jones, "Magic, Meaning, and Leadership: Weber's Model and the Empirical Literature," *Human Relations* 54/6 (2001): 753.

17. Thomas F. O'Dea, "Five Dilemmas of the Institutionalization of Religion," *Journal for the Scientific Study of Religion* 1/1 (October 1961): 34.

18. Ibid., 32.

19. Edgar H. Schein, *Organizational Culture and Leadership* (San Francisco: Jossey-Bass, 1990), 209–10.

20. Hirsch, *Forgotten Ways*, 114–16.

21. Michael heard Tony Campolo tell this story in a presentation many years ago.

22. Adopted from online podcast notes by Canadian writer and speaker, Bruxy Cavey, available at http://www.themeetinghouse.ca/podcast/TMH.rss.

23. From Addison's exceptional but unpublished work on Christian movements. Material used with permission. See also his blog on movements called *World Changers* at http://www.steveaddison.net/.

24. Robert E. Quinn, *Change the World* (San Francisco: Jossey-Bass, 2000), 61.

25. Ibid., 138.

26. Lawrence Cada et al., *Shaping the Coming Age of Religious Life* (New York: Seabury, 1979), 92.

27. Raymond Hostie, *The Life and Death of Religious Orders* (Washington, D.C.: Center for Applied Research in the Apostolate, 1983), 277.

28. Ibid., 278.

Chapter Four

I've Got a Picture of Jesus

It's been said often enough, but it bears repeating: without the real human Jesus of Nazareth, we are at the mercy of anybody who tells us that "Christ" is this, or that.
—N. T. Wright

Our passion for Jesus is the only passion that will not destroy us.
—Larry Crabb

To embrace the radical traditionalism we have been discussing requires a rediscovery of our foundation—the person, Jesus. It will require us to let go of our much-loved but inaccurate assumptions about him and be prepared to venture back to the Gospels to see him in all his strange radicalness. We don't for one minute assume that this will be easy for many Christians. The benign images of gentle Jesus, meek and mild, have comforted and encouraged many believers. But we ask you to reacquaint yourself with the biblical record and to be brave enough to encounter the disquieting, unsettling, perplexing, unfamiliar Jesus found there.

It has been said that God made us in his image, and we returned the favor (was it Voltaire?). This innate tendency to co-opt God to our own egos and agendas is deeply embedded in the human condition. An illustration: Some time ago Michael was speaking at a conference and was teamed with a worship leader for each of his sessions. Michael was calling the participants to the reJesus project with all its implied radicalism. The worship leader, though, was on an entirely different page. He spoke about Jesus as a cuddly, fatherly type, as all-gentle, all-kind, all-forgiving. He led the audience through a visualization experience in which they were to imagine themselves returning home to Jesus, feeling his strong, warm embrace around them. They were invited to cuddle him, secure in his love and knowing he adored them like his gorgeous little boys or girls. You can imagine the disconnect when Michael stood up after this and spoke about the wild, radical, mysterious, revolutionary Messiah from Nazareth!

In fact, the shift required by the participants to get from the warm, sentimental Jesus of the worship leader to the wild, revolutionary Jesus of the keynote speaker was so great that Michael and the worship leader met for breakfast the next day to try to integrate their approaches as best they could. During this conversation, the worship leader spoke about growing up in a cold and austere German family, with a distant, unpleasable father. All his life he had tried to fulfill his father's high standards, only to fall short time and again. It was through discovering the unconditional love of Jesus that he finally felt free from the scathing and debilitating self-criticism that he had inherited from his childhood. This experience had been so formative that it had shaped his whole view of Jesus. His Jesus had become an end-lessly loving daddy-figure, a sentimental parent who was proud of his son and who cheered him on and was thrilled with his every achievement no mat-ter how small. Can you see how our understanding of Jesus can be so easily shaped by our own psychospiritual needs? Show me your Jesus, and I'll tell you who *you* are.

So, was the worship leader wrong? Doesn't Jesus love us uncondition-ally? Of course he does, but we need to know what it means for Jesus to love us lest we romanticize it and thus distort the type of love that Jesus has for us. Is it soft and sentimental? Doesn't Jesus' understanding of love involve action and sacrifice more than just feelings? And besides, is that really all there is to Jesus? If hugs and kisses were the sum total of Jesus' character, why would anyone have wanted him dead? No one wants to kill a big ball of daddy love, do they? Jesus' character must at the least be viewed through the knowledge that his whole public ministry was marked by a resolute march toward the cross. Death becomes him! He embraces it early in his ministry and barely flinches from it all the way to Golgotha. We don't mean to sound insensitive to the terrible craving for acceptance that many people are left with because of poor parenting. Jesus unquestionably meets that deep need. But if we limit Jesus to the meeting of our psychological needs, we end up following only part of Jesus. That's how we get this daddy-hunger Jesus.

Earlier we talked about the distorted view of Jesus promulgated by the Ku Klux Klan. Since their deepest need is to justify their fear and loathing of blacks and Jews, they construct racist Jesus. Similarly, many churches have constructed Jesuses who meet their needs. There is a schmaltzy Jesus, or a middle-class Jesus, or a meek and mild Jesus who speaks in platitudes that don't upset their closely controlled lives. And then there is that annual cultural distortion, baby-in-a-manger Jesus, a harmless little child that everyone can "oohh" and "ahhh" over without having to take seriously. And so it goes. Our concern here is not to suggest that Jesus doesn't address our deep longings and needs but rather to affirm that he can never be limited to meeting those deep longings. Sometimes he challenges those needs. Many of us are familiar with the scene in C. S. Lewis's *The Lion, the Witch, and the Wardrobe*, when Lucy is about to meet Aslan the lion, the allegorical Christ figure in the books. She asks Mr. Beaver, "Is he safe?" "'Safe?' said Mr. Beaver . . . 'Who said anything about safe? 'Course he isn't safe, but he's good. He's the King, I tell you.'"[1] Following Jesus is never safe when it comes to our culturally adopted lifestyles, but it is always good.

To be sure, there are times when the word we hear from Jesus is, "I have desired to gather your children together as a hen gathers her brood under her wings." But at other times it might just as well be, "Do you not perceive or understand? Are your hearts hardened? Do you have eyes, and fail to see? Do you have ears, and fail to hear?" Both these statements appear on the lips of Jesus. The first one, from Luke 13:34, refers to his love for the people of Israel, and the second, from Mark 8:17, is directed in frustration toward his disciples. Our point is that Jesus was more than willing to express his disappointment and annoyance at his friends as well as his love and compassion. We need to remember that even though he deeply loved his disciples (John 17, for instance), he also continued to surprise, amaze, frighten, disturb, and challenge them. To limit Jesus to a spiritual tap that can be turned on and off according to our need for affirmation is a terrible mistake. It leads to us remaking Jesus in our image, rather than us being molded to his likeness.

In *Talladega Nights*, Will Ferrell, in typical over-the-top style, plays the fictional Nascar champion, Ricky Bobby. In a mostly inane film, filled with ridiculous set pieces, one scene surprises us. Ricky Bobby sits down to dinner with his wife, Carly; his two sons, Walker and Texas Ranger; his father-in-law, Chip; and his racing partner, Cal, and says grace. Addressing his prayer to "dear Lord baby Jesus," Ricky begins with thanks for the bountiful harvest of Dominoes, KFC, and Taco Bell set before him, as well as for his family and his best friend, Cal. He then asks Jesus to use his "baby Jesus powers" to heal Chip's bad leg, at which point his wife, Carly, interjects:

Carly: You know Jesus did grow up. You don't always have to call him "baby."

Ricky: I like the Christmas Jesus best and I'm sayin' grace. When you say grace you can say it to grown-up Jesus, teenage Jesus, bearded Jesus, or whoever you want . . . [continues praying] Dear tiny Jesus, with your golden fleece diapers, with your tiny little fat balled-up fist . . .

Chip [yelling]: He was a man! He had a beard.

Ricky: Look, I like the baby Jesus version the best. Do you hear me?

Inspired by this discussion about Jesus, Ricky's friend Cal decides to throw in his favorite image as well:

Cal: I like to picture Jesus in a tuxedo T-shirt, cos it says, like, I wanna be formal, but I'm here to party too. I like to party, so I like my Jesus to party.

Walker: I like to picture Jesus as a ninja fighting off evil samurai.

Cal: I like to picture Jesus with, like, giant eagle's wings, and singin' lead vocals for Lynard Skynard with, like, an angel band, and I'm in the front row, and I'm hammered drunk.

After Carly puts an end to the theological discussion by asking Ricky to finish saying grace, he continues praying: "Dear eight-pound, six-ounce infant Jesus; don't even know a word yet, just a little infant so cuddly, still omnipotent, we just thank you . . ."[2]

The bulk of Ricky's prayer is an expression of gratitude for his hot wife, his success on the track, and the millions of dollars he's made in endorsements (he even fulfills his contractual obligation to mention his sponsor Powerade). The whole scene is a farcical reminder of the temptation felt by those who don't read the Gospels to fashion Jesus in their own image.

To paraphrase Anne Lamott, you know you've remade Jesus in your own image when he hates all the same people you hate! We have all tried to shoehorn Jesus into our own agendas, making him hate those we hate, whether it's gays, Muslims, liberals, Catholics, fundamentalists, or postmoderns. But not even his own community could compel Jesus in that way. In Luke 4, Jesus commences his public ministry in his hometown with a reading from the scroll of the prophet Isaiah. The first half of his sermon that day is often repeated in churches today; having read of the day of the Lord, he impetuously announced, "Today this scripture has been fulfilled in your hearing" (Luke 4:21). The second half of his message, however, is rarely celebrated today. But it is every bit as radical as his announcement that he is the fulfillment of the prophecy made in Isaiah 61. It is so radical, in fact, that his audience was prepared to murder him. What does he say?

He plucks from the pages of 1 and 2 Kings two stories that have appeared in so many children's Sunday school curricula that their potency has been leached from the narrative. And yet they are both subversive and radical stories. In the first, he alludes to Elijah's retreat to the home of the widow at Zarephath in Sidon (1 Kgs 17:8–24). Of all the widows in Israel to whom God might have sent Elijah, he chose to provide him with sanctuary in the home of a Sidonite, says Jesus. But furthermore, as if to press his case even harder, Jesus jumps to 2 Kings 5 and the healing of the leprous Aramean warlord, Naaman. Of all the lepers in Israel, God chose to heal the leader of one of their enemy's armed forces. What do the widow at Zarephath and General Naaman of Syria have in common? They were both outsiders, enemies, despised by Israel. And yet it is to both of them that the grace of God is revealed. Indeed, in the widow's case, it is through her that God's grace is revealed. Jesus picks two characters he knows his Sabbath-day audience in Nazareth would have hated, and he dares his audience to admit that God loved them as much as anyone in Israel. He will not be co-opted, even by Israel, to a cause fueled by hatred and racism.

Later, the religious leaders of Israel send an emissary to try to trick Jesus into making politically inflammatory statements against Rome. We know how cleverly Jesus repels their trick with his statement, "Give therefore to the emperor the things that are the emperor's, and to God the things that are God's" (Matt 22:21), but it's the emissary's opening line that caught our eye: "We know you are sincere, and teach the way of God in accordance with the truth, and show deference to no one; for you do not regard people with partiality" (Matt 22:16).

No doubt, these are falsely flattering words. But we can't help but notice the irony of Jesus' enemies correctly identifying the fact that he cannot be swayed by the agendas of others, no matter who they are. So, why do we constantly persist in trying to co-opt him for our purposes?

Having said that, we are not foolish enough to suggest that knowing Jesus is a purely objective task. Of course, we all bring our own needs, hopes, and longings to our quest to understand Jesus. The poet Robert Frost once wrote, "Heaven gives its glimpses only to those not in a position to look too close." Here we have a deeply insightful understanding of Christian revelation. Those of us taken by Jesus have, in faith, glimpsed him. However, when we try to describe the content of that glimpse, the vision and the viewer inevitably become one. Though the glimpse is real, we are not in a position to sort out where it ends and we begin. We have the Gospels to provide us with the parameters outside of which we mustn't stray lest our glimpse of Jesus be more about us than about Jesus. And of course, we have the Holy Spirit.

The apostle Paul was bold enough to claim that if we are in the Spirit of God, "we have the mind of Christ" (1 Cor 2:16). If this is true, then any supposed necessity of separating ourselves in our subjectivity from the objective reality of Jesus Christ is questionable. So-called pure objectivity is a fallacious quest. We are always subjectively (personally) involved in the knowledge of God because God cannot be known in pure objectivity. In fact, objective detachment from the object of faith, which is Jesus Christ, is not consistent with a biblical way of knowing (see ch. 5). It is also out of our subjectivity that we can discover who the real Jesus is, for his mind is present in the world. But it is present only in his followers, as a gift of the Spirit. Bringing both to bear—our objectivity and our subjectivity—is more likely to yield a clearer glimpse of Jesus than either one alone.

⟵ Vandalizing Our Portraits of Jesus

One of the best ways to expose our co-option of Jesus to our own personal, religious, and cultural agendas is to interpret the many images of him that we entertain. The artistic talent of the Spanish painter Bartolome Murillo first emerged when, as a boy, he vandalized his parents' much-loved icon. Murillo converted the holy and other-worldly image of Jesus the shepherd boy into the depiction of a playful, rough-and-ready Spanish child. With the intuition of a child, young Murillo couldn't bear the almost frightening image of the pristine holy boy that hung in his childhood home. He had to rescue Jesus from the gilt frame and put him back on the dusty streets of Seville. We respond to this story strongly.

The thought of the young Murillo vandalizing his family's icon stays with us and informs a good deal of what we do. We see ourselves as iconoclasts, as holy vandals, defacing the church's cherished but unhelpful images of Jesus. Some of these images are relatively benign, like the daddy-love Jesus of the worship leader just mentioned. Others are sinister, like the KKK's Aryan Christ. But they are both inaccurate. And it's their inaccuracy that leads many people off in an unhelpful trajectory. Allow us to apply our vandals' spray cans to some of the classic glimpses of Jesus.

The Bearded-Lady Jesus

In the early 1850s, William Holman Hunt, one of the founders of the avant-garde Pre-Raphaelite movement, painted an immeasurably popular picture, *The Light of the World*. In this image, Jesus is standing outside a closed, heavy, wooden door, under a stone archway. He gently raps on the door with the back of his open hand. In his other hand he holds a jewel-encrusted lantern. The scene is dark, and behind him can be seen wild woods with twisted branches silhouetted against the setting sun. It seems that Jesus has braved an inhospitable terrain to make it to this ivy-covered door. Hunt said, "I painted the picture with what I thought, unworthy though I was, to be by Divine command, and not simply as a good subject."[3] The picture is certainly reminiscent

Jesus. *The Light of the World*, William Holman Hunt. Oil on canvas over panel.

of the text we mentioned earlier: "I am standing at the door, knocking; if you hear my voice and open the door, I will come in to you and eat with you, and you with me" (Rev 3:20).

It's hard to quantify the popularity of this image. At the turn of the twentieth century, it toured Canada, Australia, New Zealand, and South Africa and was seen by thousands. In our homeland of Australia more than five hundred thousand people saw it in Sydney and Melbourne in a time when the combined populations of those cities was fewer than a million people. Across the United Kingdom, postcard-sized copies were made, and people couldn't get enough of them. They carried the image like a keepsake or a relic. Servicemen were given copies to keep in their uniforms, a physical reminder of the closeness of Jesus to them in their time of battle. The Salvation Army composer, Sir Dean Goffin, was inspired by the painting to compose his most famous piece, also entitled *The Light of the World*. Hunt's original is now in a side room off the large chapel at Keble College, Oxford, and he painted a large copy toward the end of his life, which is now in London's St. Paul's Cathedral.

A closer examination of Hunt's Jesus reveals some interesting observations. For example, the wooden door has no exterior handle. It can obviously only be opened from the inside, adding weight to its portrayal of the passage from Revelation 3. Furthermore, Jesus is somewhat feminized. He is wearing a silk ball gown (we're not sure what else you'd call it) and a royal red robe or cape. He has a golden crown on his head, flattening his glorious blond, shoulder-length hair. His beard is blond, too, and his serene gaze makes him look more like a mythic English king than a Middle Eastern radical. In his genuine attempt to portray Jesus' kingly grandeur, Hunt has cast him as King Arthur or Richard the Lionheart perhaps, a wise, unruffled, beautiful English monarch. A classic co-option.

William Holman Hunt was to influence the popular perception of Jesus more than just about anyone else in Western cultural history, even, dare we say it, the Gospel writers. His rendering of the door-knocking Jesus as a blond, bearded royal was seared into the public consciousness of Britons and carried throughout the British Empire as far away as South Africa, Australia, and New Zealand, until today. Hunt's rendering heavily influenced the most common image of Jesus you can find—Warner Sallman's painting, *Head of Christ*. We don't have permission to include it in our book, but it is easy to find on the Internet. (We suggest you Google the artist and painting title to see if you recognize this.)

We call it the bearded-lady Jesus. Flowing blond locks swept back from the face, high cheekbones, groomed eyebrows, full lips, with heavenward gazing, gentle eyes—he's beautiful. But is this a valid biblical representation of Jesus? Or is this a mere fantasy object for an overly sentimental, cultural Christianity? This is the inoffensive Messiah, clean and tidy, pleasing to the eye. This is no disturber of our souls. This image of Jesus reflects a spirituality that is anchored in an adoration of the wonderful Christ, the unattainable Jesus.

A few years back, when Michael was teaching a seminar to Salvation Army officers in New Zealand, he noticed that most of the members of the audience were wearing black T-shirts with the revolutionary slogan, "I'll fight," emblazoned in red across the back. This was an allusion to a famous sermon by the Salvation Army founder, William Booth, who claimed that while there was poverty, alcoholism, and suffering on the streets of London, he'd fight it with all his might. It's a dramatic and motivational slogan. But hanging on the wall in the seminar room, dominating the whole space, was the picture of Jesus shown above. Michael pointed this out and asked whether the Jesus depicted in that painting would ever fight against anything, let alone get down into the filthy alleys and laneways of nineteenth-century London to serve the poor. One officer present admitted that the bearded-lady Jesus probably informed their Christology far more than the example of William Booth, a holy warrior if ever there was one.

The bearded lady in these paintings exudes an abstracted serenity, gentleness, and peace. And yet the Jesus we meet in the Gospels is at times frustrated, disappointed, annoyed and, worse still, angered. He is full of holy pathos. He exasperated his rivals, unsettled his friends, and drove his enemies mad. Says Alison Morgan, "Jesus was a difficult and uncooperative revolutionary who so threatened the established order of the day that there seemed to be no option but to have him executed."[4]

Spooky Jesus

Another series of images of Jesus that affects the imaginations of many can go under the heading of what we call spooky Jesus. They are similar to the bearded-lady Jesus in that they present a somewhat feminized picture of Christ, but they go further by adding a variety of highly symbolic, ethereal elements to the picture. These immensely popular portrayals of Jesus present him as an otherworldly being, swathed in swirling haloes and unearthly auras (probably to ensure that the viewer would not miss the fact of his divinity). This Jesus seems almost heretical. Why? Because these images seem to portray Christ's divinity at the expense of his humanity. It's as if his God nature can be barely contained by his ill-fitting human shell. It is almost as if he is one of those aliens who take on a human disguise in the movie *Men in Black*. Every now and again the alien breaks through the skin to reveal the otherworldly creature who has co-opted a human vehicle, a disposable pod, for his purposes.

Jesus. *Sacred Heart,* Pompeo Batoni.
Oil on canvas.

The early church worked hard to ensure that while it affirmed Jesus' divinity, it did not lose sight of his complete and total humanity. And it was right to reject any notions that diminished his humanity. Portrayals like spooky Jesus can rightly be labeled docetic (the heresy that claims that Jesus only seemed to be a human but was not) and should be rejected as such. When we look at the Jesus of the Gospels, we find that in fact this was exactly what Jesus was not. The incarnation emphasizes the fact that Jesus' humanity so contained the divinity of Jesus that his family, his neighbors, his friends, and even his disciples did not fully realize that God was present in the human person that they encountered in Jesus—so hidden was his divinity in his humanity. Glowing halos, exposed hearts, and dramatic posturing—all regularly included in these depictions—take us away from the Gospels rather than toward the real Jesus.

If the William Holman Hunt Jesus is a benign, insipid, emasculated man, then spooky Jesus is an otherworldly and distant being. One raps respectfully at the door to your heart, while the other waits serenely for you to approach him. The Hunt Jesus cares, while the Romanesque Jesus knows! If we asked you to show us your Jesus and you said he looked like spooky Jesus, we'd guess you feel most comfortable with the intangible, wise, ethereal, otherworldly, composed aspects of Jesus.

And yet the Jesus we meet in the Gospels is at times frustrated, angry, and disappointed. He is not always serene, his emotions held masterfully in check. Nowhere is this more movingly portrayed than on the night of his betrayal and arrest. After celebrating Passover, the grand Hebrew story of exile and restoration, Jesus and his friends take a late-night stroll in the garden called Gethsemane. There, as he prepares himself for the sacrifice he is about to make, Jesus asks, even begs, his Father three times for some alternative course. Far from the unflinching automaton he can sometimes be portrayed as, Jesus is filled with anxiety and uncertainty. Having asked his dearest friends to wait with him and pray during this his darkest hour, he expresses such sadness and loneliness when they fall asleep: "Could you not watch with me and pray for just one hour?" More than sadness, we can sense his frustration and annoyance at their abandoning him for sleep.

Scott Peck once noted that one of the chief reasons for his trusting the Gospels was their all-too-real description of Jesus. In his agnostic days, before reading them, he had assumed that the Gospels were simply works of hagiography, exaggerated accounts of this mythic holy man, invented by those of his followers committed to creating a cult of personality around him. However, when Peck first read the texts themselves, he was astonished to discover that the Jesus in their pages was nothing like the Romanesque icons he had seen before. He was richer, more textured, more authentically human than any invented folk hero could possibly be. In fact, Peck went on to conclude that the Gospels must be true. If they were inventions by Jesus' followers, those followers would have invented a better messiah than the one found in the Gospels. By that he meant that they would have invented a flawless messiah, one who never showed fear, sadness, or anger. That he isn't a "perfect" Jesus was proof enough that the Gospel writers were faithful reporters, not cunning inventors.

Ordinary Galilean Jesus

N. T. Wright was noted for having said that after the novelist and amateur New Testament scholar A. N. Wilson had finished with Jesus, all we were left with was "a moderately pale Galilean."[5] In fact, Wilson epitomizes that approach to Christology that seeks to strip away all the historical dogma only to find a simple Galilean holy man who had no idea he was launching a major new faith movement by his folksy parables and general good nature. In his surprisingly popular book, *Jesus: A Life*, Wilson concludes rather dramatically that if Jesus "had foreseen the whole of Christian history, his despair would have been even greater than it was when he cried out, 'My God, why hast thou forsaken me?'"[6]

According to Wilson, Jesus didn't think he was the messiah, far less the second person of the Trinity. He was born in an ordinary fashion in Nazareth, not Bethlehem. He taught an inner morality, and his kingdom was more a kind of indestructible inner kingdom than any external reality. He tried to raise the status of women, and he opposed extreme Jewish nationalism. However, when some people tried to foist certain messianic pretensions upon him, he was arrested by the Romans and summarily executed. He stayed dead and was buried in Galilee. Ultimately, he failed. His message was not taken up. When his brother James set about rehabilitating his damaged reputation by reassuring his followers that all had happened according to the Scripture, some people mistook him for his dead brother and a rumor began circulating that Jesus had been resurrected. But the resurrected Jesus was no more than James, who bore a striking family resemblance to his now-deceased brother the *hasid*, or holy man.

For Wilson, Paul is the great inventor of Christianity. Paul took the sayings of Jesus and the passion of the earliest Christians and constructed the complex theology of the New Testament, moving it far away from the simple teaching of Jesus. And the rest is history!

Wilson's speculation gives us a Jesus who is an ordinary itinerant storyteller and religious guru. He probably married (some writers believe he married Mary Magdalene and fathered children or a child with her). Jesus is damned with faint praise. He was a "great teacher," "a good man," "a holy man." What this means is he was an ordinary man, and the only way to explain the incredible movement of Jesus followers that combusted soon after his death is to give the credit to someone else. That someone is the villain of the piece, the dastardly Apostle Paul. He took Jesus' uncomplicated folk Judaism and perverted it into the complex system known today as Christianity.

Jesus. Computer Model.
From the BBC's *Son of God.*

The picture above was created for a BBC special on Jesus in 2001. Forensic scientists took a skull from first-century Palestine and, using the reconstructive techniques currently employed by police investigators when trying to determine the identity of an unidentified skull, constructed this face. They added facial hair in keeping with what historians know of the fashion of the time and colored its skin to reflect Middle Eastern men today. The BBC wasn't claiming that this is the face of Jesus. Rather, they pointed out that this is what a typical Jewish man in Palestine looked like two thousand years ago. The heavy brow, swarthy complexion, and thick features are a world away from the bearded lady or the Romanesque Jesus. According to Wilson, this is the Galilean we mistook for the savior of the world.

Suffice to say, this is an image of Jesus that's not too popular in churches. Try this: conduct an exercise with church folk or even seminarians. Display a number of images of Jesus, including the ones we've looked at here, and ask them to rank the images from favorite to least favorite. It has been our experience that in almost every case, the BBC Jesus ranks last. Church folk seem to prefer their Jesus to look more impressive than this guy. However, we strongly suspect that outside the church, more and more people are being taken by the ordinary Galilean of Wilson. For instance, Robert Funk from the Jesus Seminar paints Jesus as a radical, gadfly, and social deviant who serves up some alternate construction of reality through his esoteric parables. Funk's colleague, John Dominic Crossan, offers a Jesus who was setting up an egalitarian community in Galilee by free healing and meals open to all comers. For them, Jesus is more easily dealt with as a great poet or a teacher of love. Of course this only begs the question, how does the poet-cum-social-worker Jesus heal the sick? The silence is deafening.

Such attempts to domesticate and secularize Jesus are flawed from the start. When rock star Bono was challenged that Jesus could be ranked among the world's great thinkers, but that to consider him the son of God was far-fetched, he had a great response:

> No, it's not farfetched to me. Look, the secular response to the Christ story always goes like this: he was a great prophet, obviously a very interesting guy, had a lot to say along the lines of other great prophets, be they Elijah, Muhammad, Buddha or Confucius. But actually Christ doesn't allow you that. He doesn't let you off that hook. Christ says: No. *I'm not saying I'm a teacher, don't call me teacher. I'm not saying I'm a prophet. I'm saying: "I'm the Messiah." I'm saying: "I am God incarnate." And people say: No, no, please, just be a prophet. A prophet, we can take. You're a bit eccentric. We've had John the Baptist eating locusts and wild honey, we can handle that. But don't mention the "M" word! Because, you know, we're gonna have to crucify you.* And he goes: *No, no. I know you're expecting me to come back with an army, and set you free from these creeps, but actually I am the Messiah.* At this point, everyone starts staring at their shoes, and says: *Oh, my God, he's gonna keep saying this.* So what you're left with is: either Christ was who He said He was—the Messiah—or a complete nutcase. I mean, we're talking nutcase on the level of Charles Manson. This man was like some of the people we've been talking about earlier. This man was strapping himself to a bomb, and had "King of the Jews" on his head, and, as they were putting him up on the Cross, was going: OK, *martyrdom, here we go. Bring on the pain! I can take it.* I'm not joking here. The idea that the entire course of civilization for over half of the globe could have its fate changed and turned upside-down by a nutcase, for me, *that's* farfetched . . .[7]

And he's right! The secular Jesus doesn't make any sense when you read the Gospels and hear his personal claims of messiahship. For him to pull it off, Wilson has to turn Paul into the architect of the faith, scripting the false claims and putting them in the mouth of the unsuspecting Galilean. Theologian Barbara Thiering and Episcopalian bishop John Spong each developed a whole approach to biblical hermeneutics that required a sophisticated understanding of the encoding of *midrash*, explaining away Jesus' more embarrassing claims to be the Son of God. Dan Brown, author of *The Da Vinci Code*, blames the Emperor Constantine and his cadre of fake gospel writers. But if we take the Gospels' claims about Jesus seriously, we are left with exactly the dilemma Bono outlines—either Jesus is the Christ or he just thought he was the Christ.

We confess we do like Bono, but to give credit where it's due, it was C. S. Lewis who first posed this formulation for dismissing those who prefer the "good teacher" Jesus:

> I am here trying to prevent anyone from saying the really foolish thing that people often say about Him: "I'm ready to accept Jesus as a great moral teacher, but I don't accept his claim to be God." That is the one thing we must not say. A man who was merely a man and said the sort of things Jesus said would not be a great moral teacher. He would either be a lunatic—on the level with the man who says he is a poached egg—or else he would be the Devil of Hell. You must make your own choice. Either this man was, and is, the Son of God; or else a madman or something worse. . . . But let us not come up with any patronizing nonsense about his being a great human teacher. He has not left that open to us. He did not intend to.[8]

This is the "liar, lunatic, or Lord" approach and it makes a good argument: you cannot dismiss Jesus as a good teacher or an ordinary Galilean holy man. Neither can you be satisfied with the serene, bearded-lady Jesus or the more alien-like spooky Jesus. The Gospels don't allow you that.

Revolutionary Jesus

As we have noted already, the Gospel story makes clear that those who understood Jesus and his message the best were those who most wanted him dead. He was considered a threat and a danger to the religious system of Judaism but presumably also to the impressionable masses. It's hard to imagine the bearded-lady Jesus, spooky Jesus, or ordinary Galilean Jesus threatening anybody. But Jesus' contemporaries saw him as a usurper of institutional religion, a blasphemer, a heretic, a drunkard, a glutton, and a false teacher. He was an unschooled rabbi from the God-forsaken north who had run amok and begun to stir up trouble among the equally uneducated populace. In his enemies' minds he was an extremist, a radical, a revolutionary.

There have been a few attempts over the years to react against the insipid depictions of Jesus. In the 1960s, the radical Italian filmmaker Pier Paolo Pasolini, a homosexual, a communist, and an atheist to boot, made a remarkable film based on Matthew's Gospel. His Jesus is a sinister-looking man, nearly always shrouded in a dark hood, presenting his parables not as heart-warming stories but as revolutionary tracts. He is stern, brusque, and demanding, insisting that he's come not to bring peace but a sword. Pasolini presents him as a subversive, covertly moving from place to place near the Sea of Galilee, sometimes attracting a multitude, sometimes being driven away. Interestingly, Pasolini's script for the film, entitled *The Gospel According to Saint Matthew*, is taken directly from Matthew's gospel and includes a clear depiction of the resurrection. Given that Pasolini was considered an unsavory character and that his Jesus is played as an unsettling radical, this film doesn't get much play in most church circles.[9] And yet Pasolini presents a conservative portrayal of Jesus, more in keeping with the Gospels than that of the pious William Holman Hunt.

Jesus. Film still from *Il Vangelo secondo Matteo (The Gospel According to Saint Matthew)*, directed by Pier Paolo Pasolini.

Then, in 1999, at the end of the Church of England's so-called decade of evangelism, the following advertisement appeared across the United Kingdom. It portrayed Jesus as a kind of Che Guevara character on a revolutionary red banner with the slogan, "Meek. Mild. As If." We thought it was cool, but on the original posters the bottom line read, "Discover the real Jesus. Church. April 4." We suspect that those who dared to go with the idea that Jesus was a revolutionary were less likely to believe they could find him in an Anglican church on a Sunday in England on April 4, or any other day for that matter. The usual image of the local parson hardly correlates with the Che-Jesus image below.

In the correct sense of the terms, Jesus was probably more a reformer than a revolutionary. He wasn't committed to overturning the whole religious system of which he was part. Indeed, as he points out, "Do not think that I have come to abolish the law or the prophets; I have come not to abolish but to fulfill" (Matt 5:17). His work was to transform Israel, and beyond

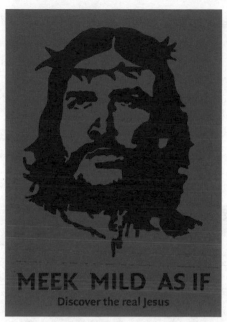

MEEK MILD AS IF
Discover the real Jesus

Jesus. Church of England poster, 1999.

that the world, not by rejecting or abolishing Israel's faith but by embodying it and calling Israel back to its true belief. Such radical reformation would have considerable impact on the structures of the religious institutions of Israel, and those beholden to such structures saw this a mile off. In this respect, Jesus is calling Israel to what we referred to earlier as radical foundationalism.

Is it any wonder that those equally beholden to the structures of the religious institutions of Christendom are just as concerned about the revolutionary Jesus being set loose in their churches! Our hope is that church leaders would recognize that Jesus doesn't want to destroy what they've got now—he just wants to reshape it radically.

Fully Human Fully Divine Jesus

One ancient icon seems to us to be more balanced. It was found in the monastery of St. Catherine in the Sinai desert. While still sporting a dramatic halo, the St. Catherine's icon depicts Jesus as tranquil and unruffled. To be sure, he has the face of a Roman scholar rather than a Palestinian rabbi, but the artist has none of the spookiness seen in other pictures of Jesus. He has painted him as an all-wise teacher. His face is not symmetrical like that in many spooky Jesus icons. It is more flawed, less lovely than the others. Such religious portraiture was rare though. The Romanesque depiction of Jesus' face characteristically portrayed him with a mask-like visage and a radically expressionistic, transfixing gaze. This, along with the halo, was supposed to convey a sense of the transcendent or the holy. Early Christian artists were conscious that Jesus was both fully human and fully divine, but when depicting him in icons, paintings, murals, and stained glass, they erred on the side of the divine, assuming that a divine human wouldn't look quite like a, well, human human.

Jesus. *Christ Pantocrator.* Icon at
St. Catherine's Monastery, Sinai.
Encaustic on panel.

⟿ The Jesus of the Age

Having attempted to debunk the many inadequate and even false images of Jesus that distort our true appreciation of him, we acknowledge that every age brings with it a new perspective on the multifaceted Jesus who has so captured the minds and hearts of millions throughout history. As selective as these images must be when viewed against his wholeness, nonetheless there is merit in surveying the effect that these images have had on forming the culture and societies of their day. Jaroslav Pelikan has done precisely that in his fine work *Jesus Through the Centuries*. In this book he reveals how each image of Jesus created by each successive era is a key to understanding the temper and values of that age—its strengths and its deficiencies. His table of contents provides us with a list of some of the successive images that have informed history over two millennia:[10]

- ⟿ *The Rabbi*: informs the early New Testament period, particularly that of Jewish Christianity.

- ⟿ *The Turning Point of History*: encapsulates the increasing significance of Jesus for the first and second centuries.

- ⟿ *The Light of the Gentiles*: highlights the pagan anticipations of Christ as prefigured in Socrates and Virgil and the other poet-philosophers of the pre-Christian period.

- ⟿ *The King of Kings*: highlights the lordship of Jesus over against the lordship of Caesar culminating in the Constantinian contract and the rise of the Christian Empire.

- ⟿ *The Cosmic Christ*: focuses on Christ as Logos, mind, and reason informing the rising Christianized Platonism of the third and fourth centuries.

- ⟿ *The Son of Man*: informs the Augustinian Christian psychology and anthropology of the fifth century.

- ⟿ *The True Image*: Christ as the inspiration for true art and architecture in the Byzantine period.

- ⟿ *The Christ Crucified*: in the Middle Ages, the cross becomes the most significant image in art and literature, emphasizing the saving work of Jesus (tenth and eleventh centuries).

↩   *The Monk Who Rules the World*: the triumph of the Benedictine vision of the world represents the triumph of monasticism.

↩   *The Bridegroom of the Soul*: the rise of Christian mysticism interprets the Song of Songs as an allegory of the love of Christ and the believer.

↩   *The Divine and Human Model*: Francis of Assisi helps restore the full humanity of Jesus and leads to the transformation of the institutional church of the thirteenth and fourteenth centuries.

↩   *The Universal Man*: the image of the Renaissance period with its rediscovery of Christian humanism.

↩   *The Mirror of the Eternal*: Christ as mirror of the true, the beautiful, and the good that features in the Reformation period.

↩   *The Prince of Peace*: the Crusades and the wars of religion also cause a resurgence of Christian pacifism, especially mirrored in Anabaptist circles.

↩   *The Teacher of Common Sense*: the quest for the historical Jesus in scholarship and philosophy of the Enlightenment period.

↩   *The Poet of the Spirit*: idealism and romantic philosophy of the nineteenth century arises in protest against orthodox rigidity and rationalist banality.

↩   *The Liberator*: applies to both nineteenth and twentieth centuries. From Marx to Tolstoy, to Gandhi and Martin Luther King Jr., Jesus' prophetic opposition to economic and political oppression and injustice is highlighted.

↩   *The Man Who Belongs to the World*: the unprecedented spread in the twentieth century of the message of Jesus means that massive populations in the Third World come into the fold. Jesus becomes a truly world figure engaging the other religions in a more significant way.

Although we think that it is just about impossible to sum up an era in one image and Pelikan's choices might seem arbitrary, nonetheless as a historian, his approach highlights the ongoing role of Jesus in shaping the culture and history of the West. But mostly it is helpful in understanding the images of Jesus that seem to capture the spirit of an age. What is most helpful perhaps is seeing that Jesus is all of the above. He is Rabbi, King of kings, Cosmic Christ, Light of the Nations, and so on. And herein lies the problem: to limit him to one image is to limit the magnificence of the person that we meet in Jesus.

⟵ What Kind of Man Is This?

Some time ago, Michael had the opportunity to conduct a regular worship gathering with a group of people who felt uncomfortable in traditional churches. They were an interesting collective of artists, writers, and cultural creatives, some of whom had church backgrounds but had rejected it all and others who had never set foot in a church building. They met for a whole summer in a cramped art gallery above a café. The gallery owners were intrigued by Jesus and had gathered a motley crew of unlikely people together to worship him. Some were unemployed. Some were working only occasionally as artists. Others were suffering with mental illness. Michael and his wife, Carolyn, would lead them through a short, simple liturgy of prayers and music, using uncomplicated symbols like stones, broken pottery, candles, and, of course, bread and wine.

One of the features of the gathering was a brief study of John's Gospel followed by a discussion about the text. John's Gospel launches right in with John the Baptist's ministry and his identification of Jesus as the Lamb of God, followed quickly by the turning of water into wine at Cana and the cleansing of the temple and Jesus' late-night conversation with Nicodemus about being born again.

What was interesting was how this group approached the text. They immediately saw things that most churched groups don't see. They saw Jesus siding with the oppressed and the marginalized. They read the scenes at the Jordan River as John and Jesus leading the forgotten, the poor, and the downtrodden out of the desert through the refreshing waters toward hope and strength. They saw Jesus' transformation of ceremonial waters into wedding wine as his subversive act of taking those religious symbols designed to separate the holy from the unholy and converting them into something delicious for all to enjoy. They identified his fury in the temple as his shattering of the institutional system that denied access and equity to the poor penitents who were forced to change their money and purchase birds for religious sacrifices. They overheard Jesus telling Nicodemus about how the transformation he was initiating began with a transformation of the heart, the inner things over which all people have control, not the outer world, which only the rich or powerful have the capacity to change.

In effect, they read the Gospel as being largely about exile and restoration (not that they would have expressed it in these terms). They read it this way because they felt like exiles from institutional religion. To these exiles who felt too dirty to attend church, the Jordan River scenes were a reminder that Jesus is calling everyone, not just the clean, to his side. To these exiles who had been told that they needed to be washed before they could approach God, the wedding at Cana convinced them that in Jesus' kingdom they were welcomed guests and that there was plenty of wine for all. Likewise, to them the cleansing of the temple presented a Jesus who would stop at nothing to demolish every religious hoop put in the way of repentant people accessing God.

In *They Like Jesus but Not the Church*, Dan Kimball reports on similar experiences he has had with unchurched people. The title of the book pretty much sums up his main point and summarizes the words of a number of young adults who are drawn to the Jesus of the Gospels but who cannot find a place in the church.[11] This has been our experience as well. That group of desperate Jesus seekers who gathered in that gallery that summer are not dissimilar to the first-century Jews to whom the Gospels were first written. They feel exiled from institutional Christianity. But they are desperate for restoration. What kind of Jesus will restore them? The pristine, pure, serene, bearded lady? He only makes them feel more guilty about their inadequacies. Spooky Jesus? He intrigues them, but ultimately he belongs in the church world of stained glass and flying buttresses, the very world they feel is off limits to them. The ordinary Galilean teacher? At least he's safe. He teaches compassion and kindness, and many exiles would prefer him to the other options, but ultimately he leads them nowhere. He might appeal to their experience of exile, but he promises no restoration.

⟵ Setting Free the Wild Man

One of the stories told about Jesus goes like this: It was said that people didn't venture down to the cliffs on the eastern side of Lake Galilee after dark. In fact, even in broad daylight, unless one had a good reason to be on the steep and desolate banks on the water's edge it was best to stay away. The wild man lived there. An insane, naked man scurried about on all fours out there. More like an animal than a man, he ate what he could scavenge from the pigs that grazed nearby and slept in the cave-tombs among the bones of the dead. His bloodcurdling shrieks could be heard day and night.

He was the stuff of local legend and lore. Parents threatened bad children with setting the wild man on to them. He has the strength of ten men, they warned; no one can hold him down. Half starved and insane, the wild man's hairy body was covered with scabs and sores. He was the object of both mirth and genuine fear among the residents of the Greek-speaking town of Gadara, and they thought that the sooner he died from starvation or infection, the better.

Jews who lived beyond this region had given them all in Gadara up for dead. This, the eastern shore of Lake Galilee, was almost entirely populated with Gentiles. It had been colonized by Greek speakers, who had built as many as ten cities there. Pious Jews had long since left the area to avoid contamination, and those who remained knew they were in pagan territory. Little wonder, some said, that it was overrun by maniacs and lunatics.

When Jesus stepped out of his boat onto the beach near Gadara, he must have suspected what he was in for. Strange it must have seemed to many Jews that he, such a renowned prophet, would even bother with Gadara. Leave them to their own devices, they would have sniffed. They are not ours, or God's, concern.

It's no mistake that Jesus disembarks at the desolate stretch of shoreline under the steep cliffs near the town. In every likelihood he has spotted the wild man from his boat as it approached land. His pathetic wailing and scampering about on the cliffs would have made him conspicuous, to say the least. Where other boatmen would have put to shore far from this madman, Jesus makes a beeline toward him. And no sooner do his feet touch the soil than the wild man rushes him. This might have scared off many an unwary traveler, but Jesus, something of a wild man himself, is unmoved.

"What do you want with me, Jesus, Son of the Most High God? Swear to God that you won't torture me," he shrieks. Such a knowing request betrays his condition. He is a demoniac, meaning that his personality is under the mastery of an evil power or powers. The effect is the destruction of human character. He has been brought to isolation from society, stripped of his moral integrity, and reduced to a state of utter physical degradation.

This man, despised and rejected by men, has not just stumbled fortuitously upon Jesus but has been sought out by him. The demons declare themselves to be in great number. "I am called Legion," cries the pathetic man, overwhelmed by evil forces who have the audacity to beg Jesus to cast them not into hell but into a nearby herd of swine. And remarkably, Jesus, having negotiated with demons, agrees to their request and sends them skittling into the pigs, who end up plunging over the cliffs into the lake and drowning.

What kind of Messiah accedes to the wishes of demons? What kind of Messiah destroys the income of a local swineherd? It would be like blowing up a grocer's corner store! These poor farmers don't deserve to watch their bloated, drowned pigs floating in Lake Galilee, do they? Shouldn't the Messiah be on the side of the poor? The demons get more courtesy from Jesus than do the swineherds. What kind of prophet is this?

This is the kind of prophet who finds clothes for the wild man, who dresses him and feeds him and treats him with the dignity and respect, the attention and love every human being deserves. When they come running to see what's happened, the locals find dead pigs, destitute farmers, and the untamed, naked wild man now clothed and in his right mind. The bizarre scene scares the daylights out of these pagan people. Strong magic has come to their shores, and they beg the strange magician to leave the area quickly.

As Jesus climbs into his boat, the wild man takes his arm. "Let me come with you. There's nothing for me here. I will serve you all my days."

Yet while the demons' request was granted, the wild man's is denied. Forced to remain in the Gadarenes, he goes on to be confirmed as part of local lore forever as the wild man who was rehabilitated by the even wilder Messiah from Nazareth.

Is it any wonder than Jesus is at home among the wild things? He inaugurated his public ministry by fasting for forty days in the wilderness where the wild beasts roam. He is untamed and unfettered, and his ministry is indicative of this. It runs amok wherever he goes. Indeed Jesus conducts his ministry as a kind of fugitive. As we've seen, after his inaugural sermon in Luke 4, he is manhandled toward a cliff in an attempted assassination. He evades the baying mob, but his public ministry is then conducted in a renegade fashion. Then in Mark 3, when Jesus returns to his old hometown, the neighbors are repulsed by his teaching, declaring him to be insane ("He has gone out of his mind"). Even his family are so outraged by his behavior that they attempt to restrain him for his own good. They are embarrassed by his wild ideas. In John 7, his brothers rebuke him because they see him as skulking around in Galilee: "No one who wants to become a public figure acts in secret. Since you are doing these things, show yourself to the world" (Luke 7:4). Later in that same chapter (v. 32), when the Pharisees send out temple police to arrest him, he evades capture and continues on the run.

Somehow we ignore these indications that Jesus' public ministry was operating "under the radar" with a band of impressionable young men by his side. One of his inner circle was Simon the Zealot. The Zealots were an underground anti-imperialist movement dedicated to driving the Romans out of Israel. They wanted political freedom but also they wanted a purified, traditionalist theocratic Jewish state free from the interference of pagan Rome. As well as the militant Simon, Jesus also attracted James and John. Some New Testament scholars think that their nickname, "the sons of thunder," may link them to the insurrectionists as well. Furthermore, some of Jesus' first followers had been disciples of the ascetic and ferociously anti-social John the Baptist. Having attracted these disaffected radicals to his side, Jesus was seen as a danger to society.

And why wouldn't he be? Even his friends were somewhat frightened by him. When Jesus asks them what people are saying about him, they reply that some think he is a resurrected John the Baptist, or even Elijah (Luke 9:18f). They're not saying they think he is a real softy, a big, gorgeous guru of love and goodwill. They think he's a resurrected wild man, for that's surely what both John and Elijah were when alive. Indeed these rumors had reached even King Herod, who had had John executed (Luke 9:7). John the Baptist back from the dead! That would be a frightening sight.

Our point is that to reJesus the church, we need to go back to the daring, radical, strange, wonderful, inexplicable, unstoppable, marvelous, unsettling, disturbing, caring, powerful God-Man. The communities around us are crying out for him. They are turning up in droves to hear the Dalai Lama speak. They are buying mountains of books on popular theology. They are traipsing over sacred sites across the globe. They are searching for the promised one, the one who offers them restoration and peace. The church needs to find itself in league with this Jesus, staring at him in amazement and saying, as Peter did, with a trembling voice, "What kind of man is this?" Even the wind and waves obey him. Even the wild demons obey him. Even the Pharisees quake at the thought of what he might unleash if left to his own devices.

⟵ Notes

1. C. S. Lewis, *The Lion, the Witch, and the Wardrobe* (New York: Macmillan, 1981), 74.

2. *Talladega Nights: The Ballad of Ricky Bobby*, directed by Adam McKay (Culver City, Calif., Sony Pictures, 2006).

3. C. Forbes, "Images of Christ in Nineteenth-Century British Paintings in the Forbes Magazine Collection," *Magazine Antiques*, December 2001, 12.

4. Alison Morgan, *The Wild Gospel* (Oxford: Monarch, 2007), 36.

5. N. T. Wright, *Who Was Jesus?* (London: SPCK, 1992), 37ff.

6. A. N. Wilson, *Jesus* (London: Sinclair-Stevenson, 1992), quoted in Wright, *Who Was Jesus?* 38.

7. "Bono: Grace over Karma," excerpt from *Bono: In Conversation with Mischka Assayas* (New York: Riverhead, 2005), ChristianityToday.com, August 8, 2005. Cited 1 August 2008. Online: http://www.christianitytoday.com/music/interviews/2005/bono-0805.html.

8. C. S. Lewis, *Mere Christianity* (New York: Macmillan, 1952), 55–56.

9. Interestingly, this film was included in the 1995 Vatican list of films "suitable for viewing by the faithful."

10. Jaroslav Pelikan, *Jesus Through the Centuries* (New Haven, Conn.: Yale University Press, 1999), vii–ix.

11. Dan Kimball, *They Like Jesus but Not the Church* (Grand Rapids, Mich.: Zondervan, 2007).

Chapter Five

The Shema Schema
(One God, One Love)

*Monotheism is a outcome of the exclusive claim of
Yahweh, rather than a conceptual hypothesis resulting
from human effort to gain a unitary view of his world.*
—Paul Minear

*R. Joshua ben Korba said: Why does the section
"Hear, O Israel" (Deut 6:4–9) precede the section
"And it shall come to pass if ye shall hearken
diligently to my commandments"? So that a man
may first take upon himself the yoke of the kingdom
of Heaven and afterward take upon him the
yoke of the commandments.*
—The Talmud

All this talk about Jesus, discipleship, and the church raises a whole set of questions relating to a broader understanding of God. Where is the place of God in a discussion on Christology and the missional church? We mean to turn our attention to this very question, and in doing so we hope to frame the discussion within the most fundamental revelation of God in the Bible, namely, that he is One and that he claims us and that this claim excludes all other claims for ultimate loyalty. In effect, we are going to look at biblical (existential) monotheism and its implications for a missional worldview, as well as some of the practical outworkings of it for life and faith. Monotheism, interpreted from within the biblical worldview, is the belief that the one God, Lord and Creator of all, has rightful claim to sovereignty over all that he has created. Viewed in this way, Jesus' teachings of the kingdom of God are one way of expressing the claim of the one God over all creation.

The reader might well be tempted to dismiss this chapter as being overly theological and therefore choose to skip it to get to the more practical stuff. We believe this would be a serious mistake, not because the practical isn't important but because so much of the practical stuff is bound up directly with our understanding of God. This goes to the issue of worldview—if we go wrong on monotheism, our most elemental view of God, the whole enterprise is threatened. We ought to be mindful once again of William Temple's warnings about the nature of theological error when he noted that if our conception of God is radically false, then the more devout we are the worse it will be for us. We believe that the fundamental correction for the church at the dawn of the twenty-first century must be a christological one that will in turn revolutionize our missiology as well as our ecclesiology. But we must be patient, and we need to be as accurate as we can, because when one is journeying to the moon, one degree off at launch and we will miss it by thousands of miles. If this is not already obvious, this theological corrective must take place in the realm of Christology. But to understand Christology properly, we need to probe the most basic assumption in the biblical revelation of God, namely, the assumption that God is One and that he redeems and claims us in and through Jesus the Messiah.

⟵ One God

The representative text on this topic is what Jewish people call the *Shema*. "Hear, O Israel: The Lord our God, the Lord is one; and you shall love the Lord your God with all your heart, and with all your soul, and with all your mind, and with all your strength." As a righteous Jew, Jesus himself affirms that there are no greater commandments than these (Mark 12:31).

The word *shema* is the first word in the text of Deuteronomy 6:4–9, and it means "hear" or " pay attention." This call to attention highlights what follows. And what follows is more than simply a statement about God and God's relationship to the people of God (and it is that). It also contains within it the fundamentals of the worldview of the Bible because it ties together a distinct way of ethical living with a distinct understanding of God. The *Shema* also assumes the whole idea of a covenant relationship between the players—a deeply personal and well-defined connection between God and the people Israel. Observant Jews of all varieties confess the *Shema* three times a day, thus highlighting its nature as a prototypal summary of biblical faith. This text is of essential importance because it contains the guiding idea of God that is basic to Jewish faith, is assumed by all the writers of the New Testament, and is adopted into the faith of Islam.

This concept of the oneness of God represents a striking contrast to that of the religious thought of the cultures that surrounded Israel where the multiplicity of gods in turn led to great upheaval and tension in human life. For polytheists, though a person might carry out his religious duties with care, he or she could not be guaranteed any security, for if there was strife among the gods, this would radically affect human life. Though a given god might promise much to the individual person, a more powerful god might still bring disaster. The resulting tension often led to a deep pessimism in religious life and thought. This is not as theoretical as it sounds at first. The average modern polytheists-next-door also lack an integrating center of life. They live under the rules of economics, nationalism, sex, family, and whatever other idols they set up. And make no mistake; these are idols that can dominate a person's life and consciousness. History is clear about that. People will kill for these if necessary. These idols compete with one another and demand loyalty and obeisance, but they can never deliver ultimate meaning to life. Because life is fragmented, distributed among the many, it therefore allows no unified vision of reality to emerge. In radical contrast to the belief in many gods, Yahweh is the one and only God who redeems his people and subsequently requires that they love him as he had already loved them.[1] And the nature of this God and the form this love of God should take is made known to us in Scripture, nature, and history. He is good, holy, just, and compassionate, and he requires us to be the same. To be in relationship with him therefore brings meaning, focus, moral vision, and an ultimate reality to human life.

This revelation of God as One speaks not only of the uniqueness of God (over against the many) but also the unity within God and therefore the world God has created. The God of the universe *is* the God of history. We assert that this understanding of God lies at the root of the whole biblical worldview. It clearly motivates and inspires the faith of the New Testament. Monotheistic statements permeate the New Testament, whether they are statements of faith in the one God (1 Cor 8:4–6; Eph 4:6; 1 Tim 2:5; Rom 3:30; Jas 2:19), the only God (Rom 16:27; 1 Tim 1:17; 6:15; Jude 25; John 17:3), or the God from whom all things derive (Rom 11:36; Heb 2:10; 1 Cor 8:6; Rev 4:11). These affirmations demonstrate a complete continuity with the Old Testament and its fundamental proclamation of existential (Deut 5:7) and theoretical

(Deut 4:35) monotheism.² And as such it forms the most basic assumption from which apostle, prophet, priest, and king operate.

But this concern with monotheism is especially present in the teachings of Jesus where he places strong emphasis on the affirmation of one God.

Release to the Captives

William Wilberforce

William Wilberforce is accredited with leading the campaign for the abolition of slavery in the British Empire in the early nineteenth century. A descendant of a wealthy family, a member of the British House of Commons, and a man with a weak constitution, Wilberforce perhaps seems an unlikely little Jesus. But his conversion to evangelical faith in 1784 led to his joining the Clapham Sect, a group of evangelical and abolitionist members of the Anglican Church. It was in this group that Wilberforce's interest in social reform was piqued. In 1789 he made his first speech against the slave trade, which launched him on what would become a monumental political battle to end slavery, a struggle dogged by many failures and setbacks. It wasn't until 1807 that the Abolition of the Slave Trade bill was finally passed through both British Houses of Parliament. Though celebrated as a milestone in the abolitionist cause, outlawing the slave trade didn't actually end slavery itself, and many slave traders continued to flout the new laws. Wilberforce helped launch a new phase of the campaign and sought to end human slavery for good. Exhausted by the campaign and the parlous state of his health, Wilberforce retired in 1825. In 1833 he received news of the impending passing of the Slavery Abolition Act. "Thank God that I should have lived to witness a day in which England is willing to give twenty million pounds for the abolition of slavery," he is quoted as saying. He died two days later. As a little Jesus, Wilberforce is commended for his unstinting effort to abolish slavery and promote equality among races in a turbulent time.

In Mark 12:28–34, Jesus responds to a question about the greatest commandment by directly quoting the *Shema* (Deut 6:4–5), thus affirming the primacy of monotheistic faith. Yet the fullness of this quotation, with its emphasis on total devotion to God, and the addition of a "second like it," the loving of one's neighbors as oneself, draws out the ethical consequence of faith that is so distinctly in *Shema* faith.

In Mark 10:18–19 this same idea is stressed, for the affirmation of God's unique goodness ("No one is good but God alone") is immediately followed by a list of ethical imperatives that derive from the uniquely good God. The monotheistic confession was thus taken seriously by Jesus, not because there was a pervasive rational challenge to it but because its ethical implications were so serious. Dedication to the one God, according to Jesus, must be demonstrated by living out God's ethical demands.[3] Scot McKnight's *Jesus Creed: Loving God, Loving Others* explores how the foundational monotheism in the *Shema* informs Jesus' teachings and the New Testament.[4]

This connection between belief in the one God and the way of life in the believer has been given the rather unappealing label *ethical monotheism*. We prefer, for reasons that will become obvious, to call it existential monotheism. And what it means is that inherent in the whole notion of monotheism, genuine relationship with the biblical God must result in a lifestyle consistent with the nature of the covenant God.[5] So the *Shema* is not so much a statement about the unity and oneness of God as it is a statement about the relationship that God has to Israel and the church.

So we can see that linked with ethical monotheism is the whole spirituality of the people born of this revelation. Therefore discipleship, worship, and mission must take a direct cue from the claim of the one Lord over our lives. This has far-reaching consequences for us, because, as we shall see, it also implies the obliteration of all the life-cramping dualisms (e.g., sacred and secular, the body and the spirit) that have plagued Christian thinking in the Western tradition. This can be represented something like this.

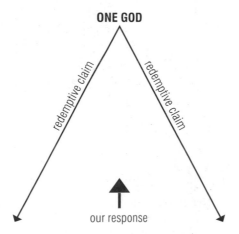

The diagram shows our view of God at the top, and our response at the bottom. Our response is the way we act based on our view of God. The above illustrates the unifying and all-compassing nature of the claim that

God makes over the lives of his chosen people. Everything is caught up into the redemptive lordship of the One. We use the term "existential" here because for us it best describes the dynamics of biblical monotheism, not so much as a philosophy or doctrine but as the impact that an encounter with the one God has on the whole lives of those who truly encounter him.[6]

⟵One Love

Monotheism, as the biblical players experienced it, is not so much an attempt to probe the inner nature of eternal Being but rather a response to an encounter with the living God. There is a clear, direct, and indissoluble link between God and the lifestyles that ought to emerge from an encounter with God. But biblical faith in God moves us beyond mere ethics and intellectual knowledge of God to something far more impacting and all-embracing.[7] The whole of life is caught up, focused, and directed in the God encounter. To attempt to avoid this far-reaching claim that God makes on our lives is to miss a truly godly experience. To try and explain the situation created by God's visit, we can do no other than exclaim, "the Lord our God, he is the one Lord." This is a profoundly existential confession, an act in which our whole being, our very lives, are drawn together and concentrated.

There is a gulf of difference between the existential view of monotheism and the philosophical one. The philosopher poses the question of the nature of God in a form quite alien to the outlook of the biblical writers. The philosopher makes the problem one of intellect rather than of action; he or she views the problem speculatively to gain objective understanding of a concept of God rather than existentially in terms of personal involvement with God.[8] To us who claim the name of Jesus, only one power is sovereign—the God we encounter in our Lord Jesus Christ. And we are called to respond with our lives. As Paul Minear writes:

> The sole sovereignty of God is realized only by stern struggle with other gods, with all the forces that oppose his will. This is to say that, to the biblical writers, monotheism begins not as a stage of metaphysical speculation, not as a final step in the development out of polytheism, not as the merging of all gods into one (as in Hinduism), but when one God becomes the decisive reality for a particular man and thereby calls for the dethronement of all his other gods.

> This helps to explain why early Christians found in the total obedience of Jesus a supreme and final manifestation of God, a manifestation of which by its very

nature transcended history, judged history, and redeemed history. It points to the reason why, in dying to the world, they experienced true knowledge of God and true power from God. And this message of the oneness of God intensified their struggle against false gods. To them, the conflict with heathen gods had entered its final stage. Everywhere their testimony is ambivalent: there are no such gods for us, yet there are many daemonic powers that are attacking us most viciously. Their ambivalence in the struggle between God and upstart deities will disappear only when all others have been subdued by Christ and brought within the sovereignty of God.

Christian belief does not consist in saying "there is one God." The devil knows that! Christians respond to their God by faith in his deeds, by trusting in his power, hoping in his promise and passionately abandoning themselves to do his will. Only within the context of such a passionate vocation does the knowledge of the one Lord live. And this knowledge necessitates rather than eliminates the struggle with the devil and all his works. To paraphrase Kierkegaard, only in unconditional obedience, spurred by infinite passion, infinite resignation, infinite enthusiasm, is such "monotheism" wholly manifested in human existence, as for example, in Jesus.[9]

Seek First the Kingdom

Beyond the defining encounter with the One who claims us, the existential approach gets us much closer to what the Bible teaches about discipleship and genuine belief in God. And all these aspects come into clearer focus in Jesus' teaching on the kingdom of God. Viewed from the angle of existential monotheism, the kingdom of God can be viewed as "the business, or working, end" of the claim of the One God over all of life.[10]

The New Testament writers' use of the phrase "the kingdom of God" is another way of saying that God is One, and that he is indeed King, and that he claims all and rules over all. We miss it because we don't understand monotheism the way the first-century Jews did. While there might be a difference of opinion over Jesus' use of this phrase, most scholars would agree that the kingdom of God refers to the active reign of God everywhere and over everyone. It is the activity of God in all spheres of life, especially in the church, but also well beyond it. We like the way Eugene Peterson puts it:

> The "political" metaphor, "Kingdom," insists on a gospel that includes everything and everyone under the rule of God. God is no religious glow to warm a dark night. Christ is no esoteric truth with which to form a Gnostic elite. The

Christian faith is an out-in-the-open, strenuous, legislating, conquering total-ity. God is sovereign: nothing and no one is exempt from his rule.[11]

It is easy to see how the concepts of monotheism and the kingdom of God are related. The way the earliest Christians expressed this was by restat-ing Israel's ancient belief in the kingdom of Yahweh and by attaching the active function of kingship/lordship to Jesus. Seen in this light, the church's elemental confession that "Jesus is Lord" captures all the meaning and sig-nificance of the biblical teaching on the kingdom of God. Reconfiguring our previous diagram, we can frame it as follows.

Our view of God is that Jesus is Lord, and the kingdom of God is the arena in which we respond to God's sovereign rule over this world. All is included (and nothing is excluded) in this claim. Once again the all-encompassing nature of existential monotheism comes to the fore.

⟶ You Shall Be Holy Because I Am Holy

Because the claim of God penetrates so deeply into the human heart and into every aspect of life, it must by its nature provoke a deeply personal response in return. The *Shema* binds the believer to a love of God that de-mands nothing less than heart, soul, and strength as the appropriate re-sponse to the initiating love of God. We cannot encounter God and walk away unchanged and unmotivated. We cannot confess with our lips and not fol-low with our lives. The call to an appropriate holiness is implied in all true knowledge of God ("be holy, for I am holy," Lev 11:44). In other words, a true encounter with the one God generates a life-embracing, all-encompassing ethic. Anything less and it is not a biblical view of God.

For instance, Mark Sayers, comrade and commentator on culture and the gospel, suggests that while the vast majority of people in Western contexts say they believe in some form of god,[12] the god they believe in is so distant and their idea of him/her/it is so vague that it fails to generate any transforming impact. Sayers calls this the "break-glass-in-case-of-emergency-god," the being we invoke when we get into trouble or experience some form national disaster. But this god of the popular mind is so remote that it fails to have any practical impact on daily life whatsoever. In other words, popular ideas of god, whether they are new religious movements or vague notions of a higher power, almost universally fail to engender a way of life as response . . . an ethic, an ethos, a Way.

But this view of God as distant leads to a lack of engagement with God (indicated by the broken lines leading to and from the idea of God in the diagram). This creates a vacuum in the life of an individual, and so other things rush in to fill the vacuum. In our day, consumerism is the chief idol: the provider of meaning, identity, community, and purpose. In other words, the spiritual quest for happiness (the good life) is mainly pursued through the blessings of consumption. Sayers thus rightly notes that consumerism provides us with a definite form of spirituality.[13] But this combines with the other factor that kicks in as a result of the practical irrelevance of the deity, namely, the deification of the self. With the loss of the holy Other that is God, the self becomes the sole source of authority and thus the only real basis of ethics, guidance, and choices. When this happens, we end up in a vacuous prison of pleasure where the self is trapped in radical bondage to the not-so-tender mercies of the marketers. The god of mammon rears its ugly head again. To illustrate, consider the diagram on the following page.

And Christians are not exempt from this trivialization of God and the resultant deification of the self. In fact, an independent observer could be forgiven for believing that Western Christianity is consumerist to the core. But surely any diminishing of the claims of the one true God, and any deification of the self, is nothing more than another form of religious idolatry. Recall chapter 4, where we discussed the various images that Christians entertain of Jesus. Now apply these images (e.g., bearded-lady Jesus, spooky Jesus, or the iddy-baby Jesus of *Talladega Nights*) to the top of the diagram above. It is not hard to see the impact that this will have on life. For instance, there is

**DISTANT/VAGUE
IDEA OF GOD**

**WE VIEW
SELF AS
GOD** ⟵⟶ our response **WE EMBRACE
CONSUMERISM AS
SPIRITUALITY**

an iconic image of Jesus that came from the film *Dogma*. It is called "buddy Jesus." Buddy Jesus is a view of Jesus that minimizes him to being my pal, mate, a friend who covers my back. There is no reverence here, only bland familiarity. But if our primary image of Jesus is that he is my homeboy, my buddy, then we shouldn't be surprised that the religion that develops around this is a false and profoundly consumerist one.

So what does true spirituality as response look like? How do we love the Lord with heart, soul, mind, and strength, and pass that spirituality on meaningfully to later generations, as the *Shema* suggests (Deut 6:5–9; Matt 22:37–40)? Allow us to suggest a couple of broad ways.

Spirituality Beyond the Sacred and Secular

One of the outcomes of a truly monotheistic view of the world is the annihilation of the dualistic category of sacred and secular. If one God is the source of reality and the reference point for life, how can life be fragmented? When we truly claim Jesus as Lord, how can we claim that some areas of life are non-God areas . . . secular? But this is a tempting thing because integrating life under the one Lord is an arduous task. But integrate we must if we believe as true monotheists. Paul Minear suggests that the biblical writers constantly fight

> against a false separation of sacred from secular, against any reduction in the territory under divine rule. It has often been observed that in neither Testa-

ment can ethics and religion be separated. One finds an ethical religion and a religious ethic precisely because every aspect of life is seen from a single centre, and every aspect is therefore potentially religious and no aspect is *per se* religious.[14]

Glocal (combining global with local) apostle Bob Roberts refers to the domains of our lives and asserts that the kingdom extends to all the domains (religion, science, politics, art, business, education, agriculture, security, family).[15] He sees that mission must entail an engagement in each and every domain and should not be limited to church and merely religious issues, as that would be to limit the activity of the kingdom to that of the church. And yet we know that the kingdom of God is God's activity in and throughout the whole cosmos, including the human and all the domains of human society. Clearly there can be no false sacred-secular divide here. One of the tasks of the church, says Roberts, is to learn how to engage in all of life in order to transform the world.

> We've segmented [our understanding of] how God works. And we've done so to our own detriment. Only when we see the bigger picture of how the pieces fit together can there be any flow or continuity. I call this way of learning, *domain jumping* [and it is] the means to bring together what was previously considered separate . . . instead of learning and mastering only one domain or specialty for a lifetime, we allow one domain to naturally lead to learning in the next related domain. We're curious. We want to know how it all relates, instead of camping out on only one [the religious] domain.[16]

Glocalnet, Robert's training organization, uses what it calls a domain map to help teach church planters to know how to engage society on a practical level. The key is to help people see that their job or vocation puts them in a domain and that is, at the same time, their chief ministry. This breakthrough in terms of our understanding of God's rule in the world and our role in it only highlights how we have failed to fully comprehend the all-encompassing nature of monotheism, whereas Judaism has understood this all along.

When we associate this idea to the christological redefinition of monotheism (as we must), then our task in the world is to be Jesus' agents in every sphere or domain of society. The lordship of Jesus extends to our sexuality, our political life, our economic existence, our family, our play, and everything in between. There must be no limitation to the claim that Jesus makes over all of life. When we get this right, Jesus' lordship takes on a missional edge. "Jesus is Lord" is more like a rallying war cry than a mere theological statement.

Oneness to the One

Judaism has well understood the nature and implications of existential monotheism, and the heart of Jewish spirituality is directly tied to the *Shema*. Jewish people know that if God is one and that all of life comes under that claim of the one God, then the only true response is that we give all of life to God as our true act of worship. They call this task *yichud*, or unification, and it involves taking all of the disparate elements in one's life and offering them up to God. No sphere or domain or aspect of human existence is to be kept out of this equation; politics, economics, family life, religious life, all are directed toward the One. In this offering, all idolatries are renounced, no domain is seen as autonomous, all motivations are to be redeemed and directed toward God, and in so doing the worshipper unifies his or her own existence. This is true holiness (Rom 12:1–3).

Seen in this light we can say that the heart of a genuinely biblical spirituality is found in response to the holy claim of Oneness. For us, as for the Israelite, worship, discipleship, and mission are rolled into the one act of unification as response to the one God, but for us it is focused in Jesus Christ. In yet another reworking of our basic diagram, we can illustrate this as follows.

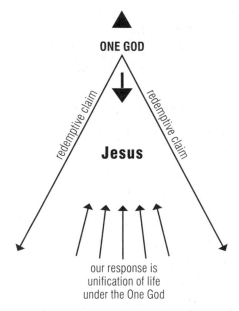

ONE GOD

redemptive claim

redemptive claim

Jesus

our response is
unification of life
under the One God

In this diagram, we see the affirmation of God and the redemptive claim of God, mediated through Jesus Christ. Our response to that claim is that we unify our lives and offer all their disparate elements toward God in and through Jesus. Here we have the spiritual meaning of worship, discipleship, and mission.

Therefore, worship as the Bible characterizes it cannot be limited to singing praise and worship songs to God. Although it includes this, it is far more all-encompassing than that. Worship is nothing less than *offering our whole lives back to God through Jesus*. It is taking all the elements that make up human life (family, friendships, money, work, nation, etc.) and presenting them back to the One who gives them their ultimate meaning in the first place. But what is discipleship if it is not the same type of action? Surely, discipleship is taking all that is me (body and soul) and over a lifetime, directing it to God through Jesus. But the discerning reader would immediately notice that this sounds like a good definition of mission as well, because mission, insofar that it involves us, entails the redemption of a lost world and bringing it back to God. This is what constitutes the biblical idea of holiness—the redemption of the everyday and of everything; oneness in response to the One.

> He who divides his life between God and the world, giving the world what belongs to it in order to save for God what belongs to Him, refuses to give God the service commanded by him, that service which consists in giving the one direction to all the energy, the sanctification of the everyday in the world and in the soul.[17]

And for us, the people of the New Covenant, it is Jesus who provides us with the model of perfect worship and true holiness. Jesus is the center point where God's claim and human response correlate. He is the perfect human being, the true Israel, who has offered up perfect worship and in his redeeming death brought God's salvation in the world. In a real sense, we are his act of worship, his offering to God. And we his people are drawn into the very life and love of God through him. And our love of God is offered through him. This is what makes us Christ-ians—one's belonging to Jesus the Messiah. And it is precisely here that Christology comes to the fore yet again. It focuses our allegiance to God in and through Jesus the Messiah. We are bound to him.

⟵ Idolatrous Views of Jesus

Clearly this calls forth a response involving the whole person—what the Bible describes as an offering of the heart. Monotheistic faith has to do with the surrender of the heart. To ask and answer the question, "What is the treasure of my heart to which I owe allegiance?" For Luther, even the word

"God," understood rightly, demands ultimate allegiance. This is what the first commandment is all about. There are strong impulses to false worship inherent in the human condition. The claim of the one true God is set against the competing claims of the many false gods. In the following diagram we see an idolatrous view of god overshadowing the true monotheism. Our response is to go off in many directions, none of them leading back to God.

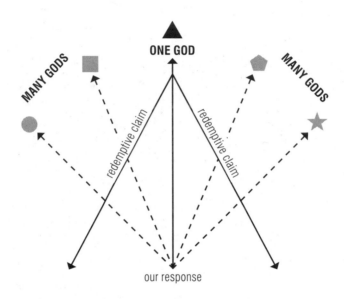

Only the true God can give unity, wholeness, and security to a human being. Therefore, the human heart, to be true to its original purpose, should have only one God. But we resist the all-encompassing claim and seek to find refuge in false gods. The question we all face is whether we will surrender our heart to the God of Israel and Jesus Christ or to an idol. In the language of Paul Tillich's existential theology, monotheism is about our ultimate concern. God, the one and only God, can be the object of our ultimate concern, since only the one God is ultimate. Without a living monotheistic faith, a person's life will inevitably be fragmentary. To paraphrase Yeats, things fall apart, the center does not hold.

Idolatry is insidious; it plays upon our deepest insecurities, appeals to our fearfulness, and therefore nourishes our fallen instinct to flee from the holy One whose love will redeem, purge, and cleanse the soul. For the person of faith, idolatry is a constant temptation, an encroachment on the true understanding of God. We can never control or manipulate the Lord. A relationship with him, while bringing utter completion to the human, paradoxically also creates a secret constant unrest in the life of the disciple. It raises a thousand questions about how we live, what we value, how we spend our money, what we do with our sexuality. The presence of God creates a constant tension in our lives, because a sort of holy terror is awakened by a contact with the Divine.

> [Our encounter with God] plunges us into an intensely dramatic participation in history. Every situation is pregnant with ultimate possibility; every moment is made explosive by the presence of infinite power. When God . . . appears, the reverberations in human existence cannot be silenced. He is not a problem to be solved; he creates problems through his nearness, his threats, his insistent demands, his irresistible intention. It is not so much that we raise questions about him, than that he raises questions of us.[18]

To encounter Jesus is to be changed by him and to embark on a lifelong journey to become like him. But to become a little Jesus is no small task. It requires real moral and spiritual effort, and few do it well. We can acknowledge without too much shame that the attempt to escape the claims of Jesus are common to all of us, no matter our situation. Hear Paul Tillich:

> Man wishes to flee from God. . . . Men of all kinds, prophets and reformers, saints and atheists . . . have had the same experience. . . . A man who has never tried to escape God never has experienced God, namely, that God who is *really* God. . . . A god from whom one can successfully flee is proved by that very success to be an idol. God is inescapable. He is God because he is inescapable . . .[19]

One of these fugitive ways is the path of idolatry. We have seen how our image of God clarifies or distorts our basic conception of God and substitutes a false experience for the true, transforming God encounter. Idolatry also invites us to give our allegiance to that which is not God, thereby fragmenting us spiritually by inviting us to give our loyalty to multiple gods. All that can be said about idolatry in relation to God can be said in relation to Jesus because Jesus is our Lord and the focal point of Christian faith.

Everyone has a god, in the sense that everyone puts something first in one's life: money, power, prestige, self, career, love and so forth. There must be something in your life that operates as your source of meaning and strength, something that you regard, at least implicitly, as the supreme power in your life. If you think your priority in life is to be a transcendent person, you will have a God with a capital letter. If you think of your highest value as a cause, an ideal, or an ideology, you will have a god with a small letter. Either way you will have something that is divine for you.

To believe that Jesus is divine is to choose to make him, and what he stands for, your God. To deny this is to make someone else your god and to relegate Jesus and what he stands for to second place in your scale of values.[20] Our way to God is through the redeeming love of Jesus Christ. Therefore, any false idea of Jesus will destroy the fabric of a New Testament faith. False ideas devastate the way of Jesus from the inside. At the least, idolatry fosters an immature following of Jesus. That is why false images of Jesus are so insidious, and this is the reason why we must strive to constantly reJesus our lives and the church.

⇐ Fifty Ways to Leave Your Lover

Human beings, including Jesus' disciples, have become artful in developing ways in which to escape from the all-encompassing claims of God in Jesus. Any discussion about true encounters with God must therefore include ways in which we try and avoid him, to qualify the God relationship, to ameliorate the tension he creates in our lives. We have found the analysis of Paul Minear in *Eyes of Faith* extremely useful, and so we use his material as a basis for this section.[21] Note how the all-encompassing nature of existential monotheism comes to the fore here.

Idolatry

Idolatry is making our own gods according to our own image and likeness. One of the basic urges of idolatry is the human desire to initiate one's own relationship to God and thereby control God. "Man worships idols precisely because of his ability to see them, to know them, to have power over them. But he can never observe God in the same way in which he can reflect on the beauty and power of his idol."[22] In becoming idolaters, we try to diminish the power and presence of God in our lives and minimize his impact on us. It's an ancient dodge.

Vacating the Arena

Vacating the arena is attempting to leave the arena of engagement and become a spectator, thereby trying to reverse the roles. God becomes the actor, and we become the critical observer. We try to become "investigators of God's claims."[23] But this attempt to escape is futile because God cannot and will not simply be observed by us. He can be truly known only by existential involvement. Key knowledge is denied to the detached observer in precisely those questions that are the most decisive in determining his destiny. Besides, people cannot forgive themselves of their own sins or even keep death away. God cannot be dodged by these means. "Existential concern expels speculative detachment."[24]

Trying to Hide

In reality there is nowhere to hide. When God invades our lives, he forces us out of our corners and into the arena. And we cannot hide from God anyway, for as the psalmist writes, "Where can I flee from your presence?" (Ps 139:7). We carry the issues deep within us. No human can fully evade the issue of God.

Religiosity

As we have seen in chapters 2 and 3, we try to escape God by attempting to "preserve mementos of God's former visits in ritual and law, to idolize these, to substitute legal observance and cultic sacrifice for 'knowledge of God' . . . The religious person is also inclined to speak of God in the third person, albeit with apparent reverence, and thus to remove himself from the magnetic field of divine compulsions. Man can forget God in the very act of speaking of him."[25] Religiosity is one of the biggest cop-outs known to the human. It objectifies God and thus seeks to control him.

Building Compartments

By building compartments the dodger consents to God's authority in the area where that seems desirable but at the same time tries to maintain his autonomy in other areas. "But God does not respect these man-made fences. Man's total existence is known by him. When he speaks, he claims total sovereignty."[26]

False Dualisms

False dualisms occur when we try to erect walls between the sacred and the secular and confining God to the sacred realm. But there is no such concept of religion in the Scriptures, "for there is no experience which as such can be defined as religious, and no experience which lies outside of the divine radius. [But] God does not call man to endorse a religion, but to view all life religiously, i.e., in its relation to God."[27]

Trying to Draw a Line Between Flesh and Spirit

As we've pointed out, the biblical God is the Creator of both body and spirit. In every personal encounter, he forces us to participate as a unit. He does not draw the false line between flesh and spirit and deal with one in isolation. We are to offer our bodies as living sacrifices.

Trying to Draw False Distinctions Between Private and Public Life

We try to distinguish between events of significance to the individual and those having social impact. But in a real way, "every event is social because it takes place within the web of personal relations and involves, in however small a compass, issues of ultimate concern."[28]

In tackling these attempts to hide, the biblical writers "fight against any false separation of sacred from the secular, against any reduction in the territory under divine rule."[29] And as disciples, we are called not to escape from God but to fully engage him, to become like him. We are the people of the way of Jesus, and as Glen Stassen and David Gushee point out, when this way "is thinned down, marginalized or avoided, then churches and Christians lose their antibodies against infection by secular ideologies that manipulate Christians into serving some other lord. We fear precisely that kind of idolatry now."[30]

↩ The Christ-Like God

Any chapter exploring monotheism must look at how Jesus changes, or rather develops, our understanding of God. We must ensure that the link between the one God of the Scriptures and Jesus the Messiah is properly understood, because this will have massive implications for the basic thrust of reJesus.

It is clear from the New Testament that Jesus fundamentally alters the way we understand everything about God and faith. He "affects every aspect of Christian doctrine and gives distinction to its understanding of God, humanity, sin, salvation and the eschaton (the end times)."[31] To make this claim, Dennis Kinlaw focuses mainly on those texts in which Jesus reveals the nature of his eternal and intimate relationship to God. He particularly focuses on the implications of Father-Son relationship in the Gospel of John. Chapters 1, 5, 9, 10, 14, and 17 are saturated with texts about Jesus' insider status and knowledge of the Godhead. In these passages, Jesus claims to be the same as God, and he fully claims the attributes and functions of God. Then, in Mark 10:17 22, the confession of "God alone" is coupled with Jesus' command to "follow me," suggesting that faith in one God and following Jesus are one and the same thing (see Mark 2:7–12). In Matthew 23:9–10, the uniqueness of God, the "one Father," is paralleled by the uniqueness of Jesus, the "one master" who stands in contrast to the multiplicity of earthly masters. This point is also emphasized in 1 Timothy 2:5–6, where the contrast is between one God/one Mediator and the multiplicity of gods and mediators suggested by the Gnostic theology that Paul was combating. When we add this with the comprehensive high Christology of Colossians and Revelation, we can see how the person and work of Jesus qualify the oneness of God and yet never violate the essential monotheistic revelation of the Bible. N. T. Wright says,

> All the signs are that the earliest Christians came to the startling conclusion that they were under obligation, without ceasing to be Jewish monotheists, to worship Jesus . . . For Paul, "there is one God (the Father, from whom are all things and we to him), and one Lord, Jesus Christ (through whom are all things and we through him)" (1 Cor 8:6). This stunning adaptation of the Shema . . . emphasizing creation and redemption as equally originating in the Father and equally implemented through Jesus, encapsulates, at the earliest stages of Christianity . . . everything that later generations and centuries would struggle to say about Jesus. From here on, we must say that if Trinitarian theology had not existed, it would be necessary to invent it.[32]

And as startling as this sounds, we can say with confidence that the thinking about God in the early church did not begin with reflecting on God; it focused first on Jesus. Jesus reveals himself not only as the door into salvation (John 10:7) but also the entry point into the knowledge of the one true God. Again, Kinlaw makes this clear: "Logically this means we should begin our theological studies with Jesus, who, as John said, 'has made him [God] known' (John 1:18)."[33] This makes Jesus Revealer and Mediator at the same time (John 14:6).

Albert Nolan, another key New Testament scholar, says it this way, and we quote him at length because of the sheer relevance for our understanding of God:

I have chosen this [the Christ-like God] approach because it enables us . . . to avoid the perennial mistake of superimposing upon the life and personality of Jesus our preconceived ideas of what God is supposed to be like . . .

By his words and praxis, Jesus himself changed the content of the word "God." If we do not allow him to change our image of God, we will not be able to say that he is our Lord and our God. To choose him as our God is to make him the source of our information about divinity and to refuse to superimpose upon him our own ideas of divinity.

This is the meaning of the traditional assertion that Jesus is the Word of God. Jesus reveals God to us, God does not reveal Jesus to us. God is not the Word of Jesus, that is to say, our ideas about God cannot throw any light upon the life of Jesus. To argue from God to Jesus instead of arguing from Jesus to God is to put the cart before the horse. This, of course, is what many Christians have tried to do. It has generally led them into a series of meaningless speculations which only cloud the issue and which prevent Jesus from revealing God to us.

We cannot deduce anything about Jesus from what we think we know about God; we must deduce everything about God from what we do know about Jesus. Thus, when we say that Jesus is divine, we do not wish to add anything to what we have been able to discover about him so far, nor do we wish to change anything that we have said about him. To say now suddenly that Jesus is divine does not change our understanding of Jesus; it changes our understanding of divinity. We are not only turning away from the gods of money, power, prestige or self; we are turning away from all the old images of a personal God in order to find our God in Jesus and what he stood for.

This is not to say that we must abolish the Old Testament and reject the God of Abraham, Isaac and Jacob. It means that if we accept Jesus as divine, we must reinterpret the Old Testament from Jesus' point of view and try to understand the God of Abraham, Isaac and Jacob in the way in which Jesus did . . . We have seen what Jesus was like. If we now wish to treat him as our God, we would have to conclude that our God does not want to be served by us, but wants to serve us; . . . If this is a true picture of God, then God is more truly human, more thoroughly humane, than any human being. God is, what Schillebeeckx has called, a Deus humanissimus, a supremely human God.[34]

Luther was a theologian who truly understood this christological re-framing of God and the implications for the Christian faith. And we ought to be thoroughly thankful because in rediscovering it, he once again unleashed the power of the gospel in the Western world. Commenting on the critics of one of his most important books (*The Bondage of the Will*), Luther writes, "I have written that . . . one must look at the revealed God (Jesus) when we sing in the hymn, 'Jesus Christ is the lord of hosts and there is no other God.' But they [his theological opponents] will pass over all of these places and take only those passages in my writing that deal with the hidden God."[35] A little earlier in the book he writes, "If you have Him [Christ] then you also have the hidden God together with Him who has been revealed."[36]

We admit that this sounds a little convoluted at first, but Luther is here countering the medieval theologians' tendency to focus on ontology (the being of God, the hidden God) instead of Christology (the revealed God). Speculation about the mystery of God's inner being was so wrapped up in speculative religious philosophy that the minds of average believers were frazzled and access to the love of God through the gospel was thereby restricted. This rightly infuriated Luther. He insisted that if we want to truly see God, we need only look at Jesus, for in Jesus we have received the fullness of God, and we need look no further. Says Luther, "The only God we see is the God clothed in the promises of the Gospel."[37] Or as Jesus says, "Whoever has seen me has seen the Father. How can you say, 'Show us the Father'?" (John 14:9).

The implications of this intratrinitarian shift within the revelation of God are paradigmatic. Executive lordship is now conferred directly on Jesus, and with this shift comes a realignment of the believer's focus and loyalties. So important is this shift that the Christian faith pivots on this precise point—it is Jesus who sets Christianity apart from the other two monotheistic faiths, Judaism and Islam. Our understanding of God is now always filtered through the prism of Jesus Christ. We cannot understand God if we don't engage him through Jesus. He is the way, the truth, and the life (John 14:6).

This redefinition of biblical monotheism around the role of Jesus can be called Christocentric monotheism, because it realigns our loyalties to God around the person and work of Jesus Christ. Jesus thus becomes the pivotal point in our relation to God, and it is to him that we must give our allegiance and loyalty. Jesus is Lord! And this lordship is expressed in exactly the same way that it is in the Old Testament. It is the covenant claim of God over our lives, the unshakable center of the Christian creed and confession.[38]

Alan's grandfather used to say this ditty,

Roses are red
Violets are blueish
If it wasn't for Jesus
We'd all be Jewish

Now, it's not really true, but it does highlight the role that Jesus plays in redefining the people of God. Jesus changes everything, and this is critical to understand if we are going to recalibrate the church around the person of Jesus as we must at this point of time. Wright makes this call to reJesus our understanding of God,

Unstinting Compasssion

Mother Teresa

Few people have embodied the role of a little Jesus quite as sublimely as Agnes Gonxha Bojaxhiu, better known as Mother Teresa. When she was eighteen she joined the Sisters of Loreto in Dublin, Ireland, and, shortly after taking her vows as a nun, found herself teaching high school in Calcutta, India (known today as Kolkata). In 1948, after several years of witnessing widespread suffering and poverty in Calcutta, she received permission to leave her teaching position and work among the poor population. She opened a school for slum children, relying on volunteer and financial support. Two years later Mother Teresa was granted permission to start her own order, aiming to care for "the hungry, the naked, the homeless, the crippled, the blind, the lepers, all those people who feel unwanted, unloved, uncared for throughout society, people that have become a burden to the society and are shunned by everyone." Originally named the *Diocesan Congregation of the Calcutta Diocese* by the Vatican, the order began with only thirteen members in Calcutta. Today it is known as the Missionaries of Charity and consists of more than 4,000 nuns who care for underpriveleged, disadvantaged, and disabled persons through orphanages, AIDS hospices, and charity centers all over the world. Another focus of Mother Teresa's lifetime ministry was to provide people with the opportunity to die with dignity. Calcutta's Home for the Dying, a free hospice for the poor, provides residents with medical attention and allows "people who lived like animals to die like angels—loved and wanted." Mother Teresa herself passed away on September 5, 1997. Her way of loving those with no capacity to repay her for her kindness more than qualifies Mother Teresa as a little Jesus.

My proposal is not that we know what the word "god" means, and manage somehow to fit Jesus into that. Instead, I suggest, that we think historically about a young Jew, possessed of a desperately risky, indeed apparently crazy, vocation, riding into Jerusalem in tears, denouncing the Temple, and dying on a Roman cross—and we somehow allow our meaning for the word "god" to be recentered around that point.[39]

Among other things, this will mean that the confession "Yahweh is Lord" will transform into the primary New Testament confession of "Jesus is Lord," bearing within it the full implications and the weight of monotheistic understanding of God. And what this means in turn is that our loyalty to God must now be mediated via the person of Jesus. Paul insists that the actual function of lordship, normally associated with the Father, is now passed on to Jesus.[40] God actually saves as well as claims us in Jesus, and this claim demands the response of our very lives. Everything we are and all that we have is included in this claim. This was a realization that could not be avoided by the Confessing Church (led by Karl Barth and Dietrich Bonhoeffer) in Nazi Germany when they developed the Barmen Declaration to counter the heretical claims of the so-called Nazi Christians. They confessed

> Just as Jesus Christ is the pledge of the forgiveness of sins, just so—and with the same earnestness—is he also God's mighty claim on our whole life; in him we encounter a joyous liberation from the godless claims of this world to free and thankful service to his creatures. We repudiate the false teaching that there are areas of our life in which we do not belong to Jesus Christ but another lord, areas in which we do not need justification and sanctification through him.[41]

Here lies the interface between the disciple and God. It is through the redeeming lordship of Jesus. And when we talk of lordship, we are talking about God's redemptive claim on our lives and our existential response to this claim. And here is where it begins to impact us in a practical way. Perhaps we can illustrate it by going back to our basic diagram (see next page). Our view of God is as the one true God. Our response is an existential one, through the redemptive work of Jesus.

As in the *Shema*, we can see all the elements of monotheism are present. The link between the one God (monotheism) and lifestyle (ethics) are fully maintained. The difference between the Old Testament and the New Testament understandings of God is found in the person and work of the Messiah, hence Christocentric monotheism.

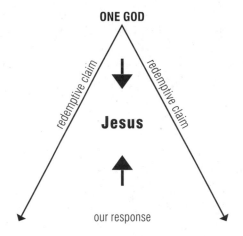

⟿A Quick Word on the Trinity

By now, any theologically sensitive reader would have asked the question, "Does all this focus on Jesus destroy the trinitarian fabric out of which comes a genuinely Christian understanding of God and the world?" The last thing we wish to do is challenge the fundamental revelation of God as triune Being. We affirm this with all orthodox Christians everywhere. Even though the later formulations are complex, overly ontological in perspective, and missionally clumsy, they are nonetheless correct in what they affirm. Rather, what we want to do here is reinstate a more primitive form of trinitarian understanding, one much closer to the trinitarianism of the New Testament than the denser philosophical formulations of the later church. This has massive implications for any church recalibrating itself along the lines suggested in this book. Renewal involves going back to basics, recovering our elemental message, and jettisoning the unnecessary in order to focus on the essential. Missiologically speaking, it is also essential that we travel lighter than we have in Christendom past. We believe we need to be as theologically unencumbered as possible so that we may more approximate the way the early Christians understood their relation to God. This has significant implication for missional movements and the rapid transfer of ideas, as Alan has demonstrated in *The Forgotten Ways*.[42]

And as for a christological center and starting point, we would argue that any understanding of the Trinity must of necessity start with Jesus because it is he who introduces us into the Trinity in the first place. Any approach to the Trinity must go through Christology and should stress the Christ-likeness of God, thus enabling us to move from the relatively known to the relatively unknown. Furthermore, to really appreciate the trinitarian revelation, we need to frame whatever understanding we glean from Jesus in the light of the Israel story that precedes the Messiah. As we noted from Wright's scholarship, without the Israel story we cannot understand Jesus properly, and once again, everything goes awry. Or to say it another way, to understand the New Testament, we must know the story that gives it meaning.[43] And so we are back to the *Shema*, the fundamental confession of Israel then and now. Any true understanding of the Trinity arises out of an understanding of the nature of biblical monotheism. Otherwise what we end up with is tritheism, which certainly is not what the Bible teaches.

In returning to the essentials in this way, we are hoping to recover the powerful dynamic, the ethos, and the faith structure of existential monotheism. This kind of monotheism tended to recede as the dogmatic and metaphysical interests of the Greek and Latin theologians became dominant and replaced the existential demands of the faith (othopraxy) with the need for orthodoxy.[44]

To Sum Up

Any examination of our own lives and communities will no doubt reveal that we are all somehow torn between the great escape, as described above, and the trembling desire to be more like Jesus, to know God more fully, and to be truly known by him in return. Ever since the fall we have been fluctuating between the desire to hide from God in the garden and to reveal ourselves to him. In Jesus, God has come to us. We know from him that God is *for* us and that it is the nature of his love that he desires to have us fully to himself. The incarnation reveals to us a God who utterly understands our condition and yet one who is able, through his sacrificial suffering on our behalf, to raise us to be the kind of people God wanted in the first place. But we must not avoid the radical place Jesus has in this schema of redemption. In Jesus, we are not only redeemed, we are claimed, and this claim, true to the existential monotheism that gives it meaning, is exclusive. We can but echo the words of Paul and make them into our confession,

> For us there is one God, the Father, from whom are all things and for whom we exist, and one Lord, Jesus Christ, through whom are all things and through whom we exist. (1 Cor 8:6)

⟿ Notes

1. "Note in particular the example of the flood account in the Gilgamesh Epic, where the flood seems to be a result of Enlil's whim. It was only through the goodness of Enki that Utnapishtim was warned and escaped from the deluge." D. L. Christensen, *Deuteronomy 1–11* (Word Biblical Commentary 6A; Dallas: Word, 1998; electronic ed., Logos Library System).

2. D. N. Freedman, "God in the New Testament," *Anchor Bible Dictionary* (New York: Doubleday, 1996; electronic ed.).

3. Ibid., electronic edition. Interestingly, the structure of Paul's letters indicates the same commitment to the unbreakable link between understanding of God with lifestyle. New Testament scholars talk about the indicative and the imperative structure of the Pauline letters. The first half deals with teaching about God, salvation, and other theological issues. The second half invariably talks about ethical issues.

4. Scot McKnight, *Jesus Creed: Loving God, Loving Others* (Brewster, Mass.: Paraclete, 2004).

5. "Today's church must not forget that the earliest theology in the New Testament is relational or existential rather than propositional or creedal." Marvin Wilson, *Our Father Abraham: Jewish Roots of the Christian Faith* (Grand Rapids, Mich.: Eerdmans, 1989), 138.

6. We are hardly alone in this. See Martin Buber, Søren Kierkegaard, Karl Barth, Helmut Theilicke, Paul Minear, Emil Brunner, John McQuarrie, et al.

7. "[M]onotheism is an outcome of the exclusive claim of Yahweh, rather than a conceptual hypothesis resulting from human effort to gain a unitary view of his world." Paul Minear, *Eyes of Faith: A Study in the Biblical Point of View* (Philadelphia: Westminster, 1946), 24.

8. To the philosopher, monotheism can be defined as "the doctrine of, or belief in, the existence of but one God." And following such a definition, one is either a monotheist or not. And whether one is or not can be determined by objective standards. People may hold to a doctrine of the existence of one God without ever involving the character of his or her personal relationship to that God. But this is not a biblical (existential) understanding of monotheism. In a strange sense, a biblical monotheism cannot even be defined, and no biblical writer attempts such a definition. At the most there is a witness to an encounter, a description of God's visit, to which a specific person (or community) responds in faith that for him (or her, or them) there is only one Lord. The effect on the person or community will be the confession that God alone is our Creator and Redeemer, that God and God alone has the right to determine our duty and demand our loyalty, that our destiny lies in God's hands alone. Others may have gods, but in reality they are idols.

9. Minear, *Eyes of Faith*, 25–26.

10. Hirsch, *Forgotten Ways*, 93.

11. Eugene H. Peterson, *Reversed Thunder* (San Francisco: Harper & Row, 1988), 117–18.

12. Notes from many discussions had with Mark Sayers during 2006—Alan.

13. See also Hirsch, *Forgotten Ways*, "'Little Jesus' in Disneyland," 106ff., and Frost, *Exiles*, 225–27, for a more thorough analysis of consumerism in relation to discipleship.

14. Minear, *Eyes of Faith*, 21.

15. See especially Bob Roberts Jr., *Glocalization: How Followers of Jesus Engage a Flat World* (Grand Rapids, Mich.: Zondervan, 2007), 40ff. This is an idea akin to Abraham Kuyper's idea of sphere sovereignty. See also Bob Roberts Jr., *Transformation: How Glocal Churches Transform Lives and the World* (Grand Rapids, Mich.: Zondervan, 2006).

16. Roberts, *Transformation*, 37–40.

17. Buber, *Mamre*, 107 8.

18. Mincar, *Eyes of Faith*, 16.

19. Paul Tillich, quoted in Minear, *Eyes of Faith*, 17.

20. Albert Nolan, *Jesus Before Christianity* (Maryknoll, N.Y.: Orbis, 1978), 166.

21. Minear, *Eyes of Faith*, 17–22.

22. Ibid., 17.

23. Ibid.

24. Ibid., 19.

25. Ibid.

26. Ibid., 20.

27. Ibid., 20–21.

28. Ibid., 22.

29. Ibid.

30. Glen H. Stassen and David P. Gushee, *Kingdom Ethics: Following Jesus in Contemporary Context* (Downers Grove, Ill.: InterVarsity, 2003), 11.

31. Dennis F. Kinlaw, *Let's Start with Jesus: A New Way of Doing Theology* (Grand Rapids, Mich.: Zondervan, 2005), 20.

32. N. T. Wright, *The Challenge of Jesus* (London: SPCK, 2000), 78, 79.

33. Kinlaw, *Let's Start with Jesus*, 27.

34. Nolan, *Jesus Before Christianity*, 165–67.

35. Martin Luther, *The Bondage of the Will*, in *Luther's Works* (ed. Jaroslav Pelikan et al.; St. Louis: Concordia, 1955–), vol. 5, 50. However, he does admit that there is a sense in which God does hide himself; for instance, in human form (the incarnation), in suffering, in a naked man on a cross, in persecution. But he does this in order to humble the pride of human reason so that he may not be found by cleverness but by faith.

36. Ibid.

37. Ibid., 48.

38. Hirsch, *Forgotten Ways*, 93.

39. Wright, *The Challenge of Jesus*, 92.

40. "[H]e [God] raised him from the dead and seated him at his right hand in the heavenly realms, far above all rule and authority, power and dominion, and every title that can be given, not only in the present age but also in the one to come. And God placed all things under his feet and appointed him to be head over everything for the church, which is his body, the fullness of him who fills everything in every way" (Eph 1:20–23 NIV). In 1 Corinthians 15:25–28 (NIV), Paul says, "For he [Jesus] must reign until he has put all his enemies under his feet. . . . When he has done this, then the Son himself will be made subject to him who put everything under him, so that God may be all in all." Cf. Hirsch, *Forgotten Ways*, 93.

41. "The Barmen Declaration of 1934," quoted from Woelfel, *Bonhoeffer's Theology*, 242.

42. See Hirsch, *Forgotten Ways*, ch. 3, for reasons why we need to distill and simplify our message in the West.

43. Jonathan Wilson, *God So Loved the World* (Grand Rapids, Mich.: Baker, 2001), 13.

44. Harnack's famous pronouncement maintained that dogma, in its conception and development, is a work of the Greek spirit on the soil of the gospel. Although Harnack seems to have thought of this work of the Greek spirit as to some extent a deterioration, he acknowledged its necessity: "Christianity without dogma, that is, without a clear expression of its content, is inconceivable." See John Macquarrie, *Existentialism* (Philadelphia: Westminster, 1972), 28–29.

Three . . . Two . . . One . . . Engage

*As civilization advances, the sense of
wonder almost necessarily declines. Such
decline is an alarming symptom of our
state of mind. Mankind will not perish for
want of information, but only for want of
appreciation. The beginning of our happiness
lies in the understanding that life without
wonder is not worth living. What we lack is
not a will to believe, but a will to wonder.*
—Abraham Heschel

*We live or die consumed by fire or fire
Our hope lies in the choice of pyre
. . . to be redeemed from fire by fire*
—T. S. Eliot

Having been claimed by the God who reveals himself in Jesus, we need to seriously consider something of the dynamic of engagement between Jesus and his people. How can we know him in the fullness of human knowledge (Eph 1:17–23)? What role does revelation play in guiding us to a true experience and life-transforming encounter with the One who saves? How do we engage the Christ of the Bible more directly? Our journey here must take us into a reconsideration of ways of apprehension and knowing, the relation between subjective and objective knowledge, direct and indirect approaches to Jesus. Most of all, we want to open up new, and yet strangely ancient, pathways into an up-to-date experience of Jesus as Lord and center of our faith.

⟿ Encountering Jesus Afresh

Much of what gets in the way of a true and life-altering encounter with Jesus can be traced to the problem of worldview. We have already seen how existential monotheism, reinterpreted christologically, radicalizes our understanding of things, but as much as a new application of worldview can change things and unify our world, another one can equally distort. This is because worldview is effectively the lens through which we engage and thus interpret the world. This issue of worldview plays itself out rather strangely in the Western spiritual and theological tradition when it comes to the understanding of knowledge, or apprehension, of God. The Western church is largely influenced by the more speculative and philosophical worldview ushered in by the Hellenistic world. The problem is that our Scriptures are formed by a significantly different way of seeing things—the Hebraic. We addressed this at length in *The Shaping of Things to Come*, which surprised some readers. Why introduce Hebraic thinking into a book on the missional church? For us, though, it goes to the heart of why the Western church has moved so far off course. The church is operating out of a Hellenistic worldview that makes it difficult to appropriate all that the New Testament is saying. If this is the case in the area of ecclesiology, it is all the more important in the study of Christology.

To try to get to the essential difference between Hellenistic and Hebraic worldview, some writers have called Greek thinking *step logic* and Hebraic thinking *block logic*. The Hellenists used a tightly contained step logic whereby one would argue from premise to conclusion; each step in the process is linked tightly to the next in a coherent, rational, linear fashion. "The conclusion, however, was usually limited to one point of view—the human being's perception of reality."[1] In contrast, Hebraic thinking tended to express concepts in self-contained units, or blocks, of thought. The blocks did not necessarily fit together in an obviously linear or harmonious pattern, particularly when one block represented a human perspective on truth and another the divine. "This way of thinking created a propensity for paradox, antinomy, or apparent contradiction, as one block stood in tension—and often illogical relation—to the other. Hence, polarity of thought or dialectic often characterized block thinking."[2] This creates problems for us, trained as we are in Hellenistic approach to thinking, when we try to grasp Scripture. In reading the Bible, in recalibrating, we need to "undergo a kind of intellectual conversion"[3] from the Hellenistic to the Hebraic mind.

It surprised us to learn recently that throughout the Apollo missions to the moon, spacecraft regularly drifted off course. In fact, more than 80 percent of their journey through space was slightly off course. To conserve fuel, the spaceships drift through space, moved by the gravitational pull of the earth. Jet engines are used occasionally only when the ship is getting too far off course to readjust their coordinates and get them back on track. The occasional burst of their massive engines completes the readjustment and keeps them heading toward their destination. We think this is a useful metaphor for the church today. Many people are claiming that the church has been drifting off course and needs a burst of renewed power to get back on track. However, for spacecraft, that surge of propulsion works only if the coordinates are accurate and the flight plan is properly conceived. Today, many voices are calling the church back on track, acting like power surges for a drifting church. But our contention is that the church needs to go back to the drawing board and work again on its flight plan. If the plan is wrong, all the bursts of renewed energy will only push us further into space.

One of those areas that need to be re-examined is that of worldview. Without an appreciation of the Hebraic worldview from which the New Testament was written, we can keep surging the church's engines and keep getting more and more lost, even though it looks like we're doing the right thing. By thinking in Hellenistic terms, we construct a highly philosophical approach to our world and indeed the Scriptures. Jacques Ellul notes that our fundamental problems in perception can be traced back to a change in the basic understanding of revelation, namely, the transition from history to philosophy:

> I believe that all the errors in Christian thought go back to this [italics added]. I might say that all the theologians I have named had correct thoughts, that their theology was true, that there was not heresy in the one and orthodoxy in the other, but that all of them are caught in the philosophical circle and pose metaphysical problems. All seek an answer by way of ontological thinking. All regard the biblical text or known revelation, as points of departure for philosophy, whether by translation into philosophical terms or as references of thought. They had intellectual, metaphysical, and epistemological questions, etc., and they adduced the biblical text with a view to providing a system of answers to their questions. They used the biblical text to meet their own needs instead of listening to what it really was [saying].[4]

In other words, as Ellul goes on to explain, the shift away from the existential and historical revelation of God toward philosophical formulations diluted the nature of the truth the church proclaimed. Even though the theologians Ellul refers to expressed a profound and authentic faith marked by a concern for truth, "all this was undermined and even falsified by the initial transition of the idea of revelation" in the first place. The die was cast. Very soon the developments in philosophical thinking became stronger than the biblical truth that they sought to retain. The theologians had forgotten the essential

Revolutionary Advocacy

Rigoberta Menchú

As a little Jesus, Rigoberta Menchú is undaunted in her advocacy for the poor and the rights of indigenous groups worldwide. She is noted to have said, "The work of revolutionary Christians is above all to condemn and denounce the injustices committed against the people." She was born in 1959 to a poor Indian family in Guatemala, and as a child Rigoberta Menchú would work alongside her family on local farms and large plantations picking coffee. In her teenage years, Menchú became involved in social reform activities through the Catholic Church and played a part in the women's rights movement. During a time of intense social upheaval between upper class landowners and the country's indigenous population, the oppressive Guatemalan regime accused Menchú's family of taking part in guerrilla activities. Her father, mother, and brother were all killed by security forces within only a couple years of each other. These horrors led the young Menchú to join the Committee of the Peasant Union, an activist group that campaigned against human rights violations. She later joined the more radical "31st of January Popular Front," through which she helped educate the indigenous Guatemalan population in resistance to massive military oppression. In 1981 Menchú fled the country, but still organized resistance to oppression in Guatemala. She has become known as an advocate for the rights of indigenous peasants, refusing to keep silent about their sufferings and struggles. Her autobiography, *I, Rigoberta Menchú*, attracted considerable international attention to her undertakings. Menchú has attempted at least three times to return to Guatemala to plead the cause of the Indian peasants, but death threats have forced her to return into exile each time. She has received several international awards for her efforts, including a Nobel Peace Prize in 1992.

point that God does not reveal himself by means of a philosophical system or a moral code or a metaphysical construction but rather enters human history and accompanies his people. Ellul concludes:

> The Hebrew Bible (even in the wisdom books) is not a philosophical construction or a *system* of knowledge. It is a series of stories that are not myths intended

to veil or unveil objective and abstract truths. These stories are one history, the history of the people of God, the history of God's agreements and disagreements with this people, the history of loyalty and disobedience. There is nothing else but history . . . a history that tells us that God is with and for us, but that does not speak about God in himself, or provide any theory about God.[5]

This history-anchored worldview values the action and word of God over a philosophical construct of his character. It also requires obedience in order to truly comprehend what is being revealed. In this worldview, the Bible is read as the history of God's self-revelation. It proves that God reveals himself in real life, in observable and distinct ways that defy neat explanation or simple formulation. Under the new Hellenistic worldview, the Bible is approached differently. God's revelation was interpreted as the climax of the teaching of Socrates, and the Bible was interpreted by the intellectual tools of Greek philosophy. The Torah, for example, is seen merely as a moral code, not unlike the Twelve Tablets, a Greco-Roman legal code. What resulted was of decisive importance. Instead of listening to the text as it was, theologians tried to draw from it a coherent philosophical system, whether modeled after Plato, Aristotle, Heraclitus, or Epicurus. It all came to the same thing. The biblical stories were treated as myths from which one had to draw some abstract, universal thought. And so the Christian theological tradition embraced a philosophical approach alien to Jewish epistemology (ways of knowing).[6] The Hebraic framework for the true comprehension of revelation was thus discarded in favor of the Hellenistic. Ellul continued,

> Some will tell me that we have no option but to use our available tools of knowledge even to understand a history. This is true. But I reply that Hebrew thought had its own tools of knowledge that are fully set forth in the language. We should bow and submit and convert to these instead of forcing God's revelation into the strait jacket of Greco-Roman thinking, instead of putting it in this cage of tigers. . . . To convert! This great word has been diluted. The people of the third century and later have been converted to Christianity in morality and religion, but they have kept intact their mode of thinking. Conversion is needed in the mode of thinking, too. . . . Now metaphysics, ethics, and law have radically transformed the meaning of revelation even though formally what is advanced seems to be right, the exposition is faithful, and the interpreters are serious and devout. The problem does not lie with their faith or piety or intelligence but with an integral falsity of meaning.[7]

If we hear Ellul correctly, this is part of the process by which Christianity was essentially subverted into something significantly less, if not entirely different, from the original way Jesus set down for us. Ellul therefore calls us to a new conversion if we are to reJesus, a conversion back to Hebraic thinking in order to rediscover Jesus afresh.

⟵ Letting the Bible Read Us, Not the Other Way Around

In order to reJesus our lives and communities, it is essential that we engage God through the revelation that he has given us in Jesus. And this will mean that we must take the Bible with utmost seriousness and must read it on its own terms if we are to truly comprehend its teachings. But the Bible should not in this process replace Jesus as the focus of our faith. In a way we are not really the "people of the Book," as we are so often called—as far as we can ascertain, it was the Muslims gave us this tag. In a far more fundamental way we can claim rather that we are truly Jesus' people before we are anything else. Our focal point remains the Messiah, and we must be guided by the Bible toward a true experience and understanding of Messiah. The Bible functions something like the wardrobe in C. S. Lewis's Narnia series—it is a gateway to another world; one goes through it in order to get into the knowledge, the love, and the wonder of God.[8] With this in mind, let us look at ways in which we can perhaps renew our love and understanding of Jesus with the Bible in hand.

Part of this journey will mean that we need to learn to value what philosophers call *subjectivity* in relation to truth. And here we find Søren Kierkegaard to be most useful. Kierkegaard stressed how important it was to move beyond mere objective understandings of truth to the subjective appropriation of that truth. He argued the case in one of his books that all truth means subjective change.[9] And he meant by this that if you believe something is really and objectively true (in this case statements about Jesus and the gospel), then it must somehow affect your life. It must become personal. It must become *your* truth, or it is by definition not true. Your values and your association with truth indicate what you really believe is true.

When we look at Jesus, we find that his approach to communicating kingdom truth squares with this very biblical idea of subjectivity in relation to truth. Jesus' method of communication is unbalancing. It destabilizes the smug complacency that stands between the individual and truth. Kierkegaard says,

> Jesus' method is essential to his goal. What Jesus "teaches" cannot be taught in some more objective manner. The listener is forced to confront the full para-

doxical power of "the lesson" and in doing so, is forced to confront himself or herself.[10]

With the previous discussion of the Hellenistic worldview in mind, we feel that so much of the way we approach the Scriptures are overly rationalistic. Perhaps some of our frustration with rationalist and overly modernist approaches to reading Scripture can be highlighted by taking a look at many of our standard commentaries. In writing a book like this, one has to refer to commentaries to glean more insight on a text. But trips to the commentary shelf often prove frustrating and useless when it came to integrating Jesus and his teachings into our lives. Biblical scholars who focus on the grammar, structure, and etymology of a passage and then carefully compare what other scholars have said couch their writings in a language laced with the assumptions of objectivity: the attempt becomes an exercise in investigating God rather than God investigating us. But following a purely rational, linear, historicist approach, we cannot hope to get at the true meaning of a text.

The problem is that the method dictates the outcomes! By not engaging the Jesus referred to in the text, scholars end up objectifying the Bible, making it into knowledge alone. In Martin Buber's terms, they move from an I-and-Thou stance toward an I-and-It in relation to the Scriptures. And herein lies many of our problems when it comes to engaging the God in and through Scripture; we lack the spiritual mechanisms to get beyond the written word to God's own self, and so we get stuck in the wardrobe. We have so attached ourselves to a Cartesian approach to knowledge (the viewpoint of the autonomous, objective, knower) that we have lost the art of participation in the text, of somehow finding ourselves in the text. James calls Scripture a mirror in which we see our true selves (Jas 1:22–25). To use it in an attempt to mine objective knowledge about God is to fall foul of the very thing he warns us about in this text. We think much of what goes by the name biblical exegesis (the critical explanation of a text of Scripture) does exactly this.

Our commitments to exegesis are now so one-dimensional that we no longer know how to connect with the Bible in a much more personally engaged manner. We suggest that alongside the task of exegesis (which we must do), we need to learn the spiritual art of *reading ourselves into the text*, participating in it, normally forbidden to the academic approach. We think that we have much to unlearn in regard to our approach to Scripture, and therefore the God of the Scriptures, and much to relearn as we seek to reJesus our lives and churches. This is not as far-fetched as it might seem at first. Any literature major at college is introduced to the art of reading himself or herself into the fictional text. The reader is invited to take the part of certain agents or players in a novel to try and assess the emotional and human richness of the material. When applied to our engagement with the Scriptures, this approach adds human warmth, pathos, perspective, and a generally richer reading of the text. And as we have already seen, this is part of what Ignatius Loyola demanded of his Jesuits.

One of the ways in which people have tried to overcome the distance between written text and dynamic Word as addressed to us is the use of the ancient practice of *lectio divina*, Latin for "divine reading." The Bible is the Word of God, which is always alive and active, always new. *Lectio divina* is a traditional way of combining prayer and reading the Scriptures so that the Word of God may penetrate our hearts and that we may grow in an intimate relationship with the Lord. It is a natural way of prayer and was developed and practiced by the early monks and then developed by the first Carmelite hermits. It involves a way of reading the Scriptures whereby we gradually let go of our own agenda and open ourselves to what God wants to say to us. It is a way of praying with Scripture that calls one to study, ponder, listen, and, finally, pray from God's Word. Any passage of Scripture can be encountered using *lectio divina*, as long as the passage is not too long. *Lectio divina* is not the same thing as exegesis but is a personal reading of the Scripture and application to one's life. After quieting our hearts and laying our cares aside, worshipers engage the text. *Lectio divina* involves the following four "moments" or readings.

1. *Lectio*: the worshipper is invited to read the passage out loud, per-haps several times. It is best to read the Word of God slowly and reflectively so that it sinks into us.

2. *Meditatio*: After the second reading, we think about the text we have chosen and ruminate upon it so that we take from it what God wants to give us. The reader is called to gravitate to any particular phrase or word that seems to be of particular importance.

3. *Oratio*: This involves a response to the passage. The worshipper opens his or her heart to God. This is not an intellectual exercise but an intuitive conversation or dialogue with God. Here we let our hearts speak to God. This response is directly inspired by our reflec-tion on the Word of God.

4. *Contemplatio*: This involves listening to God. We free ourselves from our own thoughts, both mundane and holy. We open our mind, heart,

and soul to the influence of God. We rest in the Word of God and wait quietly and listen at the deepest level of our being to God speaking within us with in a still small voice.

Any conversation must allow for both sides to communicate, and this most unfamiliar act is allowing oneself to be open to hearing God speak. One of the biases that we bring to the Bible, and one that blocks the possibility of true conversation, is the assumption that we read it. We are the active party. The Jewish approach to Scripture is that we don't read the Bible but rather that it reads us! Our standard practice is to assume we are its interpreter and therefore the arbiter of its meaning. Jewish approaches reverse this: we are not the interpreter, but rather it is the Torah that interprets us. This is because it is God who addresses us in Scripture, hence the idea of revelation that is so important to a biblical worldview. "It is not so much that we' raise questions about him, but that that he raises questions of us."[11]

God addresses us and challenges us personally in and through Scripture. When it comes to the Word Become Flesh, Jesus as the incarnated *logos*, we see this whole questioning played out in dynamic ways. The kingdom presses itself upon the world in Jesus. The rule of God challenges the false claims to loyalty that so easily ensnare us. Jesus in his teachings and actions is constantly driving us back to our assumptions, forcing us to play our cards, bringing us to account, demanding that we respond to the redeeming love of God expressed through him. What is clear is that when we engage Jesus, we never get to objectively interpret him—he does not allow us that epistemological luxury. In Jesus, love is on the offensive, wooing us into the transforming encounter with God. Just try bringing Jesus and the Bible into conversation with any latent middle-class consumerism you might have. In any genuine encounter with Jesus, we can either respond in faith and obedience, cut and run, or take the fire out of the issue by reinterpreting the Bible to suit our understandings. Ever heard yourself saying, "Oh it's not what it means literally, Jesus is actually saying . . ." Just see what most preaching does with the kingdom way expressed in the Beatitudes, the Sermon on the Mount, or the rich young ruler—we emasculate the text by spiritualizing it or domesticating its direct implications.

⟵ Hebraic Ways of Knowing

We need to broaden our capacities to know God and to engage him through the text of Scripture. Because of issues relating to worldview, as previously discussed, we feel that we have to address this issue if we are to re-encounter the Jesus of the New Testament afresh.

The Hebraic approach to the knowledge of God includes the ways of the heart, of obedience, of wonder, of action, as well as the intellectual life of a person. We will look mainly at two, namely, the way of the heart and the way of action, because clearly these have implications when it comes to a mission that is funded by a sense of the immediacy of God. Jesus wants our hearts and our lives, and this he gets when we open ourselves to his invading love and when we act in his name.

Orthopathy, or the Way of the Heart

As we have seen, engagement with Jesus must move us beyond being spectators to participants. If we wish to become like him, we must learn to actively participate in Jesus, actively applying him and his teachings to our lives. We cannot be disinterested spectators when it comes to Jesus. In fact, in the encounters described in the New Testament, the desire of people to remain neutral observers is in a real sense the real sin (the rich young ruler, Pilate). It is those who allow Jesus to get at them who end up entering the kingdom. The Pharisees want to check him out, objectify him, line him up against their understandings of the faith, and because of this they are judged for their hardness of heart, for holding themselves back from what God is doing in Jesus.

And the heart is the issue. When the Bible uses the word "heart," it includes not only the source of emotion but of will, loyalty, and commitment. In many ways the heart determines our actions, not just our feelings, and it's critical to engage the heart when dealing with God (e.g., Ps 101:4; Isa 29:13; Matt 15:8). On this matter, the great revivalist Jonathan Edwards said:

> The Holy Scriptures every where place religion very much in the affection; such as fear, hope, love, hatred, desire, joy, sorrow, gratitude, compassion, and zeal. . . . It is an evidence that true religion lies very much in the affections, that the Scriptures place the sin of the heart very much in *hardness of heart*. . . . Now by a *hard* heart is plainly meant an *unaffected* heart, or a heart not easy to be moved with virtuous affections. . . .[12]

Without the heart, we cannot comprehend God. Besides, none of the really great things in human life spring only from the intellect but rather from the heart, which can embrace what the mind cannot. The great anonymous mystical work *The Cloud of Unknowing* says it this way: "Only to our mind is God incomprehensible, not to our heart." Following this spiritual logic, prayer affords us a certain kind of knowledge, one that cannot be attained through merely rational means.[13]

Most people reading this book would be aware of the distinctive meaning of the Hebrew word for knowledge, a word that is used for sexual intercourse, as well as for knowledge of God. The original meaning of the Hebrew verb "to recognize, to know," in distinction from Western languages, belongs not to the sphere of reflection but to that of personal contact.

In biblical Hebrew, in order to know something, one doesn't observe it, but one must come into contact with it. This basic difference is developed in the realm of a relation of the soul to other beings, where the fact of mutuality changes everything. At the center is not a perceiving of one another but a contact of being—intercourse. This theme of knowing rises to a remarkable and incomparable height in the relation of God to those he has chosen.[14]

Closely allied to this way of knowing is the role played by passion or affection in spirituality. Passion requires participation, involvement, faith. Søren Kierkegaard can say, "If passion is eliminated, faith no longer exists."[15] The truth of God can be found only by such a passionate search and by applying one's whole personality existentially. The criterion of the genuine search for truth is what Kierkegaard called *inwardness*, which requires an intense personal concern with it to be able to understand and assimilate it. Perhaps more widely known for this kind of approach was the American revivalist preacher Jonathan Edwards, made popular by his spiritual classic *The Religious Affections*. Edwards maintained that if the heart is left unmoved by God, no abiding action can, or will, take place. At its core, spirituality, what he called true religion, must redeem and direct our spiritual passion. It must involve the heart. And then he goes on to affirm that all great actions spring from the heart:

> I am bold in saying this, but I believe that no one is ever changed, either by doctrine, by hearing the word, or by the preaching or teaching of another, unless the affections are moved by these things. . . . In a word, there is never any great achievement by the things of religion without a heart deeply affected by those things. . . . True religion is placed in the affections.[16]

These are bases of motivation as well as the means to know God. Essentially what we are trying to say here is that we have to engage our heart to truly understand Jesus, but also to become like him and to follow him over the long haul. The emotional connection with God provides us with distinctive insights into God that cannot be gained from any other source.

In fact, prayer and worship grant to the worshipper a real, if highly subjective, knowledge of God. Prosper of Aquitaine (ca. 390–436) stated it this way: *lex orandi, lex credendi, lex vivendi*—how we worship reflects what we believe and determines how we will live. The law of prayer or worship is the law of life. Or, even more popularly rendered, as we worship, so will we live . . . and as we worship, so will we become! "Worship expresses the faith of the community, but it also helps form it. Doctrines grow out of people's actual life of prayer and worship, that is, their actual relationship with God."[17] Once again the function of orthopathy comes to the fore. Prayer is a form of knowledge that cannot be gained by any other means.

Orthopraxy, or the Way of Action

We have previously written of the idea that action is a form of sacrament,[18] so we will not repeat all that here, except to affirm the basic idea that when we respond to God in actions done in his name, we meet with him in a new and fresh way. The rabbis teach that we are never alone when we do a holy deed because we partner with God in the redemption of the world. In other words, a deed done in his name is a means of grace, a sacrament. As we state in *The Shaping of Things to Come*:

> . . . our actions, or more particularly our missional deeds, also confer grace. In fact, this could be the case even more so than the standard (somewhat abstracted) sacraments of the Christendom church. Humans have the freedom to protest against human suffering by *acting* to alleviate it. But it is the act itself, when done in the name of Jesus, that bestows something of the grace of God, not only to the beneficiary, but also to the benefactor. Grace goes two ways: such an action pulls a person away from their own self-involved concerns and directs them missionally toward other human beings in such a way that they, the person acted upon *and* the person acting, find God in a new way.[19]

Elie Wiesel, the Nobel laureate and luminous Jewish writer, has a character in one of his books affirm the sacramental value of the human, and humanizing, deed:

> If you could have seen yourself, framed in the doorway [Pedro once said to Michael], you would have believed in the richness of existence—as I do—in the possibility of having it and sharing it. It's so simple! You see a musician in

the street; you give him a thousand francs instead of ten; he'll believe in God. You see a woman weeping, smile at her tenderly, even if you don't know her; she'll believe in you. You see a forsaken old man; open your heart to him, and he'll believe in himself. You will have surprised them. Thanks to you, they will have trembled, and everything around them will vibrate. Blessed is he capable of surprising and of being surprised.[20]

Such deeds are not only sacramental but are themselves revelatory. That is, they reveal God in his goodness. There is a talmudic saying that may be interpreted as meaning that revelation resides within the deed itself: "From within his own deed, man as well as nation hears the voice of God."[21]

Hebraic faith puts such an emphasis on the sacramental nature of deeds that even if we don't understand why we should do it, or whether we doubt God, or don't wish to do a *mltzvah* (a holy deed), we are encouraged to do it anyway, because God will change us when we act in his name. The key to this form of knowledge is obedience. Helmut Thielicke says it like this, "Only conformity to God's will can open up access to knowledge of the figure of Christ."[22]

The New Testament epistle of James exhorts us to precisely such sacramental action in the world.

> Humbly accept the word planted in you, which can save you. Do not merely listen to the word, and so deceive yourselves. Do what it says. Anyone who listens to the word but does not do what it says is like a man who looks at his face in a mirror and, after looking at himself, goes away and immediately forgets what he looks like. But the man who looks intently into the perfect law that gives freedom, and continues to do this, not forgetting what he has heard, but doing it—he will be blessed in what he does. If anyone considers himself religious and yet does not keep a tight rein on his tongue, he deceives himself and his religion is worthless. Religion that God our Father accepts as pure and faultless is this: to look after orphans and widows in their distress and to keep oneself from being polluted by the world. (Jas 1:21–27, NIV)

Theoretical knowledge of spiritual truth is never commended in Scripture. In fact, as we can see, it is explicitly discouraged and condemned. As mediated through a Hebraic worldview, the understanding of Christian knowledge is indissolubly linked to experience. The follower of Jesus broadens his or her knowledge through experience or action, and his or her knowledge is to be expressed as experience or action. The Bible always aims at responsibility and responsiveness toward God. It is part of the conditions of God's covenant (e.g., Exod 24:7; Jer 11:3) as well as the momentous parting words of commission under which we live (Matt 28:18–20).

The command to obey is not because God wants to have it over us, but because, at least in terms of Hebraic worldview, it always confers knowledge of God that cannot be gained by any other means. Indeed, obedience is the

Transformative Suffering

Eva Price

Eva Price was a Midwestern American wife who in 1889 agreed to accompany her husband Charles into missionary service in the remote interior region of China. With their young sons, Donnie and Stewart, the Prices were sent to an isolated mission in Shansi. Located on a bare, windswept plateau, the mission was brutally hot in summer and freezing cold in winter. The area housed open sewers, piles of festering garbage, and contaminated wells that spread smallpox and typhoid, to which both Price sons succumbed within the first few years. The mission was not a successful one and the Prices returned to the United States in 1897 with little to show for their work but the deaths of their beloved sons. Out of this sorrow and disappointment, however, Eva Price emerged a new person; although the first mission had taken their sons' lives, she later willingly returned to China with Charles, "stripped to the soul by the fires of suffering." She sensed that she was supported by the indescribable love of Jesus and wrote, "My capacity for loving has enlarged in all the discipline of sorrow. . . ." Eva Price was a little Jesus not simply because of the suffering she endured in her short life, but because she was able to transform her suffering into a rare ability for the deepest compassion. She had been awakened into life just in time to meet her death; both Price and her husband were killed in the Boxer Rebellion shortly after their return to China.

evidence that knowledge of God has been received and understood. In the Bible, the real test of what you know is how you live. Something goes seriously wrong with our capacity to integrate or even comprehend Scripture if we do not obey but just study it. This is so because the disciple is called beyond right belief (orthodoxy) to a direct relation to Jesus as well as to the Scriptures. But the Scriptures also point directly to Jesus Christ. So discipleship, as well as the Scriptures, find their true interpretive center in Jesus.

The surprising fact is that when one looks at the Gospel records, it is clear that "Jesus did not ask for homage but obedience. He always had much more to lose from his friends than from his enemies. Admiration has always blunted his sword. It serves to dull the original outrage of his mission. Veneration assumes that we know what kind of man he really was and that we approve of his demands. It blinds us to their radicalism and inoculates us against being wounded by them. In fact, our well-speaking makes him vulnerable to his own curse: 'Woe to you when all men speak well of you, for that is what their fathers did to the false prophets.'"[23] We think what is being pointed to here is true. Nowhere does Jesus call us to worship him in the Gospels; what is clear is that he does demand obedience. Understood from a Hebraic perspective, obedience is the worship we should render him. When we merely approve of Jesus, take his side as if we can agree intellectually with what he is saying, we can easily domesticate his demands, making them into mere sayings and aphorisms of a wise man. They are far more dangerous and demanding than that.

According to Bonhoeffer, any other approach to the Scripture serves only to provide the believer with an escape from the clear call to obedience. Bonhoeffer can therefore speak of discipleship as a "problem of exegesis" and goes on to say, "By eliminating simple obedience on principle, we drift into an unevangelical interpretation of the Bible."[24] So, orthodoxy is not enough. As followers of Jesus, we have to start obeying long before we know and understand much of him whom we obey. More than that, if we take obedience out of the equation, we cannot even hope to truly understand the Bible. Calvin can claim that only when the Scriptures are believed and obeyed do sinful people even begin to have an epistemological foundation for true knowledge: "all right knowledge of God is born in obedience."[25]

Along similar lines, Ellul writes:

> We are saved by grace, not by works. Hence we cannot glorify works. Yet doing them is indispensable, for they are prepared in advance by God, they are in his "plan," and we are created to do them (Eph 2:10). In Paul, then, practice (praxis) is the visible criterion that we have seriously received grace and also that we have entered effectively into God's plan. For Paul, as for Jesus, practice is the touchstone of authenticity. We are in the presence here of something that is constant across the centuries.[26]

↩ Not Forgetting Orthodoxy

Ancient theologians came up with the potent slogan *lex seqendi, lex credendi*, which means that the law of following is the law of belief. This means that not only worship but also Christian life, ethics, and mission are centered in Jesus Christ and that following Jesus is a source for understanding him. This concept also suggests that Christian doctrines about Jesus arose in part out of the experience of following him. "Christians found themselves in a relationship of following and obedience to Jesus Christ and found life within this relationship. That believing flows out of following underscores the necessity that theology, like Christian life itself, must be Christ-centered."[27] We must remember this lest we slip into an ideology about Jesus rather than a true following of Jesus. Ideology is never enough.

We have noted that by itself orthodoxy, or mere creedal belief, is insufficient for a true knowledge of God. However, we are not suggesting that orthodoxy is unimportant. Far from it. We believe that right belief is an essential element of any discipleship in the way of Jesus. But we also believe that the church needs to reinterpret what it means by right belief and confession. The church nearly always sees orthodoxy as a commitment to propositional truth, assuming that the knowledge of God is received through purely the cognitive functions. We are convinced that our thinking about God must be right if we are to come to a full appreciation of God, but it must be complimented by othopraxy and orthopathy if we are to come to be in a full-orbed, biblical engagement with God. This can be depicted in the following way.[28]

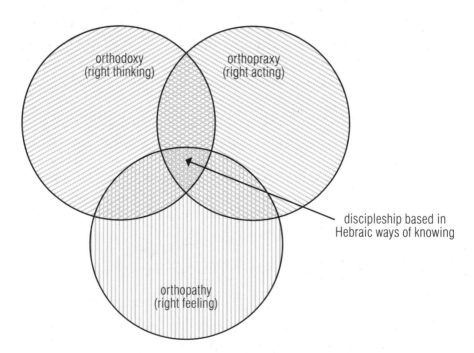

orthodoxy
(right thinking)

orthopraxy
(right acting)

orthopathy
(right feeling)

discipleship based in
Hebraic ways of knowing

As can be seen, it is in the nexus between orthopraxy, orthopathy, and orthodoxy that a true and full appreciation of God is to be found. In the place where all three intersect, we are less likely to make the mistakes that occur when we favor one over the others. If we adopt a commitment to orthopraxy alone at our worst we become tireless (and tired) activists, burning ourselves, and others, out while relying on our own efforts to please God. If we foster orthopathy to the exclusion of the others, we can end up as impractical mystics or experience junkies, so focused on contemplation and personal spiritual experience that we become of no use in the kingdom of God. But as we well know, if our primary or exclusive interest is in orthodoxy (as is the case in many churches today), at our worst we are arrogant bibliophiles, ideologues, no different from the Pharisees, worshipping our doctrine and our theological formulations over a genuine encounter with the Jesus revealed in Scripture. It is in the place where the ways of head, heart, and hand overlap that we find our way to Jesus. Or as John Wimber constantly reminds us in his writings, a true understanding of God required no less than Word, Works, and Wonders interacting together.

As we saw in the previous chapter, this is what the *Shema* (Deut 6:4–9) aims at and what Jesus directly affirms as being at the heart of discipleship and knowledge of God (Mark 12:28–34). We are to love God with all our heart, mind, will, and strength.

To illustrate this we can look to Luke 7, where Jesus encounters some Jewish elders sent by a Roman centurion to request that he heal the soldier's servant. When you read the Gospels and look to see who Jesus was personally impressed with, the number is not great. John the Baptist was one; Jesus called him the greatest of all prophets. And this centurion was another. It's a little disturbing to see what impresses Jesus: his cousin, a raving, ascetic lunatic in the wilderness, and a pagan soldier!

This soldier was a remarkable man, though. A military leader, probably garrisoned at Capernaum with a legion under his command, he was part of a conquering, occupying force that represented the crushing, superior, pagan imperial power of Caesar—everything the Jews despised. Romans tended to view their vanquished enemies as inferior barbarians. Israel must have seemed like a backwater to most centurions. These ancient peoples who worshipped one God and conducted ages-old rituals and embraced the strange ethical code of Moses must have appeared as foolish and childlike when compared with the sophistication of Rome.

But at some point this particular soldier had come to love Israel and its people. Using his personal resources and his ability to pull strings, he even manages to have a synagogue built in Capernaum. Surely, there would have been nothing in this for him. No one would go to such lengths to merely curry favor with the locals. Very likely he become interested in their God and their faith and their complex code of morality. The Jews of Capernaum came to say of him, "He loves our nation."

His involvement with Jesus is limited, as it turns out. They know of each other, though they don't meet. And yet the centurion has heard enough to put his complete faith in Jesus' power. His servant had fallen ill and had failed to recover in spite, one assumes, of even the finest quality health care. Knowing that a Gentile dare not speak face to face with a rabbi, and certainly not one of Jesus' standing, he asks the Capernaum elders to represent him. The small envoy rushes to Jesus' side and makes its request on the centurion's behalf. How bizarre. Jewish leaders, usually the enemies of Christ, representing a Gentile, usually an enemy of Israel, before the Messiah.

Jesus, no doubt intrigued by this request, agrees, as he does to many similar requests every day. But as they head to the centurion's home and to his dying slave, they are met by another emissary. The Roman has had second thoughts, not for his servant but about inviting the Christ into his home. The message from his friends reads, "I am not fit for you to come under my roof."

Jesus glances at the Jewish elders, "I thought you said he deserves my attention, because he built you a synagogue and he loves Israel? Now he tells me he deserves nothing, not even my presence in his home!"

The elders look furtively at each other. They are dumbfounded. What to say? They had assumed Jesus would be swayed to help the Roman if he knew he was a good man. Now Jesus feels betrayed. The Roman has told him he is not good at all! The Jews begin to suspect that Jesus, feeling duped, will not help them now.

"What, then, does he want from me?" Jesus asks the centurion's friends.

"He said that he knows about giving orders," they reply. "He is under the authority of his superior, and there are those who are under his authority. He simply sends out orders, and they are obeyed. So, he said you don't need to be physically present for your power to work. He says you transcend space and time. If you are who he thinks you are, then you are the master of the universe. Your power is universal. Just as Caesar can make decrees from Rome that are carried out around the empire, you can decree your will around the world."

An eerie hush descends upon the group. The Jewish elders blanch at this blasphemy. The Roman's friends await his response. A servant's life hangs in the balance. Jesus gazes at them in disbelief, before breaking the silence: "I'm impressed. And not just because he built a synagogue," he says, glaring at the embarrassed elders, who smile sheepishly. "But because I have never seen such faith in all Israel." And with that, far away, the servant was healed.

The centurion impresses Jesus because in him he finds that nexus between orthopraxy (the building of synagogues and other good works), orthodoxy (the right belief in the identity of Jesus), and orthopathy (the right sense of his own unworthiness and Jesus' holiness). Building synagogues doesn't guarantee Jesus' favor in itself, but it does indicate that the centurion recognizes the importance of good works, coupled with faith and humility. This man, in whom these things combine, evokes in Jesus an exclamation of joy. If a Gentile centurion can get it, then the kingdom is surely about to be unleashed across the empire.

↩ReJesus, Take Three

By making Jesus the center or the norm, we are invited to embrace that same nexus between orthopraxy, orthodoxy, and orthopathy. And let's be clear about this, when we speak of Jesus Christ as primary norm, center, foundation, we mean the whole Christ. We do not refer only to the Jesus of history or Jesus of Nazareth prior to the events of the cross and resurrection. Nor do we mean some abstracted Christ figure cut apart from the Jesus of history. "The center and foundation of Christian faith is Jesus of Nazareth, the Messiah, crucified and risen, and present with us now in the power of the Spirit."[29] There must be no sundering of Jesus' person from his work and from what he has taught and modeled. It is all one of the same phenomenon. Anything less than this total understanding of our Lord is insufficient to fund the church's mission in the world or to sustain any vital faith. Since the beginning of the church's history, we have struggled between either making Jesus into either an otherworldly object of faith or limiting him to a mere figure of history.

As we have seen, the process of reJesusing the church involves in some sense a return to Hebraic perspectives. Much of recent scholarship has involved a re-examination of the historical Jesus and his Jewishness. But the Hellenistic worldview can lead us far astray in the study of the Gospels. Some approaches reject the Gospels as the historical revelation of the Christlike

God, as texts that read us and demand a response from us, and instead examine the Gospels simply as ancient texts. Now, we don't imagine that we can do justice to summarizing the history of New Testament interpretation here,

Explosive Storyteller

Harriet Beecher Stowe

When the writer Harriet Beecher Stowe visited President Lincoln in 1862, legend claims that he greeted her as "the little lady who made this big war." Whether this legend is true or not, Lincoln's words certainly illuminate Stowe's role as a catalyst of the American Civil War, which ended in the abolition of slavery in the United States. Stowe is credited with writing one of the most socially influential and politically explosive books in English literature: *Uncle Tom's Cabin.* Completed in 1852 at the height of the abolitionist movement, Stowe's novel provided many Americans with their first glimpse into the lives of slaves on a Southern plantation and is believed to have broadened abolitionist sentiment in the North. Begun as a serial for the Washington anti-slavery weekly *The National Era,* and based on Stowe's own exposure to slavery, herself having grown up across the Ohio River from the slave-owning state of Kentucky, her book gave the abolitionist movement a deeply human face. Stowe's portraits of local social life, particularly with minor characters, reflect an awareness of the complexity of the times. *Uncle Tom's Cabin* is not just a political tract; it is also a wonderfully written piece of realist literature presenting a social and political outlook within a remarkable story format. The beauty of her stories engaged a massive readership, but the truths they revealed also divided American society, energizing the efforts of the North, and infuriating the Southern states. After the book's publication, Stowe went on to speak out against slavery in the United States. After the end of the Civil War, she established several schools and homes for former slaves. Harriet Beecher Stowe passed away on July 1, 1896. She is a little Jesus because she advocated showing mercy and freedom to the powerless and marginalized through beautiful, socially relevant stories.

but we do believe it's fair to say that most of the recent innovations in New Testament interpretation—whether they are of the popular, and rather fanciful, variety like Dan Brown's *The Da Vinci Code,* or the more scholarly type like *The Historical Jesus,* by John Dominic Crossan, and *Jesus: Uncovering the Life, Teachings, and Relevance of a Religious Revolutionary,* by Marcus Borg, and the work of the Jesus Seminar—are indebted to the model championed by Rudolf Bultmann in the twentieth century. Called form criticism, Bultmann's approach involved the dismantling of the Gospels into their various pieces for the purpose of closer scrutiny. His assumption, and one followed by Wilson, Spong, Borg, Crossan, J. T. Robinson, and many more, was that the Gospels could, indeed should, be approached in the same way that contemporary literature studies approached ancient folklore such as Homer's *Odyssey* or *Iliad*. These folk stories were told and retold over an extended period of time. When finally written down, the texts were then edited and re-edited as they passed through the hands of various interpreters over the ages. The job of the modern literature scholar was to disassemble those parts, dicing them up into their various bite-sized portions according to literary style and historical sensibility for the purposes of clarity. Form critics do the same thing with the Gospels. Each piece, or *pericope*, whether a parable, a saying, or a riddle, is separated out, and judgments are made on their authorship, intention, and authenticity.

So, for instance, if you've ever met someone who believes in the resurrection but rejects the virgin birth, or who believes in the parables of grace but rejects the parables of judgment, chances are that person has been influenced by form criticism, or at the least operates under the assumptions that many theologically liberal interpreters adhere to. Even the atheist writer Richard Dawkins has no truck with this approach, which, to paraphrase him, is like cherry picking which doctrines you like from those you don't. Of course, Dawkins thinks all of the Gospel material is religious mumbo-jumbo, and he'd prefer you threw the lot out. But at least he sees the contradictions in people who consider themselves Christians choosing which bits are binding and which are negotiable.

With Bultmannian form criticism holding such sway, it has been interesting to watch the emergence of the British scholar N. T. Wright. He has been the leading light in the third quest for the historical Jesus (Bultmann launched the so-called second quest with his 1921 book, *History of the Synoptic Tradition*).[30] If Bultmann and the many varieties of his followers pull each tiny piece of the Gospels apart and examine them under a microscope, as it were, Wright does the opposite. He stands back from them, like a patron in an art gallery stands back from a massive Monet canvas, trying to take in the piece as a whole. Not unlike Jacques Ellul, Wright says we need to recognize that the Hebrew worldview—with its innate sense of the importance of history that gave rise to the Bible and the Gospels—provides us with the best tools for examining them.

Interestingly, Wright concludes his magisterial book, *Jesus and the Victory of God*, as he began it, with the parable of the prodigal son. Only this time the parable is related to the contemporary quest for the historical Jesus. Not only is Israel like the prodigal, who has experienced exile and has returned home to be restored by their Father (via the ministry of Jesus), but those of us who have followed the unhelpful leads offered by modern form critics have found ourselves in a far land, barely surviving on the non-nutritious results of their scholarship. Wright suggests we need to return home to a more Jewish appreciation of the Gospels and their inherent integrity. Referring to Albert Schweitzer, who had claimed that Jesus comes to us as one unknown, Wright concludes,

> We come to *him* as ones unknown, crawling back from the far country, where we had wasted our substance on riotous but ruinous historicism . . . But when we approached, as we have tried to do with this book, we found him running to us as one well known, whom we had spurned in the name of scholarship or even of faith, but who was still patiently waiting to be sought and found once more.[31]

We believe, with scholars like Wright, that we can have absolute confidence in the reliability of the Gospels, precisely by coming to them as their original Jewish hearers would. But we also believe that the Hebraic worldview invites us to come to the ancient texts in a different way to the approach taken by Hellenistic thinkers. That is, we believe rather than reading the Bible, we need to allow it to read us.

As difficult as it seems, we believe that a renewed engagement with Jesus requires a radical transformation in worldview as well as that of the heart. We need to recover a biblical epistemology (ways of knowing). In order to see Jesus truly, we need to saturate ourselves in the Hebraic perspectives that both originate and sustain the biblical worldview. And we believe we have to pickle ourselves in the Gospels. They must become our primary stories and reference point. There is no truer way to encounter Jesus afresh than prayerfully cycling through the Gospels and asking God to give us fresh insight into the remarkable person we find there. We must give our hearts, minds, souls, to the One around whom history turns.

↶ Notes

1. Wilson, *Our Father Abraham*, 150. See also Thomas Cahill, *The Gifts of the Jews: How a Tribe of Desert Nomads Changed the Way Everyone Thinks and Feels* (Oxford: Lion, 1998).

2. Wilson, *Our Father Abraham*, 150.

3. R. Martin-Achard, *An Approach to the Old Testament* (trans. J. G. C. Greig; Edinburgh: Oliver & Boyd, 1965), 46.

4. Ellul, *Subversion of Christianity*, 23. Ellul's view is backed up by the analysis of Jewish theologian Michael Wyschogrod, *The Body of Faith: Judaism as Corporeal Election* (New York: Seabury, 1983), chs. 1–3.

5. Ellul, *Subversion of Christianity*, 24.

6. Wyschogrod, *Body of Faith*, ch. 2.

7. Ellul, *Subversion of Christianity*, 24.

8. This is not to say it is not authoritative for all matters of life and faith, but it is precisely because it is God's Word that it is authoritative. The Narnian metaphor was suggested by Bruxy Cavey from Toronto.

9. See Søren Kierkegaard, *Concluding Unscientific Postscript 2: Kierkegaard's Writings* (vol. 12.2; Princeton, N.J.: Princeton University Press, 1992), for a full exploration of the place of subjectivity in relation to truth.

10. Donald D. Palmer, *Kierkegaard for Beginners* (New York: Writers and Readers, 1996), 25.

11. Minear, *Eyes of Faith*, 16.

12. Jonathan Edwards, *On the Religious Affections*, in *The Works of Jonathan Edwards* (1834; repr., Peabody, Mass.: Hendrickson, 1993), I.II.4, 10.

13. Mystics often talk about the *via negative*, the way of negation, or unknowing, where one can but trust what is unknown. For example, "What can be learnt does not matter; what matters is the self-abandonment to that which is not known." Buber, *Mamre*, 87–88.

14. Martin Buber, *Good and Evil* (Englewood Cliffs, N.J.: Prentice Hall, 1953), 56.

15. Kierkegaard, *Concluding Unscientific Postscript*, 30.

16. Edwards, *On the Religious Affections*, 11.

17. Harold Wells, *The Christic Center: Life-Giving and Liberating* (Maryknoll, N.Y.: Orbis, 2004), 122.

18. Frost and Hirsch, *Shaping of Things to Come*, ch. 8.

19. Ibid., 137.

20. Elie Wiesel, *Twilight* (Suffolk: Viking, 1988), 69.

21. Martin Buber, *On Judaism* (New York: Schocken, 1967), 112.

22. Helmut Thielicke, *The Doctrine of God and of Christ* (vol. 2 of *The Evangelical Faith*; trans. and ed. Geoffrey W. Bromiley; Edinburgh: T&T Clark, 1977), 289.

23. Paul Minear, *Commands of Christ* (Nashville: Abingdon, 1972), 10. This does not mean that we believe that we should not worship Jesus, but it does force us to try understand what Jesus meant by worship. What it does mean is that our worship must be based on obedience and not just songs.

24. Dietrich Bonhoeffer, *The Cost of Discipleship* (New York: Macmillan, 1979), 83. Bonhoeffer always stressed the role of obedience in faith. He could say that "only he who believes is obedient and only he who is obedient believes." Quoted in J. A. Woelfel, *Bonhoeffer's Theology* (Nashville: Abingdon, 1970), 253.

25. John Calvin, *Institutes of the Christian Religion* (ed. John T. McNeill; Philadelphia: Westminster, 1960), 1.6.3, 73.

26. Ellul, *Subversion of Christianity*, 5.

27. Wells, *Christic Center*, 125–26.

28. We are indebted to the work of friend and colleague Stephen Said for this diagram.

29. Wells, *Christic Center*, 121.

30. The first quest for the historical Jesus was associated with the work of Albert Schweitzer and catalyzed by his best-known scholarly work, *The Quest of the Historical Jesus* (1910). Schweitzer proposed an understanding of Jesus as a primarily eschatological character, whose distinct mission was the institution of a messianic epoch. Bultmann and the second quest refuted this and consigned Jesus to the role of an earthly teacher of godly wisdom.

31. N. T. Wright, *Jesus and the Victory of God* (London: SPCK, 1996), 662.

The Church That Jesus Built

*The ultimate problem, which has caused our theological
helplessness, lies in the separation between Jesus Christ
and the Church.*
—D. Ritschl

> *The Indian is making an amazing discovery, namely
> that Christianity and Jesus are not the same—that
> they may have Jesus without the system that has been
> built up around Him in the West.*
> —E. Stanley Jones

In 2006, a somewhat eccentric pastor, Jim Henderson, made national news when he rented a soul for $504 on e-Bay after its owner offered an open mind to the highest bidder. Henderson purchased Matt Casper's soul, and he and Casper traveled around America critiquing various churches. The result is Henderson's book, *Jim and Casper Go to Church*, a survey of the different approaches to church currently being tried in the United States, all presented from the fresh point of view of an unbelieving outsider.[1] Jim and Casper visited such diverse expressions as Rick Warren's Saddleback, Bill Hybel's Willow Creek, Erwin McManus' Mosaic, Joel Osteen's Lakewood, as well as the Dream Center, First Presbyterian in Chicago, Lawndale, Jason's House, Imago Dei in Portland, Mars Hill in Seattle, The Bridge in Portland, and the Potter's House in Dallas. You can't claim they weren't looking at churches from right across the spectrum, from mega-churches to emergent churches (and a bit of everything in between).

What did they find? Well, Matt Casper's perspective certainly is fresh, uncluttered as it is by preconceptions and insider knowledge. And his comments do heighten your sensitivity to showy, nonessential forms of church. He also highlights how churches can miss Jesus' message by focusing too much on raising money or by talking in indecipherable religious jargon. But the take-home point seems to be, "Why are there such glaring discrepancies among churches regarding what it means to be a follower of Christ?" If they're all talking about Jesus, why does the Jesus they're talking about look different in different churches?

This was similar to the question posed to us by a young man who had been raised by evangelical missionary parents but who had converted in the Eastern Orthodox church in California. While he took issue with a number of the practices of the Orthodox church, he preferred its unchanged seventeen-hundred-year message and liturgy to the multiplicity of Protestant versions. "With all the evangelicals telling me they were 'just preaching Jesus' I became confused when they were all preaching different Jesuses," he complained.

In *They Like Jesus but Not the Church*, Dan Kimball fires a similar shot across the church's bow. By interviewing a number of unchurched young people in California, Kimball discovered that, far from being antagonistic about faith in Jesus, his focus group was open to such faith but skeptical that the church as they knew it had anything to teach them about it. They believed the church is an organized religion with a political agenda, is negative and judgmental in outlook, and is generally male-dominated, homophobic, and fundamentalist.[2]

Kimball describes going onto a university campus with a video camera to interview students about their attitudes to the Christian faith. Instead of asking the usual questions that a lot of campus ministries ask ("Do you believe there is only one way to God? If you were to die tonight . . ."), Kimball asked just two: "What do you think of when you hear the name Jesus?" and "What comes to mind when you hear the word Christian?" The responses were interesting.[3]

Jesus	Christians
He is beautiful	The church messed things up
He is a wise man, like a shaman or a guru	They took the teachings of Jesus and turned them into dogmatic rules
He came to liberate women	Christians don't apply the message of love that Jesus gave
I want to be like him	They all should be taken out back and shot

In summing up their attitudes, Kimball quotes Gandhi's dictum: "I like your Christ. I do not like your Christians. Your Christians are so unlike your Christ."

As should be obvious by now, we believe that Christian faith must look to Jesus and must be well founded on him if it is to be authentic. If NASA was even .05 degrees off in launching a rocket to the moon, they would miss the moon by thousands of miles. And in many ways this is the same as it applies to the gospel. Because of the fundamental role that Jesus plays in Christian identity, ministry, and mission, we believe it is critical to get this right and to constantly keep checking. Church history makes it clear that such shifts take place. But these shifts are usually inadvertent and take place incrementally as other issues press in and traditions create their own overlay, obscuring the core of the faith. Whatever the process, it results in an insidious change in the resulting religion.

Therefore we propose that church should be recalibrated around its founder, Jesus. But what would that look like? Jesus didn't found any churches. He unleashed an army of little Jesuses who went forth and founded faith communities across the known world. But Jesus fashioned a temporary community, or a proto-church, if you will. Within the DNA of his itinerant community of disciples there exists the stuff of church, but it's not until we get to the apostle Paul that we see what it looks like to embody that DNA in a more stable, indigenous faith community. Paul takes the example of Jesus and, under the guidance of the Holy Spirit, unfurls those priorities and values into what we today call biblical ecclesiology.

Here is a curious question that will highlight the issue for us: If the church had only the four Gospels to go by, what would it look like? Certainly discipleship would be emphasized, as would the prominence on living in and under the kingdom of God. There would likely be a strong emphasis on uncluttered lifestyle and adventuresome community with lots of love, faithfulness, mercy, and justice going around. Would this be an adequate expression of Christianity? Now again, this somewhat tongue-in-cheek question is not meant to displace the canon of the New Testament or dislodge Paul's God-given apostleship in the church (God forbid), but as a mental exercise it should highlight the fact that all the basics would be in place—as they ought to be—when we focus on Jesus. Indeed, what we see Paul doing, in his epistles in particular, is working on developing the implications and logical conclusions of the stuff provided by Jesus in the example of his community. It's a relief that we are not just left with the four Gospels, because God has spoken through the rest of the New Testament to help us see the fullness of all that a community of Jesus' followers should look like. Our point is that there is no disjunction between Jesus' example and Paul's ecclesiology. One is the outworking of the other. But it's all seminally there in the Gospels themselves. The renewal of the church in our time is dependent on the renewal of the gospel. And the renewal of the gospel requires the recovery of the centrality of Jesus for faith and thought. We must reJesus our theology as well as our churches.

Paul's Vision of the Jesus Community

Let's take some time to explore Paul's ecclesiology and hold it up against the lens of Jesus' example from the Gospels. In his letter to the Ephesians, Paul addresses a number of what we might call generic church issues. Unlike his correspondence to the Corinthians or the Galatians, which specifically addresses particular issues with which each church was struggling, the letter to the Ephesians includes a lot of material applicable to all churches everywhere. This is probably because it was a circular letter that was sent around to various churches in Asia Minor. According to his Ephesian correspondence, Paul saw the notion of *ecclesia* being anchored on the foundation of a series of core truths.

Jesus Is "Head over All Things for the Church" (Eph 1:22)

Here we have an intriguing phrase regarding Jesus' pre-eminence. After noting that God has placed everything under the feet of Jesus, Paul then says that Jesus has been appointed head over everything for the church. That Jesus is head over all things is clear enough, but what did Paul mean by the phrase "for the church"? It seems that Paul is saying that Jesus exercises his supreme global authority over all things in the interest of the church. That is, the rule of Jesus is for the benefit of his church. It can sound arrogant of the church to suggest such a thing, as though Jesus rules in favor of Christians over all other people. Some church leaders have spoken this way to suggest that Jesus endorses them no matter what. However, a quick read of the seven letters to the seven churches found in the book of Revelation will show that Jesus doesn't mind standing against the church at times. It seems that what Paul is saying is that the future of Jesus' pre-eminent reign is inextricably linked with the future of the church. He has the church's interest at heart.

The Church "Is His Body" (Eph 1:23)

Paul makes much more of this metaphor in 1 Corinthians. Here, he is happy simply to introduce the idea. The church is the body of Jesus. It is his spiritual body, of which he is the head. In Ephesians 1, this implies intimacy and connectedness between Jesus and his followers. In Ephesians 4, Paul uses the metaphor to commend unity within the community of the followers of Jesus. And in 1 Corinthians 12, he expands it to discuss the diversity of gifts expressed by the followers of Jesus working together in harmony. The overall idea is one of teamwork, partnership, trust, respect, and intimacy. In both our previous books, we discuss the idea of *communitas*, the intimacy and devotion that develop between a group of people when faced with a common task or ordeal. Paul suggests as much in his use of body imagery in his letters.

The Church Is "the Fullness of Him Who Fills All in All" (Eph 1:23)

Now here is a big concept of the church—hardly a reduced idea of what Jesus intended! In the previous chapter we explored the centrality of the *Shema* in Hebrew thought and life. It was a declaration that Yahweh rules over all of life in every sphere. Here, Paul is identifying Jesus with such a rule by saying that he "fills all in all," that is, everything in the world. It is a statement of Jesus' omnipresence and sovereignty. But note how he refers to the church as Jesus' fullness. In other words, the community of Jesus' followers constitutes his fullness. In a sense Paul is saying, for example, "Look at the mountains and the sea. There you will see Jesus' presence on display. But if you really want to see the fullness of his presence, look at the church!" Now, often when church leaders say such a thing they implicitly (sometimes explicitly) refer to the institution of the church: "Look at our buildings and our church services! There you will see the fullness of Christ!" This isn't what Paul meant. There were no flashy church services to look at, and very few churches had their own buildings. Paul is saying that in the organic, messy, often troubled, sometimes harmonious webs of relationship found among Jesus' followers you can see the richness and beauty and power of the fullness of Jesus.

The Church Is Part of God's "Eternal Purpose" (Eph 3:10–11)

In this beautiful section of Ephesians 3, Paul declares that God has made his wisdom known in the heavenly realms through the church:

> Through the church the wisdom of God in its rich variety might now be made known to the rulers and authorities in the heavenly places. This was in accordance with the eternal purpose that he has carried out in Christ Jesus our Lord. (Eph 3:10–11)

Now that's saying something! It implies that throughout the ages God's manifold wisdom could never be quite appreciated by the heavenly community, because it seems that God doesn't have a true relationship with the rulers and authorities in heaven. They are excluded from the unique and intimate relationship God reserves himself for with humankind. It wasn't until the church was unleashed as a community of human beings in relationship with God through Jesus that the richness of God's wisdom could be appreciated. Therefore, to all the angelic beings God displays his wisdom through the church. Do we need a greater demonstration that God's wisdom is intrinsically relational than this? God's wisdom is not merely a matter of superior cognition or greater accumulated knowledge. The wisdom of God is displayed through the webs of relationships of Jesus' followers. In James 3:17, a similar idea is presented: "the wisdom from above is first pure, then peaceable, gentle, willing to yield, full of mercy and good fruits, without a trace of impartiality or hypocrisy."

If the wisdom of God is all these things—essentially relational things—then God is able to fully express such wisdom only through relationship with his people. This was God's plan, says Paul, throughout eternity. The followers of Jesus are essential for the expression of God's wisdom.

God Is to Be Glorified "in the Church and in Christ Jesus" (Eph 3:21)

In a somewhat premature benediction, Paul declares a closing prayer over the recipients of his letter (and yet he still has three more chapters up his sleeve):

> Now to him who by the power at work within us is able to accomplish abundantly far more than all we can ask or imagine, to him be glory in the church and in Christ Jesus to all generations, forever and ever. Amen. (Eph 3:20–21)

Certainly God is worthy of all glory, and Paul identifies two sources of his glory: his son, Jesus, and the church.

"Christ Is the Head of the Church, the Body of Which He Is the Savior" (Eph 5:23)

Paul returns to the body metaphor again, if only briefly, to re-emphasize Jesus' rule over his followers and to make explicit that he is its Savior as well. Having saved the church, he can then be its head or ruler. But this is not simply a matter of ownership. This text appears in the midst of a discussion about the relationship between husbands and wives. Jesus is the head and the savior of the church, but this is expressed in distinctly relational terms.

Jesus "Loved the Church and Gave Himself up for Her" (Eph 5:25)

Jesus loves his church, just as a good husband is to love his wife. His death on the cross is his supreme act of devotion and love.

Jesus' Design Is to Present It as a Holy, Blameless Church (Eph 5:26–27)

Paul has told us what Jesus has done for his church in a past sense: he has loved the church, saved the church, and rules the church. Now he turns his attention to the future and announces that the church is a work in progress. It is Jesus' work to improve us, to slowly but surely recreate us in his image. Jesus' future design for his followers is to

> make her holy by cleansing her with the washing with water by the word, so as to present the church to himself in splendor, without a spot or wrinkle or anything of the kind—yes, so that she may be holy and without blemish. (Eph 5:26–27)

Jesus Nourishes and Cares for the Church (Eph 5:29–30)

Says Paul, "No one ever hates his own body, but he nourishes and tenderly cares for it, just as Christ does for the church, because we are members of his body" (Eph 5:29–30). In another return to the body metaphor, Paul indicates that as part of his future orientation in presenting the church blameless and radiant, he nourishes and cares for the church, supplying its needs and attending to its concerns. It seems to us that Jesus is more than involved in it than what first appears to the casual observer.

If This Is Church, We Want In

And so, whatever the church is, we want to be a part of it! We think that its true reality is far more than the religious institution it became. It is an intimate network of Jesus followers. It is saturated with Jesus.

Paul's favorite image for the church is that of a family, or to be more accurate, the household.[4] If you did a word search through his letters, you would find that he makes more references to body than to family, but if you include all Paul's use of family language (brothers, sisters, etc.), it is clear that the church as family is his favorite idea. Paul saw the church inextricably linked to Jesus and each other in a bond of deep interpersonal relationship. From this brief study of Ephesians, it becomes clear that Paul saw the church as something that issues forth from Jesus. It is a matter of what Jesus does for his followers and what they become in him doing it.

This table summarizes what we have explored so far.

What Jesus Does	What the Church Becomes
He reigns over the church	A Christlike community that reflects his character, life, and activity
He reigns over all the world	A holistic community that seeks to offer up all of life to the lordship of Jesus
His wisdom is relational	A peace-loving community that is considerate, submissive, merciful, fruitful, impartial, and sincere
He is glorified by the church	A worshipping community that exalts Jesus and declares his sovereignty
He loves the church	A devoted community that experiences intimacy with Jesus
He saves the church	A graced community that relies on the work of Jesus for salvation
He cleanses the church	A holy community that seeks after the righteousness of Jesus
He nourishes the church	A healthy community that feeds on God's Word and the ministry of his Spirit

In some of our previous books we have presented some rather pointed criticism of the way church is being done in the West.[5] This has riled some readers and led some critics to suggest that we don't love the church, but we submit to you that it is our very love for the church that motivates us to write what we do. And besides, there is a difference between liking the church and loving the church the way Jesus commands us to. To be sure, we do not *like* gatherings of strangers who never meet or know each other outside of Sundays, who sit passively while virtual strangers preach and lead singing, who put up with second-rate pseudo-community under the guise of connection with each other, who live different lives from Monday to Saturday than they do on Sunday, whose sole expression of worship is pop-style praise and worship, who rarely laugh together, fight injustice together, eat together, pray together, raise each others' children together, serve the poor together, or share Jesus with those who have not yet been set free. We do not *like* the church if it's a fractured organization with hundreds of competing creeds, names, and doctrines, teaching a multitude of contradictory beliefs and insisting on compliance with a raft of recently invented traditions. But if it's a family of Jesus followers striving, no matter how inadequately, to be Christlike, holistic, peace-loving, worshipful, devoted, graced, holy, and healthy, then we will love it with every ounce of physical and emotional strength we have.

There's a story told about a young soldier of the army of Alexander the Great who deserts his post and is tracked down and captured by Alexander's men. Normally deserters were summarily executed by these ancient bounty hunters, but according to this story, the young man was brought into the presence of the king. Alexander demanded that the deserter tell him his name. "I share the name of my king," said the soldier. "My name is Alexander." While the king went on to pardon the deserter, he did not do so before insisting, "Young man, you change your life, or you change your name."

This is as it was with the followers of Jesus. It was as if they took on his name as their own and their life had to mirror that marvelous name they now used. Likewise, the church today, we suggest. It's time to change its life or alternatively to change its name. The unconventional Christian musician Moby recently toyed with this idea in a journal entry on his website.[6] Beginning his comments with, "So, do you think that it's time to invent a new religion?" he playfully questioned whether the ways we perceive church or Christianity are so different from what Jesus had in mind that it's time to start a new Jesus-following religion all over. He said,

> I actually think that the teachings of Christ accommodate most of the new ways in which we perceive ourselves and our world.
>
> the problem is that although the teachings of Christ accommodate this,
>
> contemporary Christianity does not.
>
> here's more seriousness dressed up as flippancy:
>
> christ: acknowledging quantum realities.
>
> christianity: depressingly newtonian.
>
> Does that make any sense?[7]

He is echoing what Kimball's subjects told him, although as a Christian, Moby is more involved in the issue than are the non-Christian young people interviewed by Kimball. When many Christians hear comments like Moby's they react against what they see as a complete disregard, even disrespect,

Champion of the Poor

Dorothy Day was relentless in her commitment to social justice and peace and her devotion to the poor. Indeed, this little Jesus once said, "I firmly believe that our salvation depends on the poor." A bohemian living in New York City in the 1910s and 20s, Day began the spiritual journey that led her to the Catholic Church after the birth of her daughter. As a new Christian who had left behind the sexual mores of her contemporaries, Day retained her commitment to pacifism and the rights of the worker that were central to the bohemian culture, believing that these values were also central to the message of Jesus.

Dorothy Day

Together with Peter Maurin, in 1933 she founded the Catholic Worker movement (CW), a controversial organization dedicated to serving Christ by working for justice for those on the margins of society. The *Catholic Worker* newspaper promoted their mission, and the movement opened St. Joseph's, a house of hospitality in the slums of New York that provided the poor with accommodation and meals. Soon after, a series of farms in rural America were opened in which the poor could live in community. The movement spread quickly to other cities in the United States and then to Canada and the United Kingdom. By 1941, more than thirty independent affiliates of CW had been established, and the work continues today, with more than one hundred communities in operation. Though pilloried for her pacifism during World War II, and seen as outdated because of her opposition to the sexual revolution of the 1960s, she never budged an inch in her beliefs. Day did retain the respect of those in the antiwar movement, and she still attended protests up through the 1970s. Some hailed her as a saint, something she discouraged. "Don't call me a saint," she said. "I don't want to be dismissed so easily." Day lived at St. Joseph's, serving the poor, until her death in 1980.

for the tradition and history of the Christian church throughout the past two thousand years. But it is also worth noting that the church has seen the rise of hundreds of reforming and renewing movements from within its ranks throughout the Christian era. If we learn anything from church history, it's that raising questions about how we are to be and do church has never done the church any harm. Indeed, it has been the church's great strength that it has been able to listen to and accommodate such critique.

If we take Moby's critiques on the chin and go back to the Bible to re-discover our original DNA as a church, we find marvelous encouragement for renewal and transformation. What does it look like for a web or family of followers to become all that Jesus intends for them? What would a new religion of Jesus followers look like? This second table offers some clues.

What the Church Becomes	How
1. A Christlike community that reflects his character, life, and activity	1. by making an intentional corporate study of the Gospels to model our lives on the example of Jesus, preferring no lesser hero from our tradition
2. A holistic community that seeks to offer up all of life to the lordship of Jesus	2. by de-emphasizing Sunday and equipping all followers to hand over every sphere of their lives and every day of the week to Jesus
3. A peace-loving community that is considerate, submissive, merciful, fruitful, impartial, and sincere	3. by moving outward to serve others, knowing that community is forged by our collective commitment to a cause beyond ourselves
4. A worshipping community that exalts Jesus and declares his sovereignty	4. by understanding that worship includes singing but is never limited to it and involves a whole of life exaltation of Jesus
5. A devoted community that experiences intimacy with Jesus	5. by practicing the presence of Jesus in prayer, solitude, fasting, and missional action
6. A graced community that relies on the work of Jesus for salvation	6. by insisting continually that it is not by our own efforts that we are saved—that is, through a continual re-evangelization of believers
7. A holy community that seeks after the righteousness of Jesus	7. by learning and living the values of Jesus, as distinct from the piety of middle-class good-manners conventionality
8. A healthy community that feeds on God's Word and the ministry of his Spirit	8. by corporately devoting ourselves to the Scriptures and the exercise of the spiritual gifts

These eight action points don't require any significant collateral or specially designed facilities. They can be appropriated by any collective of believers devoted to following Jesus, and they can be lived out in the ordinary world.

⟵ Getting Back to Jesus' Community

So far so good. But remember we have derived these points from Paul's words in Ephesians. Would Jesus agree with what Paul wrote in Ephesians? There's no doubt that Paul anchors the church steadfastly to the example of Jesus, but did Jesus teach or develop a community of followers that looks like this? Let's turn our attention back to the Gospels to find out. We will take the eight action points listed above and check them against the example of Jesus.

Jesus' Community Will Follow the Example of Jesus

As implied in the early sections of this book, our point is that we don't want Presbyterians to look more like John Knox or Methodists to look more like John Wesley or Salvationists to look more like William Booth. We want all believers to look more like Jesus. We don't discount the enormous contribution made to the Christian cause by people like Knox, Wesley, or Booth, and we recognize that there's much we can learn from such leaders, but let Jesus be our guide, our Lord, and our master. This was the crux of the Jesus community as found in the Gospels. Jesus is central. It is his example to which his followers continually turn. To them, Jesus is not merely some radical rabbi whose innovative take on Hebrew philosophy they had come to appreciate. He does more than conduct outdoor theology classes. He models an alternate lifestyle. He models itinerancy (Luke 9:57–62) and complete trust in the provision of God (Luke 12:22–31). He demonstrates how to treat children (Luke 18:15–17) and women (Luke 8:1–3; 10:38–42). He provides a template for how they are to pray (Luke 11:1–2). He sends them out to duplicate his ministry of healing and preaching (Luke 9:1–6). He allows them to question him on his parables (Luke 8:9). Some of them witness his transfiguration (Luke 9:28–29); all of them witness his resurrection (Luke 24:36–37).

This was the beginning of the conspiracy of the little Jesus. He replicates himself in the lives of his first followers. He allowed them to make an intensive study of his life and ministry and then unleashed them on an unsuspecting world like a tsunami of love and grace. Without the real thing in flesh and blood, we today have his Spirit within us and the Gospels as our guide and impetus. It would follow, then, that in order to replicate his life and ministry, we must make an intentional corporate study of the Gospels. They are the staple diet of Jesus followers. Rather than milk for Sunday school children, the Gospels should be the main course at every Christian meal.

Jesus' Community Will Equip All Followers

The examples of the de-emphasizing the Sabbath in Jesus' life and ministry are many. In Luke 14 we read,

> On one occasion when Jesus was going to the house of a leader of the Pharisees to eat a meal on the Sabbath, they were watching him closely. Just then, in front of him, there was a man who had dropsy. And Jesus asked the lawyers and Pharisees, "Is it lawful to cure people on the sabbath, or not?" But they were silent. So Jesus took him and healed him, and sent him away. Then he said to them, "If one of you has a child or an ox that has fallen into a well, will you not immediately pull it out on a Sabbath day?" And they could not reply to this. (Luke 14:1–6)

Jesus was picking up on a scholarly debate of the time. It had been a topic of much discussion by Jewish scholars as to whether it was lawful to save your dying son on the Sabbath. Surely, some argued, it would be unlawful to save an ox but legal to save your own son. Such debates always occur in rarefied academic contexts where neither child nor ox is thrashing for life in a watery well. Jesus throws their scholarly disconnection back in their faces. Before them lay a man who could not walk. Without work, he would have been starving to death, reduced to begging for scraps and alms. Knowing that their answer about the legalities of Sabbath keeping would directly bear on the livelihood of this poor soul, the Pharisees are silenced by their embarrassment. Jesus, though, is a man of action. He is a man of engagement and decisiveness. Sabbath or no Sabbath, the beggar needed his touch, and he refused to stand idly by, paralyzed by theological niceties.

How amazing that the religion that bears his name has become every bit as Sabbath-centric as Jesus' opponents! So much of the Christian church focuses on getting people into the pews on a Sunday morning as its highest goal. It has created its own legalism that defines holiness in terms of attendance instead of as communion with God in every area of their week and life. It has shifted its preference to Sunday, but it is no less paralyzed by the legalism that silenced the Pharisees. How could we have missed Jesus' words in Luke 6, where after the Pharisees rebuked his disciples for eating the kernels of grain on the Sabbath, he snapped,

"Have you not read what David did when he and his companions were hungry? He entered the house of God and took and ate the bread of the Presence, which it is not lawful for any but the priests to eat, and gave some to his companions?" Then he said to them, "The Son of Man is lord of the sabbath." (Luke 6:3–5)

Jesus is locating himself as the center of the religious cult of Judaism. As we've seen, he sees himself as the physical embodiment of the temple. He does what a temple is supposed to do. Now, he proclaims lordship over the Sabbath. It is *his* day now. He was not shifting the focus of Sabbath keeping from Yahweh to himself. He *is* Yahweh! It was always his day. What he is doing is declaring lordship over all of life, including the Sabbath. In Mark's version of the same episode, Jesus says, "The sabbath was made for humankind, and not humankind for the sabbath" (Mark 2:27). His point was that the Sabbath was made to serve people, instead of people being created to serve the Sabbath. The Sabbath was a servant, not a master. He was telling them that they should apply the law of the Sabbath with mercy and thought to human need. And he was telling them he had the authority to define how they should observe the Sabbath. In short, human need (the disciples' hunger, the ill man's dropsy) is more important than blind Sabbath keeping.

Jesus sets his friends free to enjoy snacking on the rolled husks of wheat. He attends to an ill man rather than be bound by legalism. Likewise, the church today must rediscover that while regular times of retreat and reflection are essential, they are tools for use by us as required. Michael has a friend who works in a downtown office in Sydney who takes his lunch two or three times a week to a nearby cathedral to reflect on Jesus and enjoy the serenity of the place. He is free to sabbath as he wills. Jesus is Lord of all of life, of every day and every place. Hallelujah!

Jesus' Community Will Move Outward to Serve Others

Jesus' community is not a static band of learners. They are a moving, living, breathing, organic team of little Jesuses. Far from setting up camp in Nazareth and downloading a whole new worldview framed in theoretical rhetoric, Jesus hits the road with his followers, showing that community is forged by the heat of action and joint cooperation in a cause beyond themselves. They are buffeted by criticism from opponents, confused by the reactions of others, and inspired by the example of Jesus. After he sends them (and fifty-eight others) out in pairs to preach, heal, and drive out demons, they return "with joy" to report on what they have seen (Luke 10:17). They are bound to each other as a band of brothers and sisters. Jesus even takes a tax collector (Levi/Matthew) and a zealot (Simon) into his troupe. No two people would have despised each other more than the nationalistic zealots who had vowed to slaughter the Romans and their collaborators and, well, collaborators like the tax collectors. This is not unlike the elf Legolas and the dwarf Gimli in *The Lord of the Rings*. Though avowed enemies, they are drawn together in their quest to return the ring to Mount Mordor. The political and theological differences that would have normally driven Simon and Matthew apart are overwhelmed by their joint commitment to the mission of Jesus.

To be sure, there are examples of occasional or casual observers enjoying the ministry of Jesus. At the Sermon on the Mount and the feeding of the thousands, Jesus attracted large audiences. However, John points out that most people weren't able to stomach Jesus' teaching. In John 6, after the feeding of five thousand, many turned away, offended by his uncompromising instruction (John 6:60, 66). Jesus is unfazed by this, though; he is aware that few will faithfully follow him (John 6:64b–65). Jesus' community is built not with casual observers but with those who have completely thrown in their lot with him. Listen to Peter's plaintive cry when Jesus offers him the chance to also turn away: "Lord, to whom can we go? You have the words of eternal life" (John 6:68).

How can churches today resist the pull to become a spectator sport? How can they fight against, instead of be caught up by, the spirit of consumerism? Churches wanting to grow sometimes end up desperately trying to attract a greater share of the market with advertising ploys and promises of greater luxury and better religious goods and services. We heard of a church in California that gives away a Harley-Davidson motorbike each year to the person who brings the most visitors to church on Sundays. Is this the way Jesus mobilized his followers? By appealing to their greed and self-interest? Jesus fashioned a community of devoted, selfless servants who had sought to model their lives on his selflessness and service. And in so doing they became bound to each in the bonds of a common cause.

Jesus' Community Understands That Worship Is a Whole-of-Life Exaltation of Jesus

Jesus' community was a decidedly missional one. It was defined and shaped by its founder's mission to usher in the kingdom of God. The term "missional church" gets bandied about by all sorts of folks from across different denominational backgrounds and from around the world. We suspect it might mean differing things to different people. We also fear that it might be becoming the latest buzz term along with such words and phrases as emerging, emergent, fresh expressions, new expressions, mission-shaped, and so on.

Caring for the Sick

Damien of Molokai

Born Jozef de Veuster in Belgium in 1840, Father Damien traveled as a member of a missionary order in 1873 to the Hawaiian island of Molokai in order to minister to those suffering from leprosy (known today as Hansen's Disease). Nearly 1,000 lepers had been quarantined at a settlement on Molokai that was surrounded by an impregnable mountain ridge. Neglected by the Hawaiian government, the settlement had declined into a lawless, filthy, immoral "Colony of Death." Although aware of the need for ministry in the settlement, the bishop of Honolulu hesitated to send a missionary into the colony, as the missionary would surely contract the contagious disease. Father Damien, however, requested the assignment, and the bishop introduced him to the colony as "one who will be a father to you, and who loves you so much that he does not hesitate to become one of you; to live and die with you." True to this introduction, Damien did not limit his role to that of a priest, and his arrival marked a turning point for the community. He dressed ulcers, built homes and beds, constructed coffins, and dug graves. Under his leadership, basic laws were enforced, shacks became painted houses, working farms were organized, schools were erected and even a girls' choir was formed. Also true to his bishop's words, however, Damien contracted the disease. In 1884, at the age of forty-nine, Damien died with his people. As a little Jesus, Father Damien was willing to give up his own life for those who suffer.

But the missional paradigm is a distinctly biblical framework for looking at the Jesus-given and Jesus-intended shape of the global Christian movement. When we refer to the missional church, we are using the term in the same way you might say the "biblical church."

For us, the phrase refers to those communities for whom mission has become the organizing principle of all they do and are. Of course, we recognize that the church has a variety of purposes or functions. These include worship, discipleship, formation, evangelism, and fellowship. Rather than seeing mission as one of the functions of the church, missional church people see it as its central and organizing purpose. For example, rather than seeing worship as central (as most conventional churches do), there is a growing movement of us who believe that worship is richer when organized around mission. We believe we do fellowship better when organized around mission. Likewise with discipleship, teaching, and the exercise of the gifts.[8]

And what is mission? It is the outward impulse of God's people. Above and beyond evangelism or social justice, it is the irresistible propulsion of the Spirit that sends his people out to declare the lordship of Jesus in all and over all. This can be manifest in sharing the Gospel, planting churches, feeding the hungry, agitating against injustice, and more. These are missional activities. But mission itself is the overarching sentness of God's people as they infiltrate all of society and stake a claim for the unending rule of Jesus in every sphere of life.

Missional churches understand that this sending impulse infuses all of church life. By contrast, conventional churches that make worship the organizing principle usually see evangelism, for example, as the recruiting of new people to attend worship and other organization-based services. They see Christian fellowship as the building up of the worshipping community. Missional churches understand that community is best built by those in league with each other in the creative task of mission. They worship like crazy because they see God's lordship over all of life. They disciple each other in order to be better missionaries. Mission is the spark, the catalyzing energy, that makes sense of everything the church was intended to be.

Someone once challenged us that in heaven there'll be no mission, only worship. We couldn't disagree more. Sure, we won't be feeding the poor or planting churches. Those missional activities will cease when every knee bows, every tongue confesses, and every tear is wiped away. But in the world to come, we will still be charged with the task of declaring Jesus' rule over all of life. We're looking forward to that unhindered mission of the new age and to worshipping through the process of offering our world back to God.

We never see Jesus' community at worship in the conventional sense of that word. They are always on mission, though. Their worship of God happens as they go. They have put worship at the service of mission and we do well to learn from Jesus' radical example in this matter.

Jesus' Community Practices the Presence of Jesus

Does this mean that if mission is the organizing principle for Jesus' community, there are never any times for private, silent, reflective worship and prayer? Far from it. Jesus commends this very thing to his community when he says,

> "And whenever you pray, do not be like the hypocrites; for they love to stand and pray in the synagogues and at the street corners, so that they may be seen by others. Truly I tell you, they have received their reward. But whenever you pray, go into your room and shut the door and pray to your Father who is in secret; and your Father who sees in secret will reward you. When you are praying, do not heap up empty phrases as the Gentiles do; for they think that they will be heard because of their many words. Do not be like them, for your Father knows what you need before you ask him." (Matt 6:5–8)

Personal prayer, solitude, and retreat are an intrinsic part of Jesus' community. In fact, Jesus models them as an essential part of his devotional life:

> in the morning, while it was still very dark, he got up and went out to a deserted place, and there he prayed. (Mark 1:35)

> But he would withdraw to deserted places and pray. (Luke 5:16)

Even at the lowest point of his life, in the Garden of Gethsemane, he withdraws from the others to pray. In fact, if we take his words to his community in Matthew 6 seriously, his preference is that prayer not be a showy display for the benefit of others but an intense and private connection between a disciple and his or her heavenly Father.

The question about fasting needs to be addressed as well, because it was noted at the time that Jesus' community did not participate in the devotional practice of fasting, unlike that of the disciples of John the Baptist:

> Then the disciples of John came to him, saying, "Why do we and the Pharisees fast often, but your disciples do not fast?" And Jesus said to them, "The wedding guests cannot mourn as long as the bridegroom is with them, can they? The days will come when the bridegroom is taken away from them, and then they will fast." (Matt 9:14–15)

For Jesus, his presence on earth was a time of celebration, of feasting, not fasting. He acknowledges that during his three days away from the disciples, they would fast as an expression of their grief and mourning. But after his resurrection, Jesus was returned to them, and he remains with his church to this very day. This is still the hour for feasting. So, is there any provision for the practice of fasting by Christians today? Well, frankly, not much. There seems to be no injunction to do so found on the lips of Jesus. We believe that while Christians might find fasting beneficial in building spiritual muscle by the discipline of self-denial and the creation of more time for personal prayer (during the time you'd normally prepare and eat food), we see it as merely that—helpful but not required. Of course, Jesus again cautions about showy displays even in the practice of fasting, when he commends us to do it in secret (Matt 6:16–18).

Jesus' Community Insists That We Need to Be Continually Re-Evangelized

The default by so many Christians toward earning their salvation by good works and dutiful church service has to be halted, and indeed, resisted. For this reason, the followers of Jesus need to be re-gospeled on a regular basis. We think this is why Jesus told his disciples to constantly remember his sacrificial and atoning death in the eating of the so-called communion meal. Far from intending it to be a sacramental or religious feast, we think Jesus intended to connect the gospel to an everyday occurrence like eating. It is not unlike the place of the *Shema* in Israel, as we saw earlier. The core of their belief system was so radical and so countercultural in its time that Israel was commanded to

> Recite them to your children and talk about them when are at home and when you are away, when you lie down and when you rise. Bind them as a sign on your hand, fix them as an emblem on your forehead, and write them on the doorposts of your house and on your gates. (Deut 6:7–9)

In a world of aggressive polytheism, you can understand how having reminders of their monotheistic faith tied to their hands or written on their doorframes was so important. Every time you left your home and re-entered it, you would be reminded again of the liberty of the existential monotheism of Israel. We are free from the fear of unknowingly offending some obscure god, they could say. All of life was now unified under Yahweh.

Likewise, the Lord's Supper was not intended to be a peculiar liturgical rite of a religious institution. Jesus was commanding his followers to remind themselves of the freedom that comes through his death every time they tore bread or sipped wine. It was a way of being re-gospeled every day, indeed, several times a day. When Paul does present certain words to the Corinthians that might accompany a collective love feast, he is not fixing it as a distinct Christian rite as much as he is reminding the wayward Corinthians of the true tone and belief that should undergird their meals together.

Jesus communities today must never lose sight of the essential work of the cross and celebrate that work as often as they meet together. It is not our pietism or our personal devotion that sets us free. It is the unconditional love of Jesus as demonstrated in his willingness to die for our sins.

Uncompromising Commitment

Simone Weil

T. S. Eliot described Simone Weil as "a woman of genius, of a kind of genius akin to that of the saints." Weil was a French philosopher, teacher, and activist whose precocious intellect and compassion for members of the working class were apparent even from an early age. As a six-year-old during the First World War, she refused to eat sugar because it was not rationed to French soldiers. In her early teens, she mastered several modern languages and often spoke with her brother in ancient Greek. Weil's espousal of Bolshevism and Marxism as a young woman led her to become known by some as the "Red Virgin." She was dedicated to bringing attention to the plight of manual laborers and factory workers, and alternated between teaching philosophy and performing manual labor in order to better understand the needs of workers. Preferring the company of the poor, she ate in their less-fashionable cafés and shared her salary with the unemployed. After the disillusioning outcome of the Spanish Civil War, Weil eventually abandoned communist and socialist ideologies. She later became interested in Christianity, although she refused to be baptized and never formally joined the church. In 1942 she fled from Nazi occupation and relocated in England, where she died at the age of 34 of tuberculosis and self-neglect in 1943, embodying her belief that one must "decreate" oneself to return to God. Her life was one of uncompromising commitment to her beliefs.

Jesus' Community Learns and Lives the Values of Jesus

For many suburban, middle-class churches, niceness is the supreme expression of discipleship. But any cursory reading of the Gospels will serve to remind you that Jesus wasn't all that nice. He was good. He was loving. He was compassionate. But he wasn't always nice. The church must abandon its preference for good-manners piety and adopt again the kingdom values as taught by Jesus. Allow us to give you an example. Some time ago Michael wrote an article for a Sydney newspaper, commenting on the influence of Sydney's largest church, Hillsong. In the article, he defended the church against various attacks in the media, but he also gently raised his concerns about Hillsong's emphasis on prosperity doctrine (the so-called health and wealth gospel). He received an avalanche of letters and email berating him for daring to be publicly critical of another church. A significant number of these angry correspondents claimed that it was un-Christlike to criticize the church in any way. Now, whether you agree with Michael's decision to write such a thing in the media or not is beside the point. But the point is that somehow these people, most of them ministers, failed to recognize that Jesus was regularly and scathingly critical of the religious leaders of his faith community. Furthermore, Jesus' seven messages to the seven churches in the book of Revelation (Rev 2:1–3:22) contain plenty of harshly critical comment directed at the church! To claim it is un-Christlike to criticize the church is to disregard the example of Jesus.

It seems to us that this is the exemplifying of politeness, courtesy, and niceness over the values taught by Jesus. We cannot boil his radical new vision for the kingdom of God down to an expression of conventionality and good behavior. It is so much more. And it is so *unconventional* that it landed Jesus and his followers in hot water on more than one occasion. And so what are those values? An incomplete list follows:

- ⟿ meekness (Matt 5:5)

- ⟿ mercy (Luke 15:4–10)

- ⟿ peacefulness (Matt 5:9)

- ⟿ sexual propriety in marriage (Matt 5:27)

- ⟿ a non-anxious reliance on the provision of God (Matt 6:24–34)

- ⟿ the love of enemies (Luke 6:27–30)

- ⟿ forgiveness toward those who wrong you (Luke 6:31–36)

- ⟿ reconciliation (Matt 5:21–24)

- ⟿ truthfulness (Matt 5:37)

When Paul calls us to be a holy community, "without a spot or wrinkle or anything of the kind . . . holy and blameless" (Eph 5:26–27), he is not referring to our standards of behavior but to the salvific work of Jesus on our behalf. We cannot earn Jesus' love by politeness or niceness. It is offered freely, so we are free to embrace these kingdom values, liberated from any neurotic attempts to win Jesus over with our Sunday best. It is, however, these values mentioned above that should distinguish the followers of Jesus from the empire in which they find themselves. Rodney Stark, chronicler of the rise of Christianity, concludes his book with the following observations,

> Therefore as I conclude this study, I find it necessary to confront what appears to me to be the ultimate factor in the rise of Christianity. . . . The simple phrase, "For God so loved the world . . ." would have puzzled an educated pagan. And the notion that the gods care how we treat one another would have been dismissed as patently absurd. . . . This was the moral climate in which Christianity taught that mercy is one of the primary virtues—that a merciful God requires humans to be merciful. . . . This was revolutionary stuff. Indeed, it was the cultural basis for the revitalization of the Roman world groaning under a host of miseries . . .[9]

It is by our love that all people might know that we are Jesus' disciples. Any community of faith characterized by his name must be a community of peace, love, mercy, and freedom. Stark continues by exploring the ways this was manifest in the early period of the Christian era:

> In my judgment, a major way in which Christianity served as a revitalization movement within the empire was in offering a coherent culture that was entirely stripped of ethnicity. All were welcome without need to dispense with ethnic ties. . . . Christianity also prompted liberating social relations between the sexes and within the family . . . [and] greatly modulated class differences— more than rhetoric was involved when slave and noble greeted one another as brothers in Christ. Finally, what Christianity gave to its converts was nothing less than their humanity.[10]

Jesus' Community Devotes Itself to Scripture and the Exercise of Spiritual Gifts

Paul says, "No one ever hates his own body, but he nourishes and cares for it, just as Christ does for the church, because we are members of his body" (Eph 5:29–30). Jesus is therefore feeding and caring for his people throughout the ages. It is obvious the ways Jesus does this with his company in the Gospels. But how does he nourish and cherish us today? It seems to us that this is the reason why God gives spiritual gifts to the church—so that through the ministry of the Holy Spirit in our midst we are built up (nourished) and nurtured (cared for). How ingenious that the Jesus who dwells within each of us should use each of us to feed and care for each other.

In 1 Corinthians 11, Paul commends the harmonious expression of the gifts with each member playing his or her part in the building up of the church in the same way that different body parts operate as a united whole. It is no mistake that he then launches into his well-known description of love in 1 Corinthians 13, because without genuine love between the members of a church the differing expressions of giftedness would tear them apart. He is in effect commending a unity-in-diversity approach. We are better together, stronger for the ministries of each other in our lives, built up by all the gifts. When he turns his attention to the public gathering of the Corinthians he says,

> When you come together, each one has a hymn, a lesson, a revelation, a tongue, or an interpretation. Let all things be done for building up. If anyone speaks in a tongue, let there be only two or at most three, and each in turn, and let one interpret. But if there is no one to interpret, let them be silent in church and speak to themselves and to God. Let two or three prophets speak, and let the others weigh what is said. If a revelation is made to someone else sitting nearby, let the first person be silent. For you can all prophesy one by one so that all may learn and all be encouraged. (1 Cor 14:26–31)

Here is a picture of the church cooperating seamlessly with the Holy Spirit and each other, each playing their part, each making their contribution. What is one of the ways Jesus nourishes and cares for us? Via the other members of our faith community.

An example of someone who takes this seriously is Dan Kimball from Vintage Faith Church in Santa Cruz, to whom we referred earlier. He has developed a series of questions he asks of all his worship leaders as a regular way of reconnecting with the proper place of worship in the life of a faith community. Those questions are

1. Does our worship lift up Jesus as the center of our church community?

2. In our worship gathering, are the Scriptures read and taught as the normative wisdom for our church community?

3. When we gather to worship, is prayer an essential part of what we do?

4. Do our worship gatherings provide opportunities for us to express our togetherness as a community?

5. Is the communion meal a regular or central part of our worship?

6. Are the members of our church reminded of their obligations to live missional lives when they gather for worship?

7. Does the arrangement of our worship meeting allow for anyone or everyone to contribute to the whole as they see fit and according to their gifting?[11]

We wish all worship curators, rectors, ministers, and pastors were asked these questions more regularly.

⌒ A Photocopy of a Photocopy of a Photocopy

In the world to come, we will still be charged with the task of declaring Jesus' rule over all of life. Paul was intentionally seeking to replicate the model laid down by Jesus. It was as if he was taking the original Jesus community and seeking to translate it into various contexts across the world. The difficulty with the church today is that we are trying to make faded copies of Paul's copies. Try photocopying a document, then keep recopying the previous copy, and see what the image looks like after multiple generations of copying. Faded, illegible, unusable. How would you get back to the image you wanted? Why, you'd go back to the original document. Paul would hardly have been asking us to copy his copies. He was using the original as his template, and so should we. It's time to reJesus our churches so they look like copies of the pristine original.

At the beginning of this book, we shared about our visits to the great cathedrals of Rome and Moscow, and we asked how far has the religious institution of church moved from the dynamic, relational, countercultural collective first forged by the Nazarene rabbi. The eight characteristics just mentioned can be adopted by any group of Jesus followers today and lived out without any of the paraphernalia or property considered to be so indispensable by the mainstream church. We are not proposing some radical new ecclesiological model. We are not inventing some innovative new approach to being and doing church. We are calling faith communities of Jesus followers to rediscover the teaching, the example, the vision of our founder. We don't do so with contempt or disregard for the traditions developed by Christians over the centuries. Nor do we assume to have some higher or deeper insight into these matters. But we can hold up the models of church we find around us today—professionalized and institutionalized—against the example found in the Gospels and the New Testament, and we can ask some serious questions about the disjunction we find there. It us time to recalibrate the church

is

around the person of Jesus rather than around marketing ploys developed for a shallow consumeristic age.

⟵Notes

1. Jim Henderson, *Jim and Casper Go to Church* (Carol Stream, Ill.: Barna-Books, 2007).

2. Kimball, *They Like Jesus but Not the Church*, 79–89.

3. This graph doesn't occur in Kimball's book but is a summary of the responses made to him by his subjects.

4. There is a world of difference as to how we tend to interpret the word "family" and what the Bible means by "household." We tend to impose the nuclear idea of family on the Scriptures, but the Bible's idea of family is much broader and more inclusive.

5. Frost and Hirsch, *Shaping of Things to Come*; Hirsch, *Forgotten Ways*; and Frost, *Exiles*.

6. Moby, "Religion," August 12, 2005. Cited 25 September 2008. Online: http://www.moby.com/node/7007.

7. Ibid.

8. See Hirsch, *Forgotten Ways*, 40–42, 235.

9. Rodney Stark, *The Rise of Christianity* (New York: HarperCollins, 1997), 209–15.

10. Ibid.

11. See Dan Kimball, David Crowder, and Sally Morgenthaler, *Emerging Worship: Creating Worship Gatherings for New Generations* (Grand Rapids, Mich.: Zondervan, 2004), 87.

Conclusion: Read This Bit Last

There is no Gospel at all if Christ be not God. It is no
news to me to tell me that a great prophet is born.
There have been great prophets before; but the world
has never been redeemed from evil by mere testimony
to the truth, and it never will be. But tell me that God
is born, that God Himself has espoused our nature,
and taken it into union with Himself, then the bells of
my heart ring merry peals, for now may I come to God
since God has come to me.
—C. H. Spurgeon

Hey, we said to read this bit last, so if you've just bought this book and
skipped right to our conclusion, turn back and start from the beginning.
We need you to take the journey with us in rediscovering the alternate vision
offered by Jesus; the journey of defragging all the pictures of Jesus you've accumulated over the years; the journey of reencountering a Hebraic framework
for seeing and following Jesus as the visible presence of the one and only
God; the journey of exploring what a Jesus-built church would look like.

Once you've walked that road with us, then we want you to turn your
attention to the following image.

Two Men Walk into an Inn . . .

Two middle-aged men meet in an inn in a small, unremarkable village.
They embrace, their heavy, solid hands slapping each others' broad backs
affectionately. They kiss twice, on each cheek. They sit and eat, hunching
over the shared table in a conspiratorial way. The dust that coats their faces

highlights the deepening lines around their eyes. Their graying beards betray the years. They are like two old lions, warriors who've fought many a battle but live to fight another day.

Wiping crumbs from his mustache with the back of his hand, one says with a smirk, "You've gotten old quickly."

The other looks up and raises his eyebrows.

"I just mean," continues the first man, "I haven't seen you for a while, and you seem to have aged quite a bit in that time." Another smirk.

The other man starts to defend himself but instead waves his hand dismissively at his friend. "Why do I even bite at comments like that?" he smiles. "You're not exactly the strapping young fellow you used to be either, you know."

They both smile, and the first man reaches across and places his hand on his friend's arm. The tone turns serious. "It's the travel that wears me out," he confesses.

"Agreed. And the disappointment. I could bear the travel, the strange lodgings, the mishaps. But the disappointment of hearing about comrades turning from the cause or cells diverting from our doctrine, well, that's what wears me out the most. I've heard it makes me look old," he says, eyeing his friend warily.

"Very old, actually." They laugh. Silence.

After a while, the first man says, "The Corinthians still causing you a headache, Paul? Should I blame them for all your gray whiskers?"

"Headaches and whiskers are nothing, Peter. Have you heard the latest? You don't want to know. Jealousy, quarrels, and divisions. Some of them have even rejected me as an apostle. Apparently, they prefer more gifted leaders! Can you believe that? They don't understand that wisdom is from the Spirit. After even such a long time, they're still babies in Christ. Don't get me started on their list of crimes: sexual immorality, lawsuits among the comrades, abuse of freedom, tolerance of immoral brothers, taking pride in their spiritual gifts, chaotic and disorderly worship, improper theology on resurrection, and, well, just a complete lack of love. I've written them four letters about all this, and each one seems to get me into further trouble with them. I'm of a mind to stop writing and start fighting. Teach 'em a lesson with my fists that my letters obviously can't. Actually you're probably a better fighter than me. Fancy a trip to Corinth?"

"Clobbering Corinthians probably won't do the trick, comrade. Though I *am* inclined to join you," Peter smiles sympathetically.

"How is the cell at Galatia? Have you had contact with them?" Paul asks after downing a mouthful from his cup. Peter shakes his head slowly. Paul continues, "Their faith was not strong enough to resist the confusions stirred up by the teaching of the Jewish Christians about the circumcision requirement, and they doubted the gospel I preached to them. Like the Corinthians, they even doubt my authority, too."

And so it goes. Two tired men sharing back and forth, recounting stories of new cells in Asia Minor, new converts in Europe, new developments in Greece.

Finally Paul says, "Peter, I'm not sure when I'll see you again. . . ."

"You say that every time we get together."

"I know, and it's always true. But in case our paths never cross again, can you tell me about him one more time."

Peter smiles sadly, "Oh, Paul, you've heard me tell you those stories a million times. You tell them yourself better than I do."

Paul leans forward toward his friend. "Comrade, I've been beaten, abandoned, betrayed, shipwrecked, and left for dead. It's hard to think of a cell I've planted that isn't in the grip of some crisis, personal or doctrinal. I'm not well. I'm often hungry. And, well, according to some of my friends, I look like an old man. The revolution is unfolding, slowly but surely. Ah, the things we've seen. But at times it feels arduous. I long for the Lord as the watchman longs for the end of night. And there are times when I wonder whether these small, struggling cells we're planting will become the movement we dreamed of. Yes, I do wonder. Even after all I've seen and done. All *we've* seen and done . . ."

Then he fixes his eyes firmly on Peter's and says, pleading, "Tell me again."

We can imagine ourselves standing in the doorway of the ancient inn, looking into the darkened room and seeing two battle-weary warriors sharing stories of their hero, their standard, their inspiration. Would Paul and Peter have met like this and spoken in this way? Who can say? But there seems little doubt that it was the story of Jesus that inspired their work and ministry and was the lifeblood of their mission. Indeed, writing to the Romans, Paul introduces himself as "Paul, a servant of Christ Jesus, called to be an apostle, set apart for the gospel of God" (Rom 1:1). What is the "gospel of God" for which he felt set apart? Is it a set of doctrinal propositions, a revolutionary dogma, a collection of beliefs and practices centered on Jesus? In fact, it's far more. The gospel is not simply theological ideology. It is a historical event! Listen as he explains:

> [the gospel] he promised beforehand through his prophets in the holy scriptures, the gospel concerning his Son, who was descended from David according to the flesh and was declared to be Son of God with power according to the spirit of holiness by resurrection from the dead, Jesus Christ our Lord, through whom we have received grace and apostleship to bring about the obedience of faith among all the Gentiles for the sake of his name, including yourselves who are called to belong to Jesus Christ. (Rom 1:2–6)

When Paul explains the content of his gospel, it doesn't consist of propositional statements about creation, sin, atonement, and redemption. It is a recapturing of the historical story of Jesus! For Paul, the gospel *is* Jesus—his messianic credentials, his physical descent from David, his vindication by the Spirit of God, and his resurrection from the dead. This looks identical to the gospel given to us in Matthew's Gospel. In effect, Romans 1:1–6 is a *Reader's Digest* version of the Gospels.

Later in Romans, Paul offers an even more truncated version of the same message, when he writes,

> But what does it say? "The word is near you, on your lips and in your heart" (that is, the word of faith that we proclaim); because if you confess with your lips that Jesus is Lord and believe in your heart that God raised him from the dead, you will be saved. (Rom 10:8–9)

Scholars believe that this was obviously the repetition of a well-known creed of the time. If it is a simple creedal statement, then note its trajectory. It is a super-summarized version of Matthew, Mark, or Luke. Compare it with the flowery Nicene Creed from the fourth century, which refers to Jesus as "light from light, true light from true light, begotten not made, of one being with the Father." Paul has nothing to do with this airy doctrinal language. In 2 Timothy he offers his preferred version of the gospel: "Remember Jesus Christ, raised from the dead, a descendant of David—that is my gospel" (2 Tim 2:8). Events. Facts. History. This is my gospel.

Probably nowhere is this expressed more urgently by him than in his advice to the Corinthians in the conduct of their public feast:

> Now, brothers and sisters, I want to remind you of the gospel I preached to you, which you received and on which you have taken your stand. By this gospel you are saved, if you hold firmly to the word I preached to you. Otherwise, you have

believed in vain. For what I received I passed on to you as of first importance: that Christ died for our sins according to the Scriptures, that he was buried, that he was raised on the third day according to the Scriptures, and that he appeared to Peter, and then to the Twelve. (1 Cor 15:1–5, TNIV)

Jesus died for our sins. He was the fulfillment of prophecy. He rose again. He appeared to witnesses. This is our gospel, anchored in the person and work of Jesus, "the gospel I preached to you," as Paul refers to it. In fact, there seems enough evidence to suggest that most of what Paul taught to his fledgling churches were the stories of Jesus, with an obvious emphasis on the death, resurrection, and appearances of Jesus. His epistles deal with specific pastoral and theological issues, but they should be read in the light of the fact that the gospel he preached to them, the doctrine he'd immersed them in, was the Christ event, the story of Jesus. Says John Dickson,

> The importance of [these] creedal statements should not be underestimated for they are rare glimpses into the missionary proclamation of the first Christians, and of the Pauline missionaries in particular. In his letters, Paul (and the other apostles) had no reason to repeat the missionary preaching at great length. The 'gospel' tends to be a shared assumption throughout the epistles, always in the background but rarely brought to the fore.[1]

Today, too many Christians are reading Romans as though it is Paul's exposition of the gospel—creation, sin, atonement. But Romans and the other epistles were applications of the gospel rather than expositions of it. Paul is assuming the Romans remember the amazing story of Jesus he had taught them. In fact, when Paul preaches the gospel it sounds more like Acts 13 than Romans 1–3:

> When he had removed him [Saul], he made David their king. In his testimony about him he said, "I have found David, son of Jesse, a man after my heart, who will carry out all my wishes.' Of this man's posterity God has brought to Israel a Savior, Jesus, as he promised; before his coming John had already proclaimed a baptism of repentance to all the people of Israel. And as John was finishing his work, he said, 'What do you suppose that I am? I am not he. No, but one is coming after me; I am not worthy to untie the thong of the sandals on his feet.' My brothers, you descendants of Abraham's family, and others who fear God, to us the message of this salvation has been sent. Because the residents of Jerusalem and their leaders did not recognize him or understand the words of the prophets that are read every sabbath, they fulfilled those words by condemning him. Even though they found no cause for a sentence of death, they asked Pilate to have him killed. When they had carried out everything that was written

about him, they took him down from the tree and laid him in a tomb. But God raised him from the dead, and for many days he appeared to those who came up with him from Galilee to Jerusalem, and they are now his witnesses to the people. And we bring you the good news that what God promised to our ancestors he has fulfilled for us, their children, by raising Jesus . . . Let it be known to you, therefore, my brothers, that through this man forgiveness of sins is proclaimed to you; By this Jesus everyone who believes is set free from all those sins from which you could not be freed by the law of Moses. (Acts 13:22–39)

Note the following three things: first, this sermon is a virtual summary of the Gospels, particularly Mark and Luke, focusing on the events of Jesus' life. Second, there is an unmistakable corollary between this sermon and the creedal statements we previously looked at in Romans and 2 Timothy, with their emphasis on the kingly rule of Jesus. And third, there is an explicit reference to the Pauline doctrine of justification by faith, rooting it firmly in the historic event of Jesus' messianic rule, his life, death, and resurrection.

We don't wish to imply that doctrinal statements are useless. But doctrinal purity for its own sake has riven churches apart and led to the current proliferation of denominations and competing Christian agencies. For Paul, as for Peter, the gospel is Jesus and Jesus alone. Any doctrine that emerges and is developed into propositional statement must find its locus in the story of Jesus.

Did Paul and Peter ever meet in a darkened inn, share a meal, and swap stories? We don't know, but if they did, we have little doubt that the stories they would have swapped wouldn't have been the trivial or the nostalgic. We are convinced that they clung to the gospel narrative as their sole reason for being. Try to imagine those battered old lions telling those stories, reJesusing each other. Then ask yourself how desperately you cling to the gospel—not the Four Spiritual Laws, not the Bridge to Life, not a doctrinal catechism, but Jesus. And if you do cling desperately to him, then join us in our quest to reJesus our churches in this day and age.

↫ Notes

1. John Dickson, "Announcing the Christ Event: Aspects of the New Testament Gospel" (unpublished article, 2001).

Selected Resources

Bell, Rob. *Velvet Elvis: Repainting the Christian Faith*. Grand Rapids, Mich.: Zondervan, 2005.

Bonhoeffer, Dietrich. *Christ the Center*. Translated by Edwin Robertson. New York: Harper & Row, 1978.

Bosch, David Jacobus. *Transforming Mission: Paradigm Shifts in Theology of Mission*. American Society of Missiology Series 16. Maryknoll, N.Y.: Orbis, 1991.

Brunner, Emil. *The Mediator: A Study of the Central Doctrine of the Christian Faith*. Translated by Olive Wyon. London: Lutterworth, 1934.

Bryman, Alan. *Charisma and Leadership in Organizations*. Newbury, Calif.: Sage, 1992.

Bultmann, Rudolph. *Jesus and the Word*. New York: Fontana, 1958.

Burke, Spencer, and Barry Taylor. *A Heretic's Guide to Eternity*. San Francisco, Jossey-Bass, 2006.

Cave, Nick. *The Gospel according to Mark with an Introduction by Nick Cave* Melbourne: Text, 1998.

Cavey, Bruxy. *The End of Religion: An Introduction to the Subversive Spirituality of Jesus*. Ottawa: Agora, 2005.

Chalke, Steve, and Alan Mann. *The Lost Message of Jesus*. Grand Rapids, Mich.: Zondervan, 2003.

Chesnut, Glenn. *Images of Christ: An Introduction to Christology*. Minneapolis: Seabury, 1984.

Clarke, Andrew, and Bruce Winter. *One God, One Lord: Christianity in a World of Religious Pluralism*. Grand Rapids, Mich.: Baker, 1992..

Conger, Jay Alden, and Rabindra Nath Kanungo. *Charismatic Leadership in Organizations*. Thousand Oaks, Calif.: Sage, 1998.

Dickson, John. *A Spectator's Guide to Jesus*. Sydney: Blue Bottle, 2005.

Ellul, Jacques. *The Subversion of Christianity*. Grand Rapids, Mich.: Eerdmans, 1986.

Erre, Mike. *The Jesus of Suburbia: Have We Tamed the Son of God to Fit Our Lifestyle?* Dallas: W, 2006.

Frei, Hans W. *The Identity of Jesus Christ: The Hermeneutical Bases of Dogmatic Theology*. Philadelphia: Fortress, 1975.

Frost, Michael. *Exiles: Living Missionally in a Post-Christian Culture*. Peabody, Mass.: Hendrickson, 2006.

————. *Jesus the Fool*. Peabody, Mass.: Hendrickson, forthcoming.

————. *Seeing God in the Ordinary: A Theology of the Everyday*. Peabody, Mass.: Hendrickson, 2000.

————, and Alan Hirsch. *The Shaping of Things to Come: Innovation and Mission for the 21st-Century Church*. Peabody, Mass.: Hendrickson, 2003.

Grempf, Conrad. *Mealtime Habits of the Messiah: 40 Encounters with Jesus*. Grand Rapids, Mich.: Zondervan, 2005.

Gruen, Anselm. *Images of Jesus*. Translated by John Bowden. New York: Continuum, 2002.

Heim, Karl. *Jesus the Lord: The Sovereign Authority of Jesus and God's Revelation in Christ*. Translated by D. H. van Daalen. Philadelphia: Muhlenberg, 1959.

Henderson, Jim, Matt Casper, and George Barna. *Jim and Casper Go to Church: Frank Conversations about Faith, Churches, and Well-Meaning Christians*. Carol Stream, Ill.: BarnaBooks, 2007.

Hirsch, Alan. *The Forgotten Ways: Reactivating the Missional Church*. Grand Rapids, Mich.: Brazos, 2007.

Houlden, J. Leslie, ed. *Jesus in History, Thought, and Culture: An Encyclopedia*. Santa Barbara, Calif.: ABC-CLIO, 2003.

Kimball, Dan. *They Like Jesus but Not the Church*. Grand Rapids, Mich.: Zondervan, 2007.

Kinlaw, Dennis F. *Let's Start with Jesus: A New Way of Doing Theology*. Grand Rapids, Mich.: Zondervan, 2005.

Men, Alexander. *Son of Man: The Story of Christianity and Christ*. Translated by Samuel Brown. Torrance, Calif.: Oakwood, 1992.

McLaren, Brian. *The Secret Message of Jesus: Uncovering the Truth that Could Change Everything*. Grand Rapids, Mich.: Nashville: W, 2006.

————. *The Voice of Luke: Not Even Sandals*. Nashville: Thomas Nelson, 2007.

Miguez Boniño, José, ed. *Faces of Jesus: Latin American Christologies*. Translated by Robert R. Barr. Maryknoll, N.Y.: 1984.

Minear, Paul. *Commands of Christ*. Nashville: Abingdon, 1972.

————. *Eyes of Faith: A Study in the Biblical Point of View*. Philadelphia: Westminster, 1946.

Moltmann, Jürgen. *The Way of Christ: Christology in Messianic Dimensions*. San Francisco: Harper, 1990.

Morgan, Alison. *The Wild Gospel: Bringing Truth to Life*. Oxford: Monarch, 2004.

Phillips, John A. *The Form of Christ in the World: A Study in Bonhoeffer's Christology*. London: Collins, 1967.

Ritschl, Dietrich. *Memory and Hope: An Inquiry Concerning the Presence of Christ*. New York: Macmillan, 1967.

Roberts, Dave. *Following Jesus: A Non-Religious Guide for the Spiritually Hungry*. Lake Mary, Fla.: Relevant, 2004.

Samuel, Vinay, and Chris Sugden, eds. *Sharing Jesus in the Two Thirds World: Evangelical Christologies from the Contexts of Poverty, Powerlessness, and Religious Pluralism*. Papers of the First Conference of Evangelical Mission Theologians from the Two Thirds World. Bangkok, Thailand, March 22–25, 1982. Grand Rapids, Mich.: Eerdmans, 1983.

Sayers, Dorothy L. *The Man Born to Be King*. London: Victor Gollancz, 1955.

Seay, Chris, Brian McLaren, David Capes, Lauren Winner, and Greg Garrett. *The Last Eyewitness: The Final Week*. Nashville: Thomas Nelson, 2006.

Shenk, Wilbert R., ed. *The Transfiguration of Mission: Biblical, Theological, and Historical Foundations*. Scottdale, Pa.: Herald, 1993.

Stark, Rodney. *One True God: Historical Consequences of Monotheism*. Princeton, N.J.: Princeton University Press, 2001.

———. *The Rise of Christianity*. New York: HarperCollins, 1997.

Stassen, Glen H., and David P. Gushee. *Kingdom Ethics: Following Jesus in a Contemporary Context*. Downers Grove, Ill.: InterVarsity, 2003.

Taylor, John V. *The Christlike God*. London: SCM, 1992.

Taylor, Tom. *Paradoxy: Coming to Grips with the Contradictions of Jesus*. Grand Rapids, Mich.: Baker, 2006.

Walsh, Brian J., and Sylvia C. Keesmaat. *Colossians Remixed*. Downers Grove, Ill.: InterVarsity, 2004.

Ward, Keith. *Re-Thinking Christianity*. Oxford: Oneworld, 2007.

Wells, Harold. *The Christic Center: Life-Giving and Liberating*. Maryknoll, N.Y.: Orbis, 2004.

Wilson, Jonathan. *God So Loved the World: A Christology for Disciples*. Grand Rapids, Mich.: Baker, 2001.

Winner, Lauren. *The Voice of Matthew*. Nashville: Thomas Nelson, 2007.

Wright, N. T. *The Challenge of Jesus*. London: SPCK, 2000.

———. *Jesus and the Victory of God*. London: SPCK, 1996.

———. *Who Was Jesus?* London: SPCK, 1992.

Yancey, Philip. *The Jesus I Never Knew*. Grand Rapids, Mich.: Zondervan, 1995.

Illustration Credits

"Martin Luther King, Jr., 1964." Dick DeMarsico. Courtesy of the Library of Congress.

"Fannie Lou Hamer at the Democratic National Convention, Atlantic City, New Jersey, August 1964." U.S. News & World Report Magazine Photograph Collection. Courtesy of the Library of Congress.

"Sheila Cassidy." Reproduced with the permission of Darton, Longman & Todd.

Janani Luwum. Drawing by Edward S. Turner IV. Reproduced with the permission of the artist.

"Dietrich Bonhoeffer in London, 1939." Bildarchiv Preussicher Kulturbesitz. Reproduced with the permission of Art Resource/N.Y.

Søren Kierkegaard. Based on a sketch by Niels Christian Kierkegaard (1806-1882).

Alan Walker. Drawing by Edward S. Turner IV. Reproduced with the permission of the artist.

Jean Vanier. Drawing by Edward S. Turner IV. Reproduced with the permission of the artist.

Jesus. *The Light of the World*, William Holman Hunt. Ca. 1851–1853. Keble College, Oxford, Great Britain. Photo credit: HIP/ Art Resource, N.Y. Reproduced with permission.

Jesus. *Sacred Heart*, Pompeo Batoni. Il Gesu, Rome, Italy. Photo Credit: Scala/ Art Resouce, N.Y. Reproduced with permission.

Jesus. Film still from *Son of God*, directed by Jean Claude Bragand. British Broadcasting Company, April 2001. Reproduced with the permission of the BBC Photo Library.

Jesus. Film still from *Il Vangelo secondo Matteo* (*The Gospel According to Saint Matthew*), directed by Pier Paolo Pasolini. Arco Film, 1964. Every effort was made to obtain permission for the image used here. Concerned parties are welcome to contact Hendrickson Publishers.

Jesus. *Meek. Mild. As If.* Church of England poster, 1999. Church's Advertising Network (CAN). Reproduced with permission.

Jesus. *Christ Pantocrator.* St. Catherine's Monastery, Sinai. Photograph by Peter Brubacher. Reproduced with permission.

"William Wilberforce, with His Signature." Reproduced with the permission of North Wind Picture Archives.

"Mother Teresa." Evert Odekerken. Licensed under Creative Commons Attribution 2.5.

Rigoberta Menchú. Drawing by Edward S. Turner IV. Reproduced with the permission of the artist.

"Eva Price." Reproduced with the permission of the Oberlin College Archives, Oberlin, Ohio.

"Harriet Beecher Stowe." Reproduced with the permission of the Ohio Historical Society.

"Dorothy Day." Milwaukee Journal. Reproduced with the permission of the Marquette University Archives.

Damien of Molokai. Drawing by Edward S. Turner IV. Reproduced with the permission of the artist.

Simone Weil. Drawing by Edward S. Turner IV. Reproduced with the permission of the artist.

Index